Voice Over! ☆
Seiyu Academy

7

Vol.7
Story & Art by
Maki Minami

TECHNICAL ADVISORS
Yoichi Kato, Kaori Kagami, Ayumi Hashidate,
Ayako Harino and Touko Fujitani

Voice Over!
Seiyu Academy

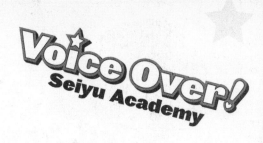

Vol. 7

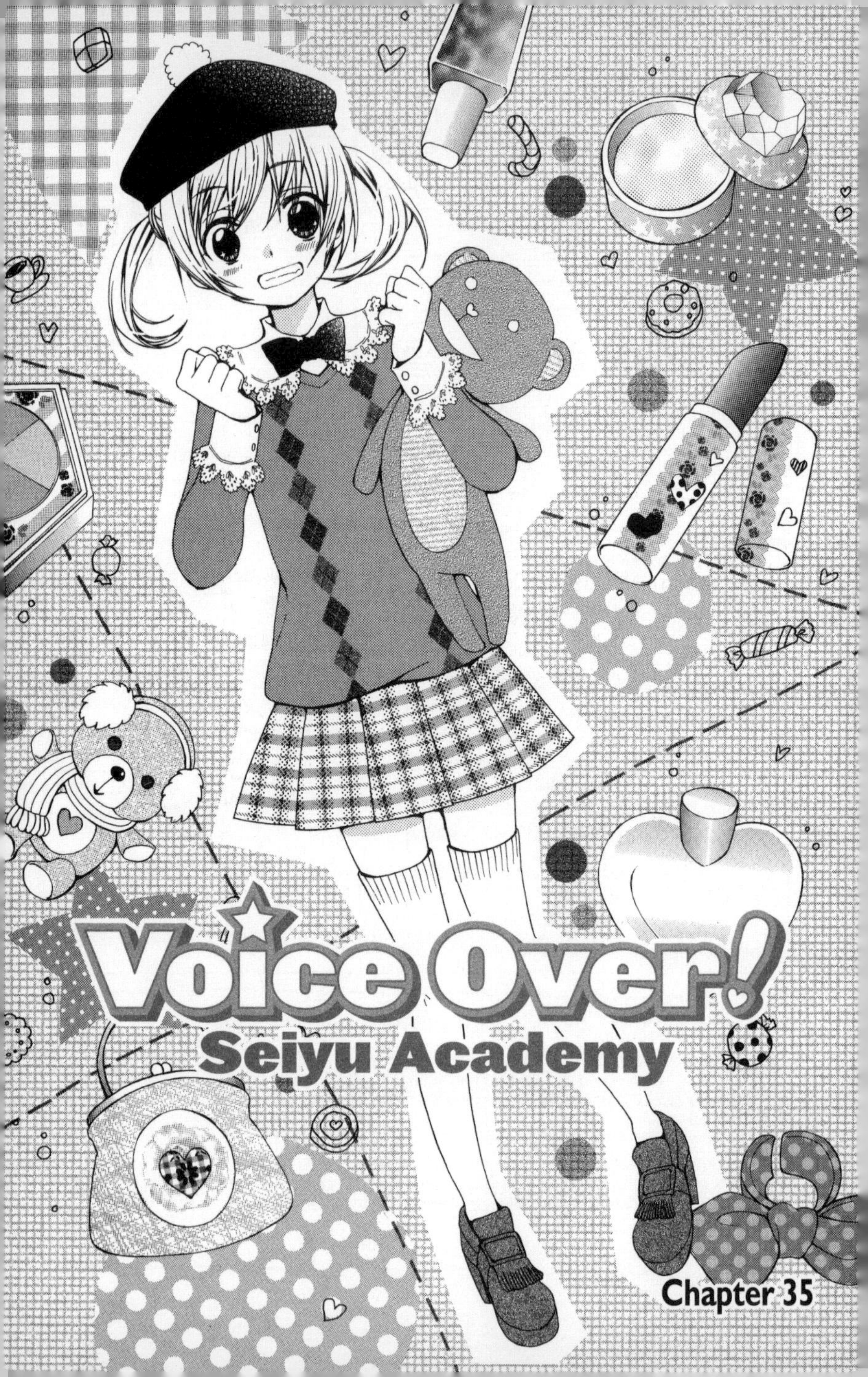
Voice Over!
Seiyu Academy
Chapter 35

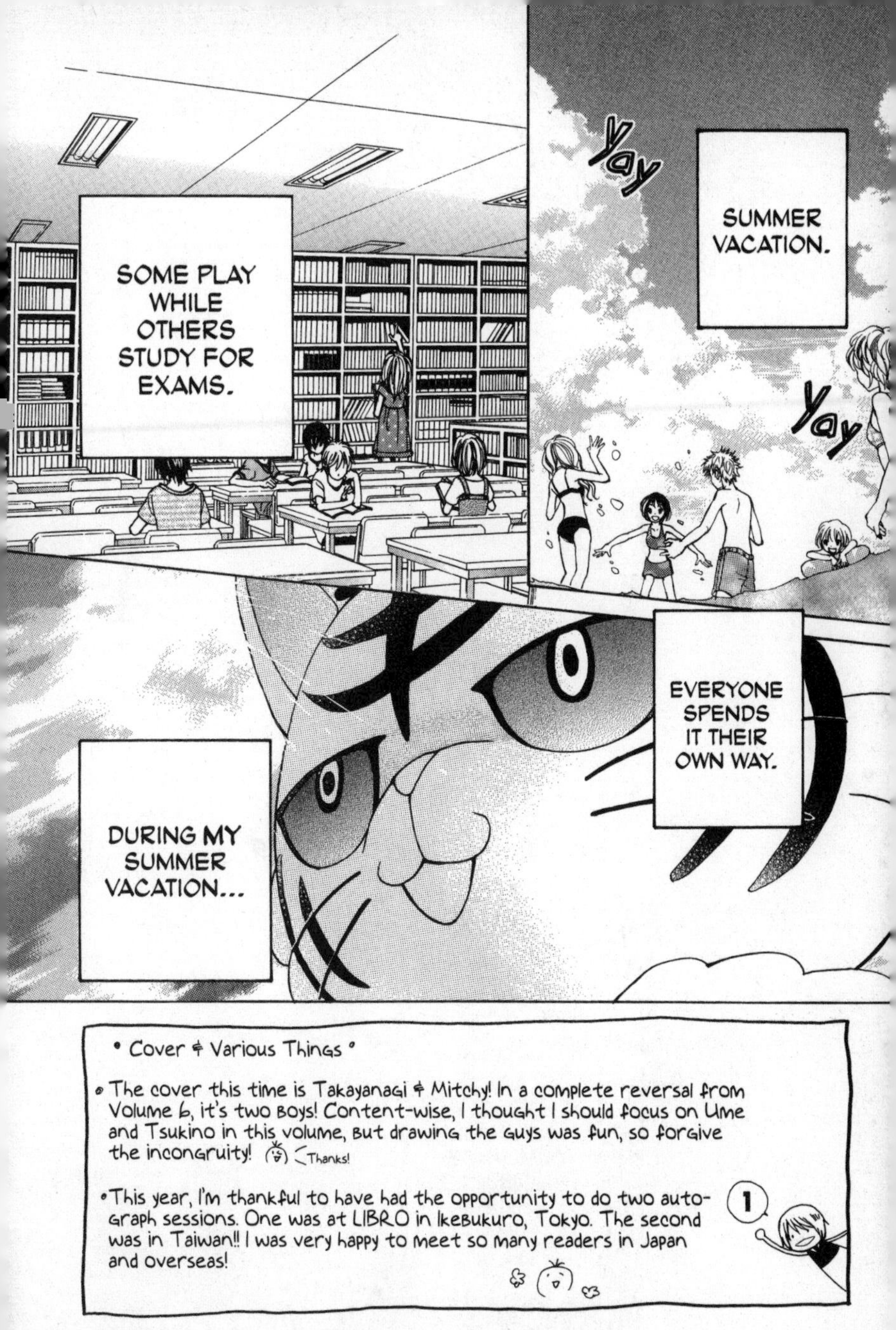
SUMMER VACATION.
Yay
Yay
SOME PLAY WHILE OTHERS STUDY FOR EXAMS.
EVERYONE SPENDS IT THEIR OWN WAY.
DURING MY SUMMER VACATION...

• Cover & Various Things •

• The cover this time is Takayanagi & Mitchy! In a complete reversal from Volume 6, it's two boys! Content-wise, I thought I should focus on Ume and Tsukino in this volume, but drawing the guys was fun, so forgive the incongruity! Thanks!

• This year, I'm thankful to have had the opportunity to do two autograph sessions. One was at LIBRO in Ikebukuro, Tokyo. The second was in Taiwan!! I was very happy to meet so many readers in Japan and overseas!

1

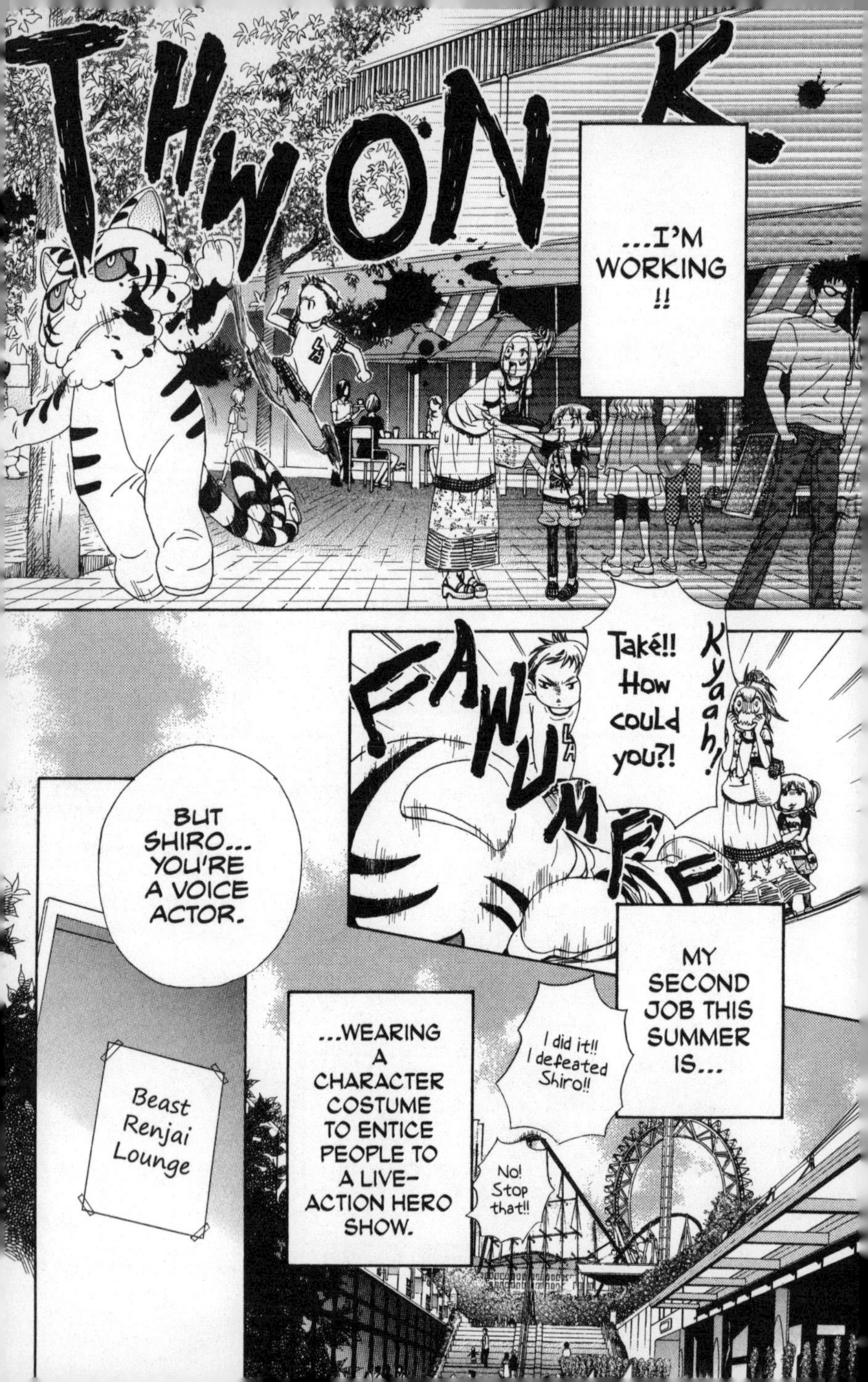
THWONK
...I'M WORKING !!
Kyaah!
Také!! How could you?!
FAWUMFF
MY SECOND JOB THIS SUMMER IS...
I did it!! I defeated Shiro!!
...WEARING A CHARACTER COSTUME TO ENTICE PEOPLE TO A LIVE-ACTION HERO SHOW.
No! Stop that!!
BUT SHIRO... YOU'RE A VOICE ACTOR.
Beast Renjai Lounge

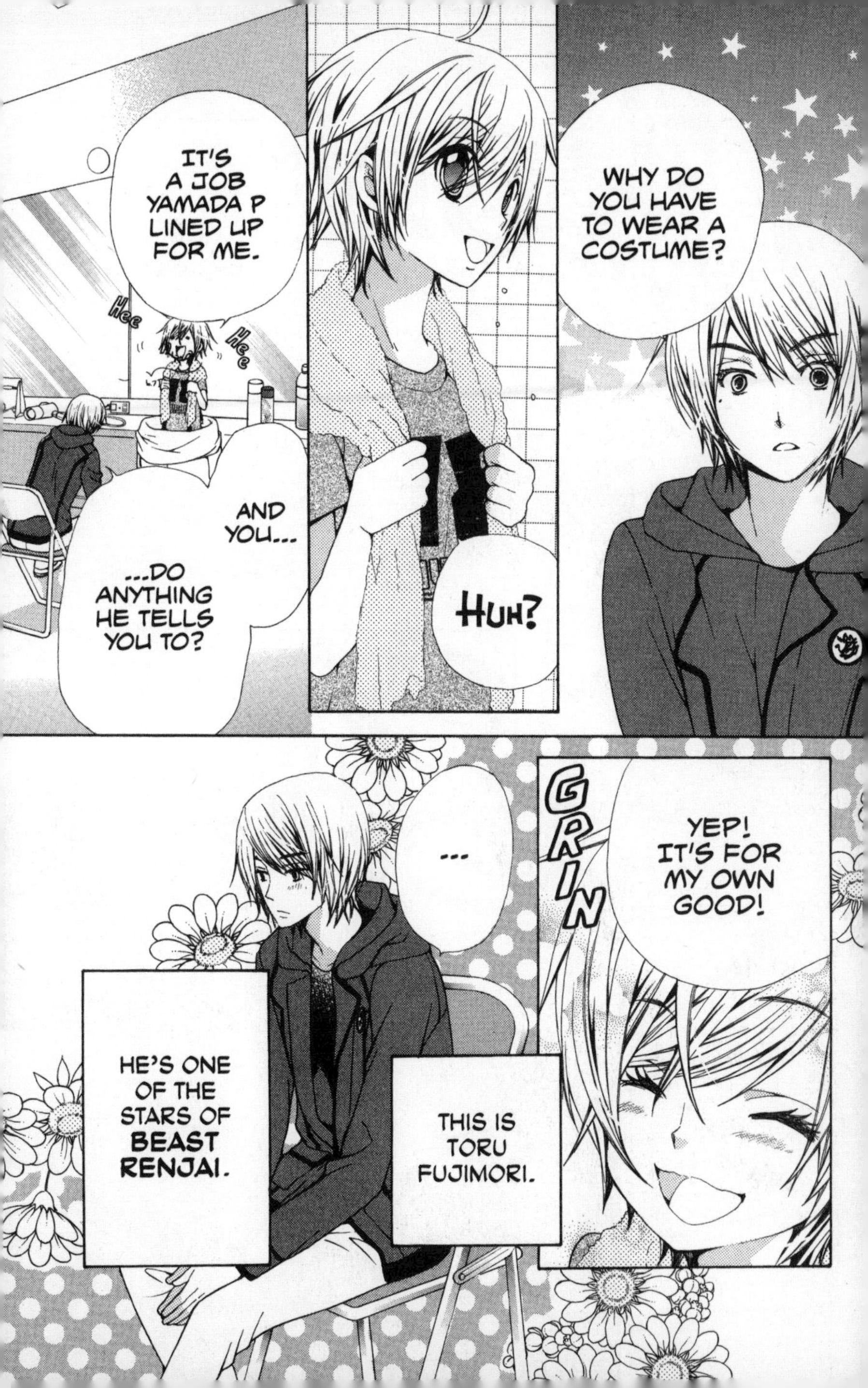
WHY DO YOU HAVE TO WEAR A COSTUME?
HUH?
IT'S A JOB YAMADA P LINED UP FOR ME.
Hee Hee
AND YOU...
...DO ANYTHING HE TELLS YOU TO?
GRIN
YEP! IT'S FOR MY OWN GOOD!
...
THIS IS TORU FUJIMORI.
HE'S ONE OF THE STARS OF BEAST RENJAI.

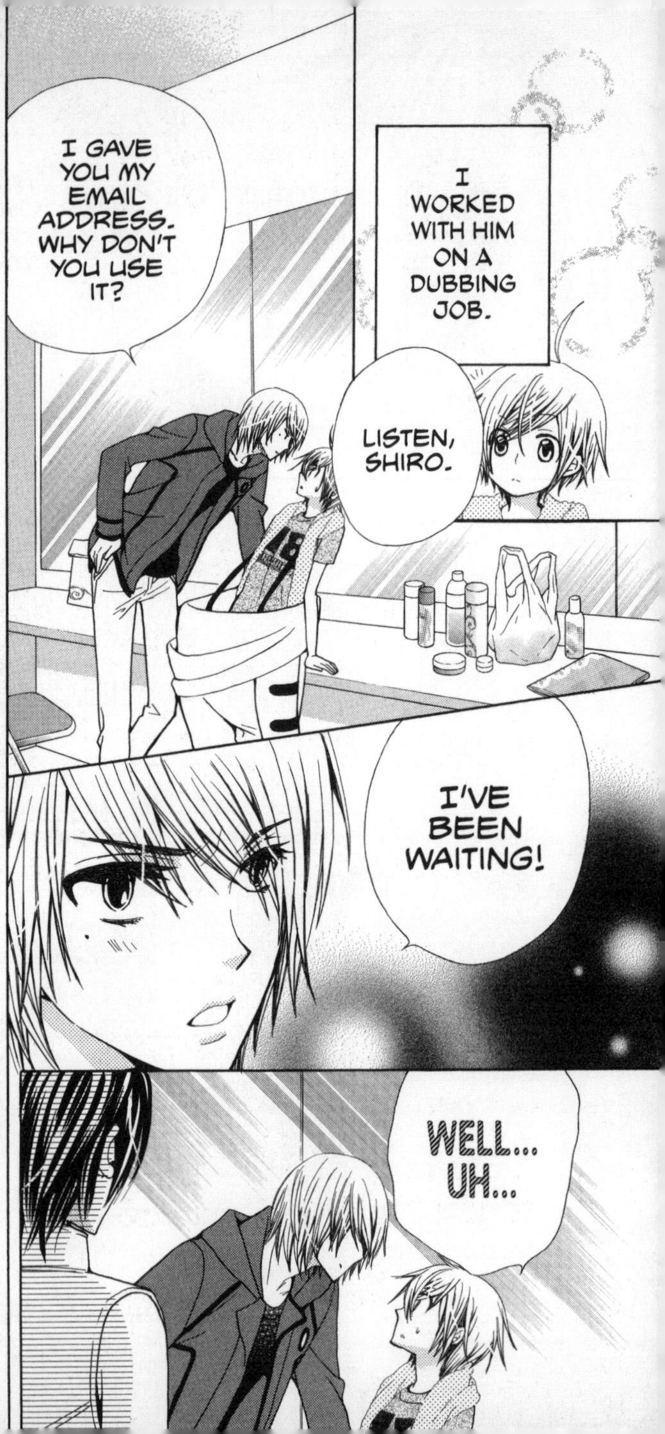
I WORKED WITH HIM ON A DUBBING JOB.
LISTEN, SHIRO.
I GAVE YOU MY EMAIL ADDRESS. WHY DON'T YOU USE IT?
I'VE BEEN WAITING!
WELL... UH...

◦ Greetings ◦

Nice to meet you & hello!!

This is Volume 7 of *Voice Over!: Seiyu Academy*! As a side note, in Taiwan they write the title like this:

聲優志願!

The character for "voice" is really neat!!

In Hong Kong, it's

爲聲優吧!

In France, it's *Seiyuka*!

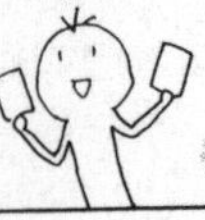

A friend who read Volume 6 said it was erotic. Is it really? Seriously?! Here's to sexy manga!!

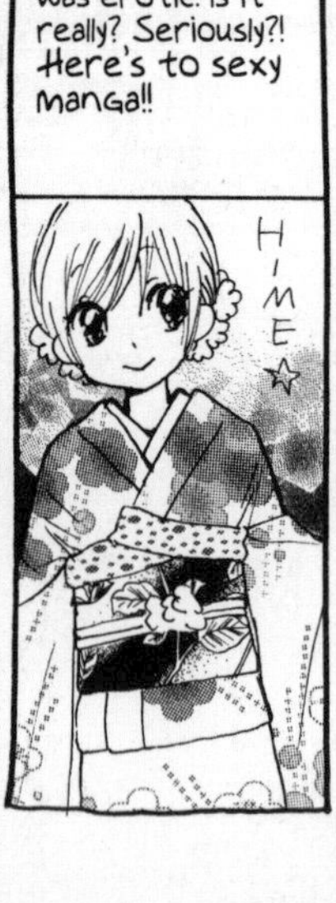
HIME☆

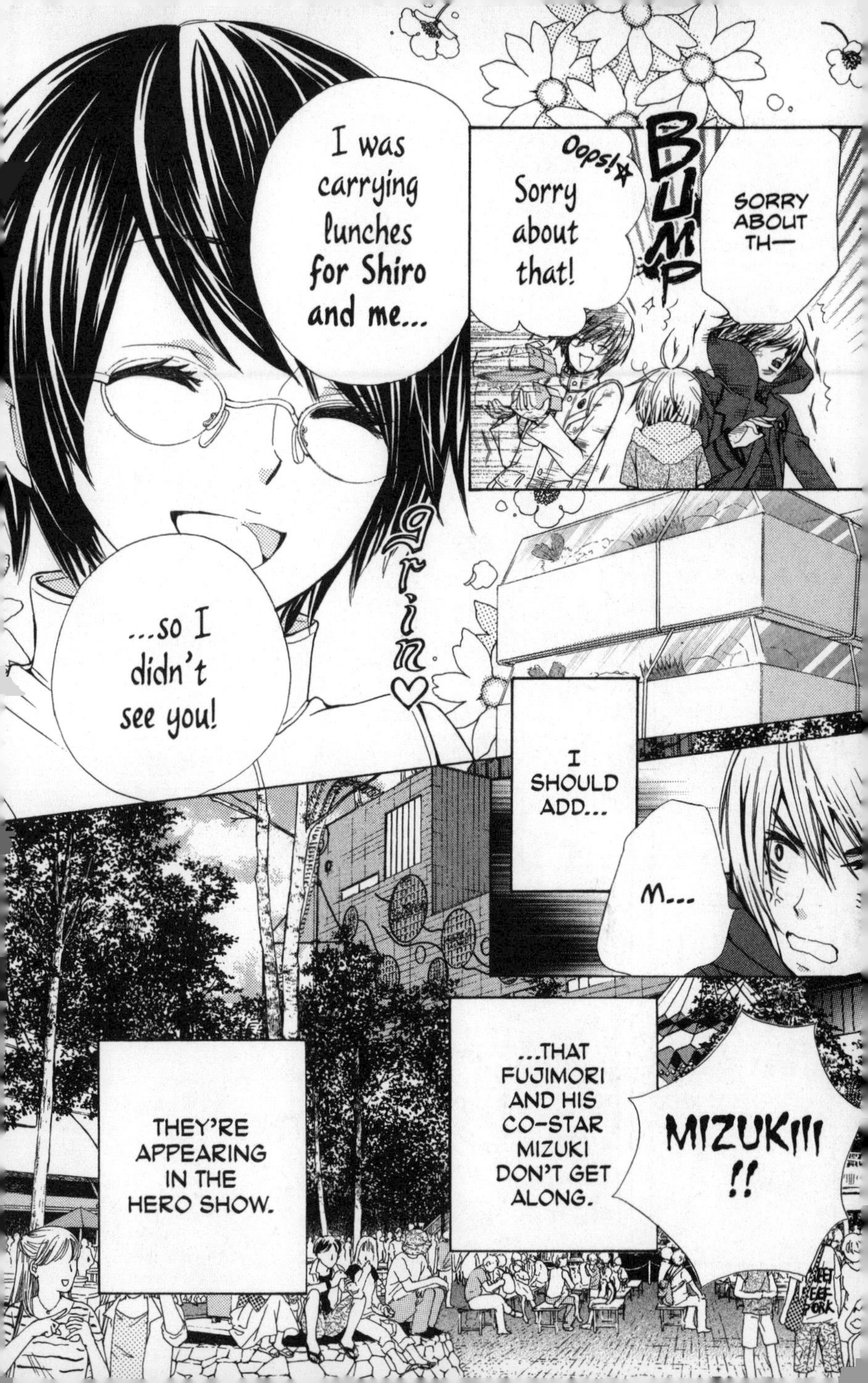
SORRY ABOUT TH—
BUMP
Oops!☆
Sorry about that!
I was carrying lunches for Shiro and me...
grin♥
...so I didn't see you!
I SHOULD ADD...
M...
MIZUKIII !!
...THAT FUJIMORI AND HIS CO-STAR MIZUKI DON'T GET ALONG.
THEY'RE APPEARING IN THE HERO SHOW.

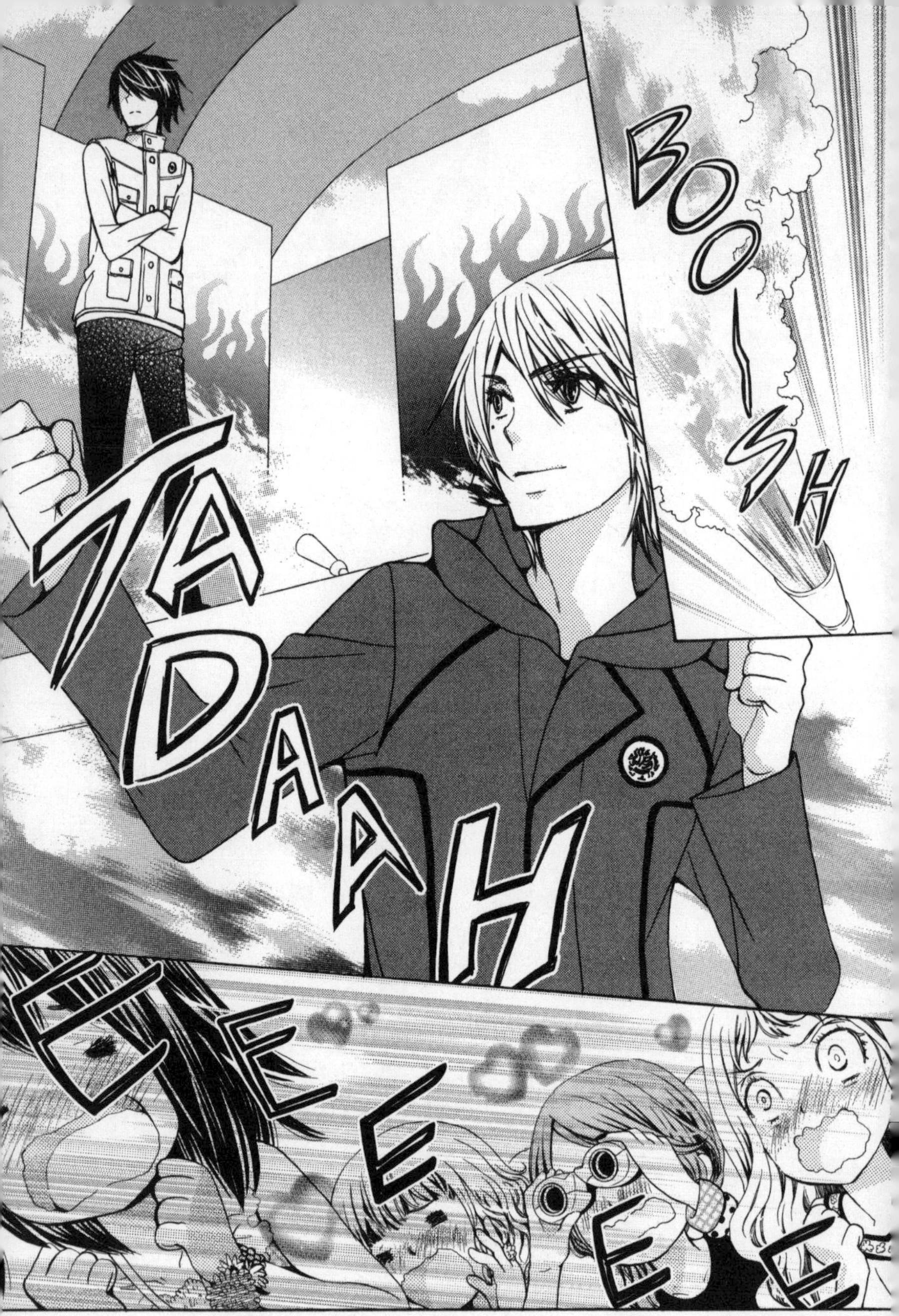
BOOOOSH
TADAAH
EEEEEE

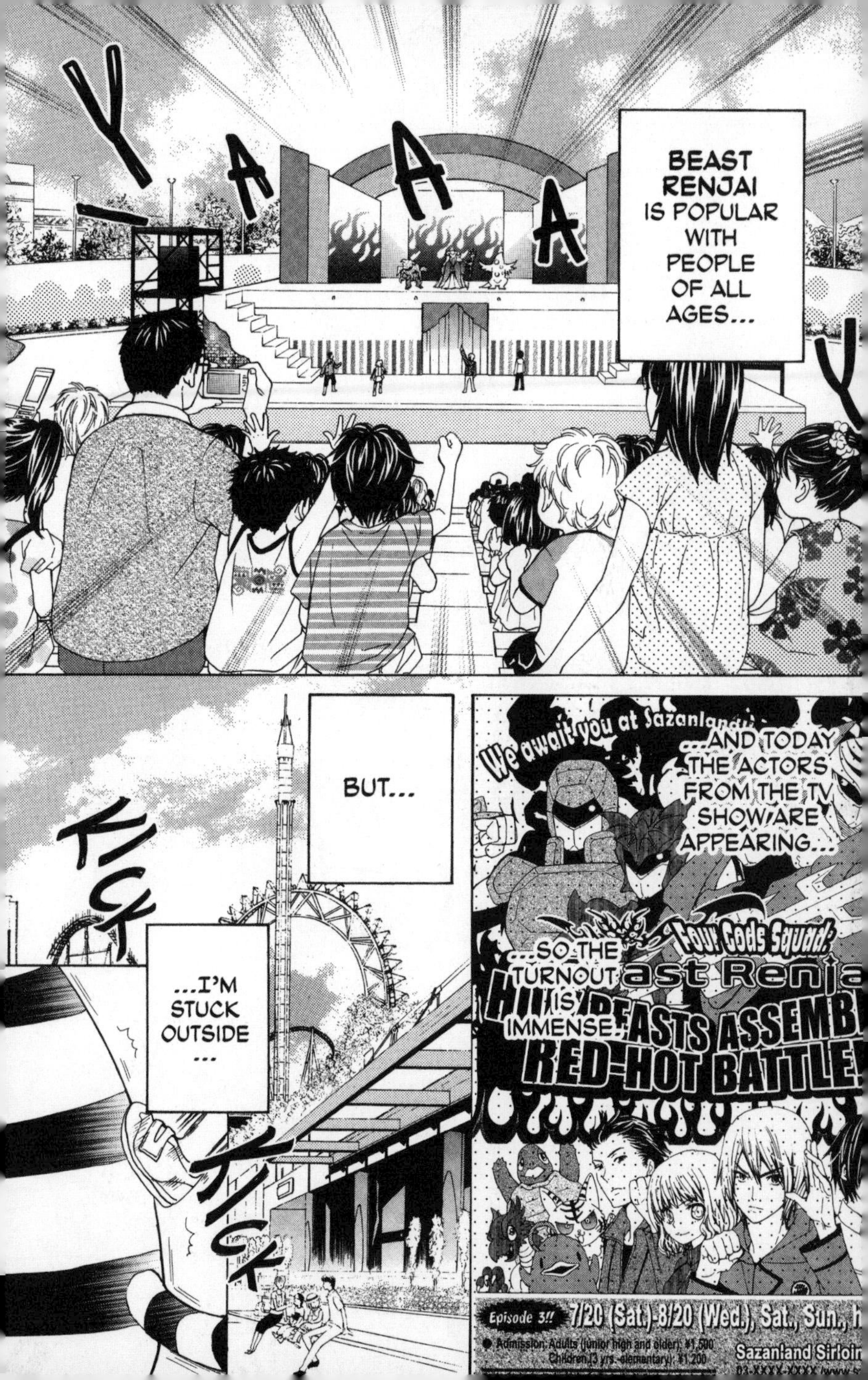
BEAST RENJAI IS POPULAR WITH PEOPLE OF ALL AGES...
YAAAY
...AND TODAY THE ACTORS FROM THE TV SHOW ARE APPEARING...
...SO THE TURNOUT IS IMMENSE.
We await you at Sazanland!!
Four Gods Squad:
RED-HOT BATTLE
Episode 3!!
7/20 (Sat.)-8/20 (Wed.), Sat., Sun.,
Admission: Adults (junior high and older): ¥1,500
Children (3 yrs.-elementary): ¥1,200
Sazanland Sirloin
BUT...
...I'M STUCK OUTSIDE ...
KICK
KICK

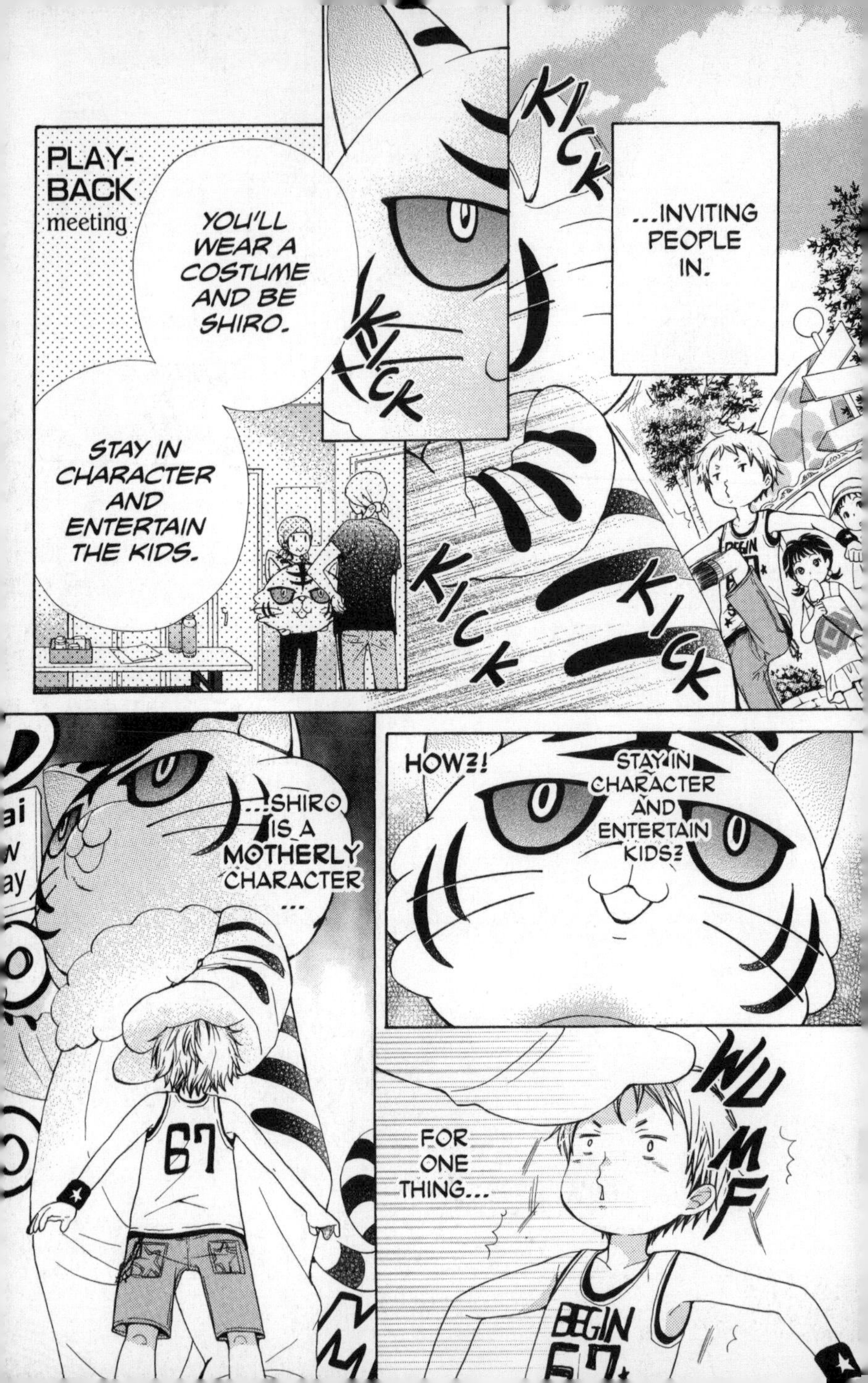
...INVITING PEOPLE IN.
KICK
KICK
KICK
KICK
KICK
KICK
PLAY-BACK meeting
YOU'LL WEAR A COSTUME AND BE SHIRO.
STAY IN CHARACTER AND ENTERTAIN THE KIDS.
STAY IN CHARACTER AND ENTERTAIN KIDS?
HOW?!
WUMF
FOR ONE THING...
...SHIRO IS A MOTHERLY CHARACTER...

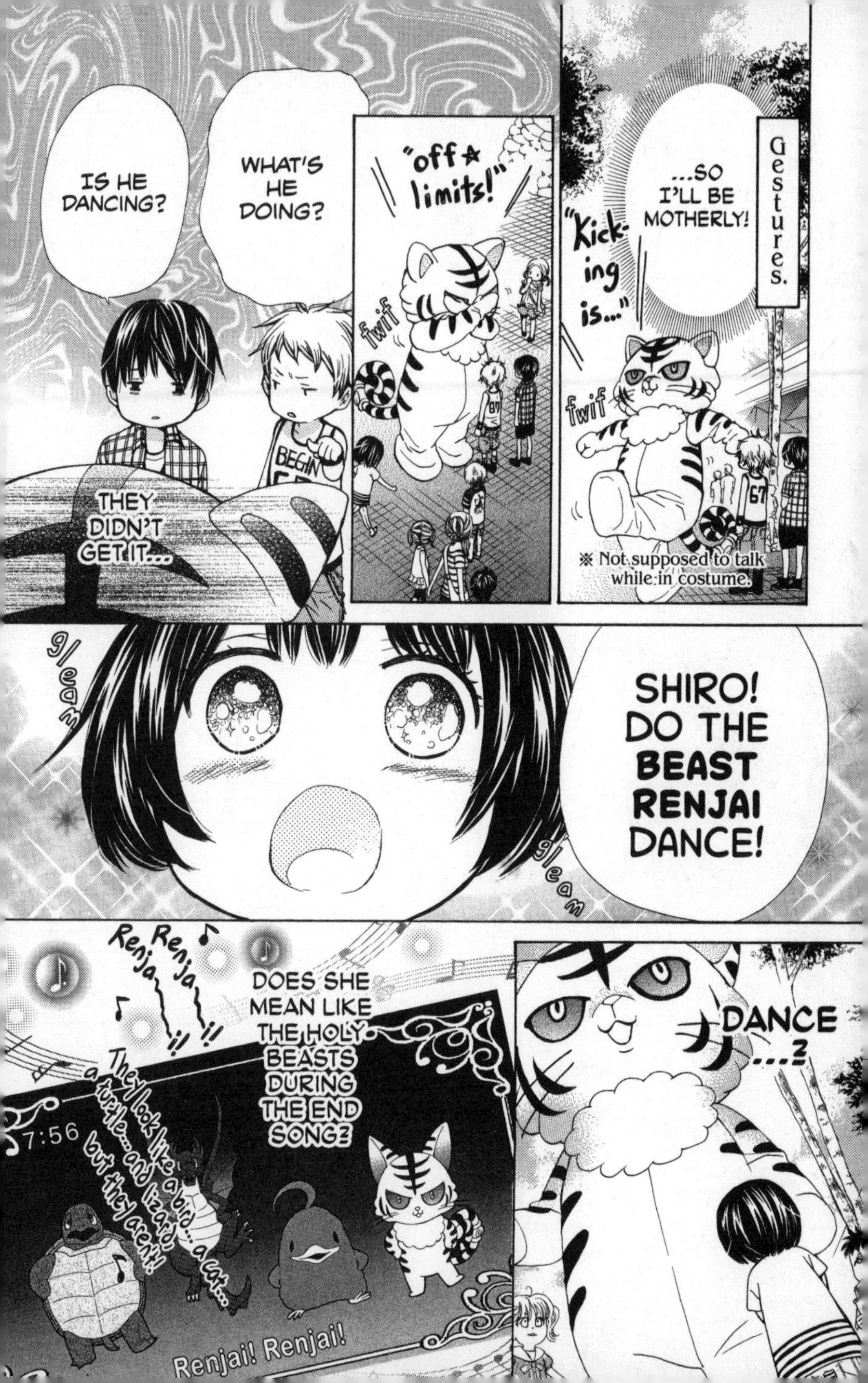
Gestures.
...SO I'LL BE MOTHERLY!
"Kick-ing is..."
fwif
※ Not supposed to talk while in costume.
"off ☆ limits!"
fwif
WHAT'S HE DOING?
IS HE DANCING?
THEY DIDN'T GET IT...
SHIRO! DO THE BEAST RENJAI DANCE!
gleam
gleam
DANCE...?
DOES SHE MEAN LIKE THE HOLY BEASTS DURING THE END SONG?
Renja~!!
Renja~!!
They look like a bird...a cat...a turtle...and lizard but they aren't!
7:56
Renjai! Renjai!

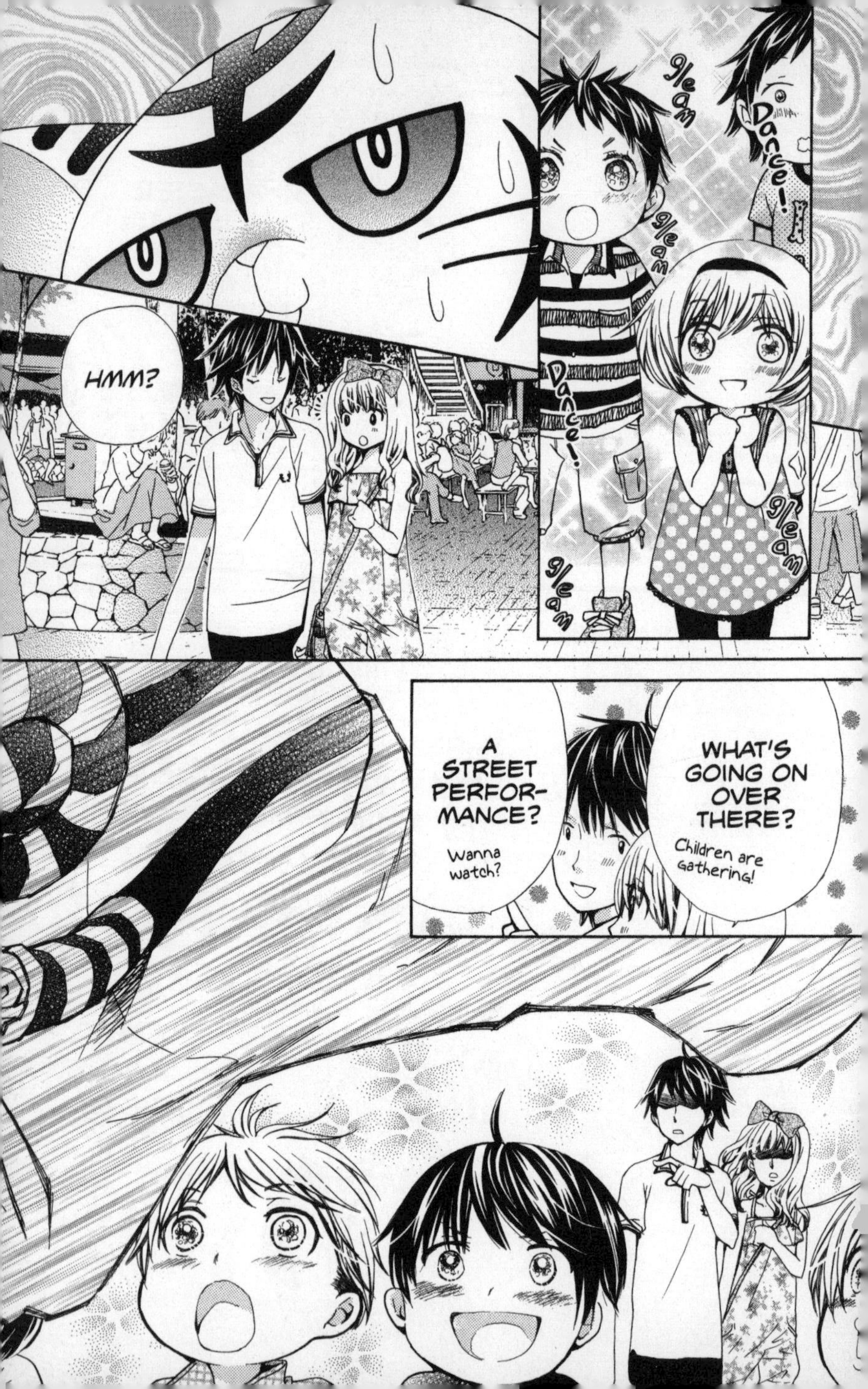

Dance!
gleam
gleam
Dance!
gleam
gleam
HMM?
WHAT'S GOING ON OVER THERE?
Children are gathering!
A STREET PERFORMANCE?
Wanna watch?

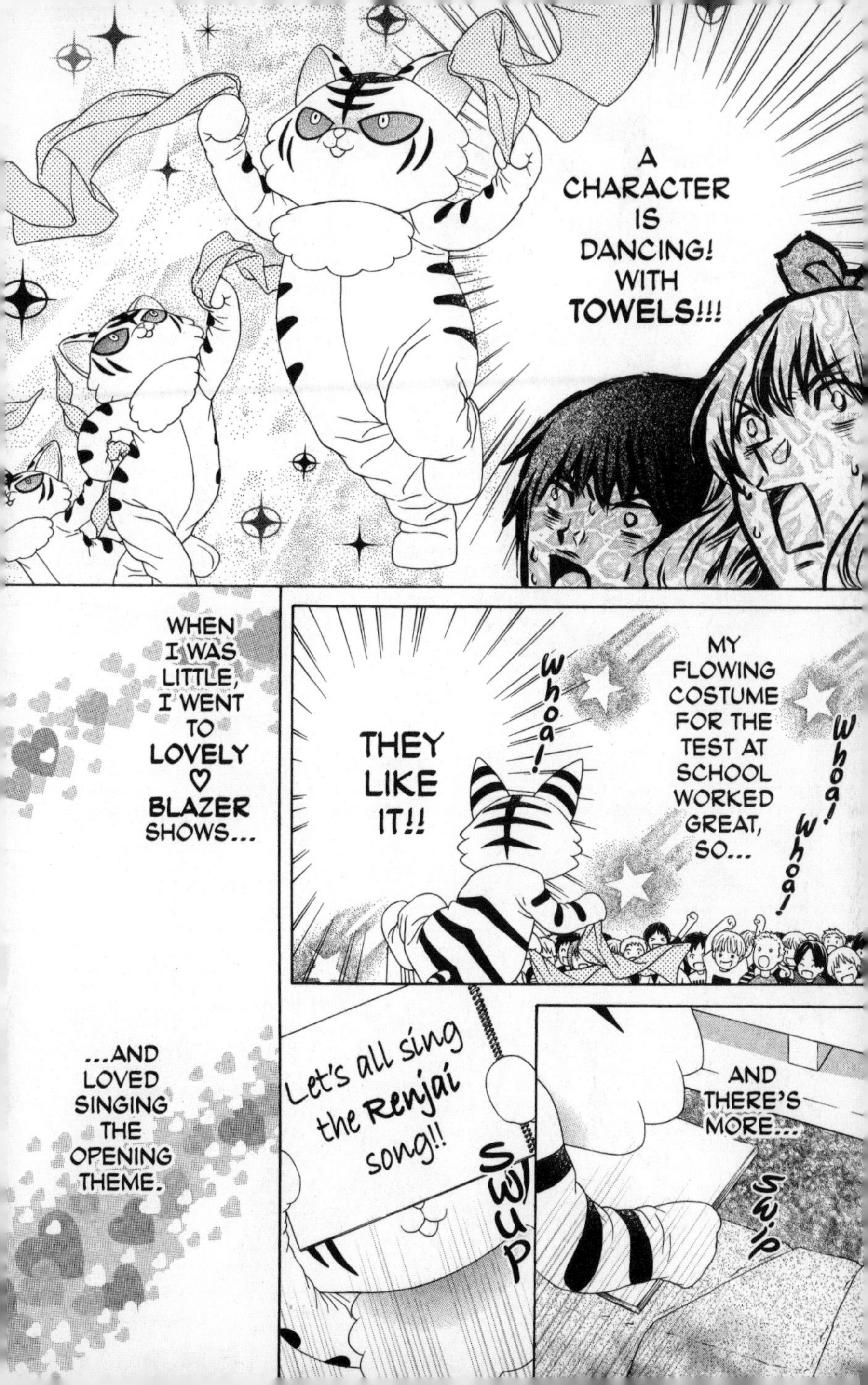
A CHARACTER IS DANCING! WITH TOWELS!!!
Whoa! Whoa! Whoa!
MY FLOWING COSTUME FOR THE TEST AT SCHOOL WORKED GREAT, SO...
THEY LIKE IT!!
Whoa!
WHEN I WAS LITTLE, I WENT TO LOVELY ♡ BLAZER SHOWS...
AND THERE'S MORE...
Swip
Let's all sing the Renjai song!!
SWUP
...AND LOVED SINGING THE OPENING THEME.

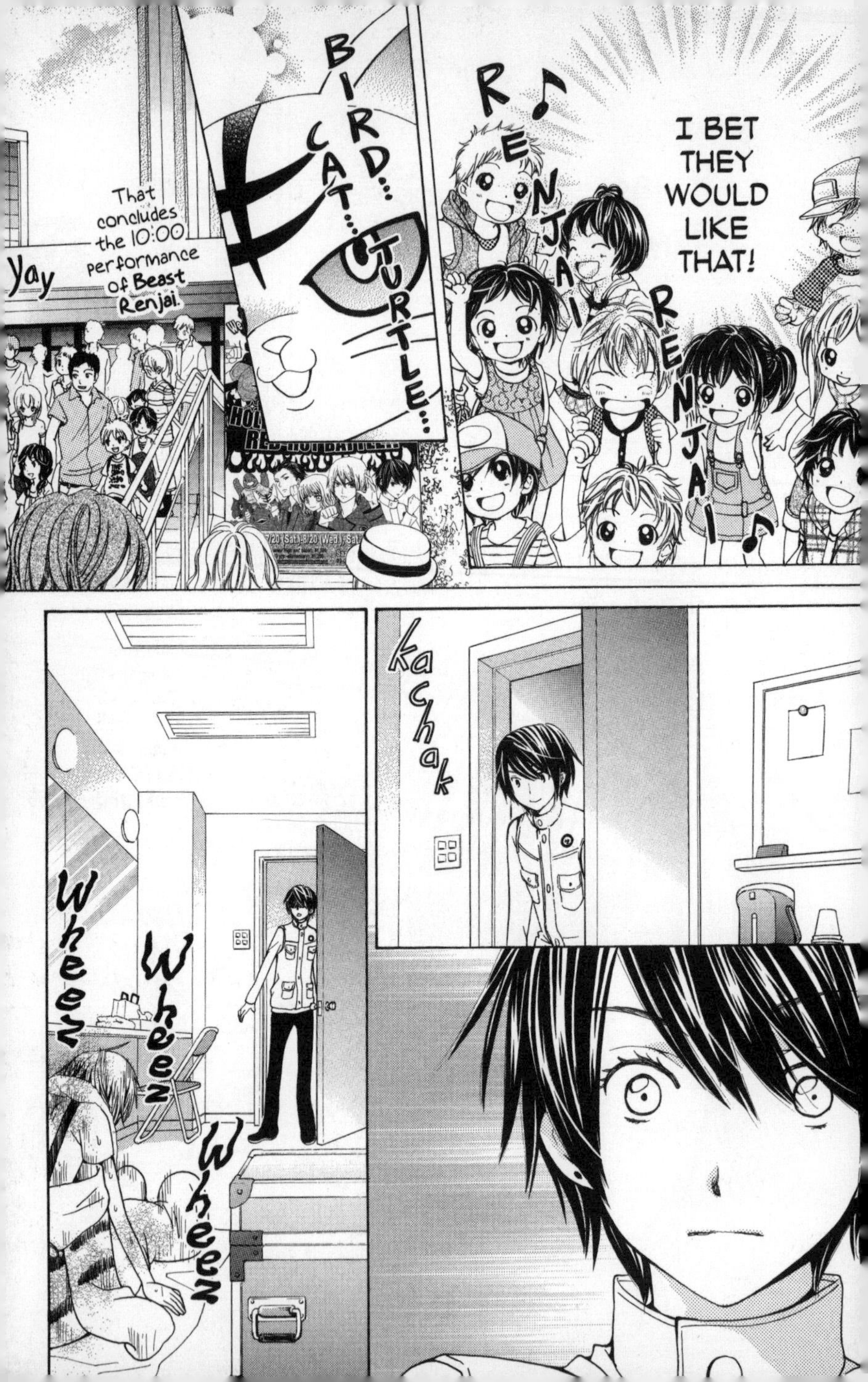

I BET THEY WOULD LIKE THAT!
RENJAI♪ RENJAI RENJAI♪
BIRD... CAT... TURTLE...
That concludes the 10:00 performance of Beast Renjai.
yay
kachak
Wheez Wheez Wheez Wheez

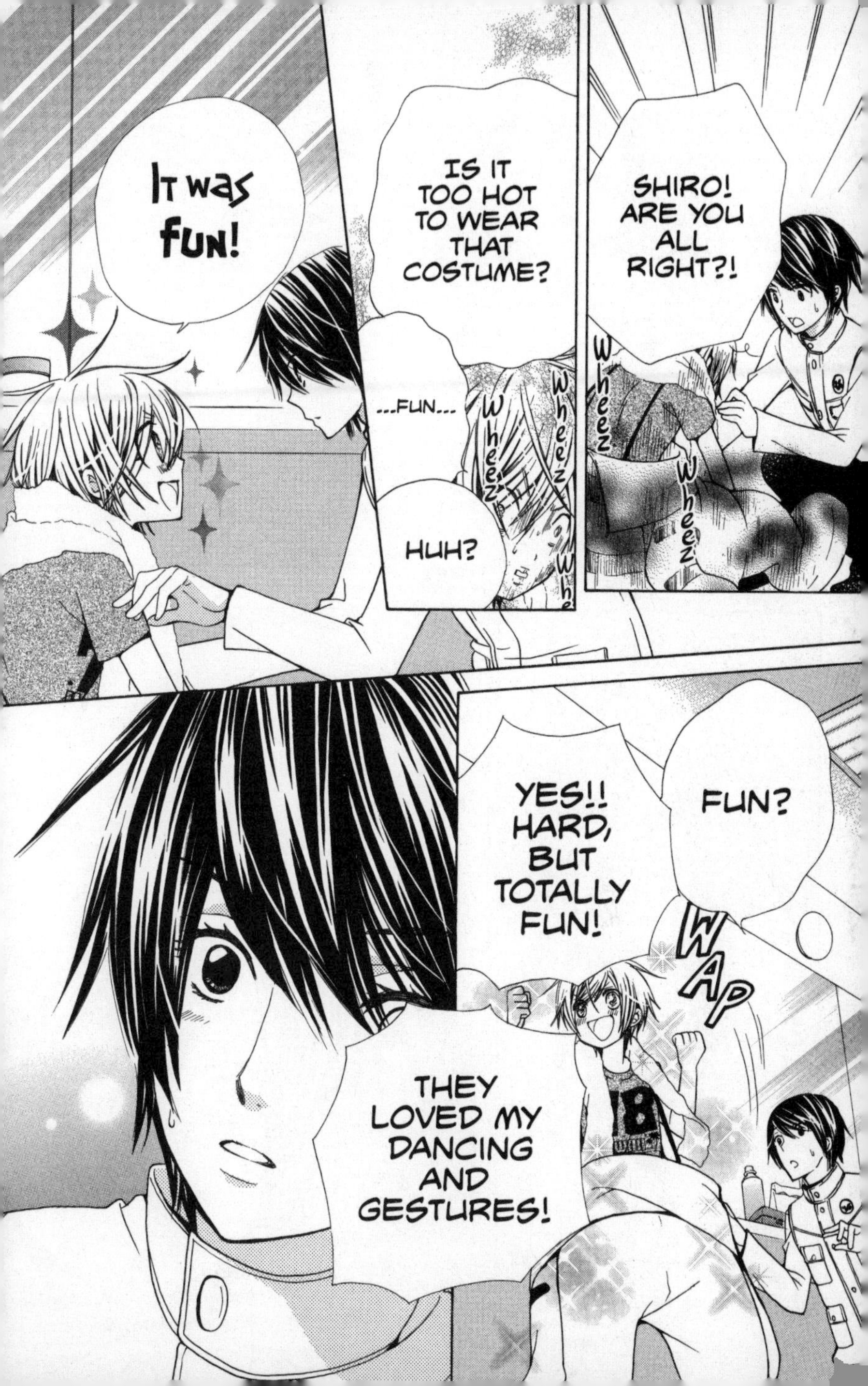
SHIRO! ARE YOU ALL RIGHT?!
Wheez
Wheez
IS IT TOO HOT TO WEAR THAT COSTUME?
Wheez
Wheez
Whe
...FUN...
HUH?
It was FUN!
FUN?
YES!! HARD, BUT TOTALLY FUN!
WAP
THEY LOVED MY DANCING AND GESTURES!

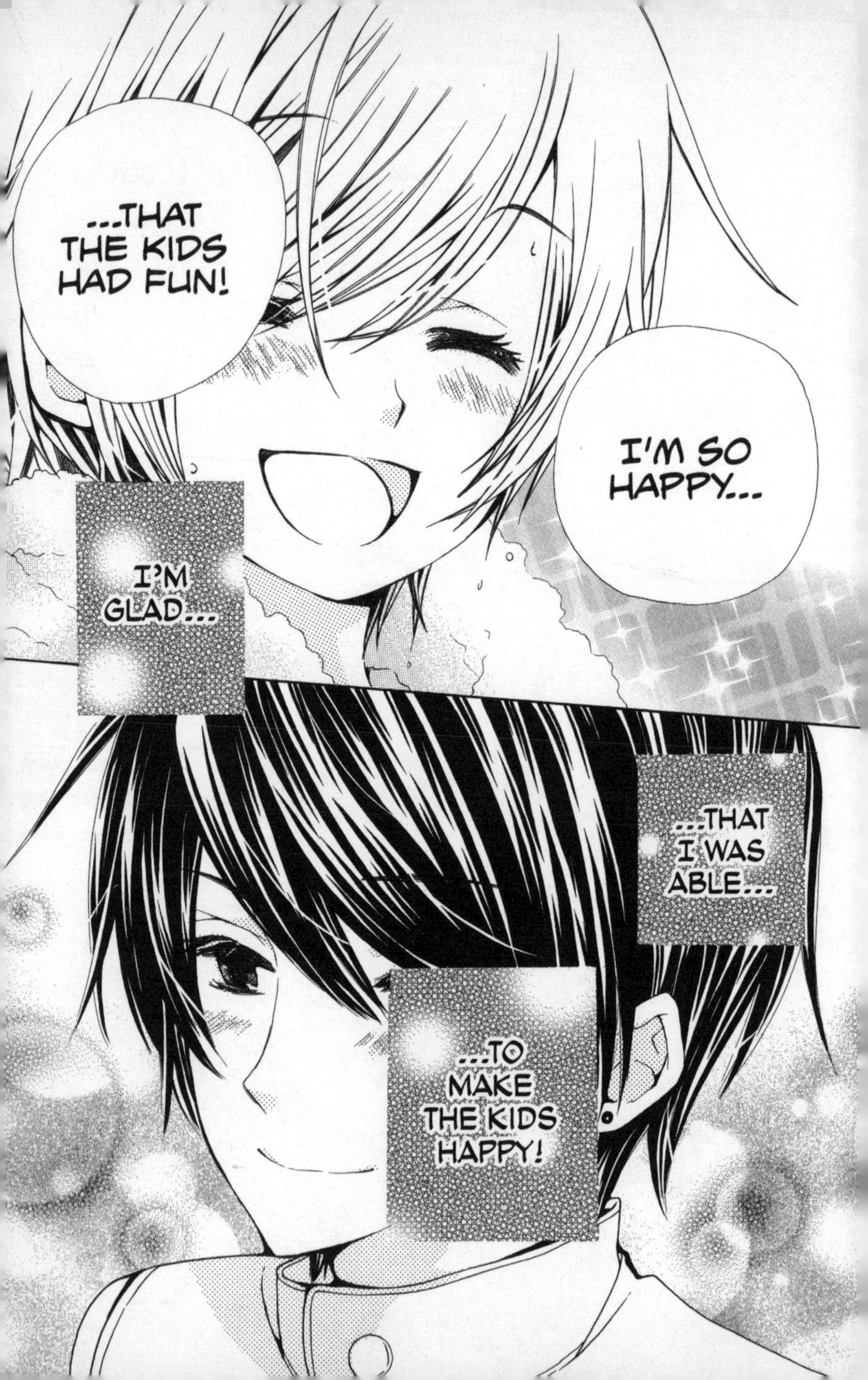
I'M SO HAPPY...
...THAT THE KIDS HAD FUN!
I'M GLAD...
...THAT I WAS ABLE...
...TO MAKE THE KIDS HAPPY!

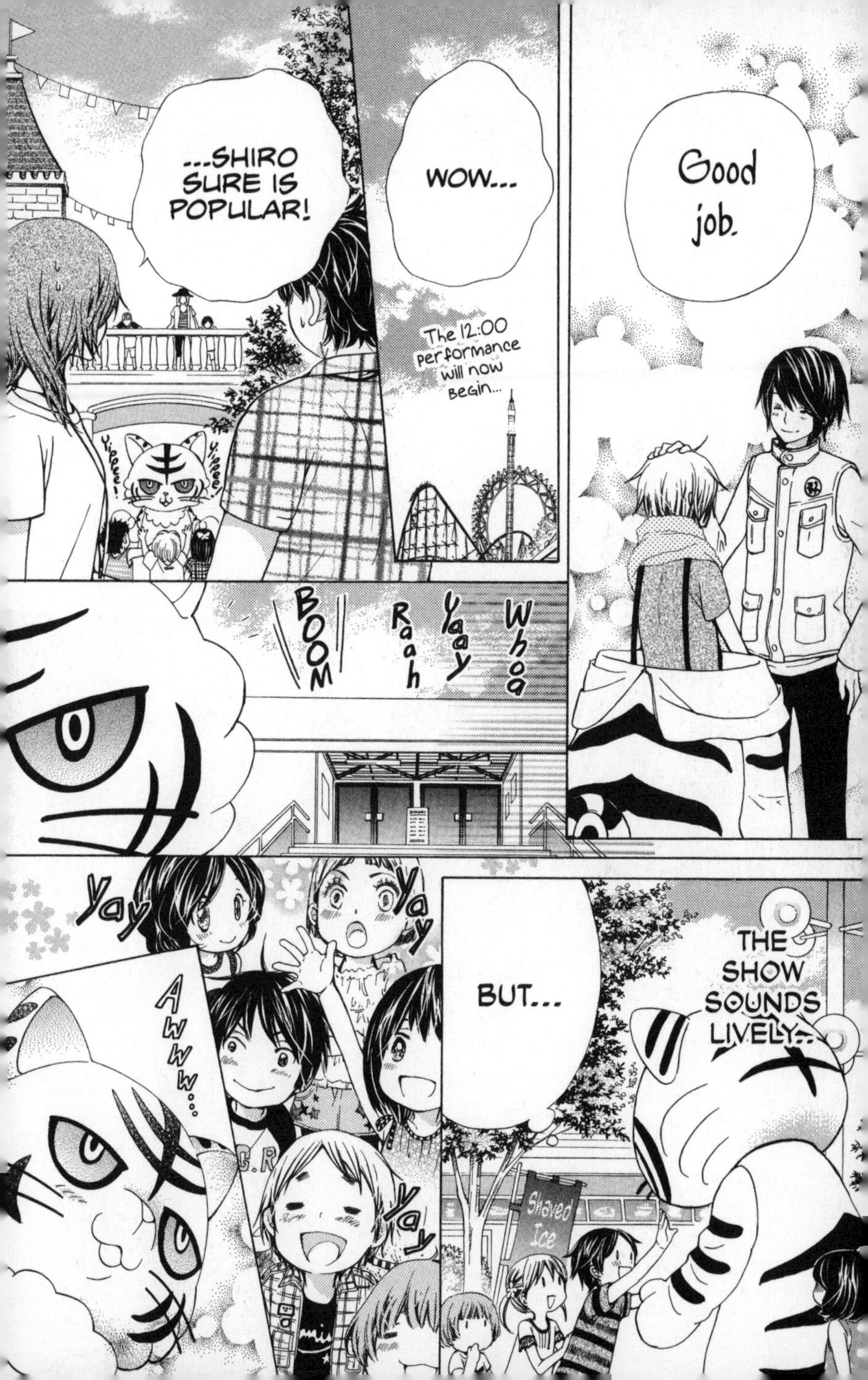
Good job.
WOW...
The 12:00 performance will now begin...
...SHIRO SURE IS POPULAR!
Yippee!
Yippee!
Whoa
Yaay
Raah
BOOM
THE SHOW SOUNDS LIVELY...
BUT...
Yay
Yay
Awww...
Yay
Shaved Ice

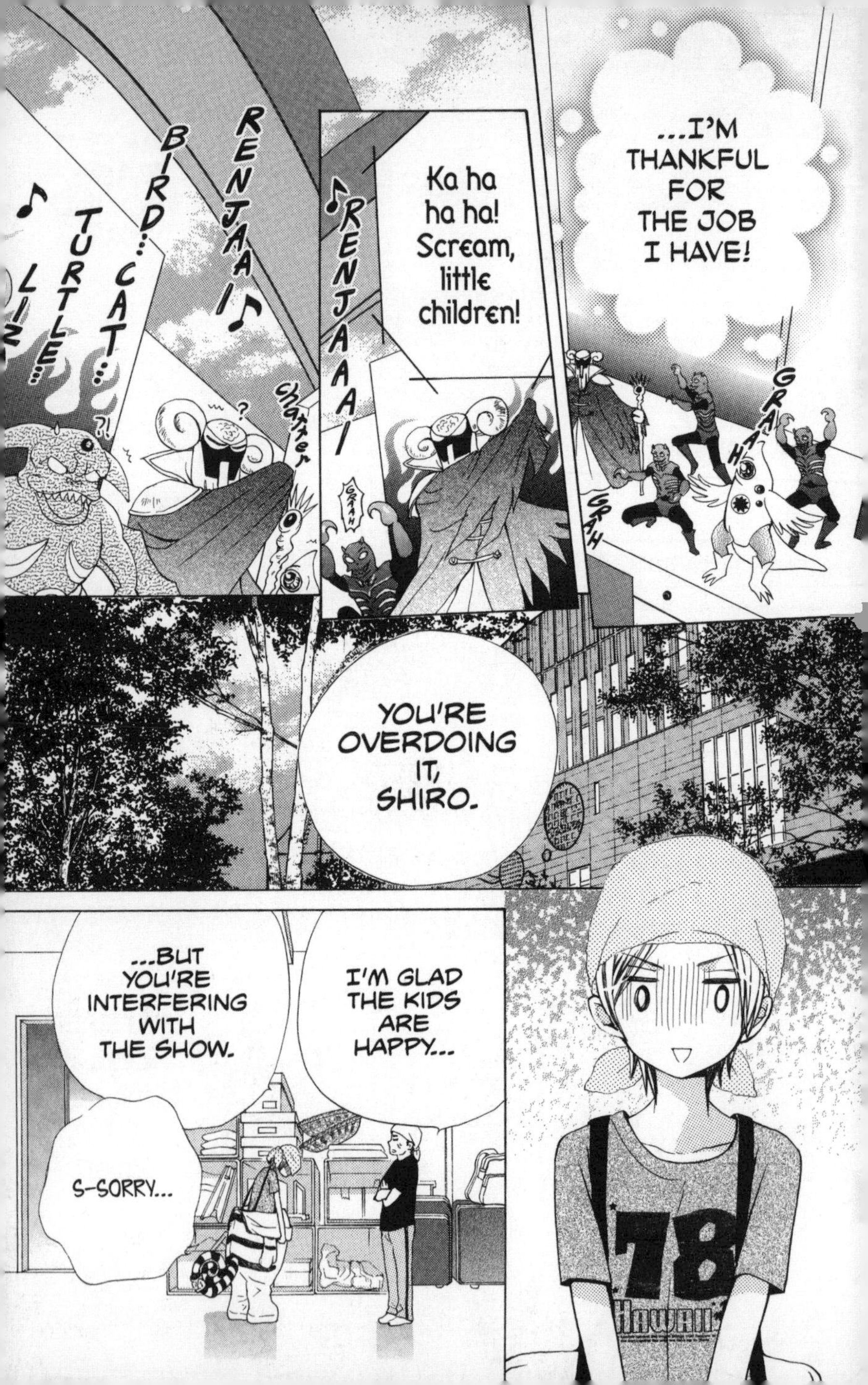
...I'M THANKFUL FOR THE JOB I HAVE!
GRAAH
GRAH
Ka ha ha ha! Scream, little children!
♪RENJAAAAI
GRAAH
RENJAAI♪
BIRD... CAT... TURTLE... LIZ
chatter
?!
?
YOU'RE OVERDOING IT, SHIRO.
I'M GLAD THE KIDS ARE HAPPY...
...BUT YOU'RE INTERFERING WITH THE SHOW.
S-SORRY...

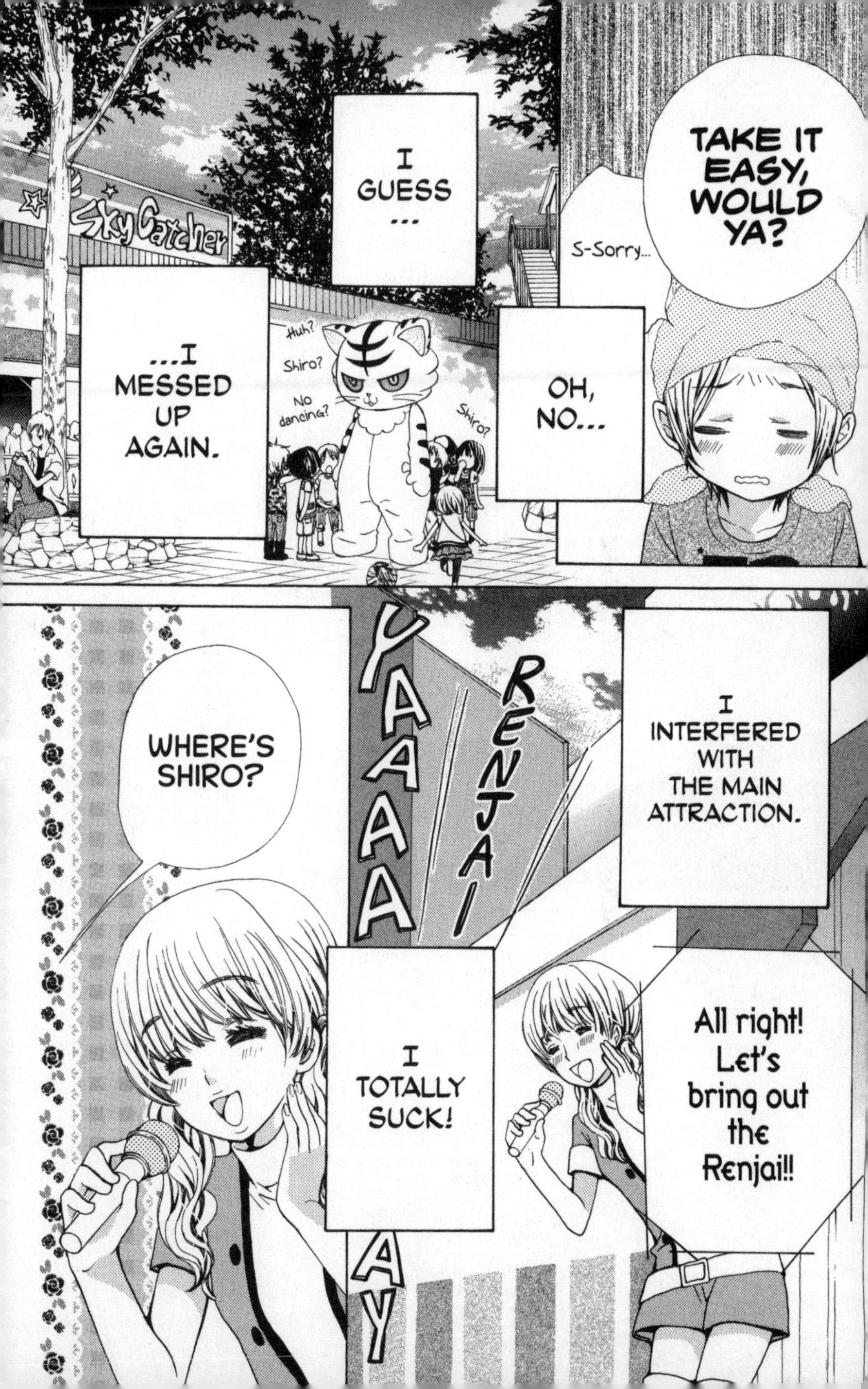
TAKE IT EASY, WOULD YA?
S-Sorry...
OH, NO...
I GUESS...
...I MESSED UP AGAIN.
Huh?
Shiro?
Shiro?
No dancing?
I INTERFERED WITH THE MAIN ATTRACTION.
All right! Let's bring out the Renjai!!
RENJAI
YAAAAAAY
I TOTALLY SUCK!
WHERE'S SHIRO?

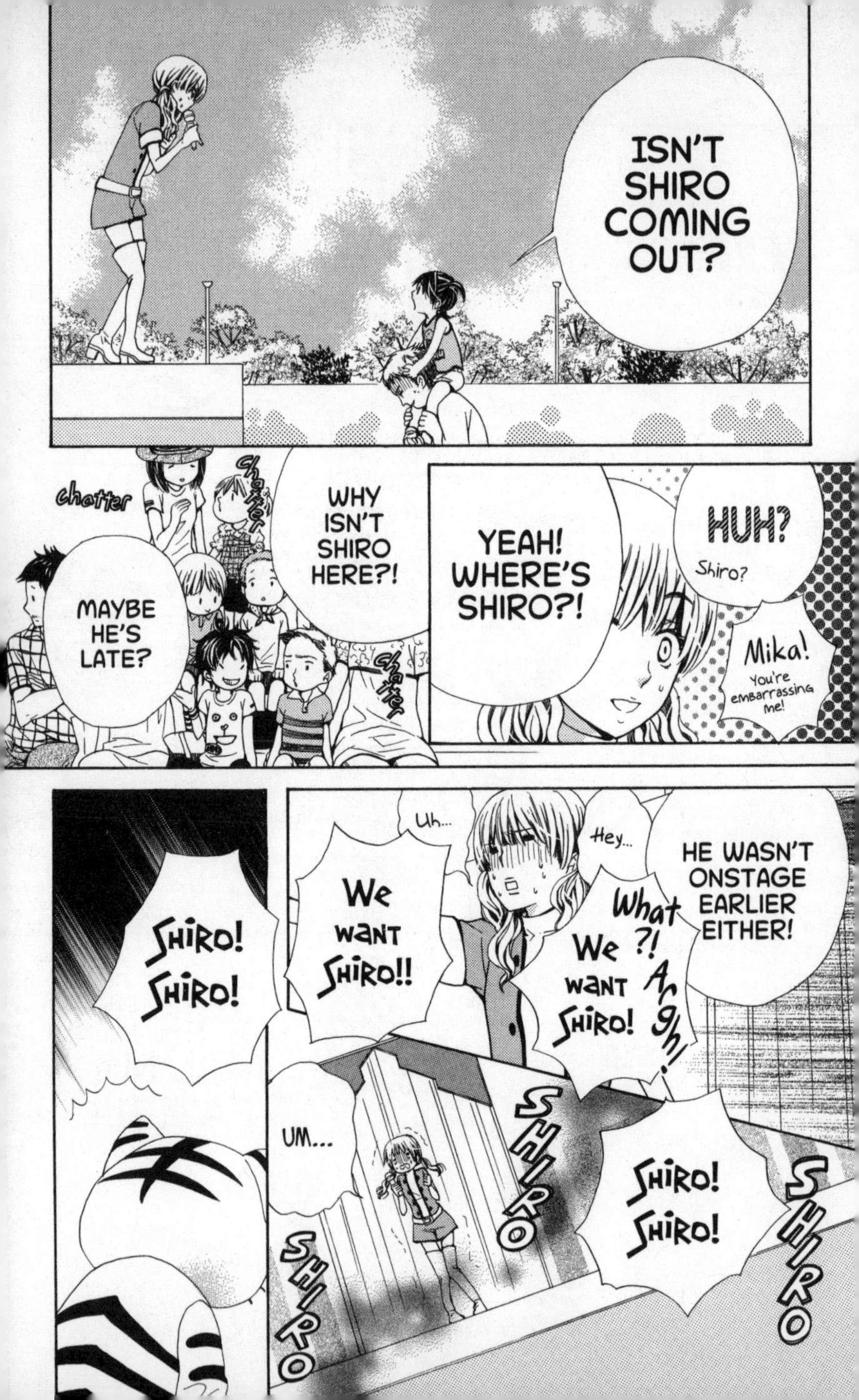
ISN'T SHIRO COMING OUT?
HUH?
Shiro?
Mika! You're embarrassing me!
YEAH! WHERE'S SHIRO?!
WHY ISN'T SHIRO HERE?!
chatter
chatter
MAYBE HE'S LATE?
chatter
HE WASN'T ONSTAGE EARLIER EITHER!
Hey...
Uh...
What?!
Argh!!
We want Shiro!
We want Shiro!!
Shiro! Shiro!
SHIRO
SHIRO
UM...
SHIRO
Shiro! Shiro!

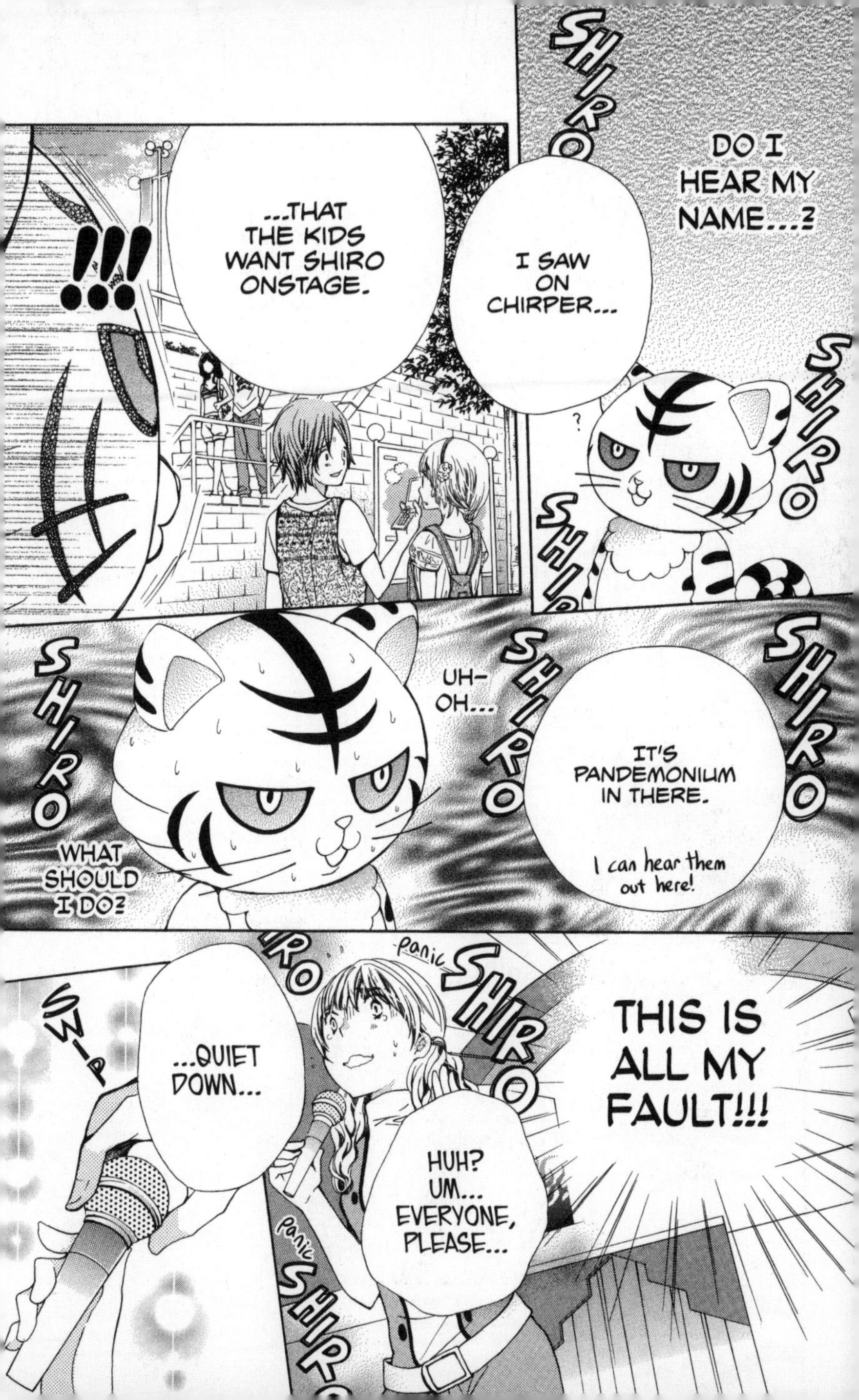
SHIRO
DO I HEAR MY NAME...?
SHIRO
SHIRO
I SAW ON CHIRPER...
...THAT THE KIDS WANT SHIRO ONSTAGE.
!!!
SHIRO
IT'S PANDEMONIUM IN THERE.
I can hear them out here!
SHIRO
UH-OH...
SHIRO
WHAT SHOULD I DO?
THIS IS ALL MY FAULT!!!
panic
SHIRO
SHIRO
HUH? UM... EVERYONE, PLEASE...
...QUIET DOWN...
panic
SHIRO
SWIP

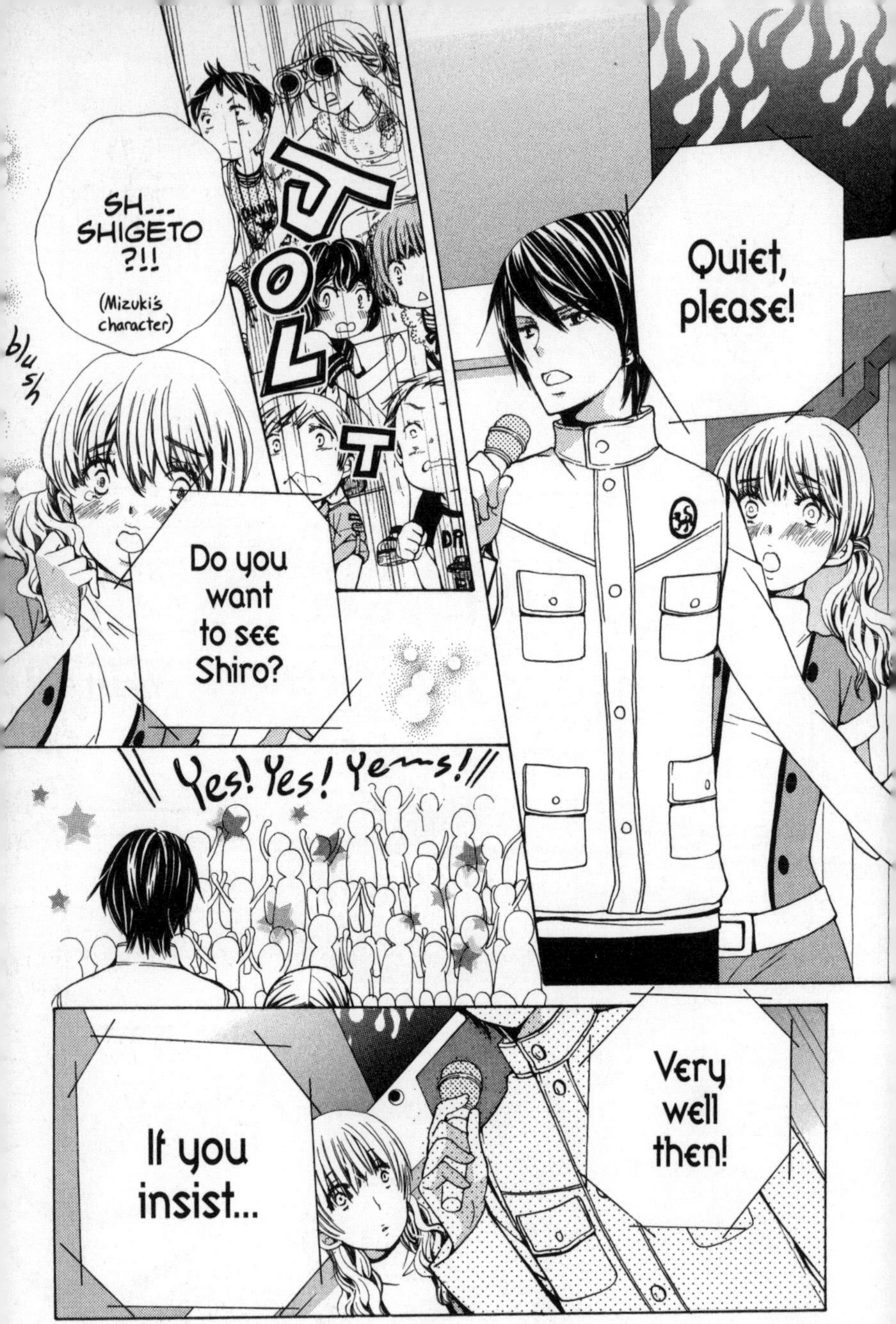
Quiet, please!
JOLT
SH... SHIGETO ?!!
(Mizuki's character)
blush
Do you want to see Shiro?
Yes! Yes! Ye~s!
Very well then!
If you insist...

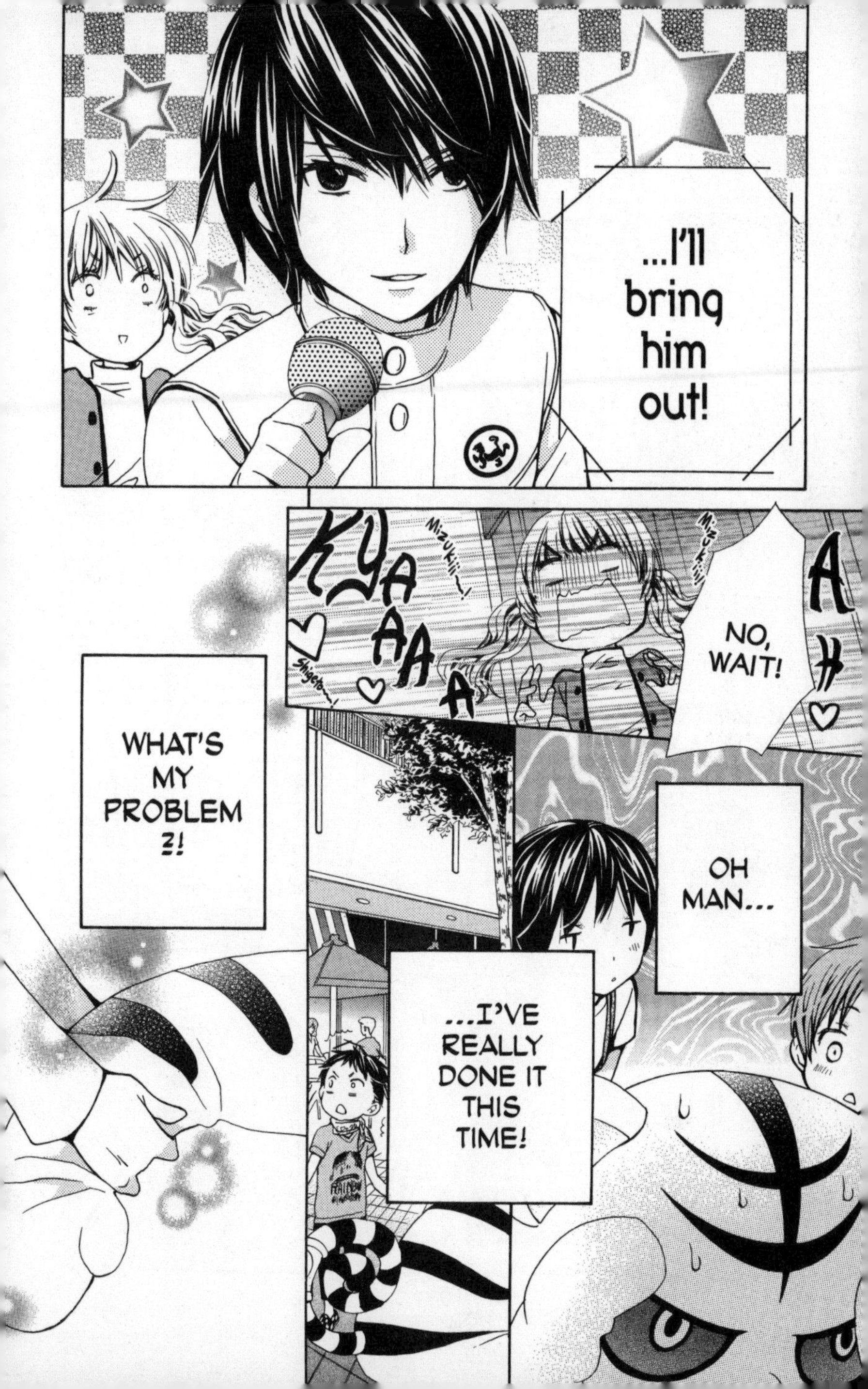
...I'll bring him out!
AH
NO, WAIT!
Mizukiii!!
Mizukiii~!
KYAAAAA
Shigeto~!
OH MAN...
...I'VE REALLY DONE IT THIS TIME!
WHAT'S MY PROBLEM?!

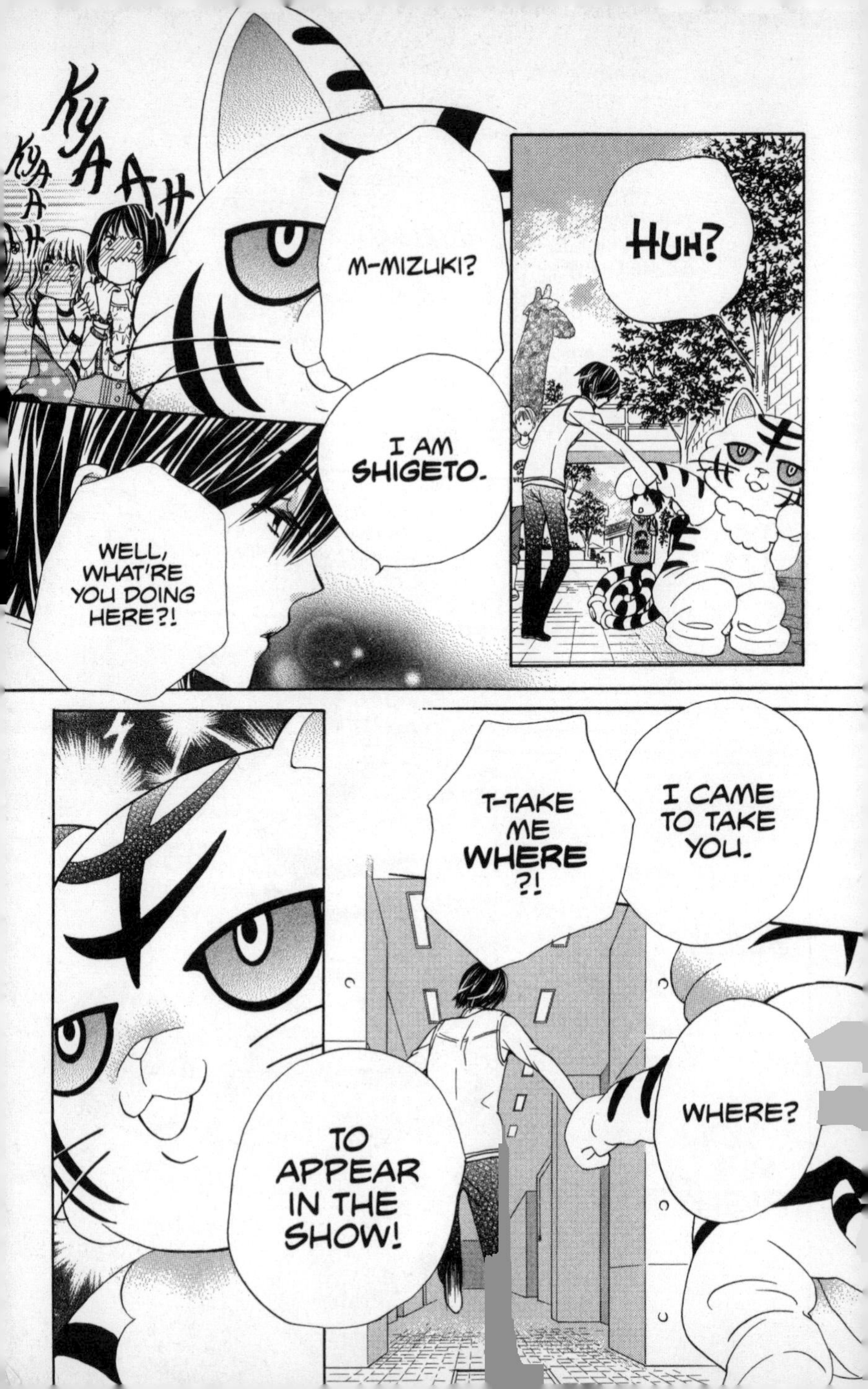
HUH?
M-MIZUKI?
I AM SHIGETO.
KYAAAHH
KYAAHH
WELL, WHAT'RE YOU DOING HERE?!
I CAME TO TAKE YOU.
T-TAKE ME WHERE?!
WHERE?
TO APPEAR IN THE SHOW!

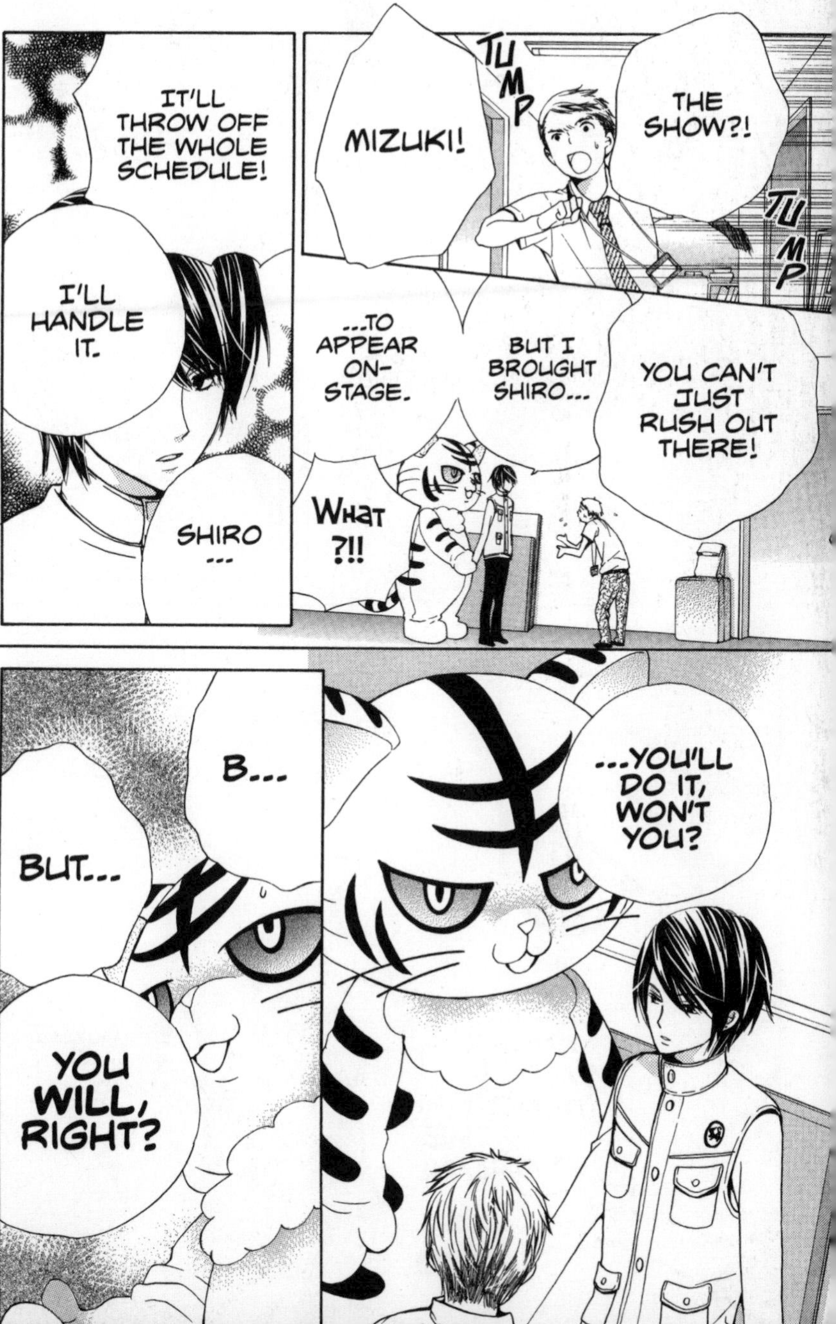
TUMP
THE SHOW?!
MIZUKI!
TUMP
YOU CAN'T JUST RUSH OUT THERE!
BUT I BROUGHT SHIRO...
...TO APPEAR ON-STAGE.
WHAT?!!
IT'LL THROW OFF THE WHOLE SCHEDULE!
I'LL HANDLE IT.
SHIRO...
...YOU'LL DO IT, WON'T YOU?
B...
BUT...
YOU WILL, RIGHT?

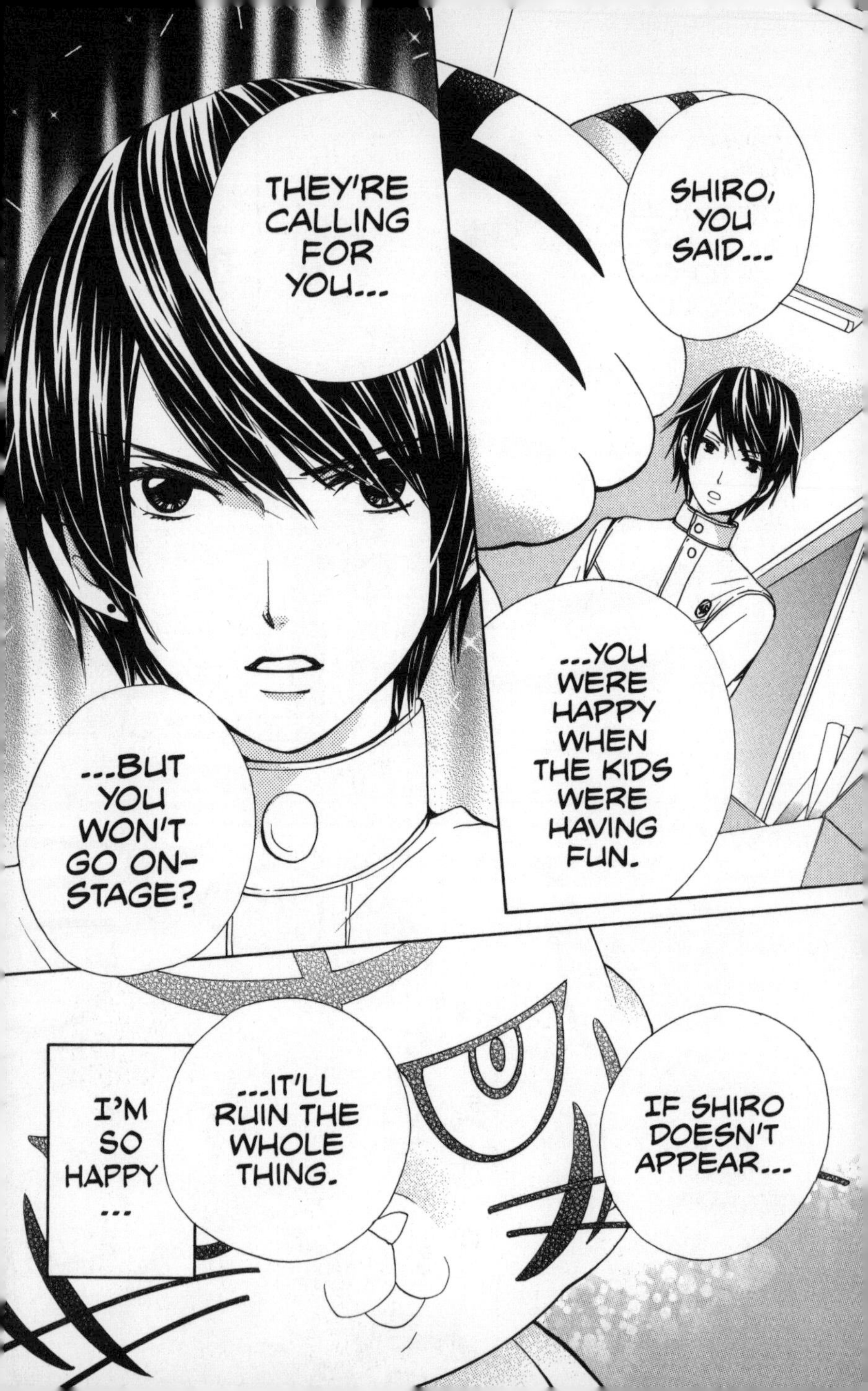
SHIRO, YOU SAID...
...YOU WERE HAPPY WHEN THE KIDS WERE HAVING FUN.
THEY'RE CALLING FOR YOU...
...BUT YOU WON'T GO ON-STAGE?
IF SHIRO DOESN'T APPEAR...
...IT'LL RUIN THE WHOLE THING.
I'M SO HAPPY ...

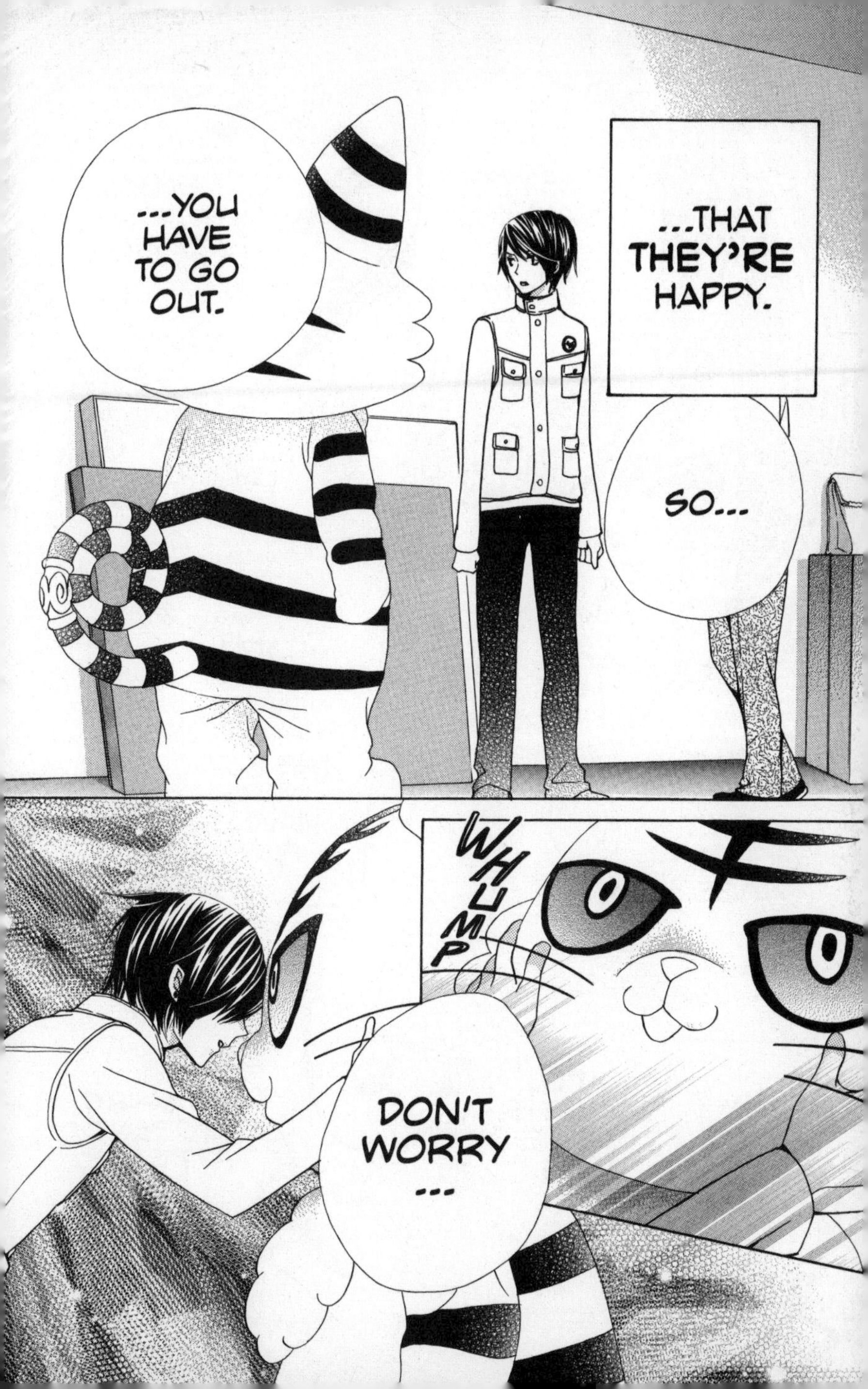
...THAT THEY'RE HAPPY.
SO...
...YOU HAVE TO GO OUT.
WHUMP
DON'T WORRY ...

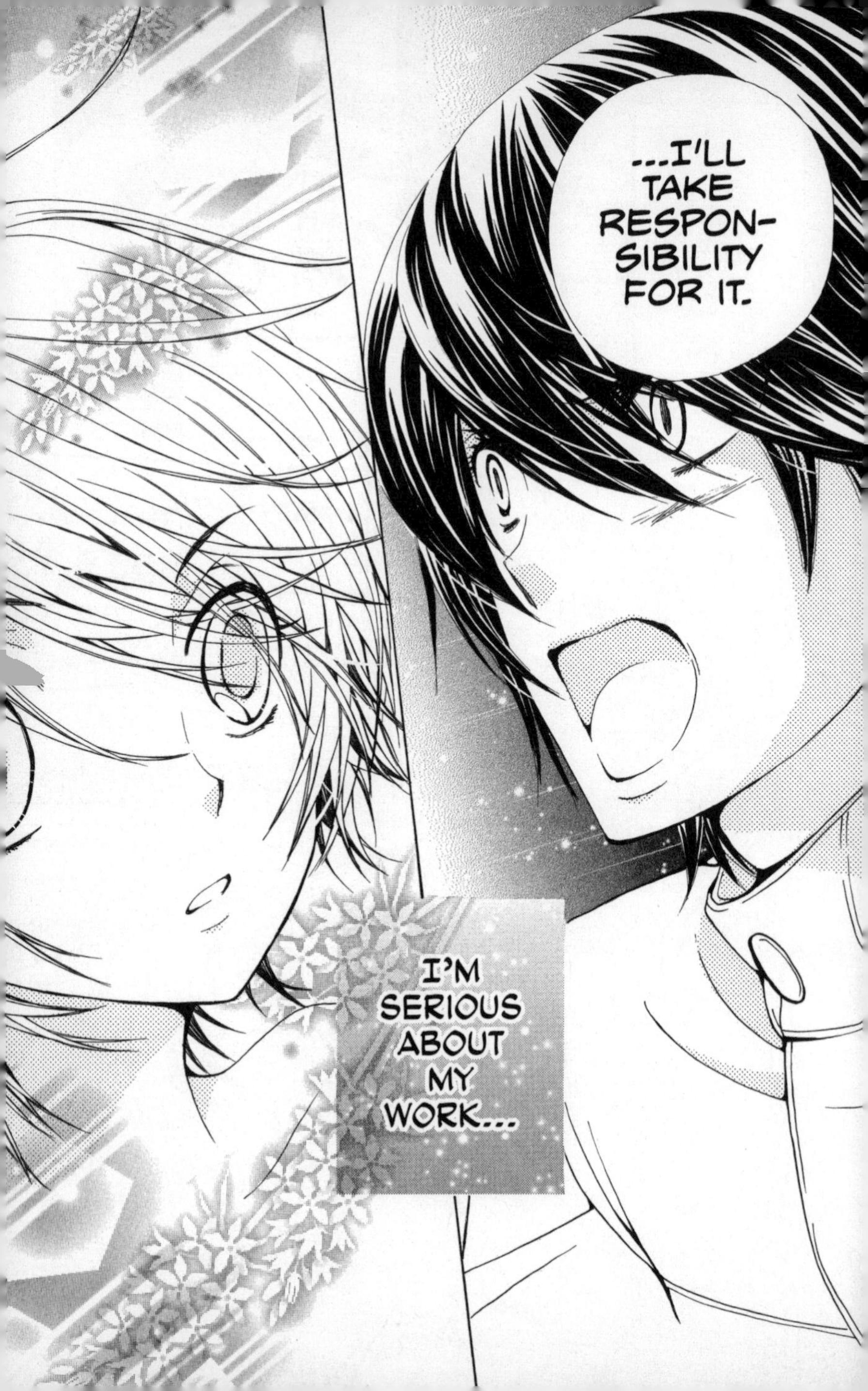
...I'LL TAKE RESPON-SIBILITY FOR IT.
I'M SERIOUS ABOUT MY WORK...

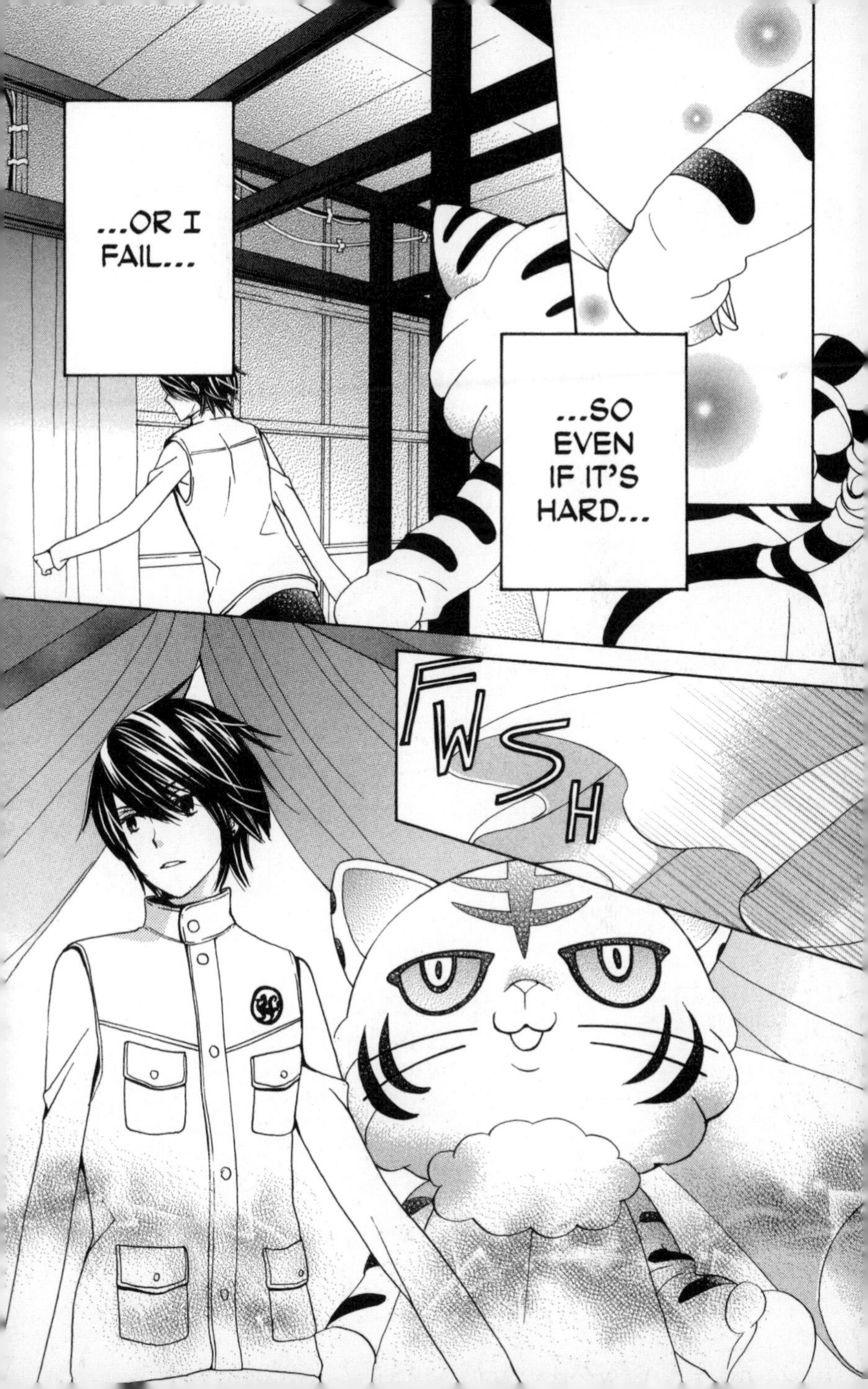
...SO EVEN IF IT'S HARD...
...OR I FAIL...
FWSH

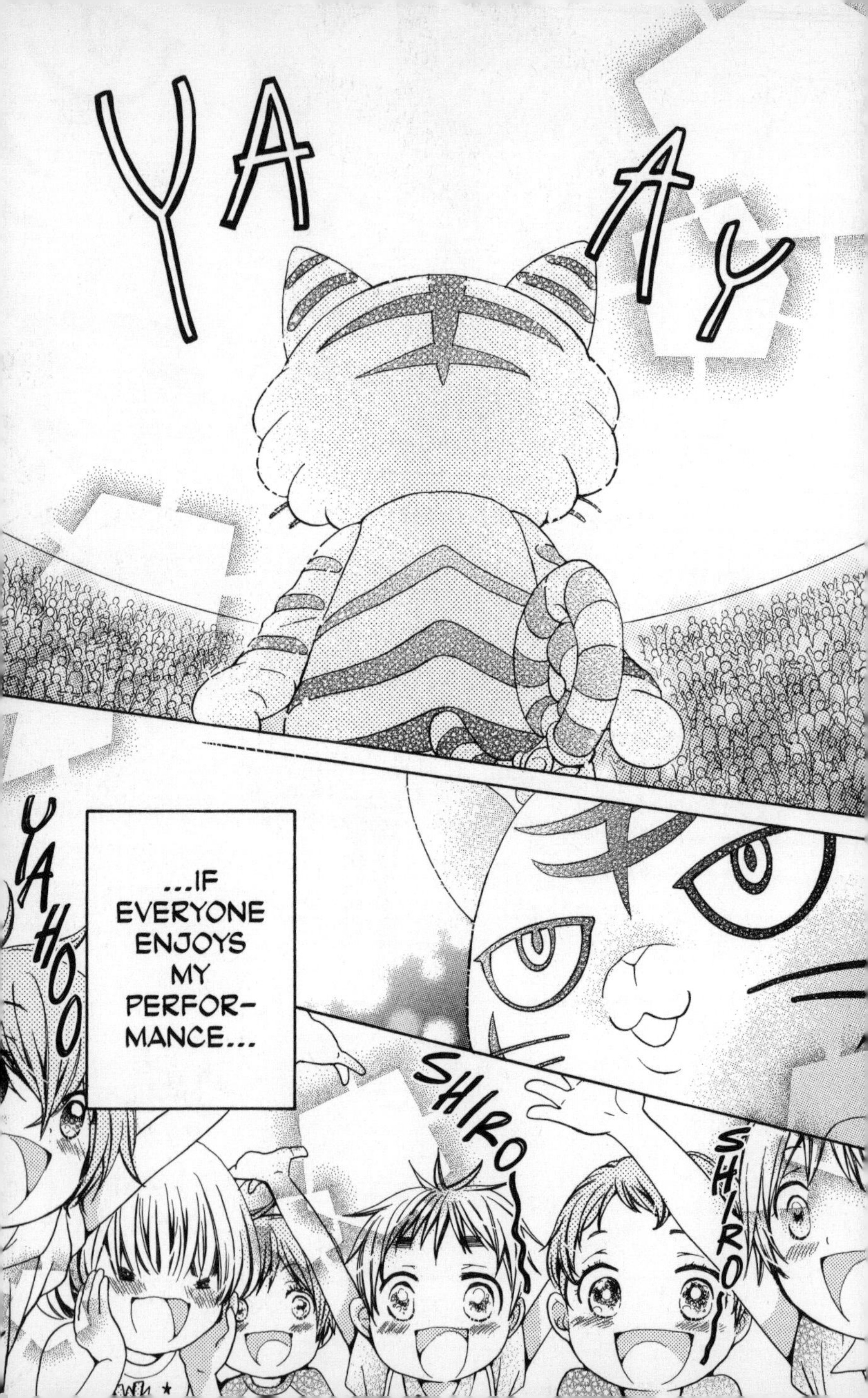
YA
AY
...IF EVERYONE ENJOYS MY PERFORMANCE...
SHIRO
SHIRO
YAHOO

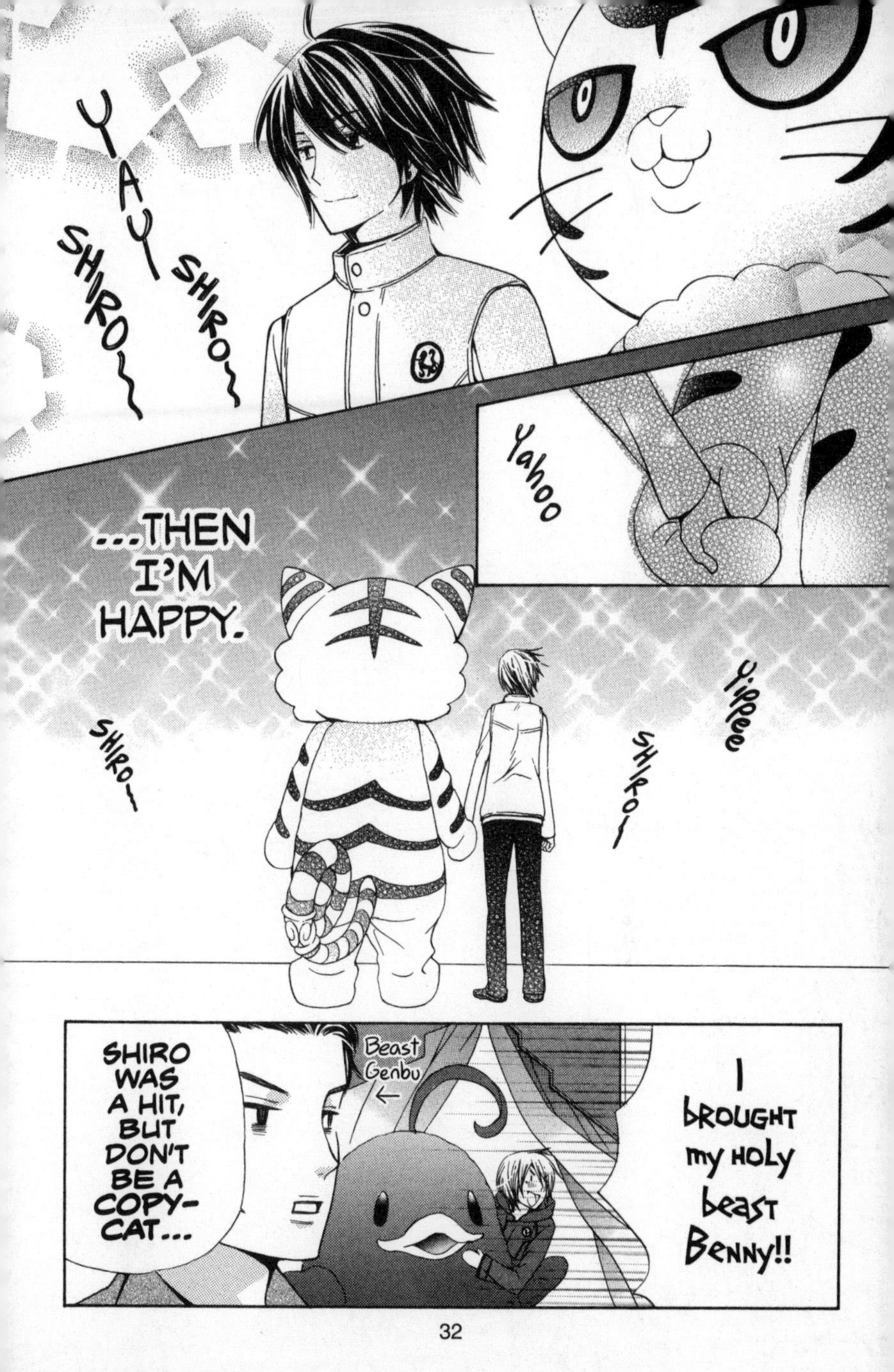
SHIRO~
YAY!
SHIRO~
Yahoo
...THEN I'M HAPPY.
Yippee
SHIRO~
SHIRO~
I brought my holy beast Benny!!
Beast Genbu ←
SHIRO WAS A HIT, BUT DON'T BE A COPY-CAT...

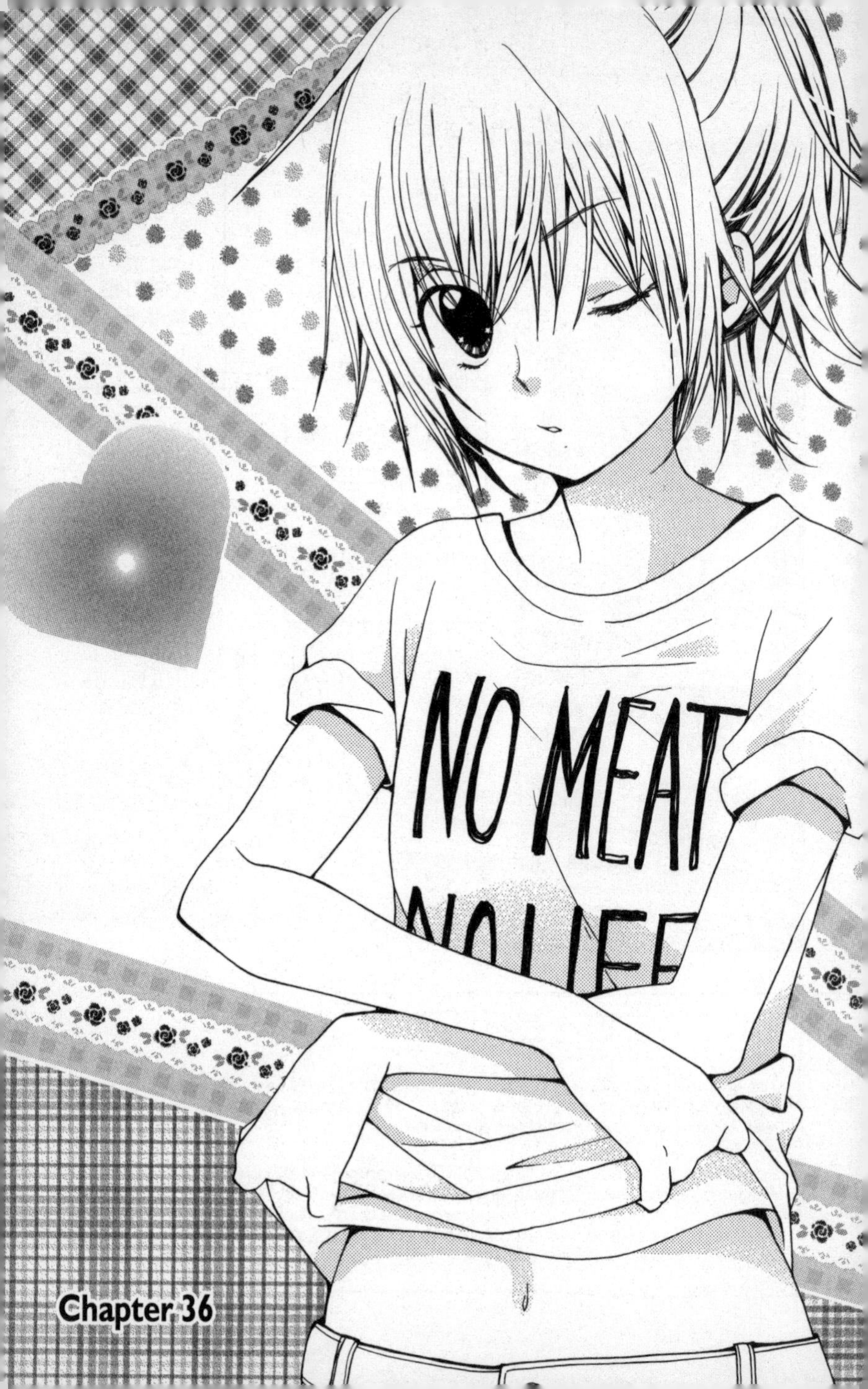
NO MEAT
Chapter 36

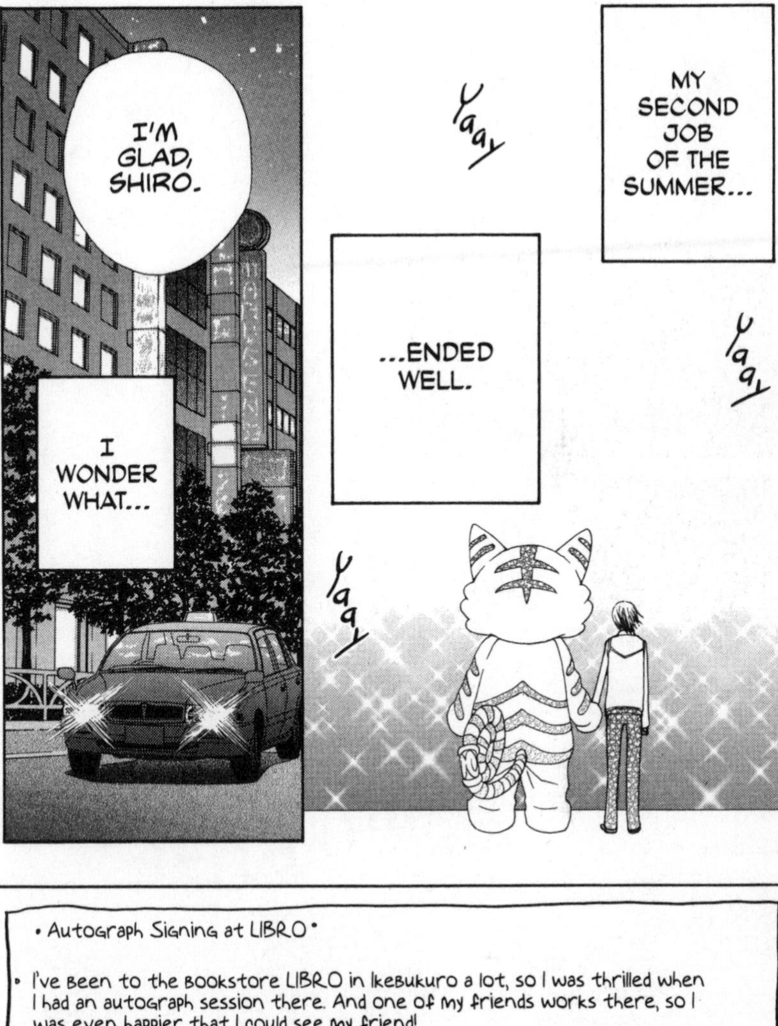
MY SECOND JOB OF THE SUMMER...
Yaay
...ENDED WELL.
Yaay
Yaay
I'M GLAD, SHIRO.
I WONDER WHAT...

• Autograph Signing at LIBRO •

- I've been to the bookstore LIBRO in Ikebukuro a lot, so I was thrilled when I had an autograph session there. And one of my friends works there, so I was even happier that I could see my friend!

- So many people came—from Yamaguchi Prefecture and Hiroshima Prefecture—and when someone from Taiwan showed up, I was floored! I'm very thankful. But I was going to do a session in Taiwan, so I guess that person was born in Taiwan but now lives in Tokyo. Or was traveling? I'm really grateful!

→ Continued

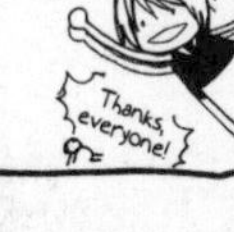
2
Thanks, everyone!

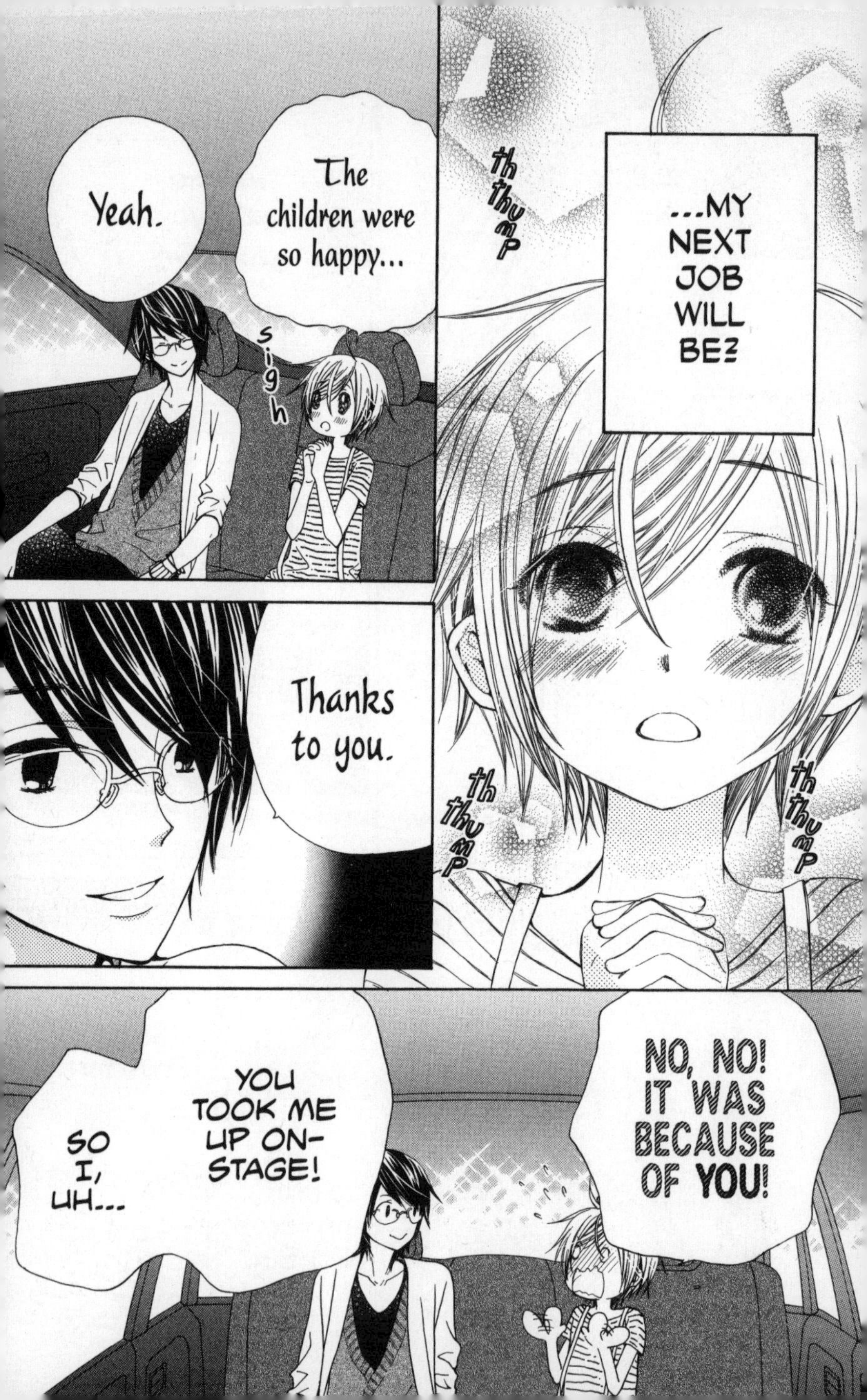

...MY NEXT JOB WILL BE?
th thump
th thump
th thump
The children were so happy...
Yeah.
sigh
Thanks to you.
NO, NO! IT WAS BECAUSE OF YOU!
YOU TOOK ME UP ON-STAGE!
SO I, UH...

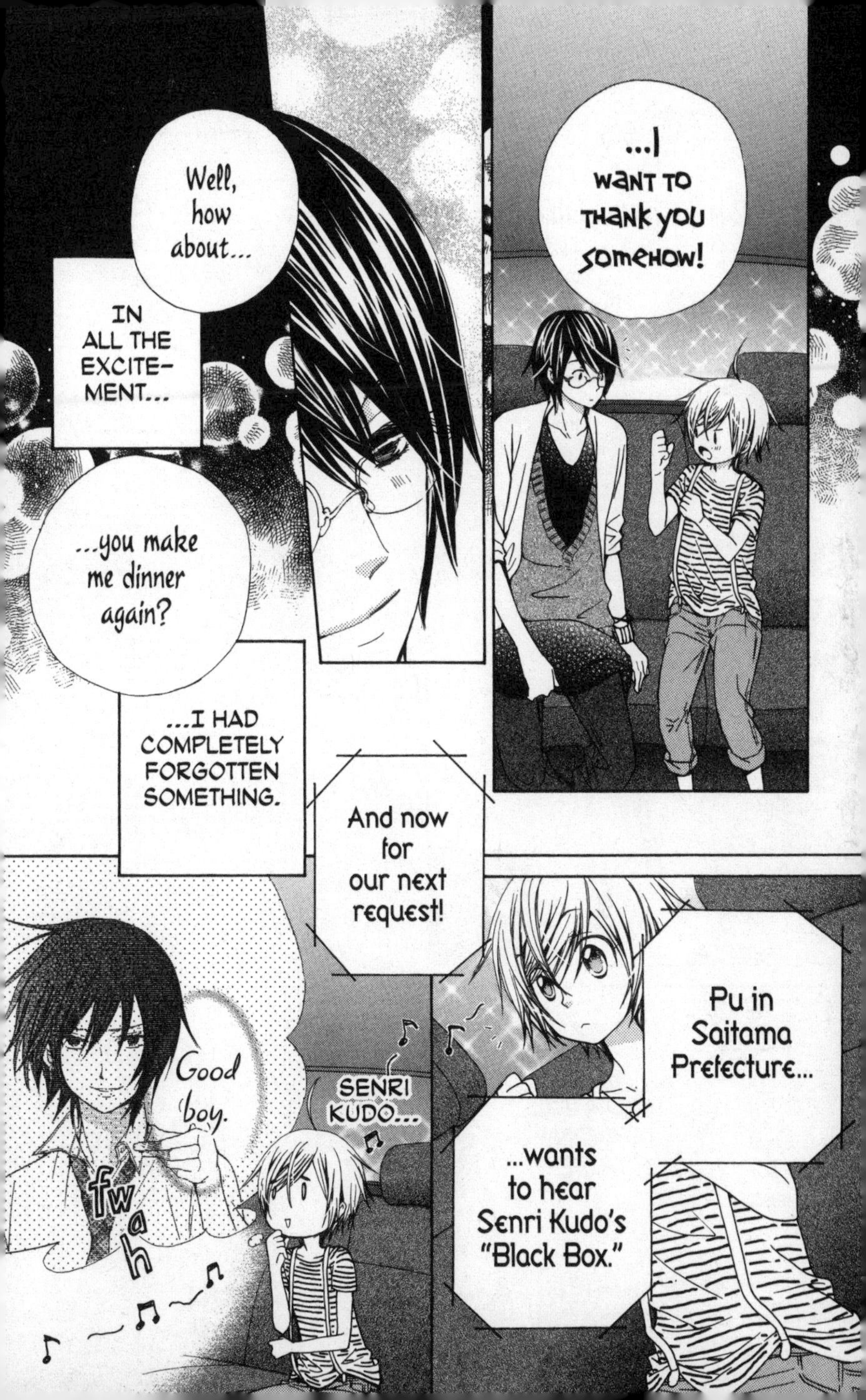
...I want to thank you somehow!
Well, how about...
In all the excitement...
...you make me dinner again?
...I had completely forgotten something.
And now for our next request!
Pu in Saitama Prefecture...
...wants to hear Senri Kudo's "Black Box."
Senri Kudo...
Good boy.
fwah

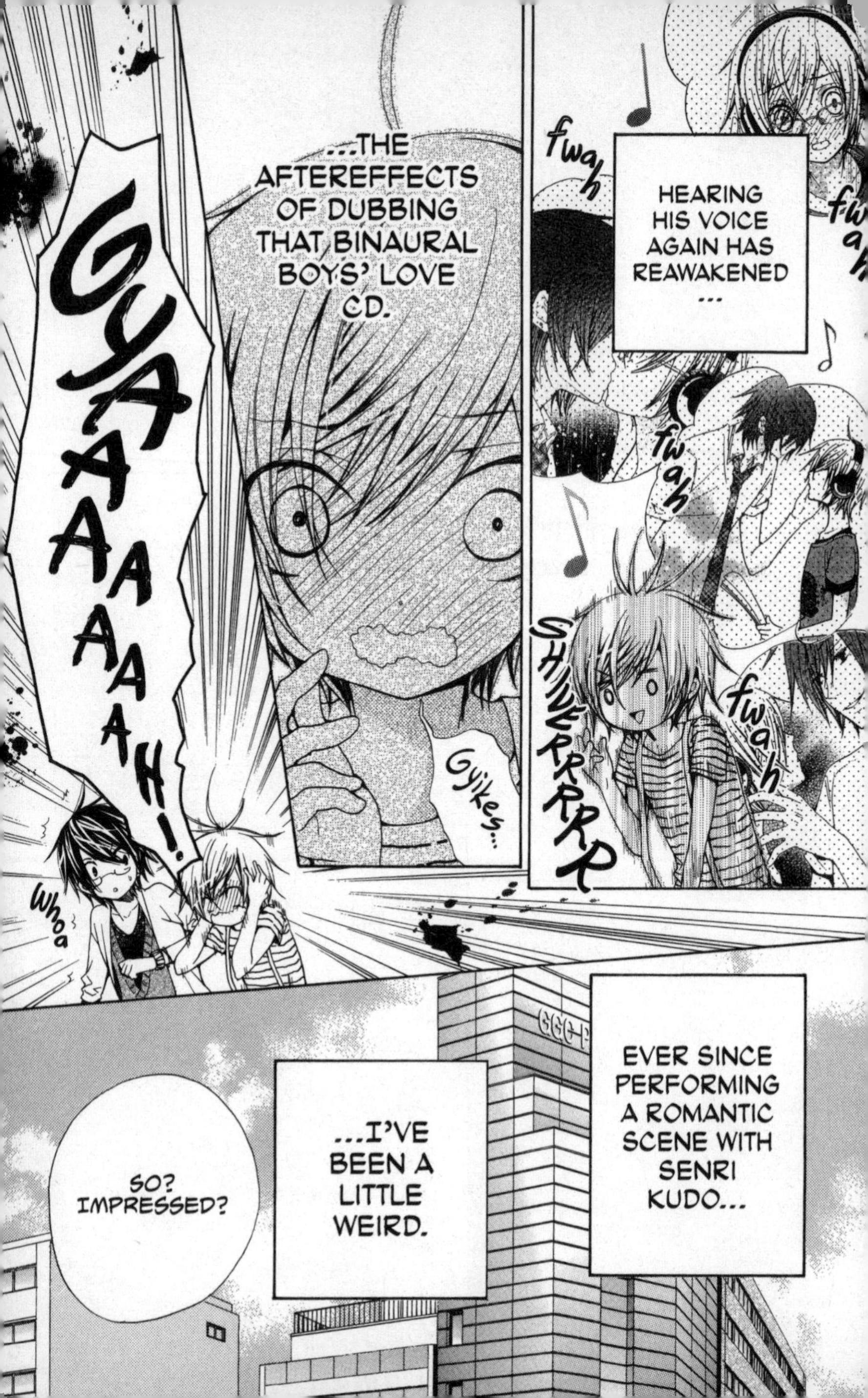
HEARING HIS VOICE AGAIN HAS REAWAKENED ...
fwah
fwah
fwah
fwah
SHIVERRRRR
...THE AFTEREFFECTS OF DUBBING THAT BINAURAL BOYS' LOVE CD.
Gyikes...
GYAAAAAAAH!
Whoa
EVER SINCE PERFORMING A ROMANTIC SCENE WITH SENRI KUDO...
...I'VE BEEN A LITTLE WEIRD.
SO? IMPRESSED?

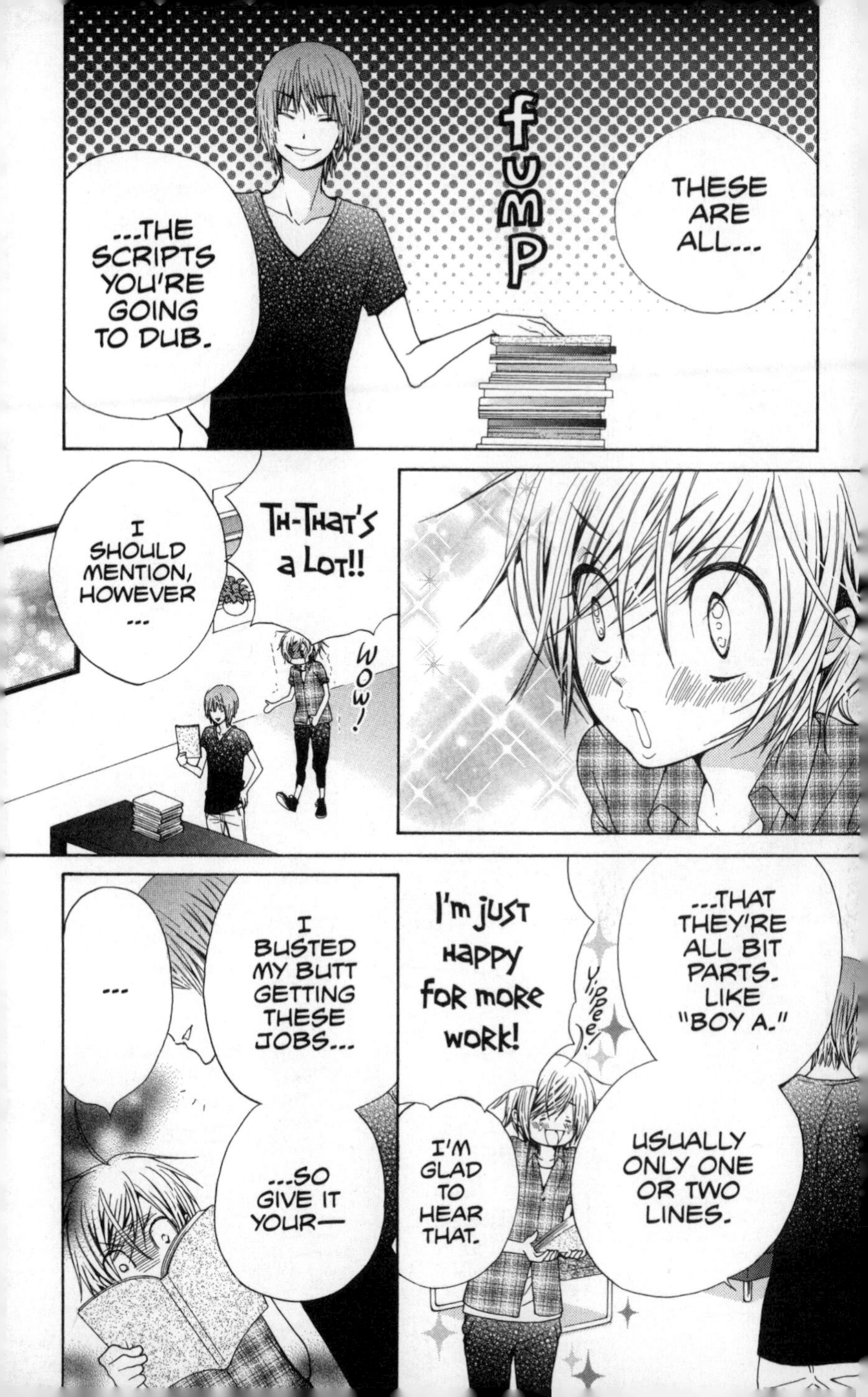
THESE ARE ALL...
FUMP
...THE SCRIPTS YOU'RE GOING TO DUB.
TH-THAT'S A LOT!!
WOW!
I SHOULD MENTION, HOWEVER...
...THAT THEY'RE ALL BIT PARTS. LIKE "BOY A."
YIPPEE!
I'm just happy for more work!
USUALLY ONLY ONE OR TWO LINES.
I'M GLAD TO HEAR THAT.
I BUSTED MY BUTT GETTING THESE JOBS...
...
...SO GIVE IT YOUR—

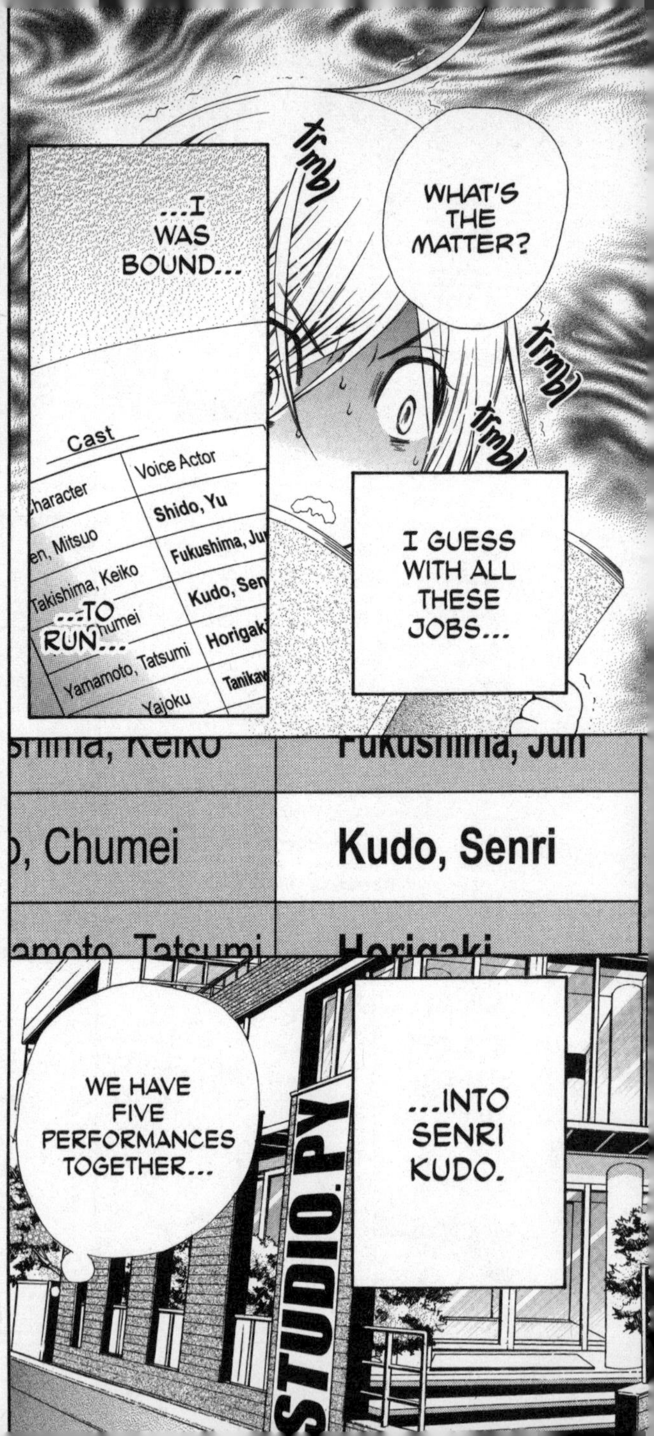
trmbl
WHAT'S THE MATTER?
trmbl
trmbl
I GUESS WITH ALL THESE JOBS...
...I WAS BOUND...
Cast
Voice Actor
Character
Shido, Yu
Takishima, Keiko
...TO RUN...
Yamamoto, Tatsumi
Yajoku
Kudo, Senri
...INTO SENRI KUDO.
WE HAVE FIVE PERFORMANCES TOGETHER...
STUDIO.PY

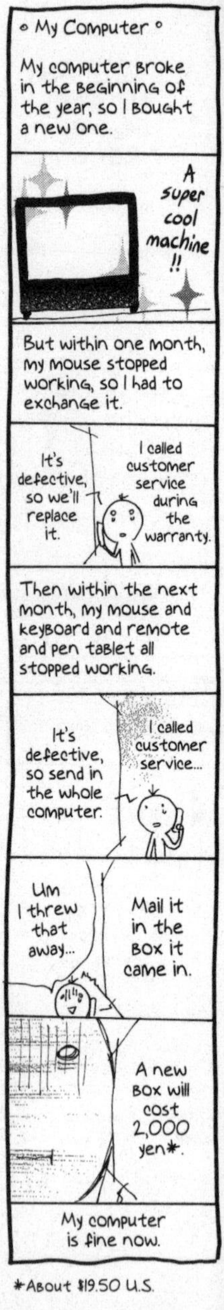
◦ My Computer ◦
My computer broke in the beginning of the year, so I bought a new one.
A super cool machine !!
But within one month, my mouse stopped working, so I had to exchange it.
I called customer service during the warranty.
It's defective, so we'll replace it.
Then within the next month, my mouse and keyboard and remote and pen tablet all stopped working.
I called customer service...
It's defective, so send in the whole computer.
Mail it in the box it came in.
Um I threw that away...
A new box will cost 2,000 yen*.
My computer is fine now.

*About $19.50 U.S.

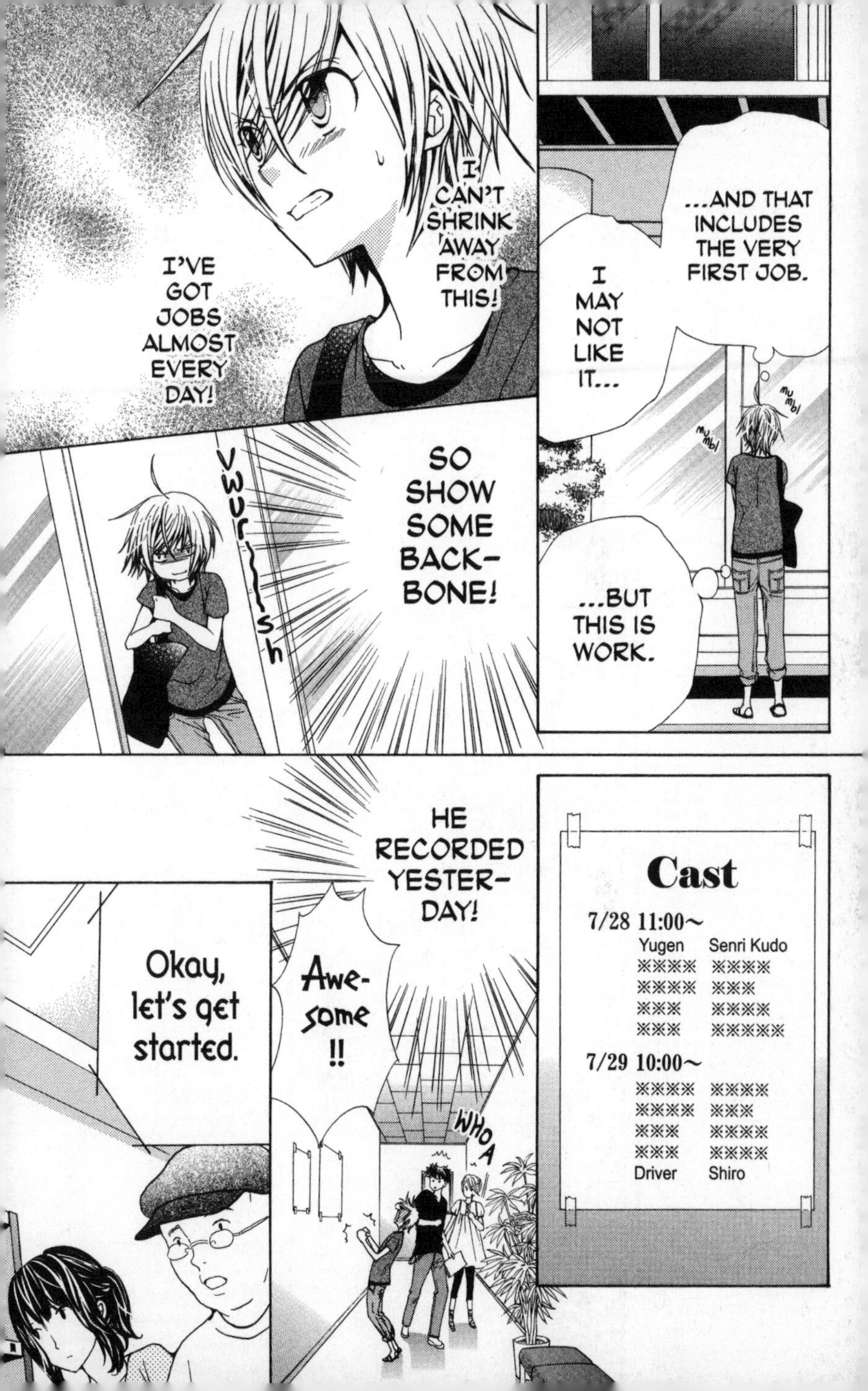
...AND THAT INCLUDES THE VERY FIRST JOB.
I MAY NOT LIKE IT...
mumbl
mumbl
...BUT THIS IS WORK.
I CAN'T SHRINK AWAY FROM THIS!
I'VE GOT JOBS ALMOST EVERY DAY!
SO SHOW SOME BACK-BONE!
Vwur~~sh
Cast
7/28 11:00~
Yugen Senri Kudo
※※※※ ※※※※
※※※※ ※※※
※※※ ※※※※
※※※ ※※※※※
7/29 10:00~
※※※※ ※※※※
※※※※ ※※※
※※※ ※※※※
※※※ ※※※※
Driver Shiro
HE RECORDED YESTER-DAY!
Awe-some!!
WHOA
Okay, let's get started.

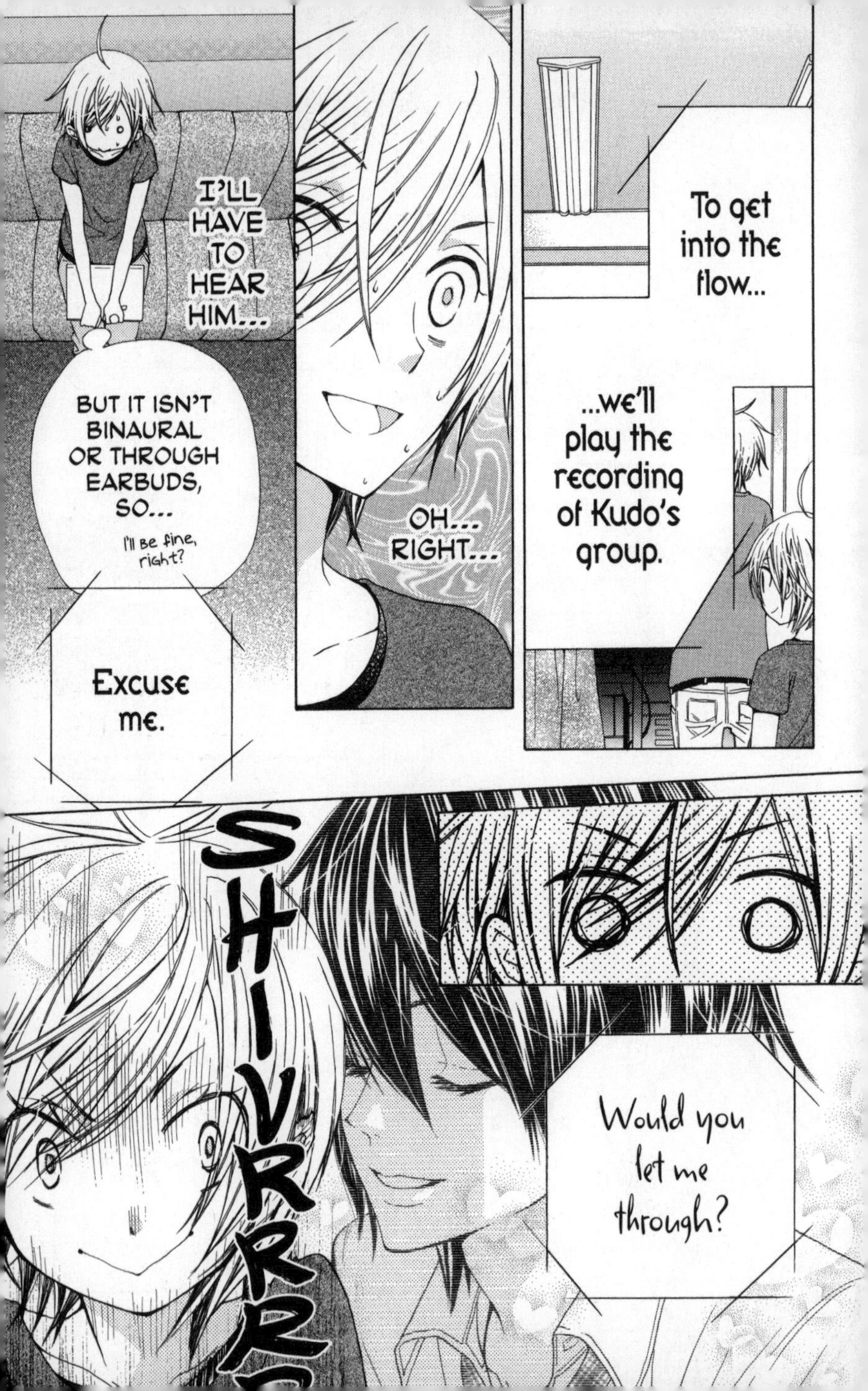
To get into the flow...
...we'll play the recording of Kudo's group.
OH... RIGHT...
I'LL HAVE TO HEAR HIM...
BUT IT ISN'T BINAURAL OR THROUGH EARBUDS, SO...
I'll be fine, right?
Excuse me.
Would you let me through?
SHIVRRRS

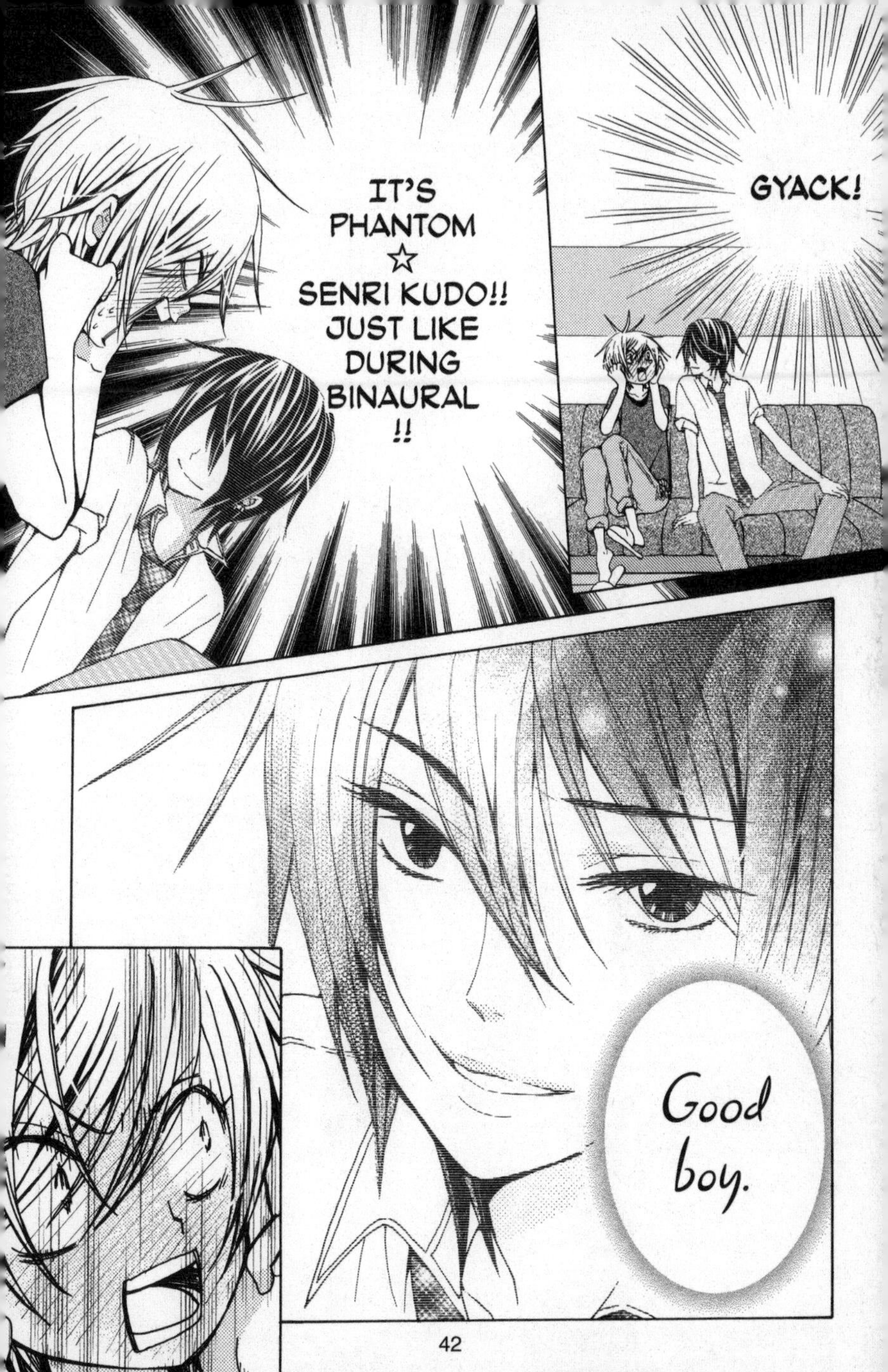
GYACK!
IT'S PHANTOM ☆ SENRI KUDO!! JUST LIKE DURING BINAURAL !!
Good boy.

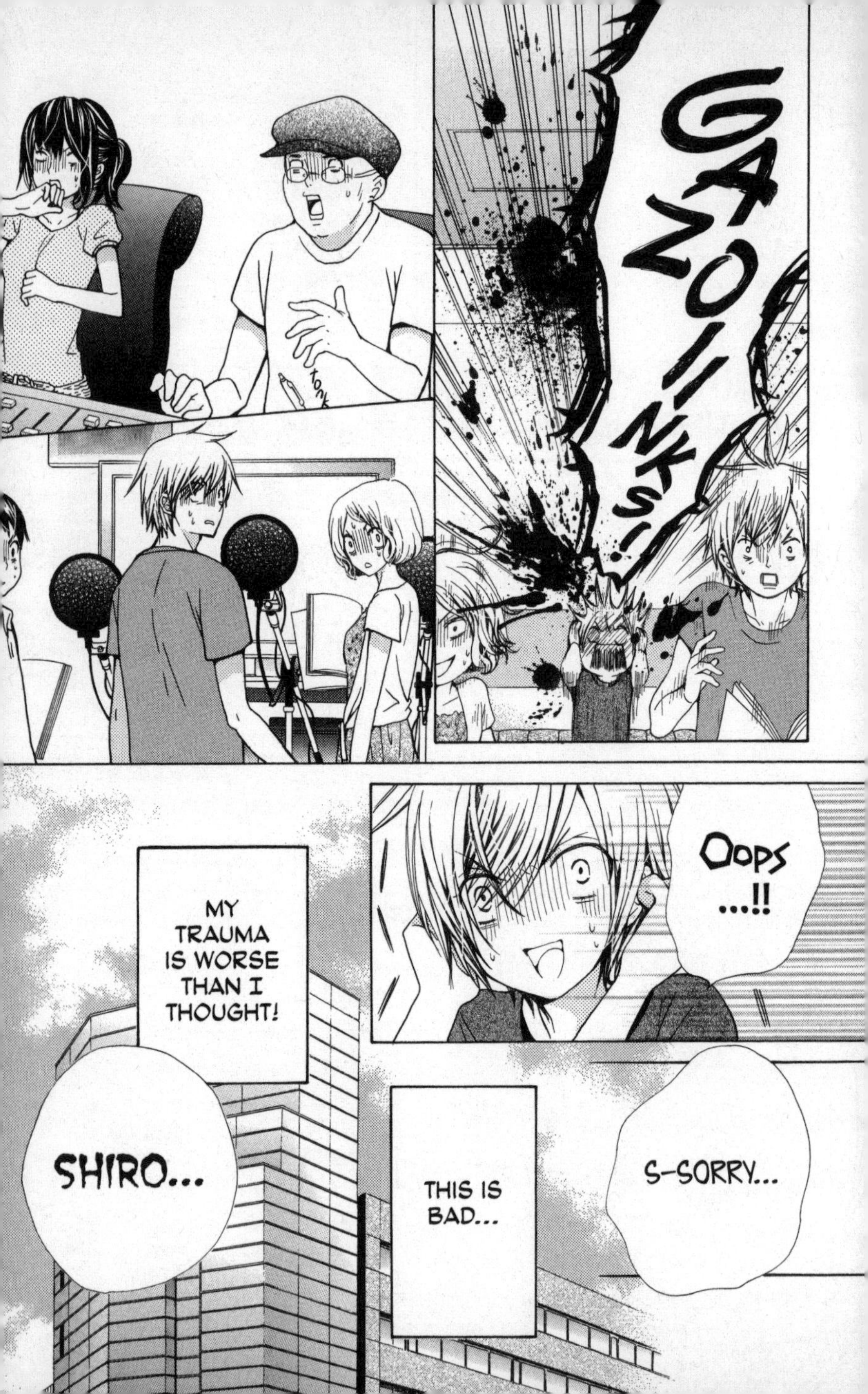
GAZOIIINKS!!
tonk
Oops ...!!
S-SORRY...
THIS IS BAD...
MY TRAUMA IS WORSE THAN I THOUGHT!
SHIRO...

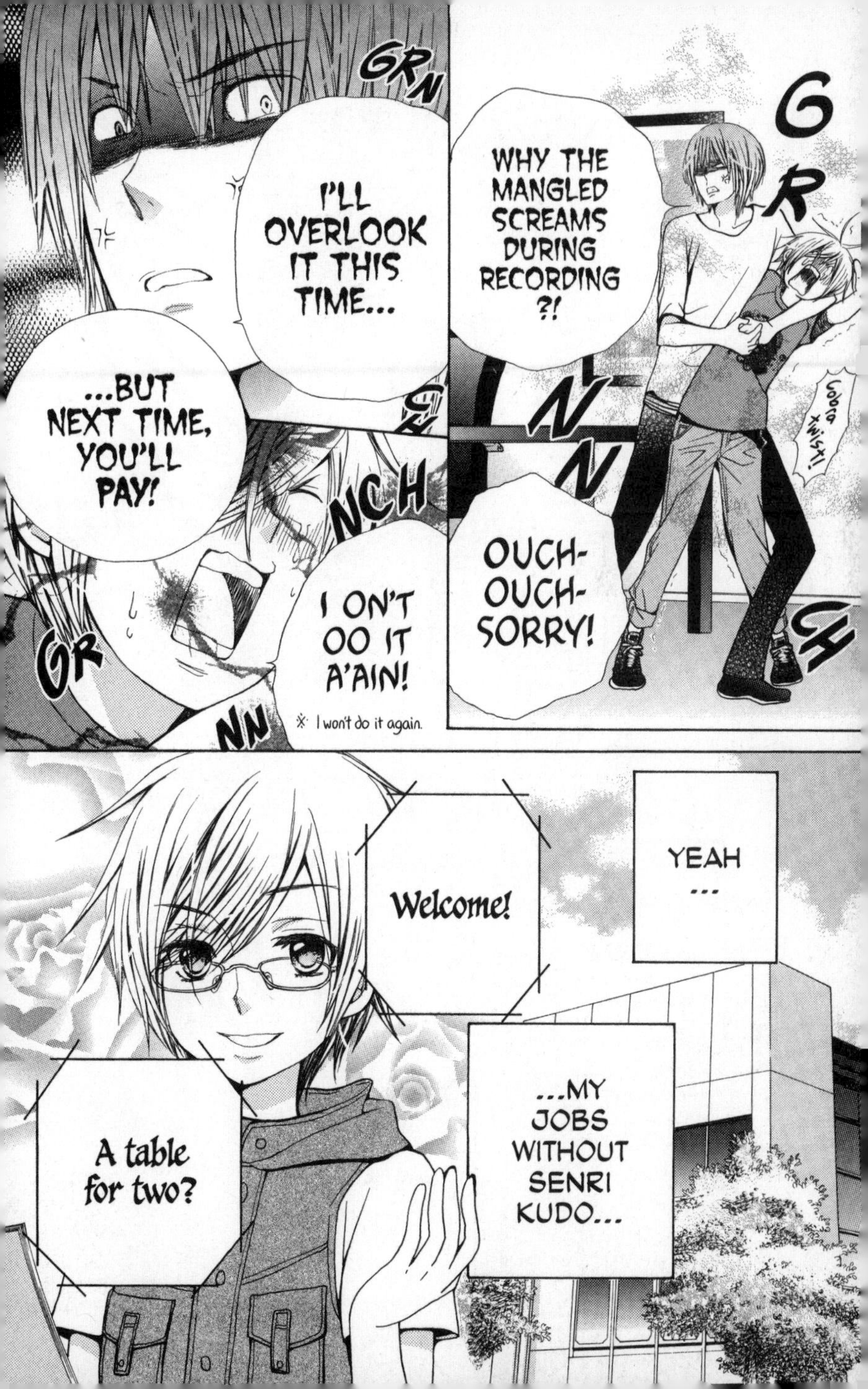
WHY THE MANGLED SCREAMS DURING RECORDING ?!
G R N N
CH
twist!!
OUCH-OUCH-SORRY!
GRN
I'LL OVERLOOK IT THIS TIME...
...BUT NEXT TIME, YOU'LL PAY!
CH
NCH
GR
NN
I ON'T OO IT A'AIN!
※ I won't do it again.
YEAH ...
...MY JOBS WITHOUT SENRI KUDO...
Welcome!
A table for two?

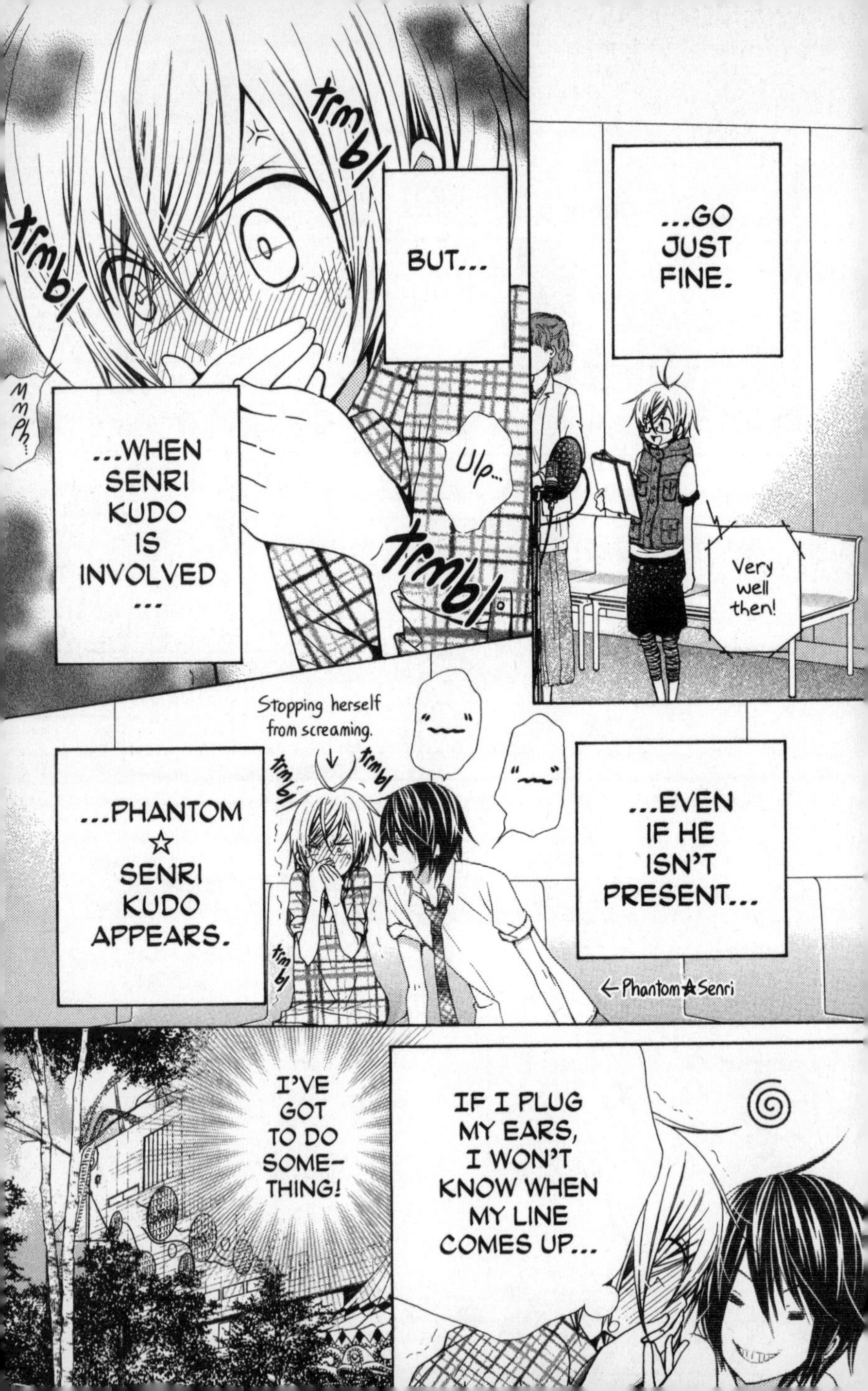

...GO JUST FINE.
Very well then!
trmbl
BUT...
trmbl
...WHEN SENRI KUDO IS INVOLVED...
mmph...
Ulp...
trmbl
...EVEN IF HE ISN'T PRESENT...
"~~~"
"~~~"
← Phantom☆Senri
Stopping herself from screaming.
trmbl
trmbl
trmbl
...PHANTOM ☆ SENRI KUDO APPEARS.
IF I PLUG MY EARS, I WON'T KNOW WHEN MY LINE COMES UP...
I'VE GOT TO DO SOMETHING!

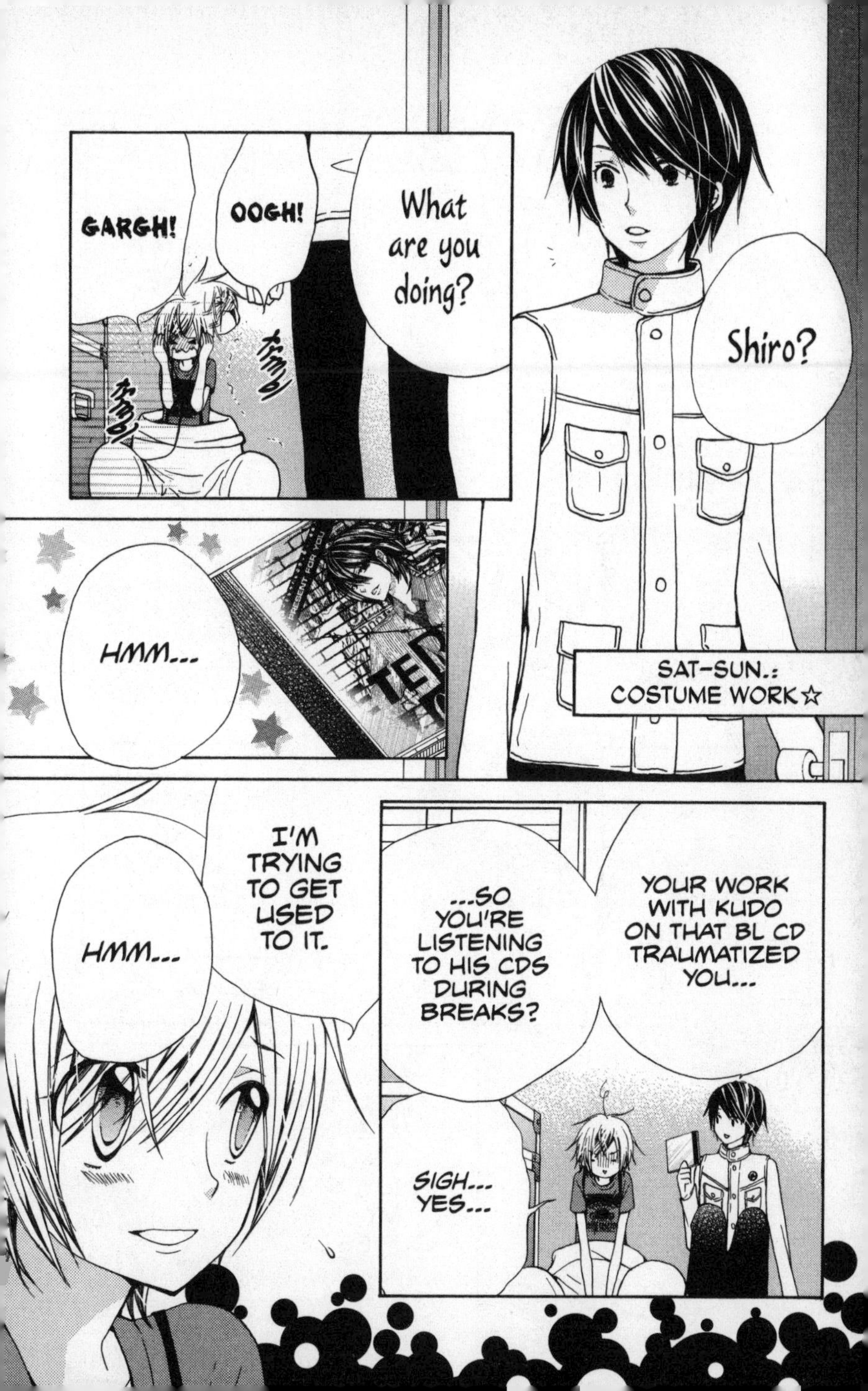
Shiro?
SAT-SUN.: COSTUME WORK☆
What are you doing?
OOGH!
GARGH!
HMM...
YOUR WORK WITH KUDO ON THAT BL CD TRAUMATIZED YOU...
...SO YOU'RE LISTENING TO HIS CDS DURING BREAKS?
SIGH... YES...
I'M TRYING TO GET USED TO IT.
HMM...

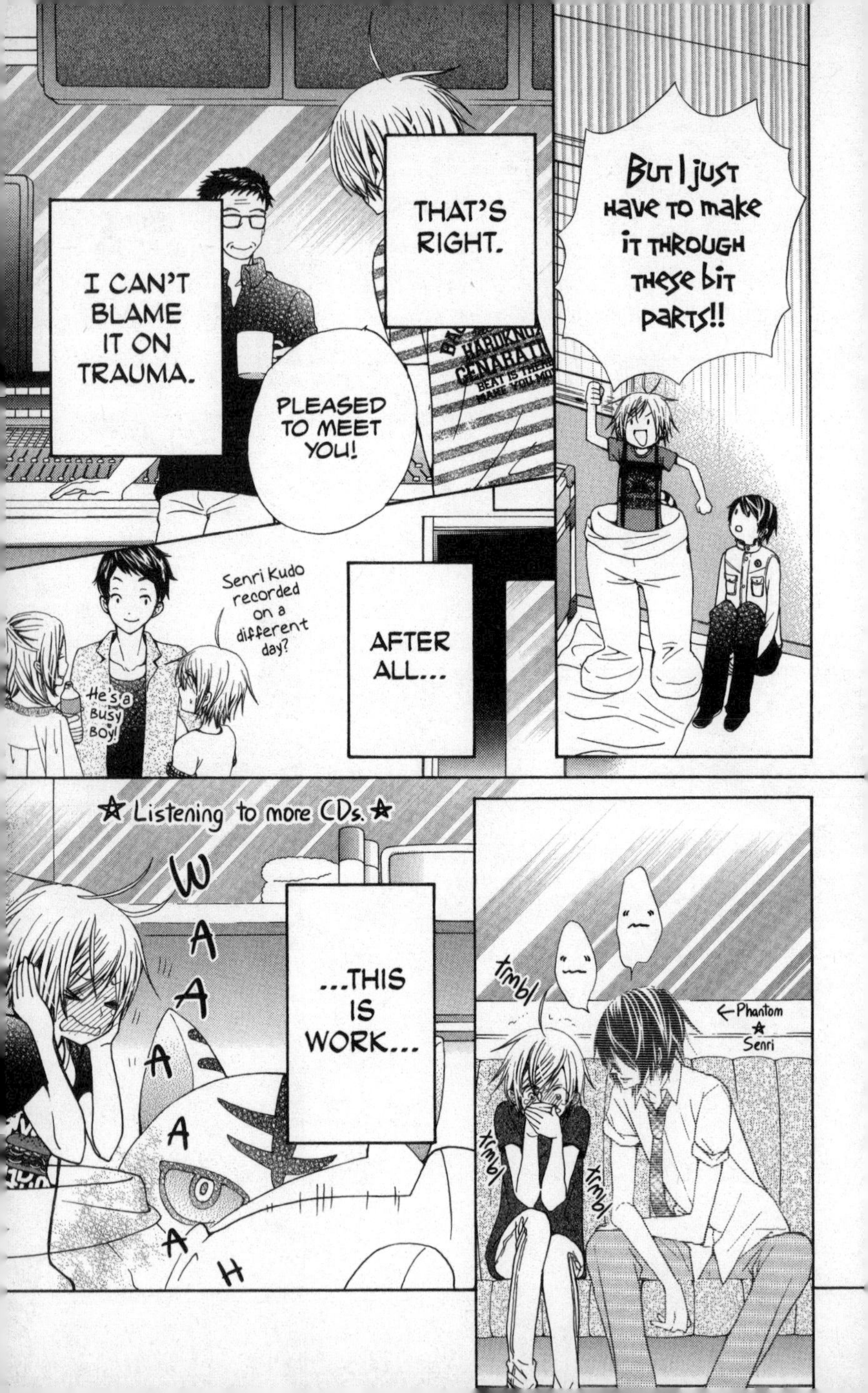

But I just have to make it through these bit parts!!
THAT'S RIGHT.
I CAN'T BLAME IT ON TRAUMA.
PLEASED TO MEET YOU!
AFTER ALL...
Senri Kudo recorded on a different day?
He's a Busy Boy!
trmbl
←Phantom ☆ Senri
trmbl
trmbl
☆ Listening to more CDs. ☆
...THIS IS WORK...
WAAAAAH

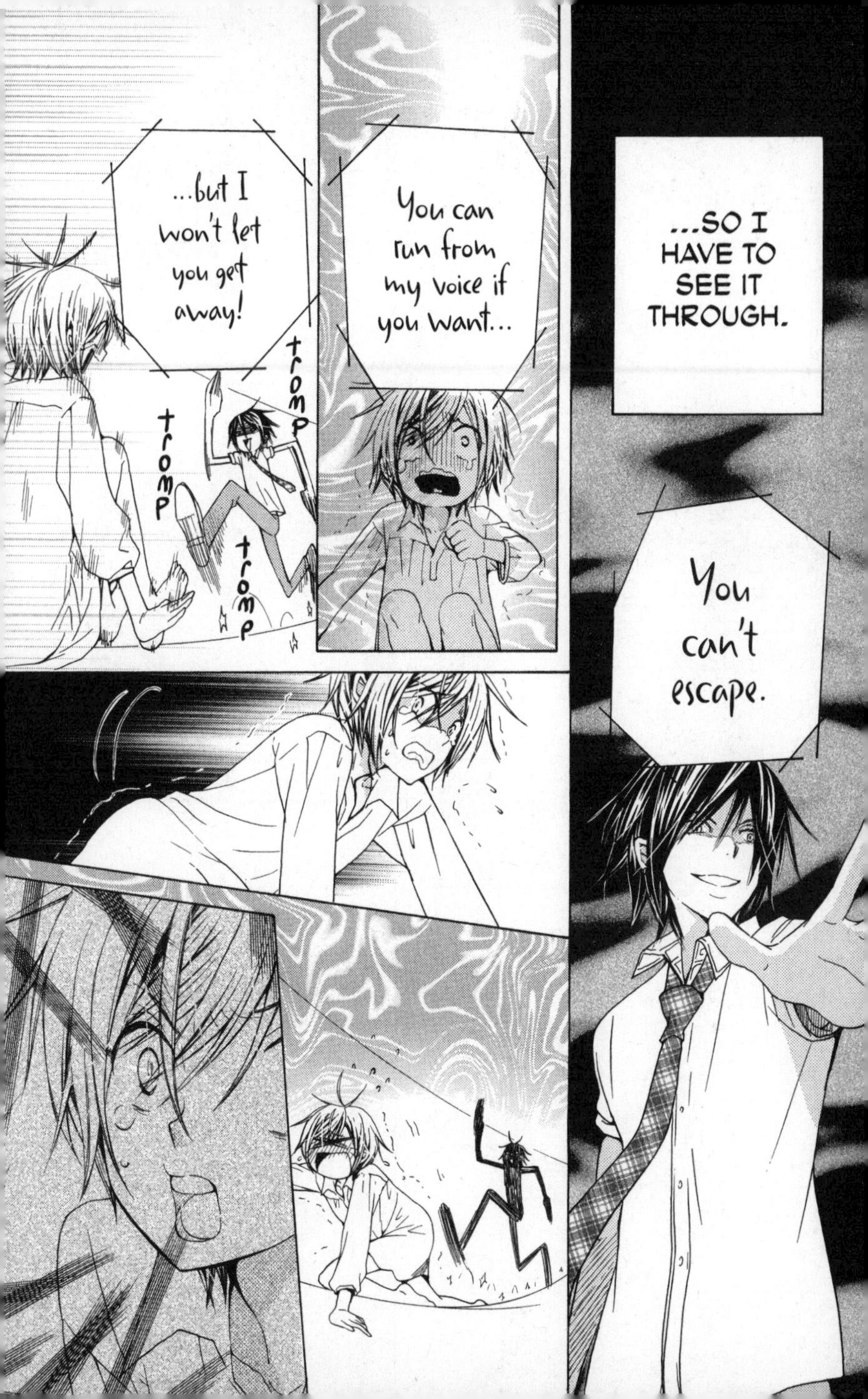
...SO I HAVE TO SEE IT THROUGH.
You can't escape.
You can run from my voice if you want...
...but I won't let you get away!
tromp
tromp
tromp

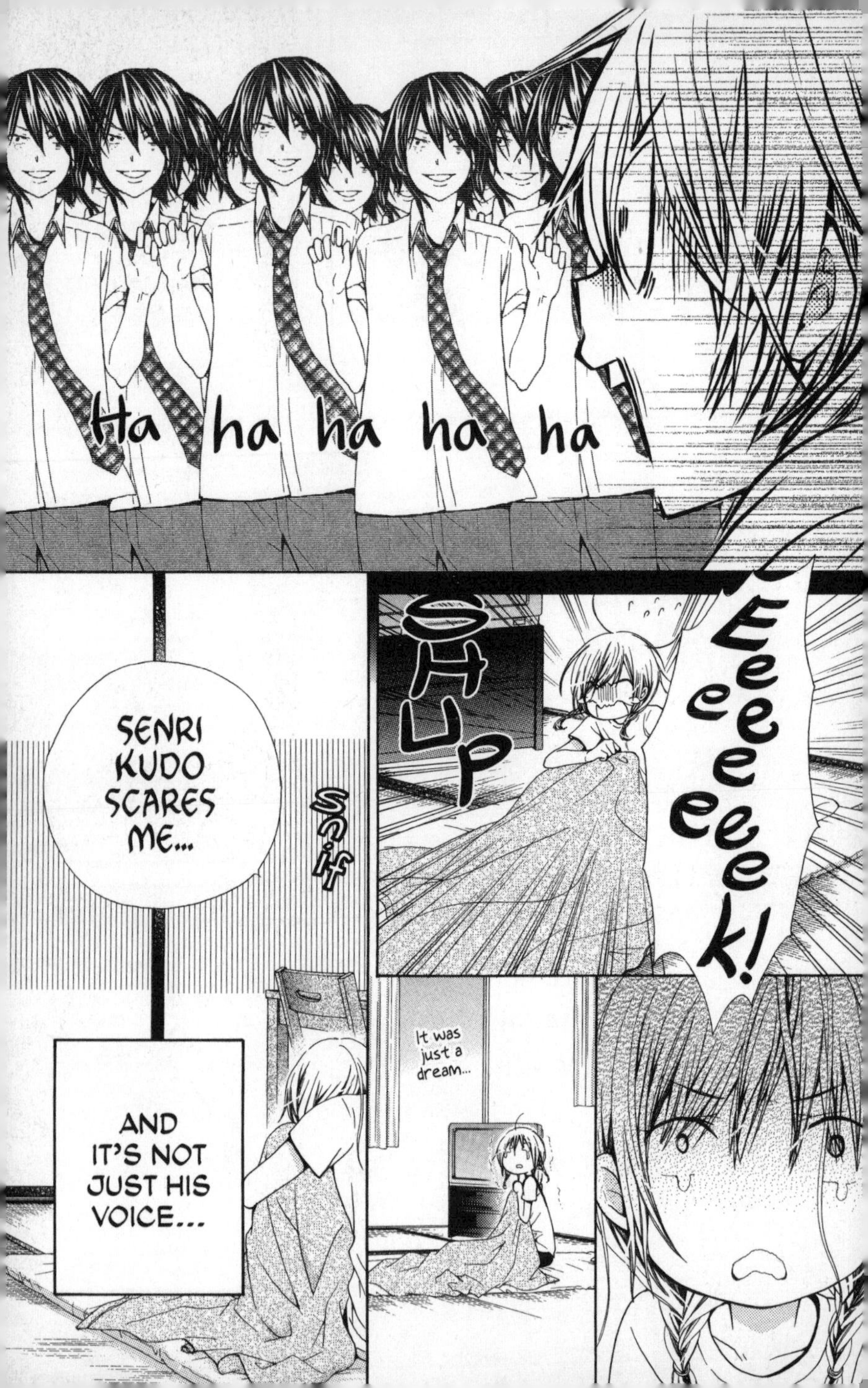

Ha ha ha ha ha
Eeeeeeeek!
SHUP
It was just a dream...
SENRI KUDO SCARES ME...
Sniff
AND IT'S NOT JUST HIS VOICE...

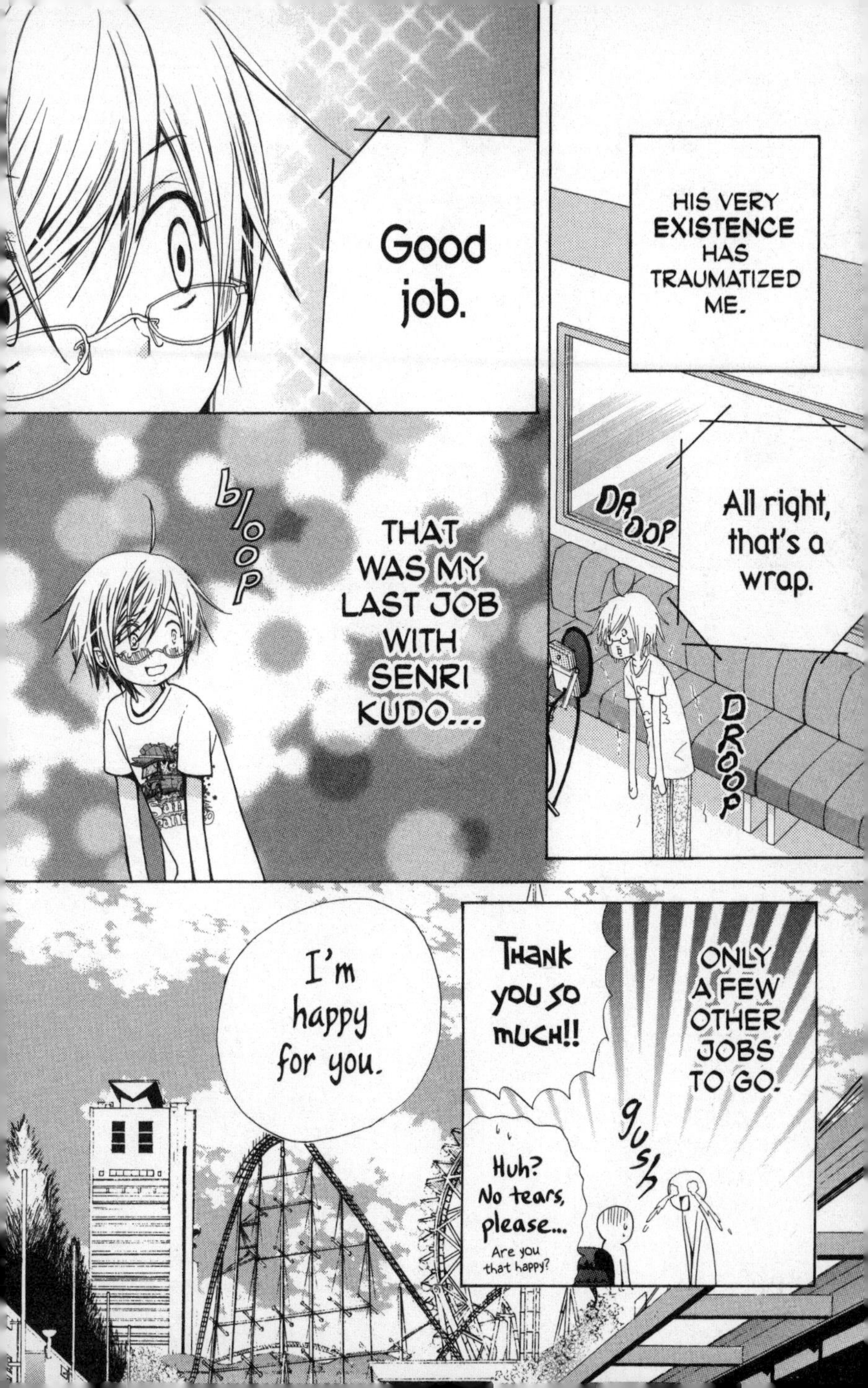
HIS VERY EXISTENCE HAS TRAUMATIZED ME.
All right, that's a wrap.
DROOP
DROOP
Good job.
bloop
THAT WAS MY LAST JOB WITH SENRI KUDO...
ONLY A FEW OTHER JOBS TO GO.
Thank you so much!!
gush
Huh? No tears, please...
Are you that happy?
I'm happy for you.

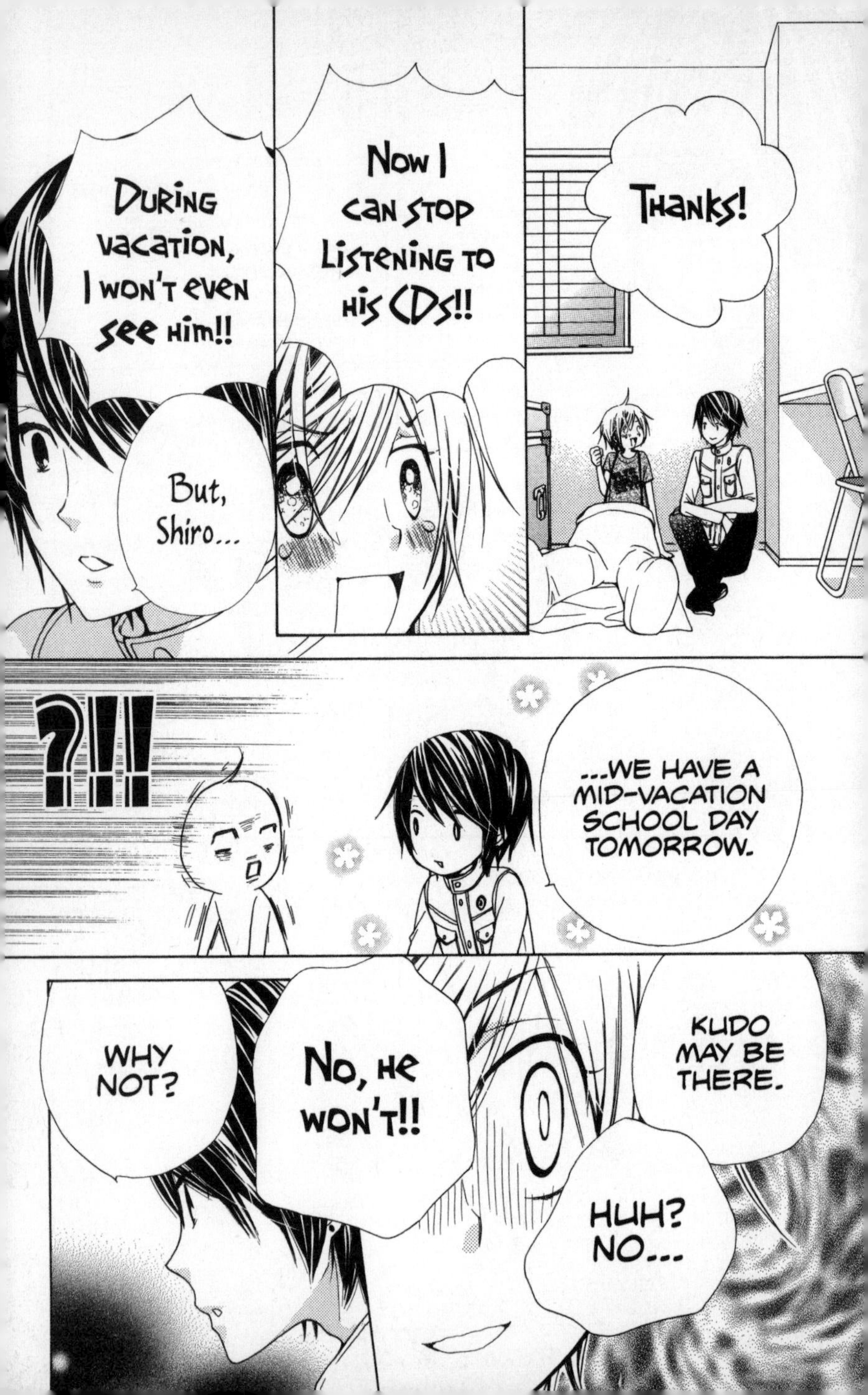
Thanks!
Now I can stop listening to his CDs!!
During vacation, I won't even see him!!
But, Shiro...
...WE HAVE A MID-VACATION SCHOOL DAY TOMORROW.
?!!
KUDO MAY BE THERE.
HUH? NO...
No, he won't!!
WHY NOT?

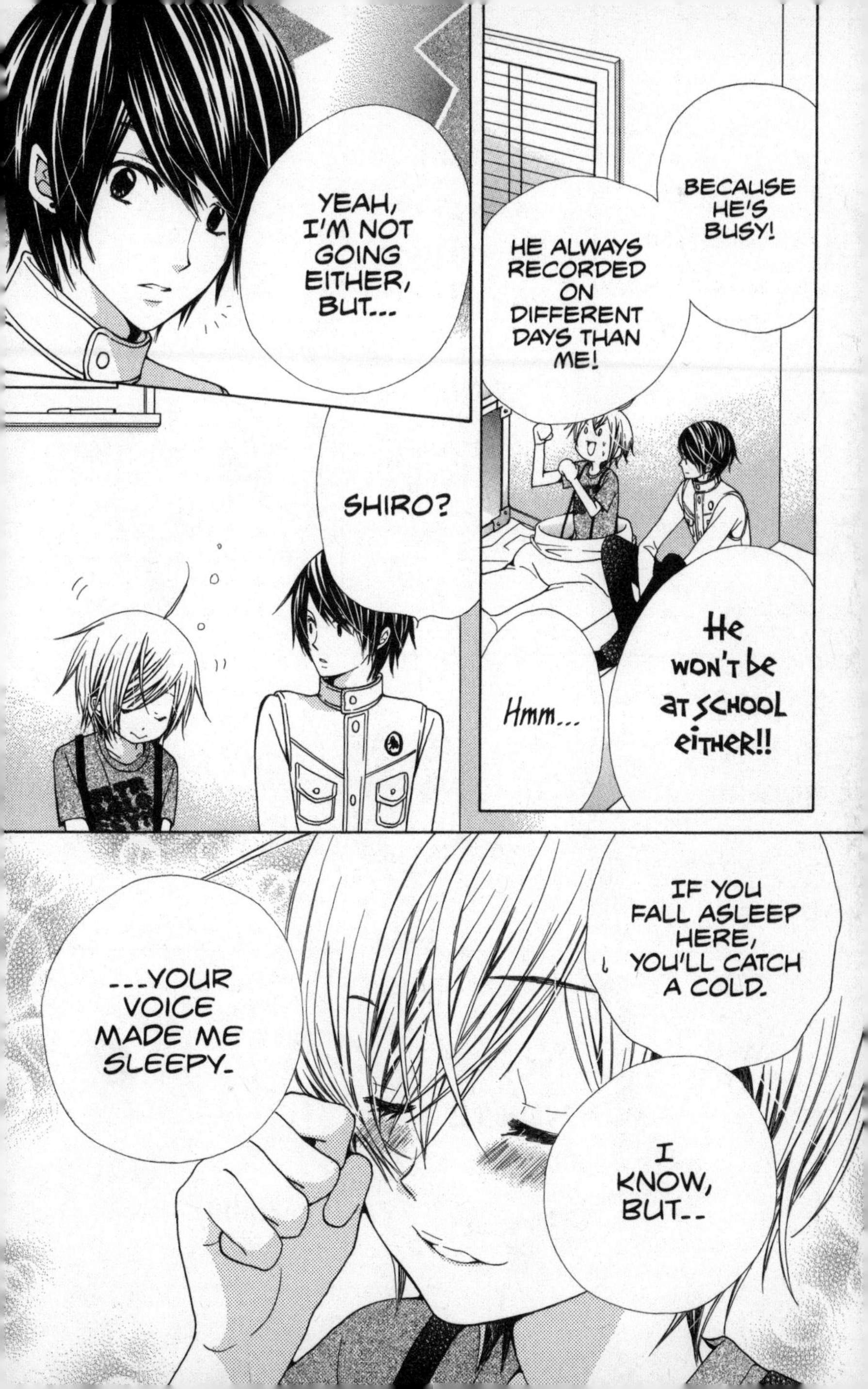
BECAUSE HE'S BUSY!
HE ALWAYS RECORDED ON DIFFERENT DAYS THAN ME!
He won't be at SCHOOL either!!
Hmm...
YEAH, I'M NOT GOING EITHER, BUT...
SHIRO?
IF YOU FALL ASLEEP HERE, YOU'LL CATCH A COLD.
I KNOW, BUT...
...YOUR VOICE MADE ME SLEEPY.

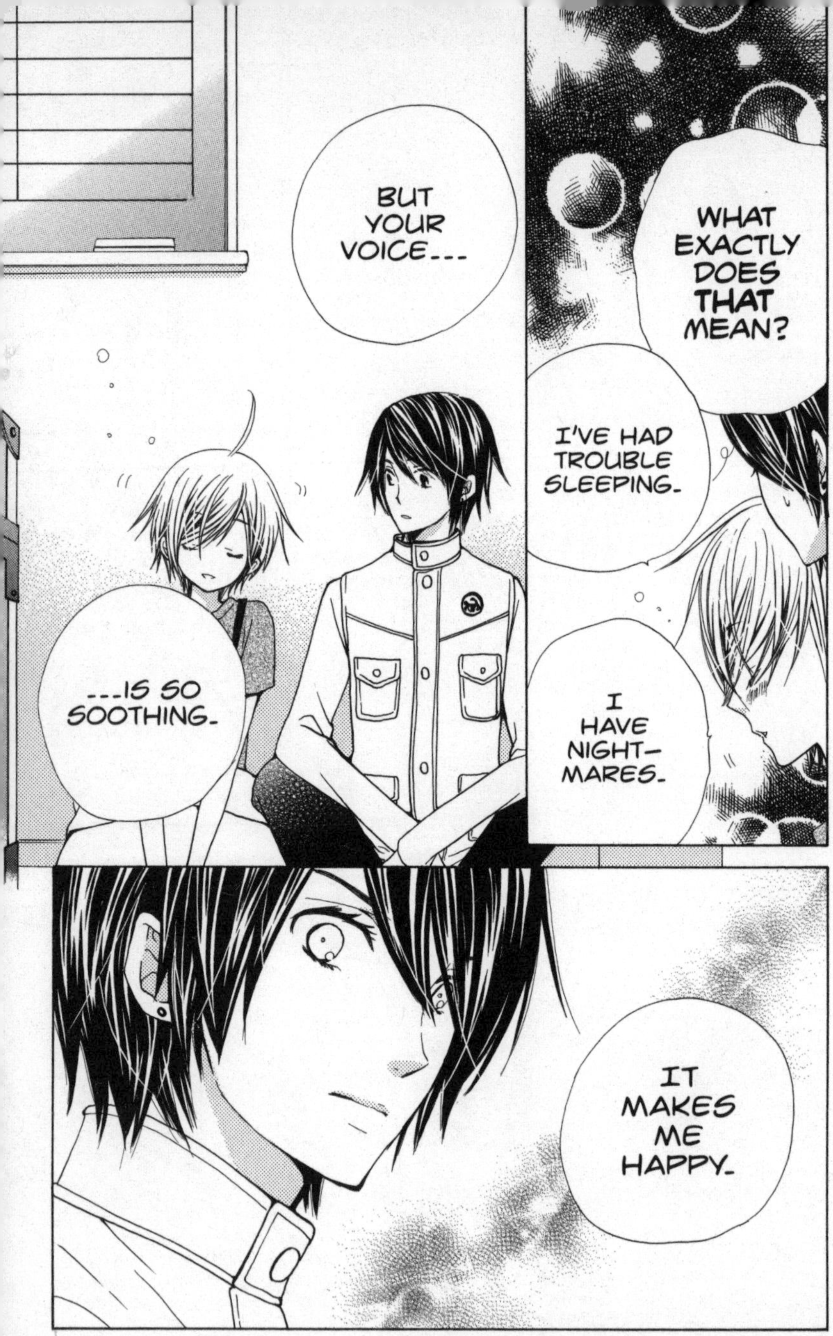
WHAT EXACTLY DOES THAT MEAN?
I'VE HAD TROUBLE SLEEPING.
I HAVE NIGHT-MARES.
BUT YOUR VOICE...
...IS SO SOOTHING.
IT MAKES ME HAPPY.

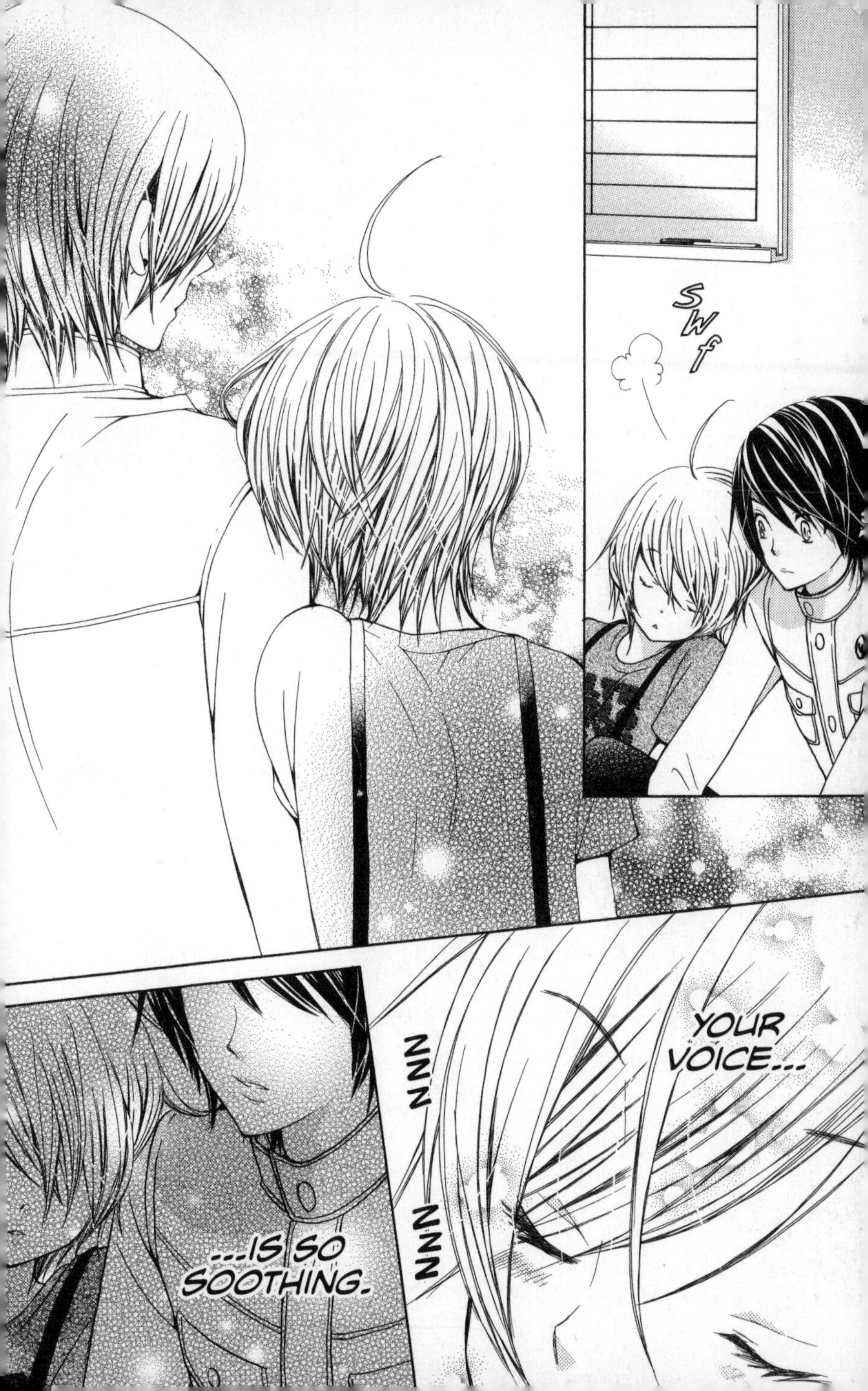
SWF
YOUR VOICE...
NNN
NNN
...IS SO SOOTHING.

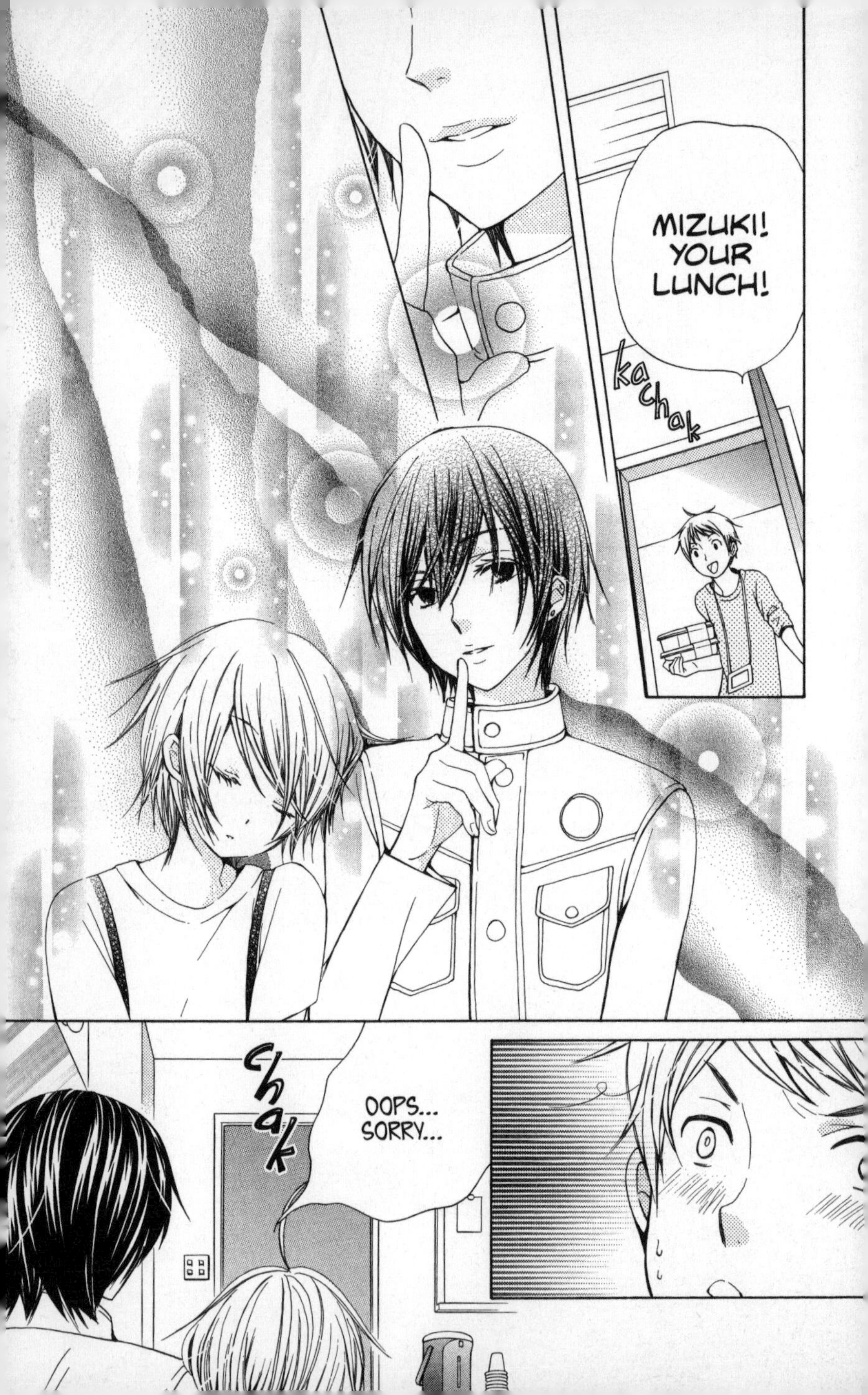
MIZUKI! YOUR LUNCH!
kachak
OOPS... SORRY...
chak

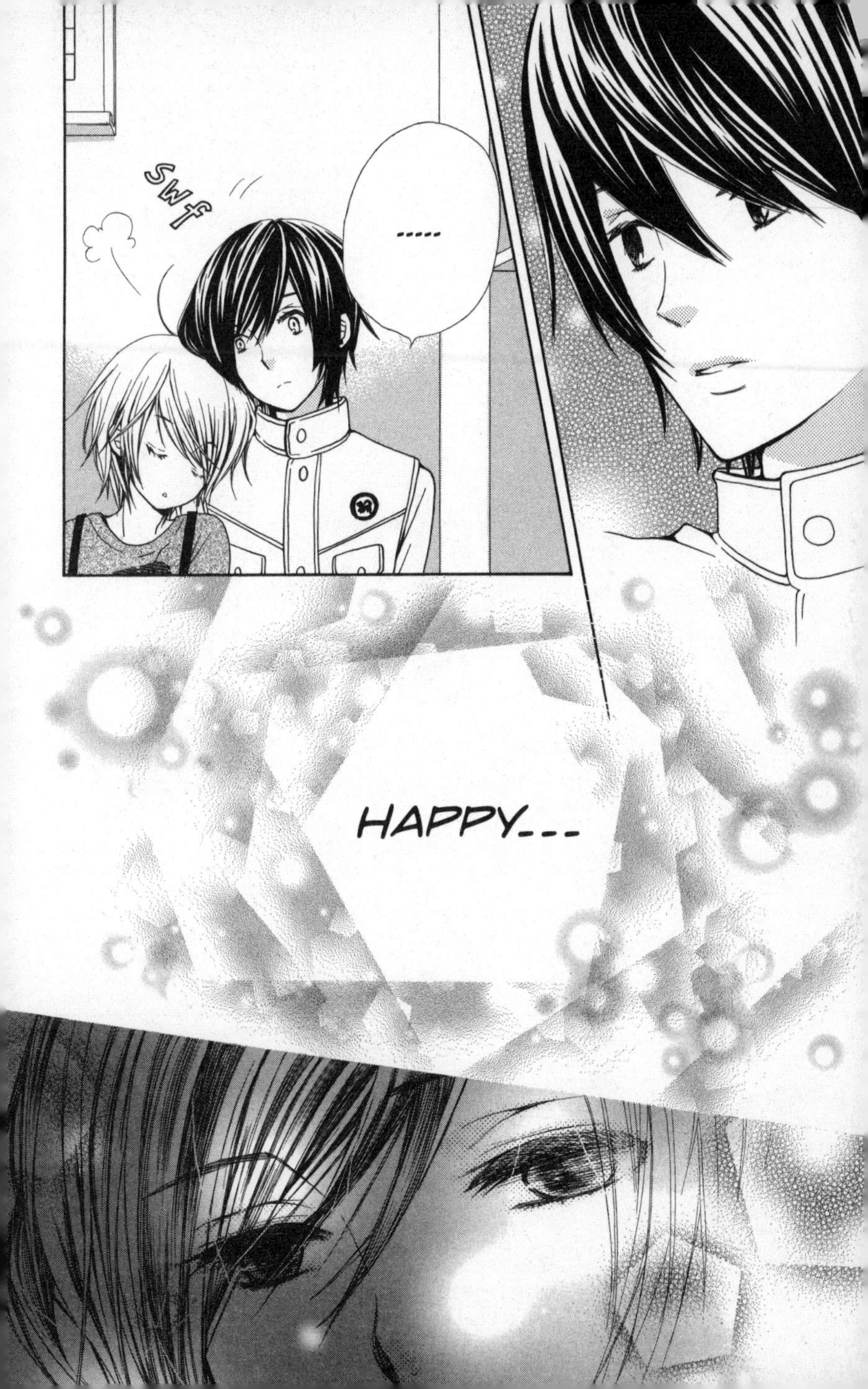
Swf
......
HAPPY...

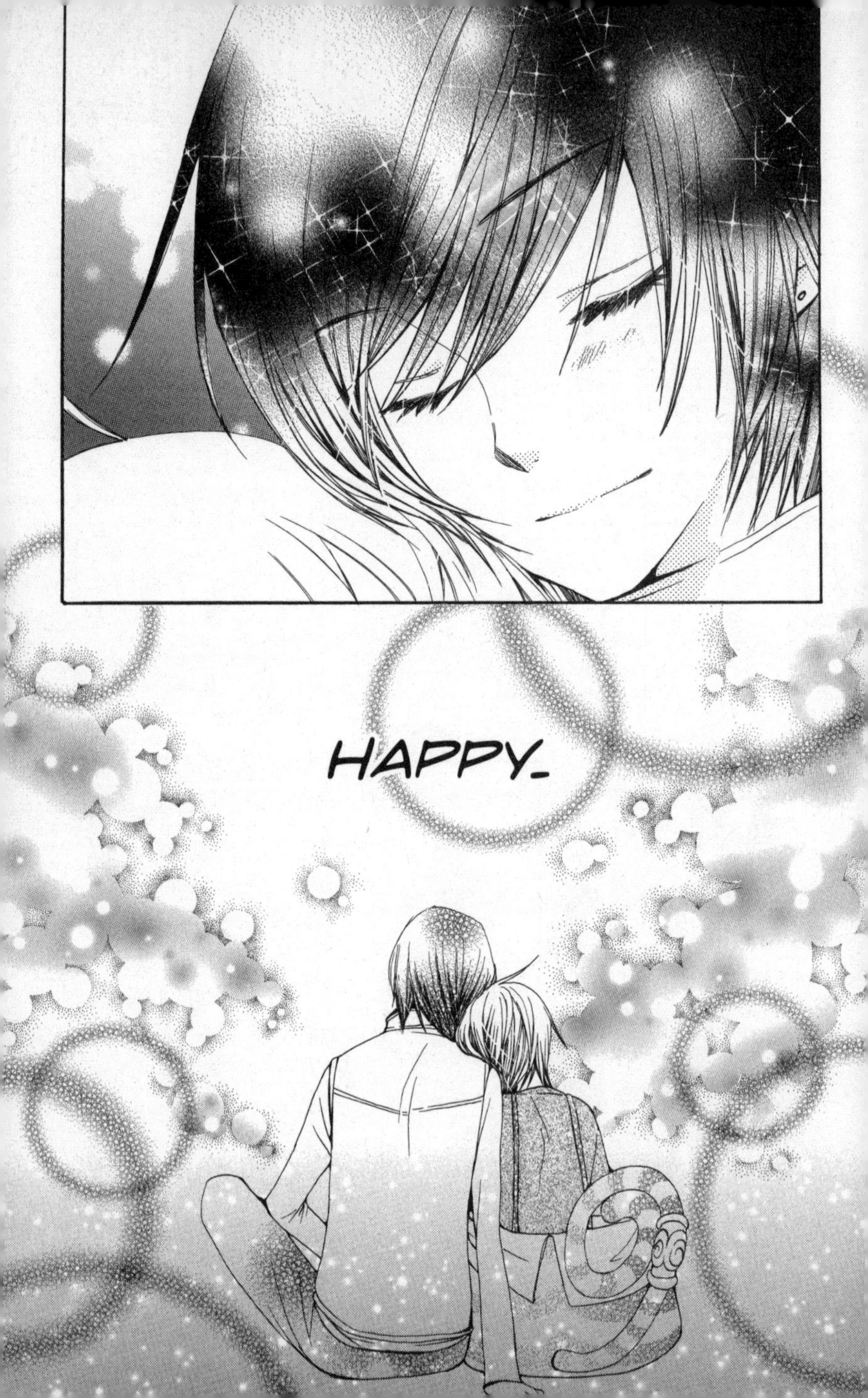
HAPPY_

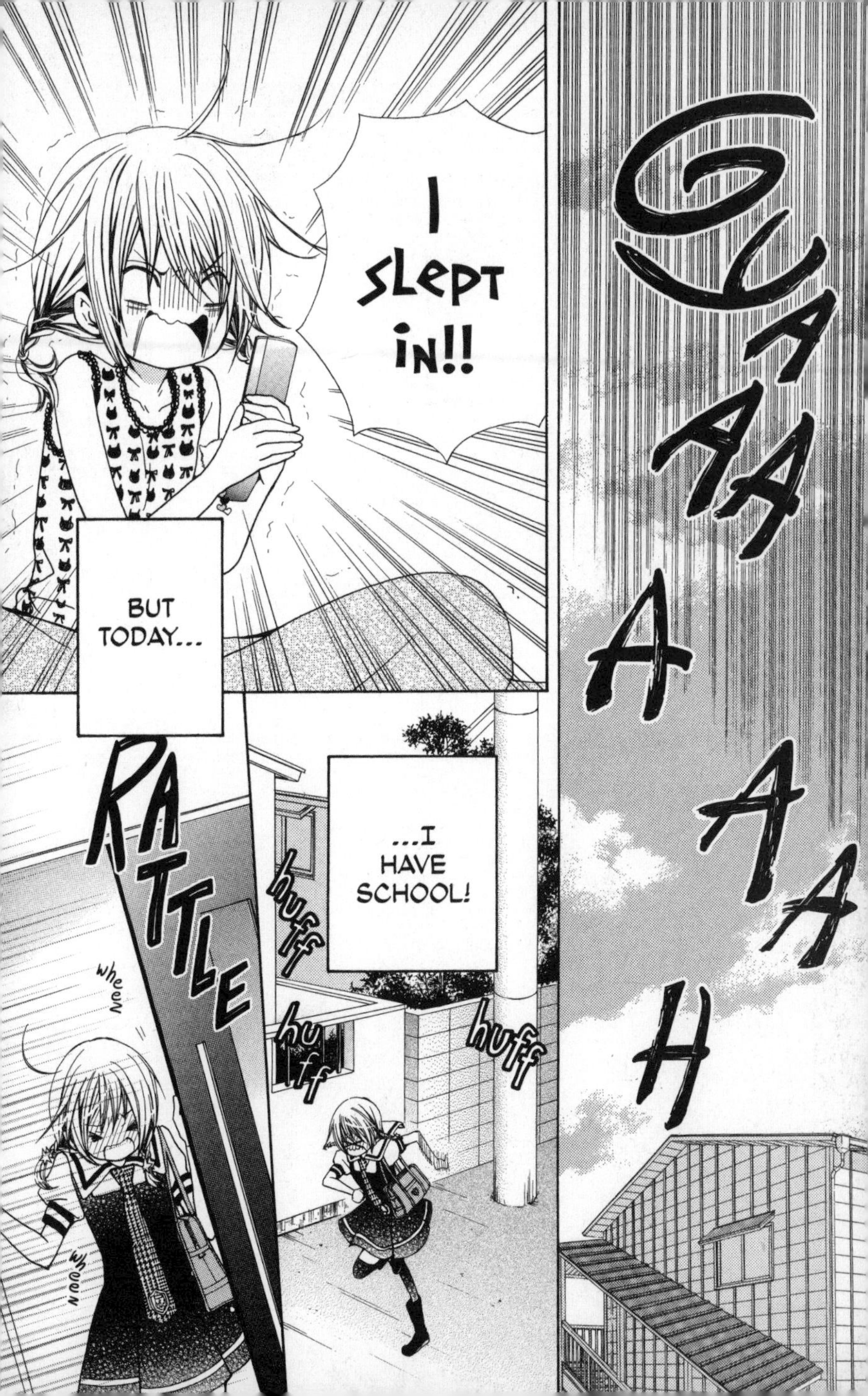
GYAAAAAAH
I SLEPT IN!!
BUT TODAY...
...I HAVE SCHOOL!
RATTLE
huff
huff
huff
wheeen
wheeen

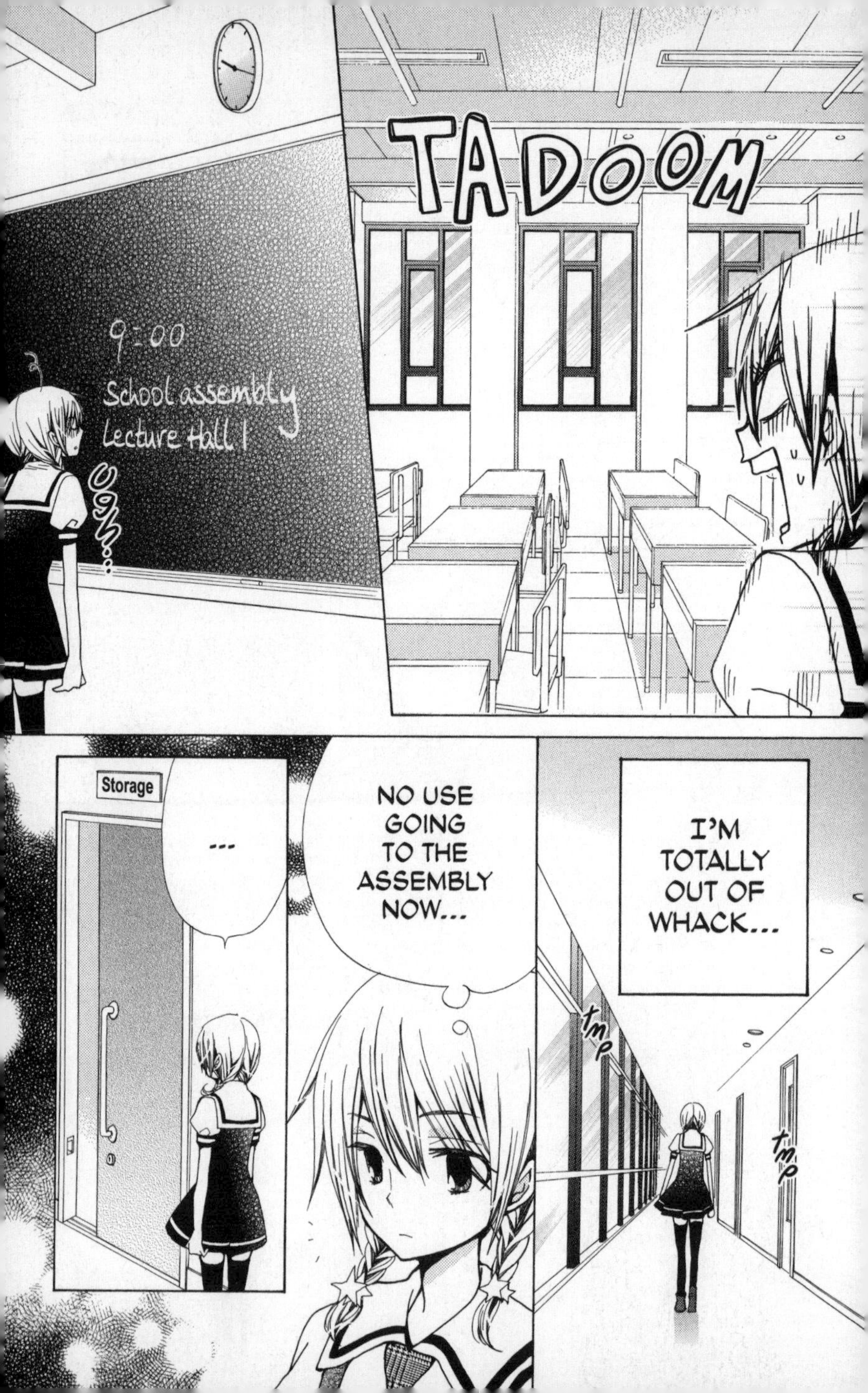
TADOOM
9:00
School assembly
Lecture Hall 1
Ugh...
I'M TOTALLY OUT OF WHACK...
tmp
tmp
NO USE GOING TO THE ASSEMBLY NOW...
Storage
...

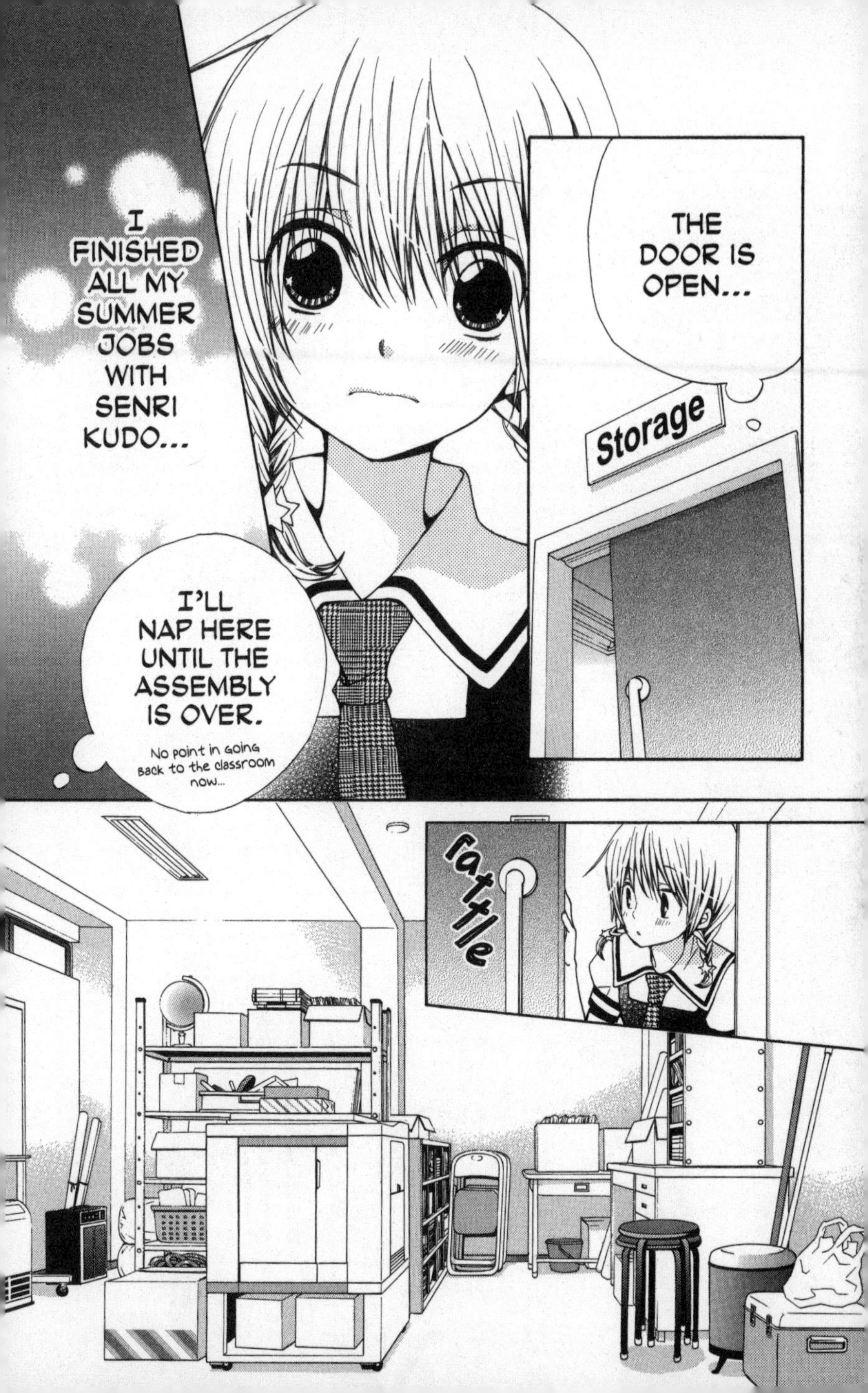
THE DOOR IS OPEN...
Storage
I FINISHED ALL MY SUMMER JOBS WITH SENRI KUDO...
I'LL NAP HERE UNTIL THE ASSEMBLY IS OVER.
No point in going back to the classroom now...
rattle

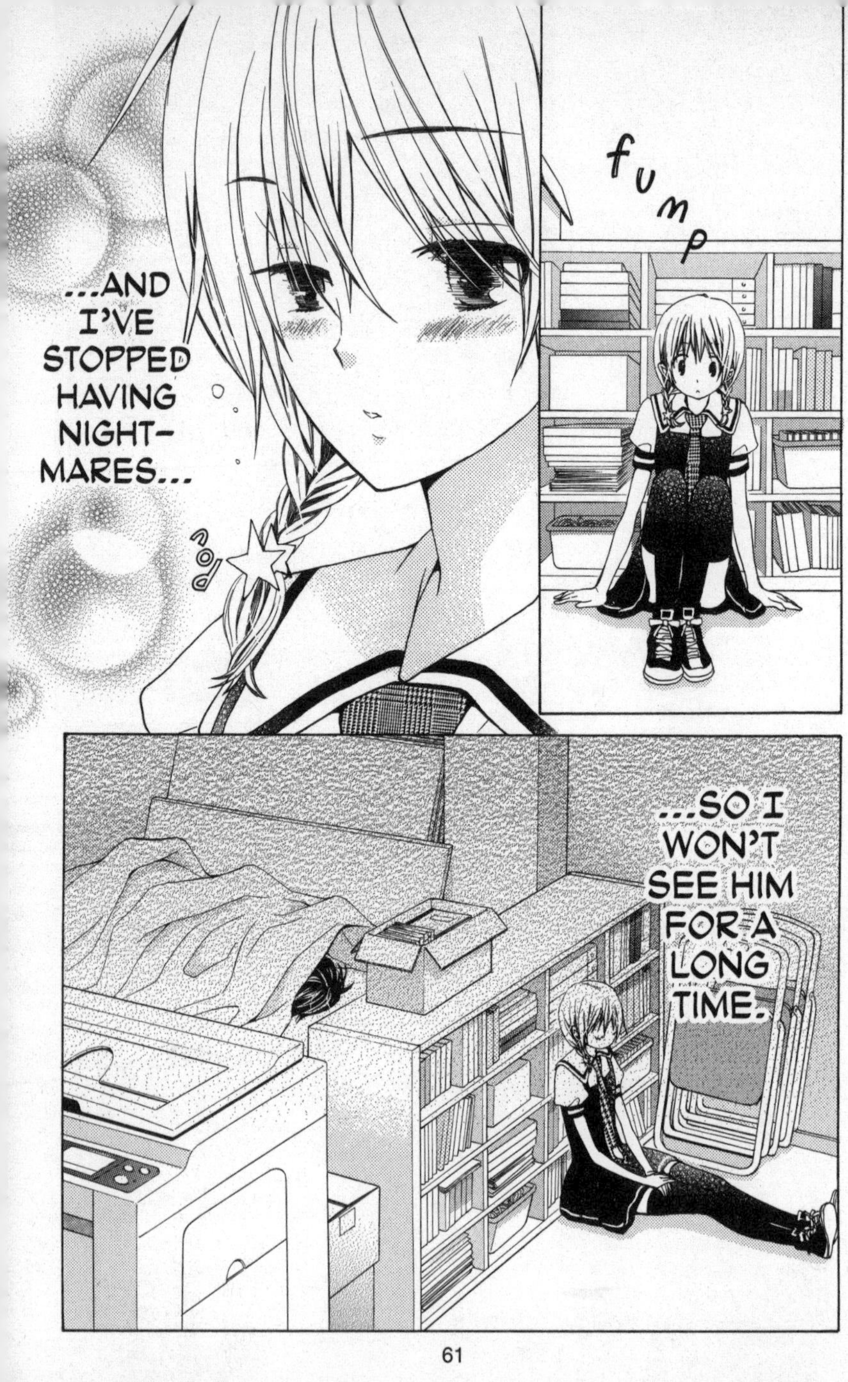
fump
...AND I'VE STOPPED HAVING NIGHT-MARES...
...SO I WON'T SEE HIM FOR A LONG TIME.

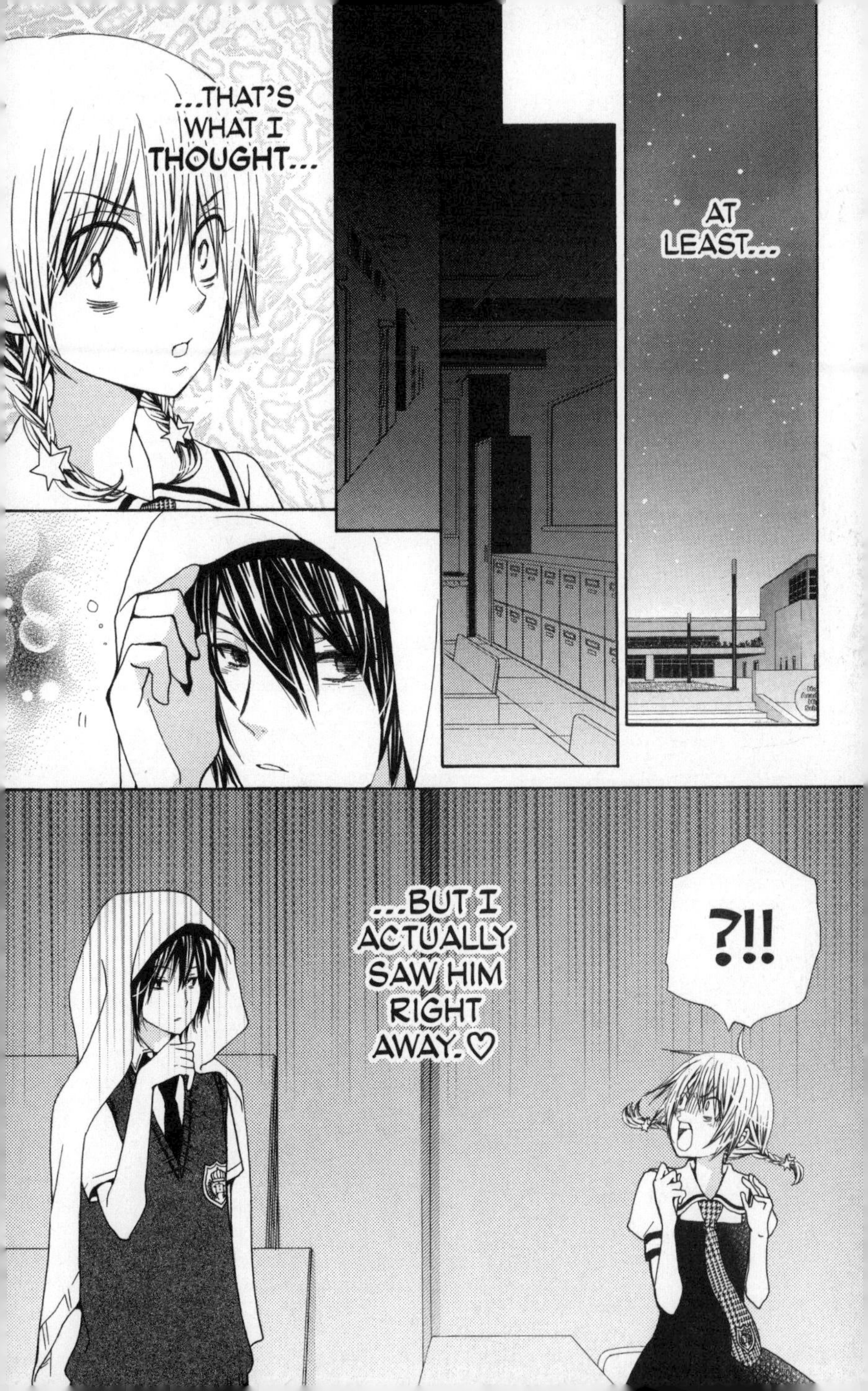
AT LEAST...
...THAT'S WHAT I THOUGHT...
?!!
...BUT I ACTUALLY SAW HIM RIGHT AWAY. ♡

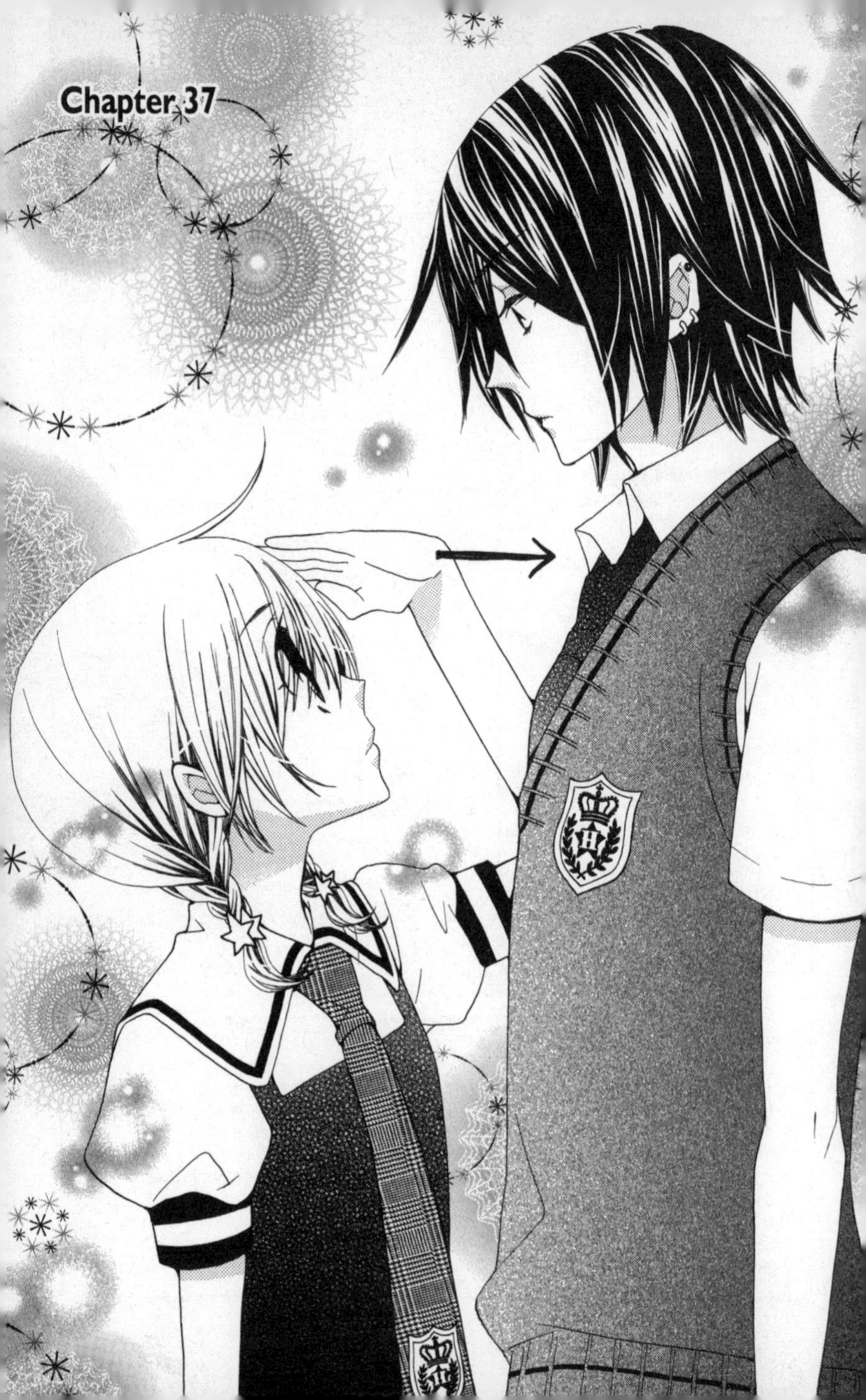
Chapter 37

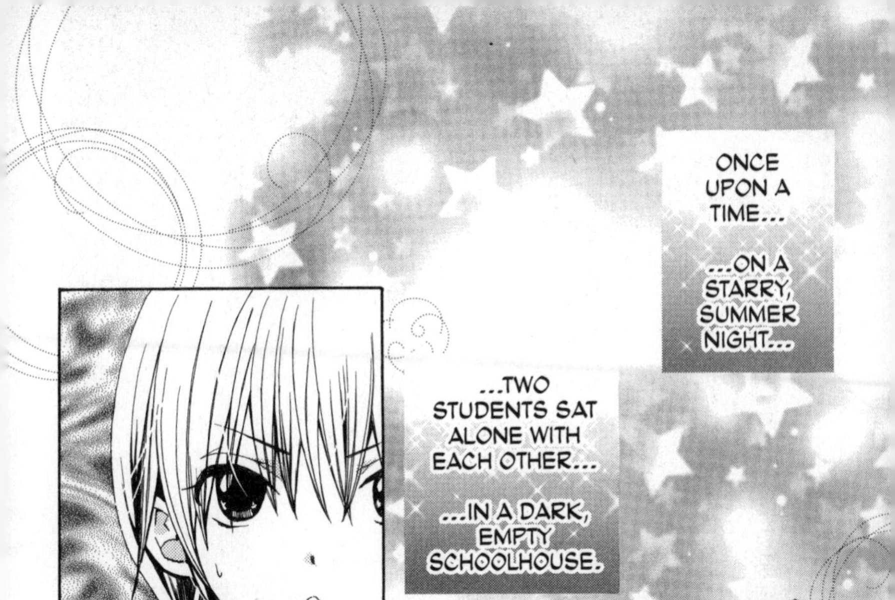
ONCE UPON A TIME...
...ON A STARRY, SUMMER NIGHT...
...TWO STUDENTS SAT ALONE WITH EACH OTHER...
...IN A DARK, EMPTY SCHOOLHOUSE.
TRULY, TRULY ROMANTIC.
BUT THAT DEPENDS...

• Autograph Signing at LIBRO •

It was fun talking to everyone who came because they gave me lots of encouragement and told me which characters they like. When someone said they liked Senri, I thought, "I'm so glad for Senri." My assistants say Mizuki is creepy, so when someone said they love him, I thought, "I'm so glad (and so on)." I was surprised to see more male readers than I expected. Most of the letters I receive are from women. I didn't think I had many guys readers, so that was unexpected. I'm so happy!! A lot of the guys said they like Tsukino!! Thank you, everyone!

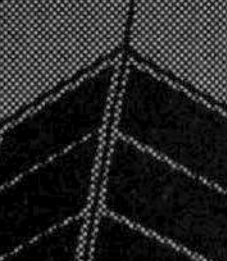
Thanks for the letters and presents!
3

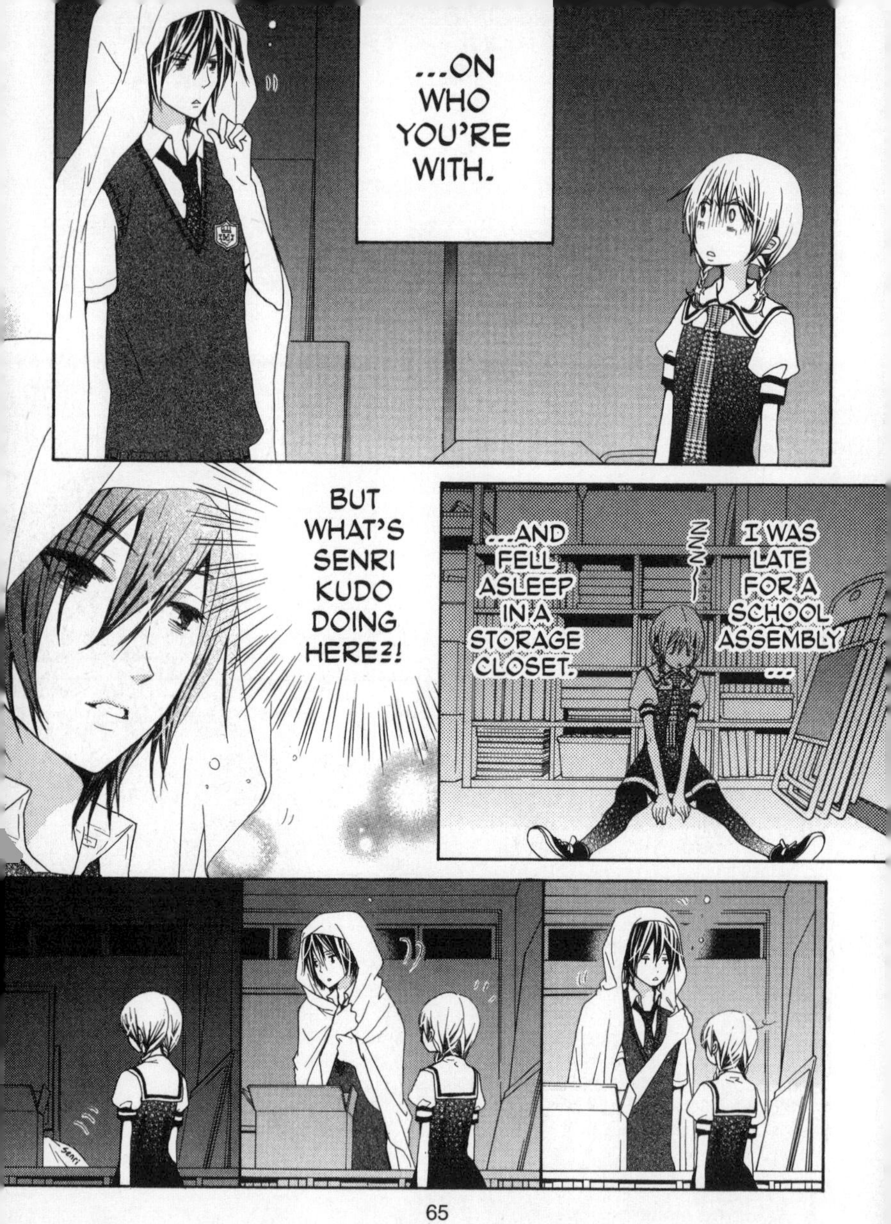
...ON WHO YOU'RE WITH.
I WAS LATE FOR A SCHOOL ASSEMBLY...
NNN~
...AND FELL ASLEEP IN A STORAGE CLOSET.
BUT WHAT'S SENRI KUDO DOING HERE?!
senri

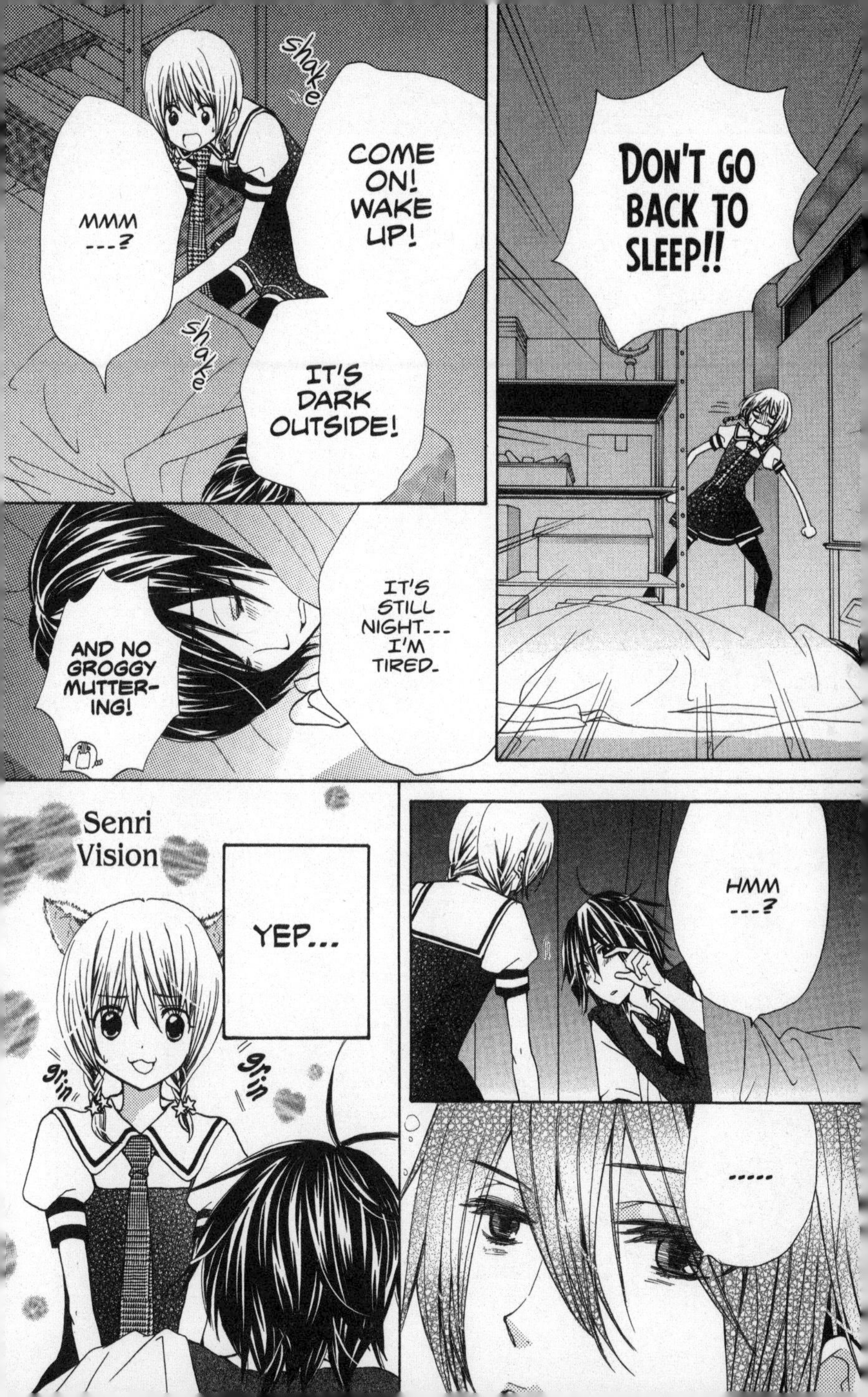

DON'T GO BACK TO SLEEP!!
shake
COME ON! WAKE UP!
MMM...?
shake
IT'S DARK OUTSIDE!
IT'S STILL NIGHT... I'M TIRED.
AND NO GROGGY MUTTERING!
HMM...?
.....
YEP...
Senri Vision
grin
grin

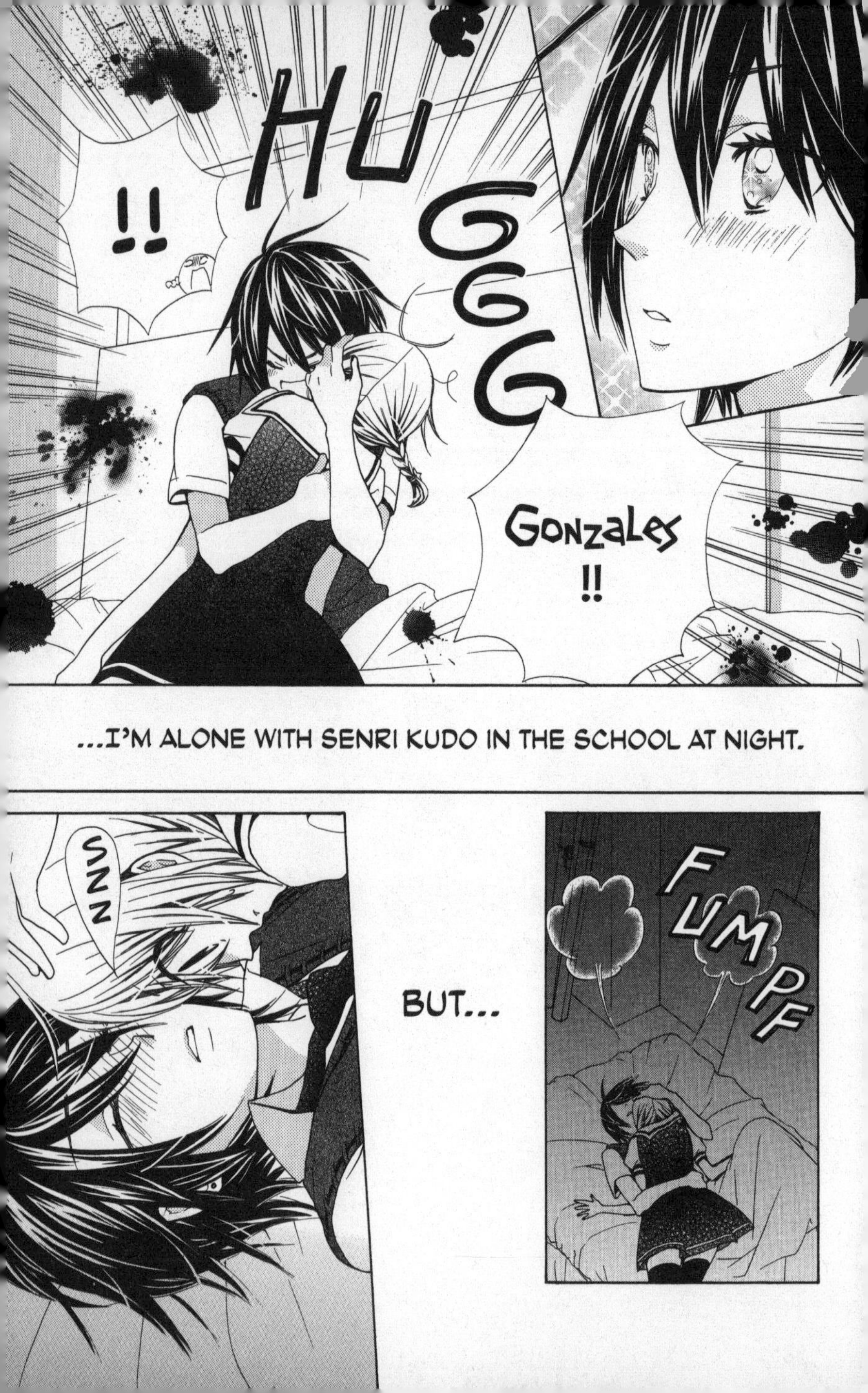
Gonzales !!
HUGGG
!!
...I'M ALONE WITH SENRI KUDO IN THE SCHOOL AT NIGHT.
FUMPF
BUT...
SNZ

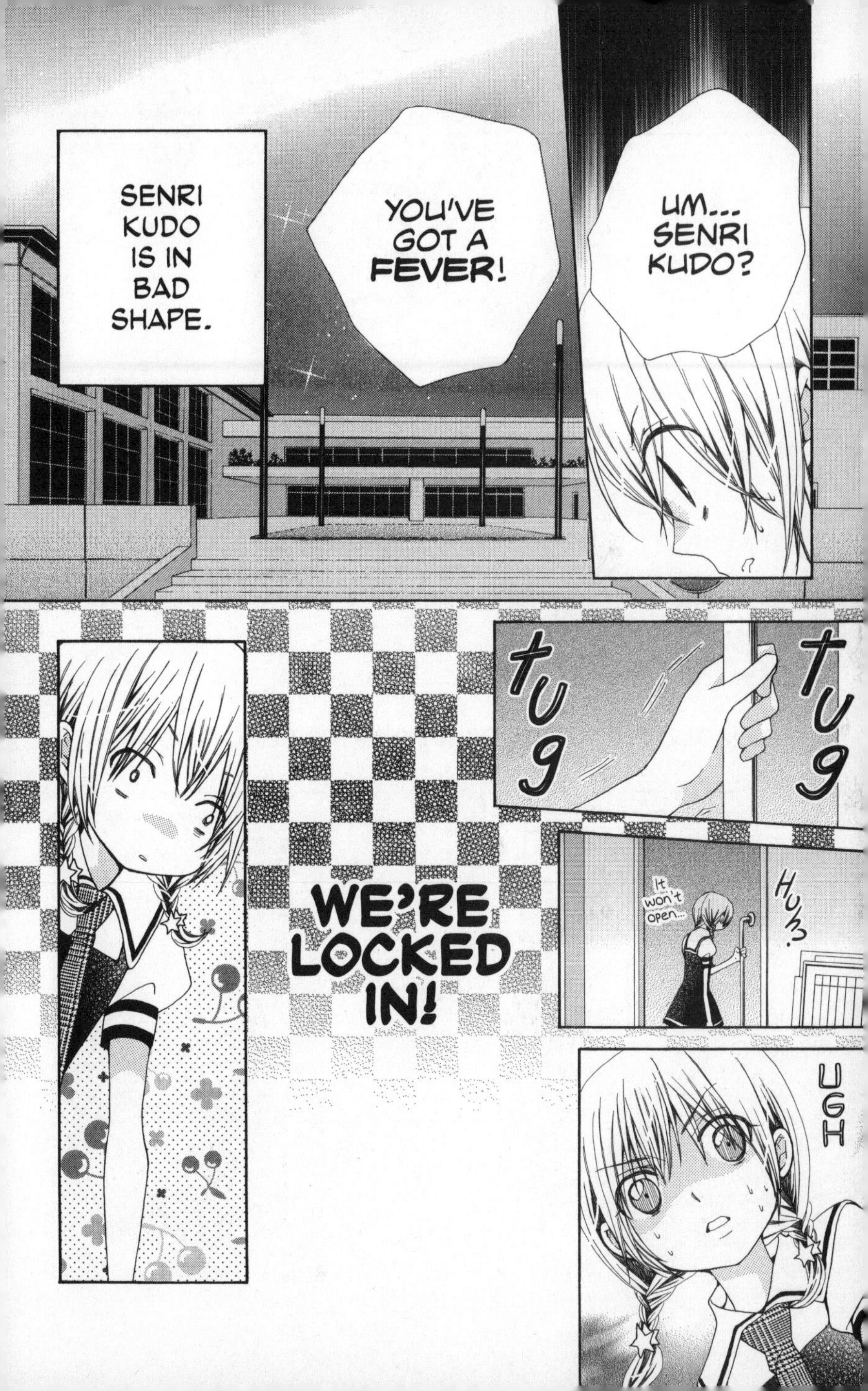
UM... SENRI KUDO?
YOU'VE GOT A FEVER!
SENRI KUDO IS IN BAD SHAPE.
TUG
TUG
HUM?
It won't open...
UGH
WE'RE LOCKED IN!

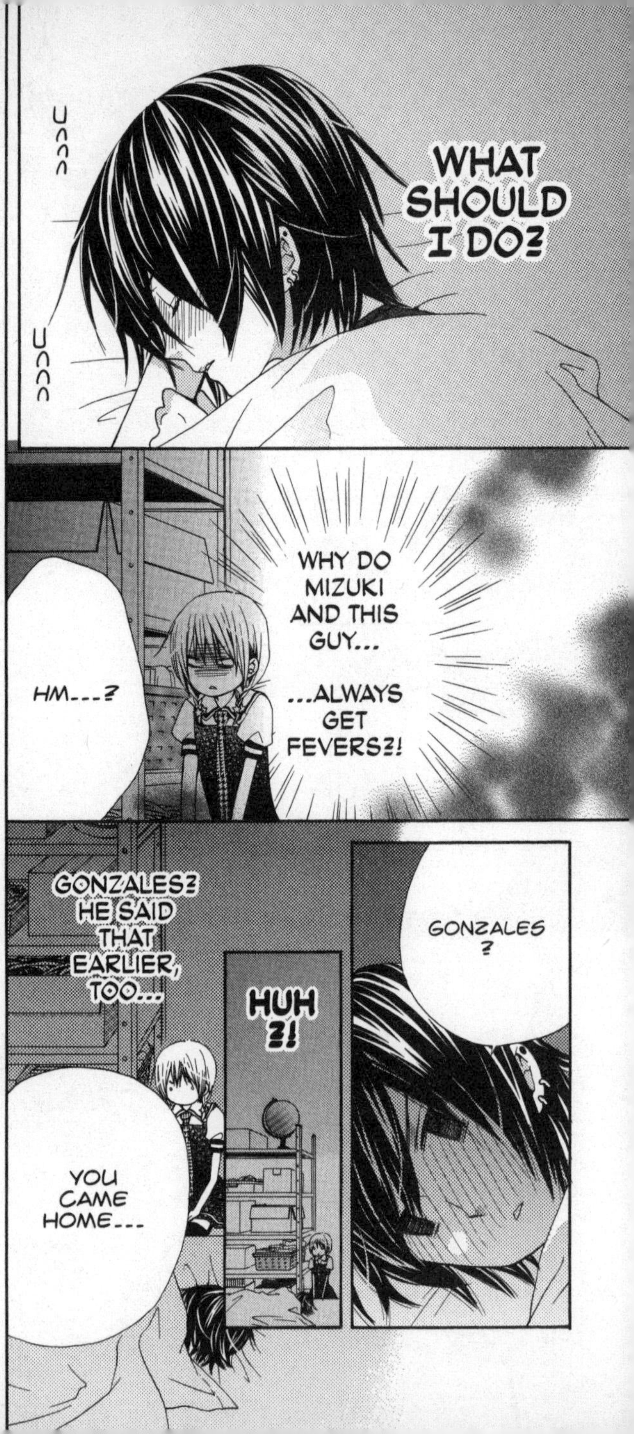
WHAT SHOULD I DO?
Unnn
Unnn
WHY DO MIZUKI AND THIS GUY...
...ALWAYS GET FEVERS?!
HM...?
GONZALES?
HUH?!
GONZALES? HE SAID THAT EARLIER, TOO...
YOU CAME HOME...

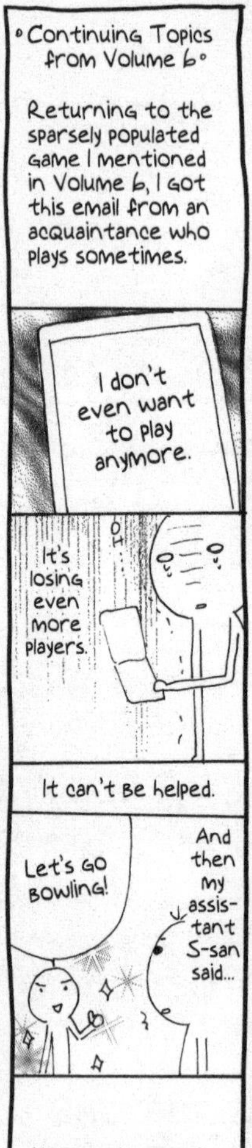
•Continuing Topics from Volume 6•
Returning to the sparsely populated game I mentioned in Volume 6, I got this email from an acquaintance who plays sometimes.
I don't even want to play anymore.
OH...
It's losing even more players.
It can't be helped.
And then my assistant S-san said...
Let's go bowling!
My worst score is a total of 37 for two games, so I said "No way!" But I'm really happy for the invitation, so I think I'll go.
No, I'll definitely go!

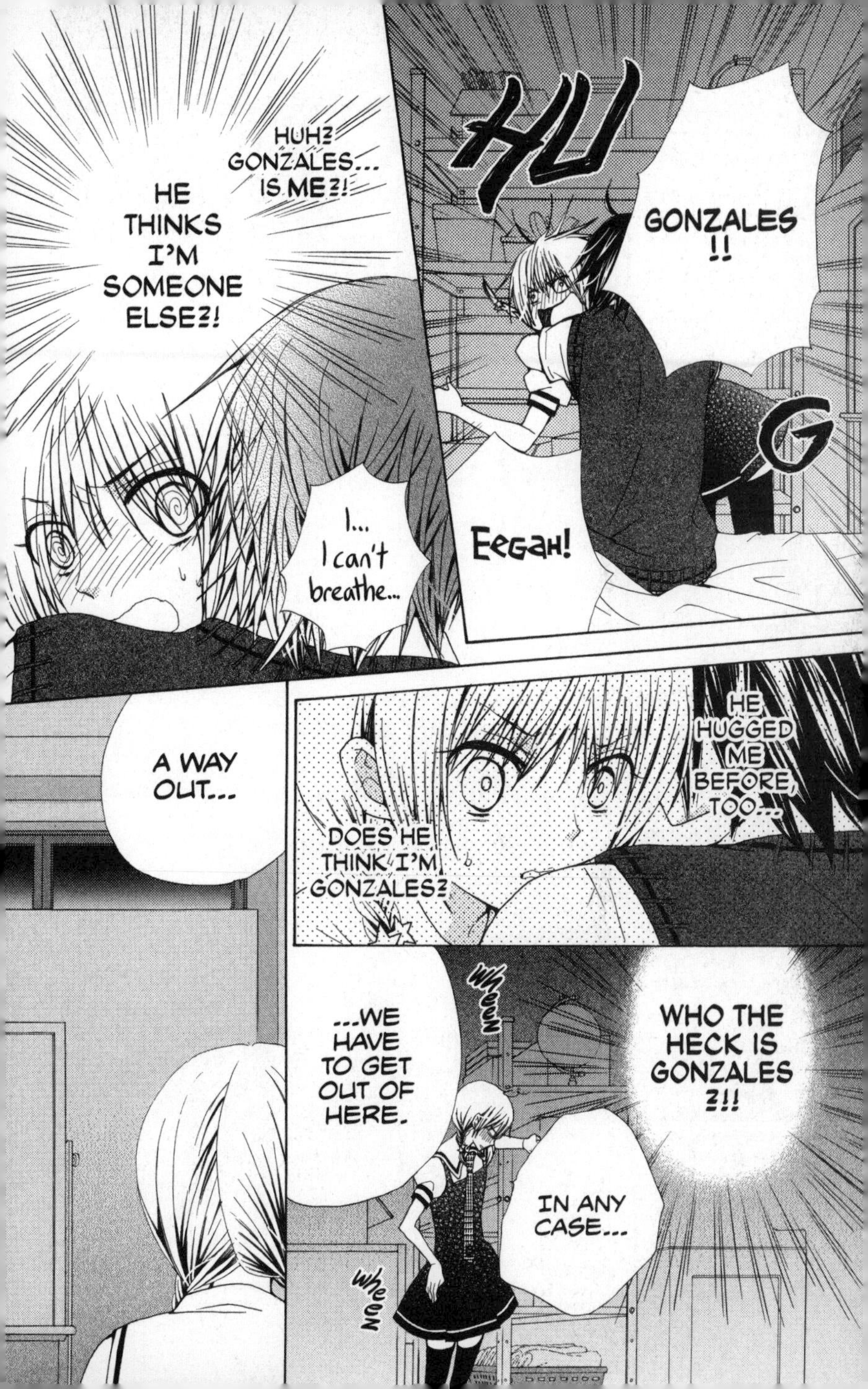
HU
GONZALES !!
G
Eegah!
HUH? GONZALES... IS ME?!
HE THINKS I'M SOMEONE ELSE?!
I... I can't breathe...
HE HUGGED ME BEFORE, TOO...
DOES HE THINK I'M GONZALES?
WHO THE HECK IS GONZALES ?!!
IN ANY CASE...
...WE HAVE TO GET OUT OF HERE.
wheen
wheen
A WAY OUT...

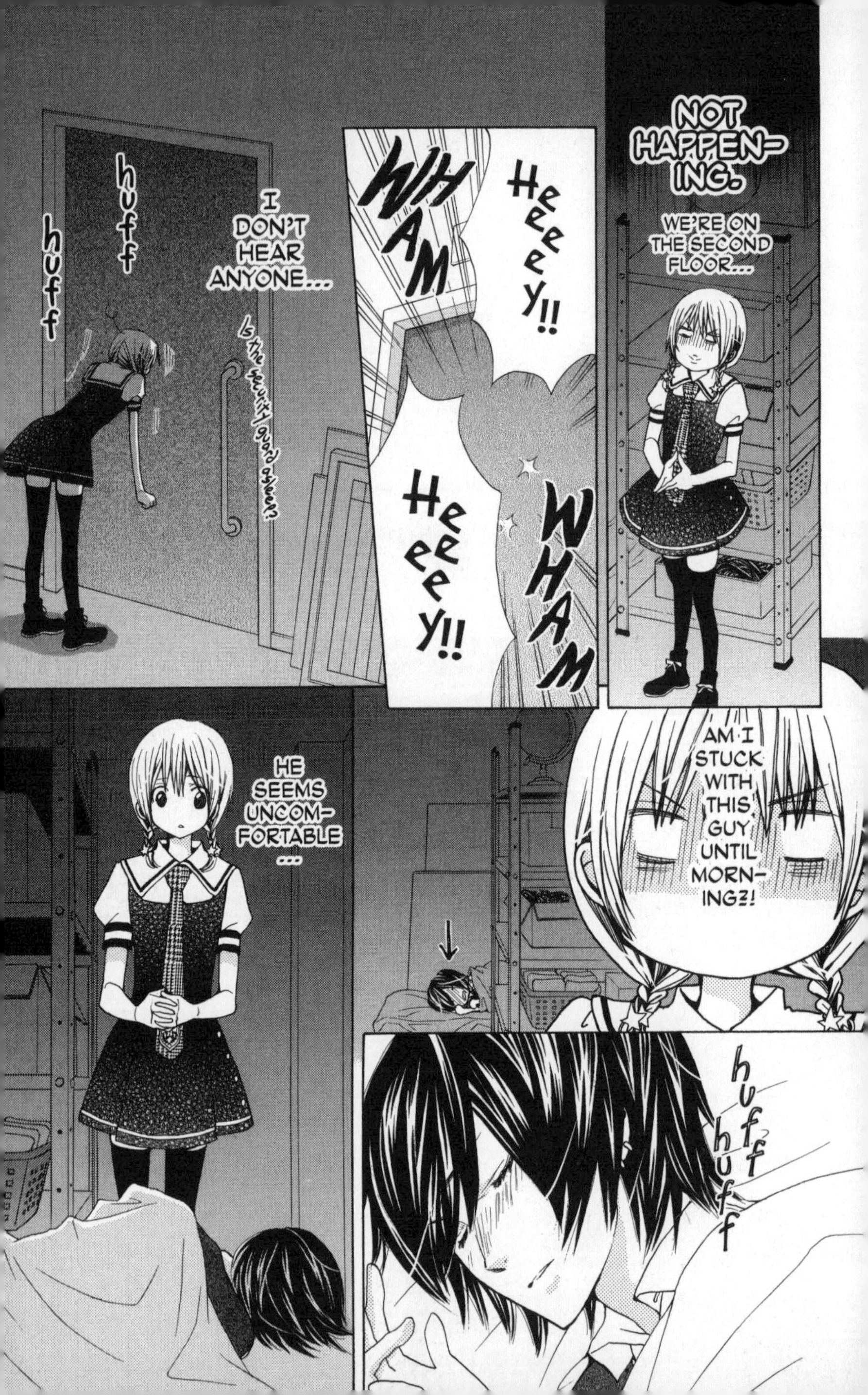
NOT HAPPEN-ING.
WE'RE ON THE SECOND FLOOR...
WHAM
Heeeey!!
Heeeey!!
WHAM
I DON'T HEAR ANYONE...
Is the security guard asleep?
huff
huff
AM I STUCK WITH THIS GUY UNTIL MORN-ING?!
HE SEEMS UNCOM-FORTABLE...
huff
huff

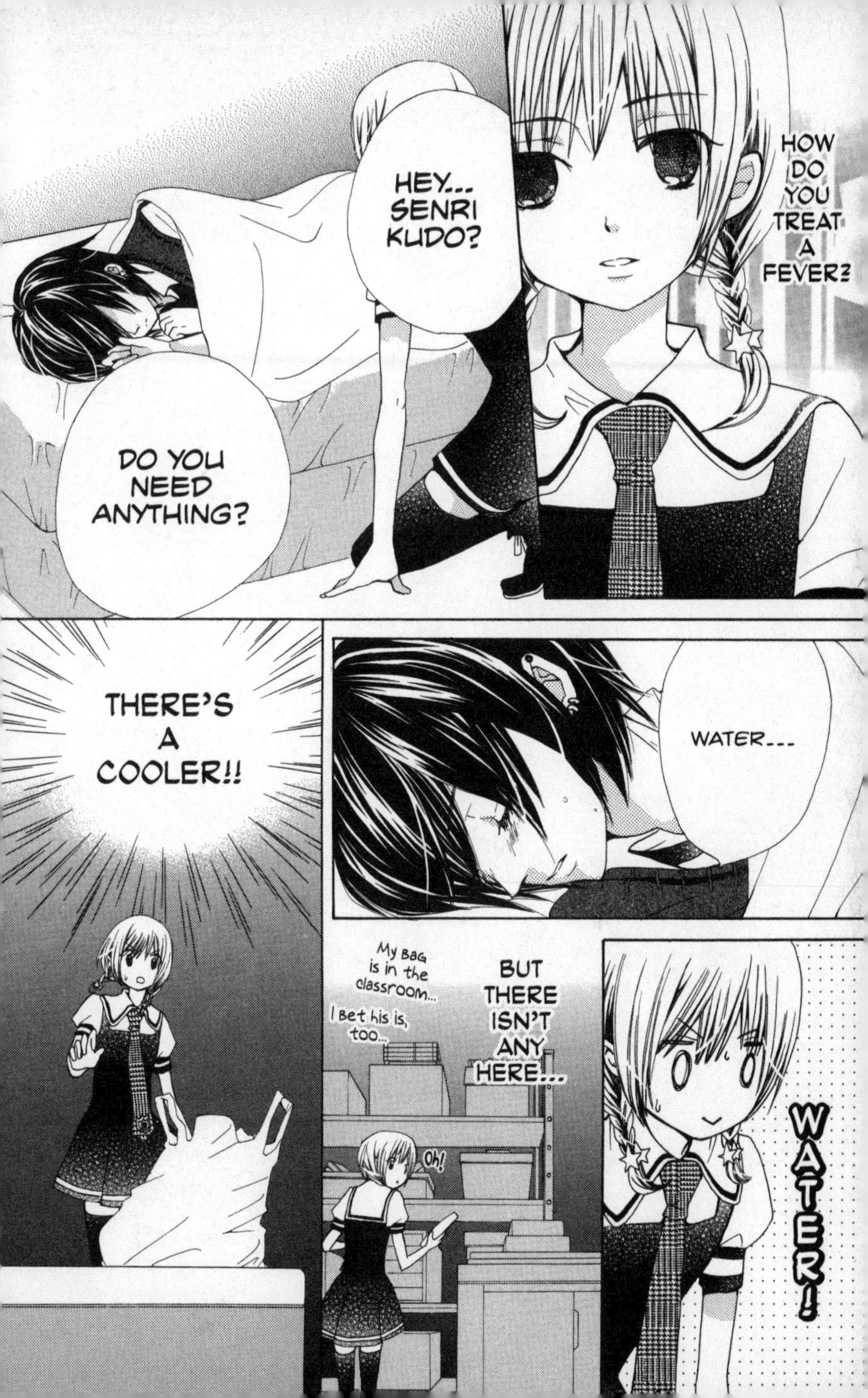
HOW DO YOU TREAT A FEVER?
HEY... SENRI KUDO?
DO YOU NEED ANYTHING?
WATER...
WATER!
BUT THERE ISN'T ANY HERE...
My bag is in the classroom...
I bet his is, too...
Oh!
THERE'S A COOLER!!

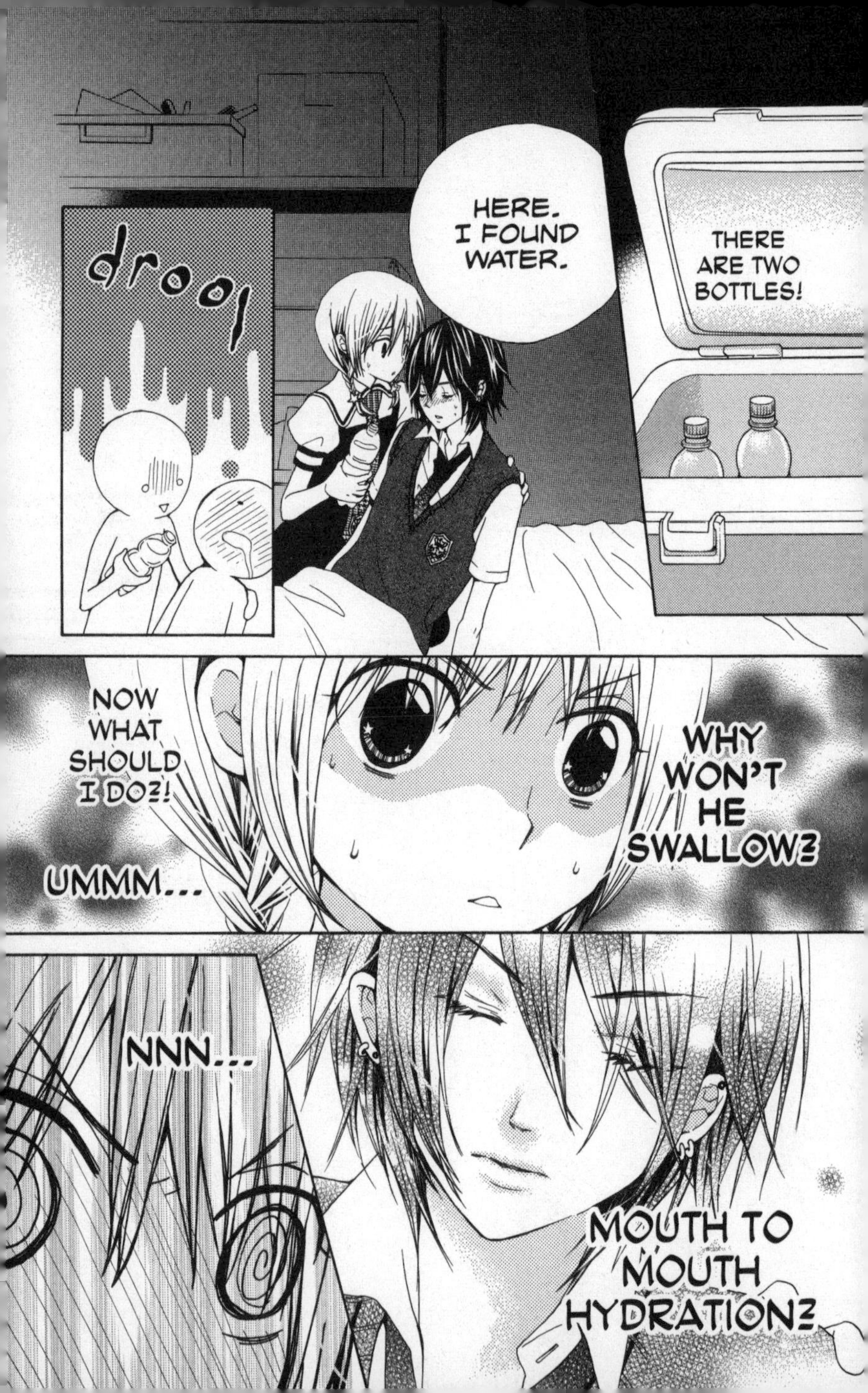
THERE ARE TWO BOTTLES!
HERE. I FOUND WATER.
drool
WHY WON'T HE SWALLOW?
NOW WHAT SHOULD I DO?!
UMMM...
MOUTH TO MOUTH HYDRATION?
NNN...

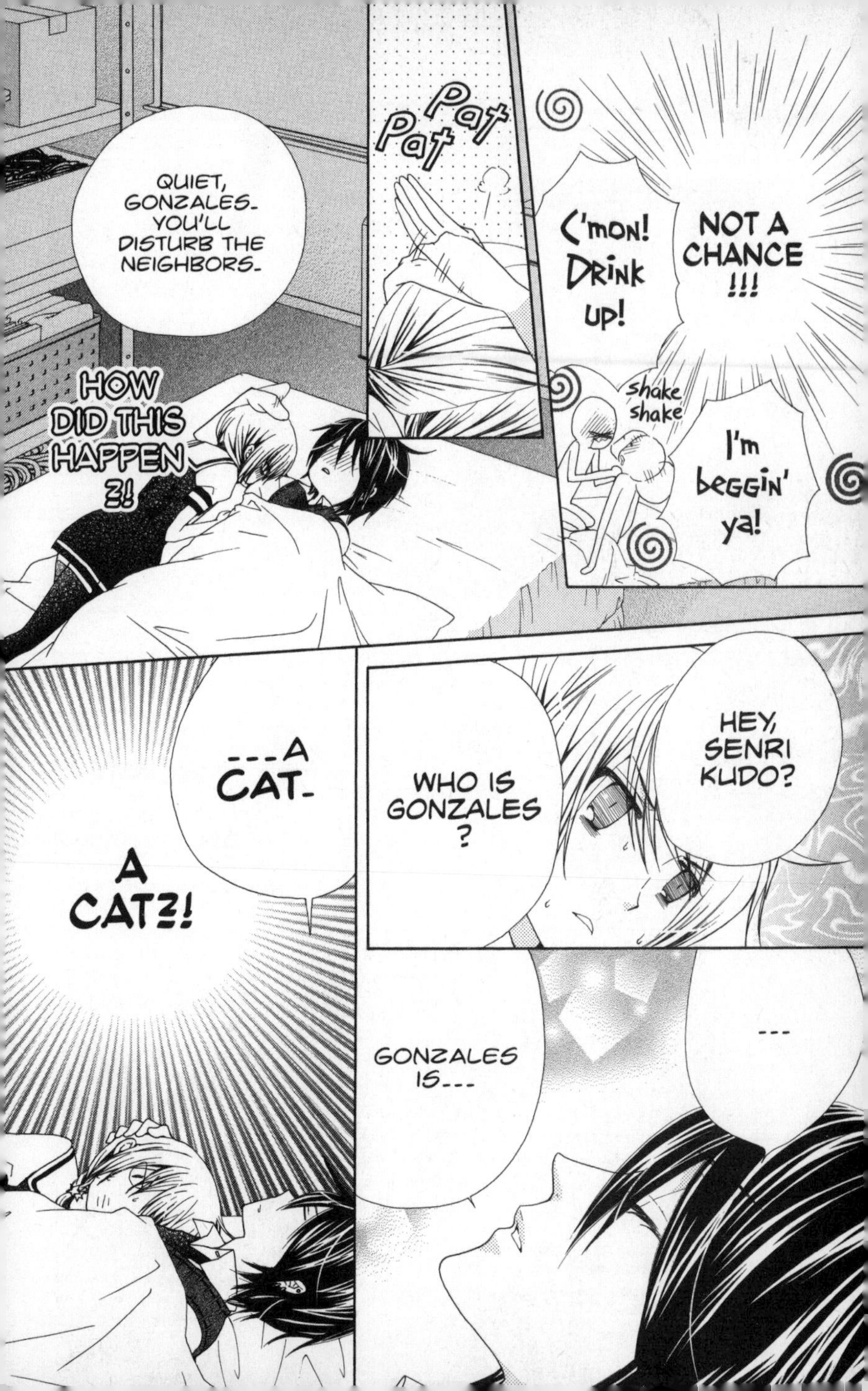
NOT A CHANCE!!!
C'mon! Drink up!
shake shake
I'm beggin' ya!
Pat Pat
QUIET, GONZALES. YOU'LL DISTURB THE NEIGHBORS.
HOW DID THIS HAPPEN?!
HEY, SENRI KUDO?
WHO IS GONZALES?
...
GONZALES IS...
...A CAT.
A CAT?!

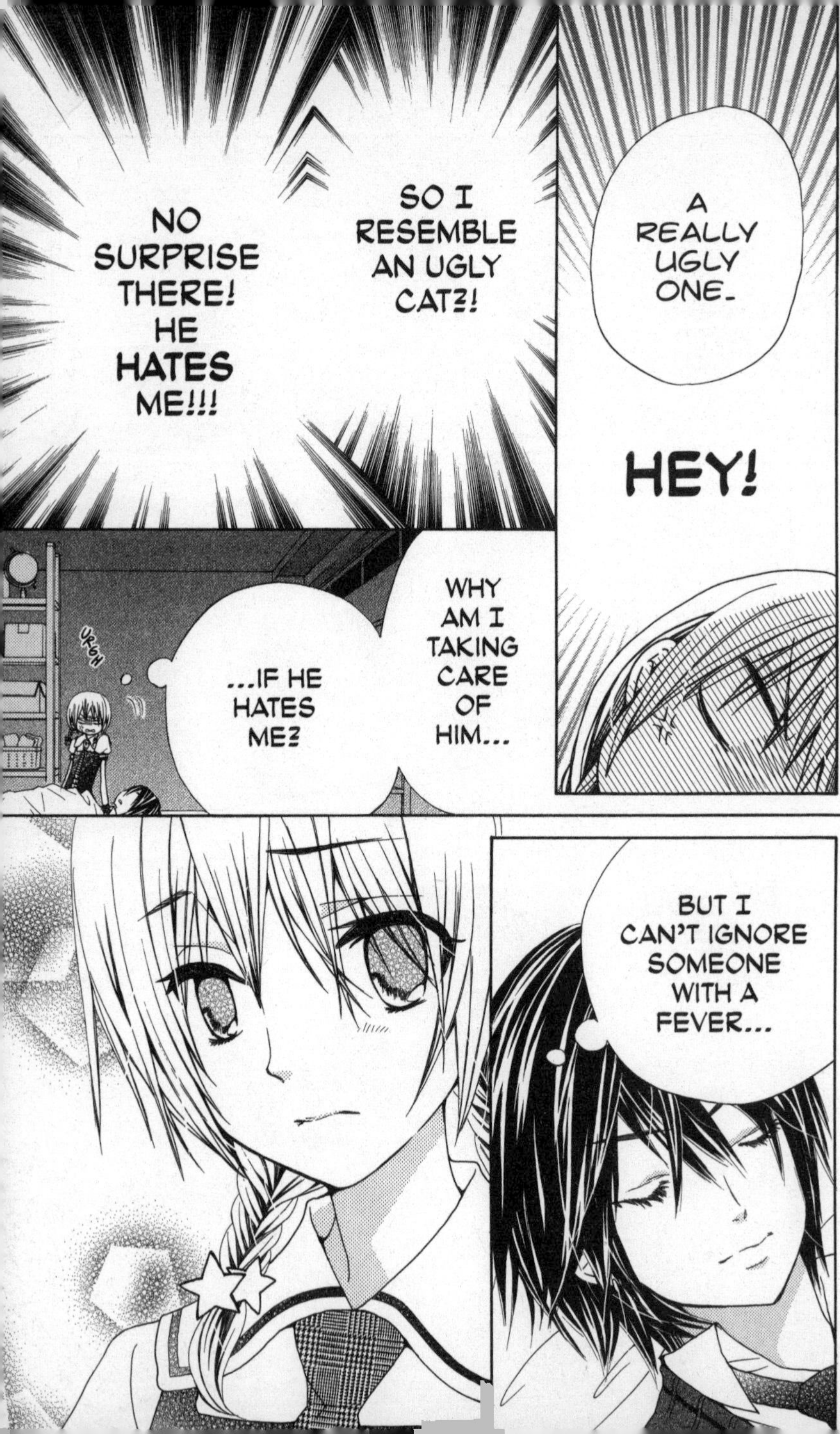
A REALLY UGLY ONE.
HEY!
SO I RESEMBLE AN UGLY CAT?!
NO SURPRISE THERE! HE HATES ME!!!
WHY AM I TAKING CARE OF HIM...
...IF HE HATES ME?
URGH
BUT I CAN'T IGNORE SOMEONE WITH A FEVER...

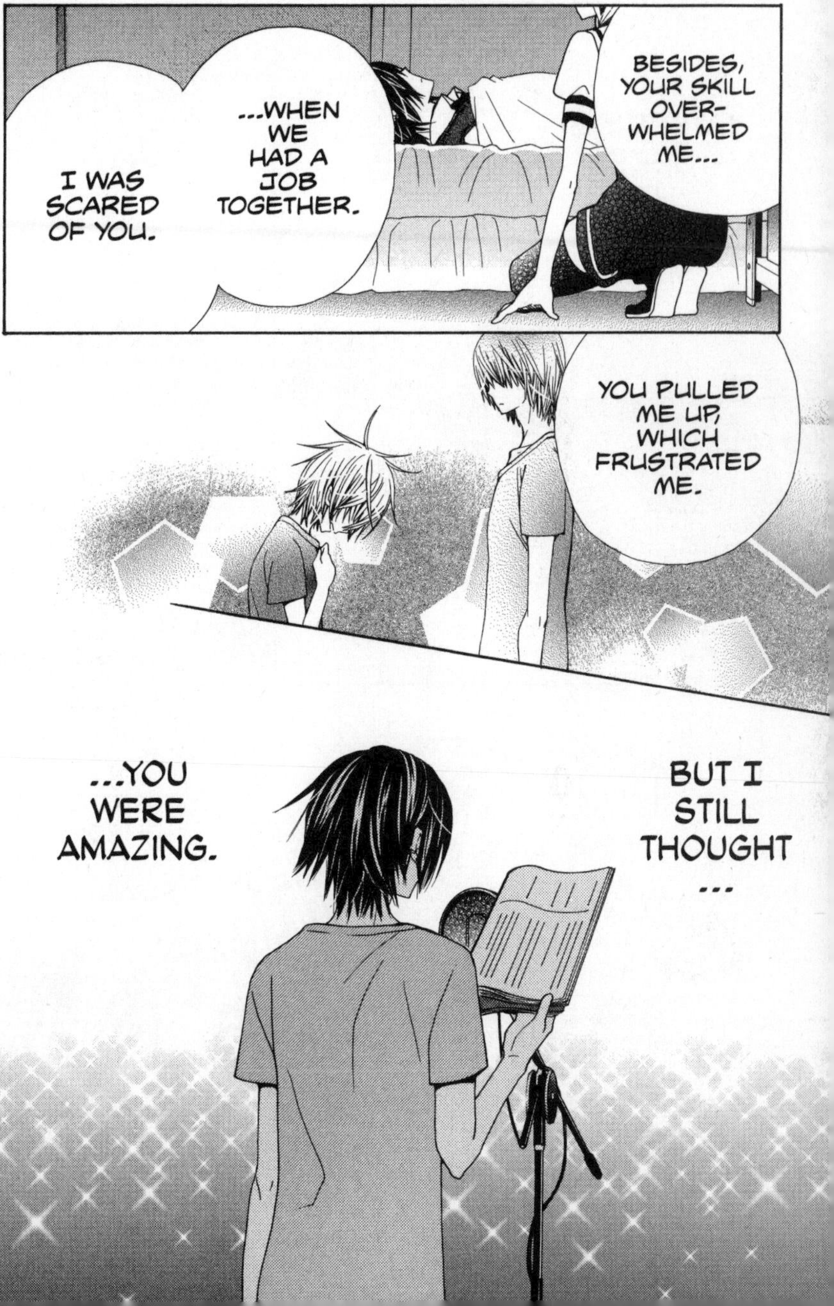

BESIDES, YOUR SKILL OVER-WHELMED ME...
...WHEN WE HAD A JOB TOGETHER.
I WAS SCARED OF YOU.
YOU PULLED ME UP, WHICH FRUSTRATED ME.
BUT I STILL THOUGHT...
...YOU WERE AMAZING.

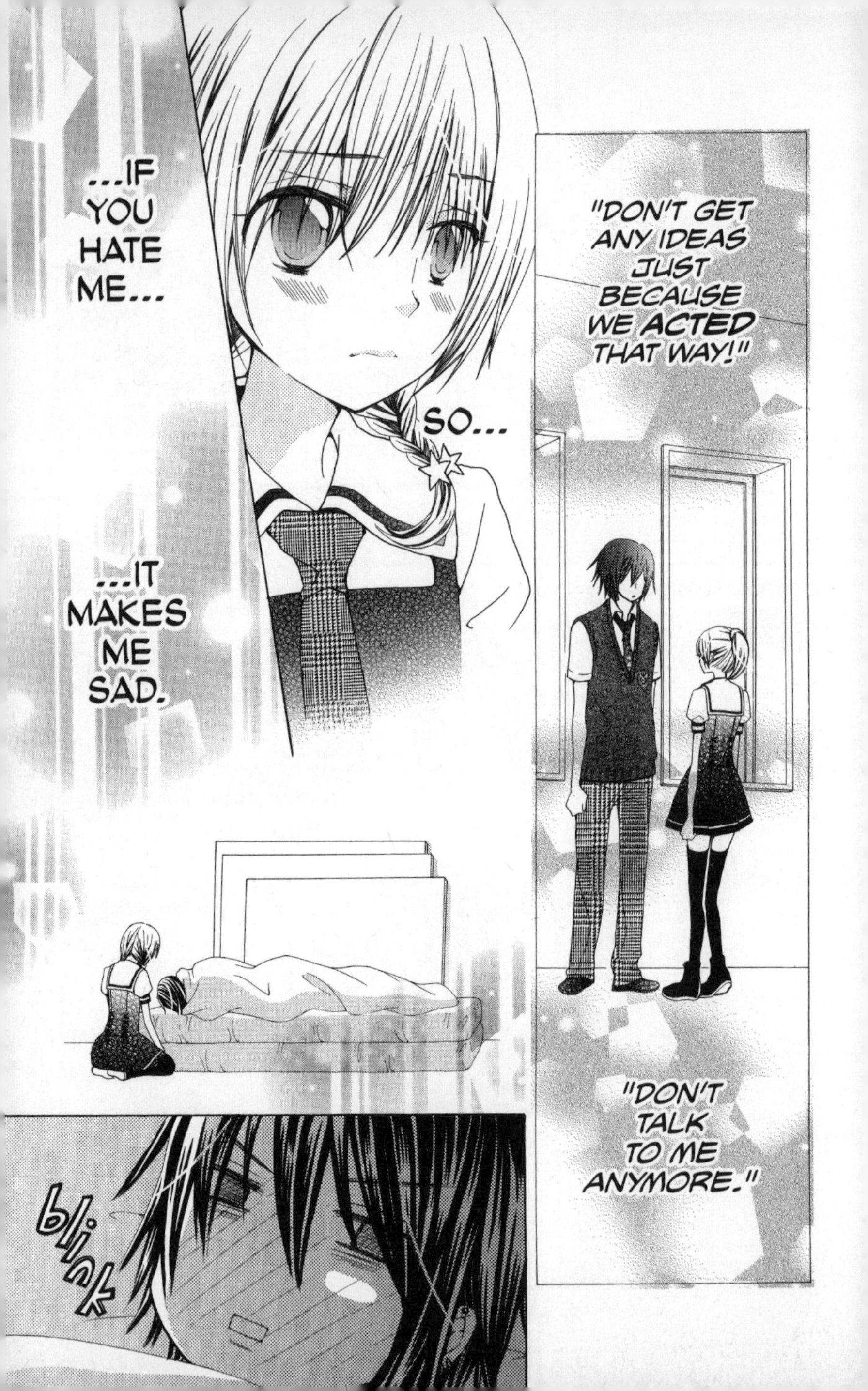
"DON'T GET ANY IDEAS JUST BECAUSE WE ACTED THAT WAY!"
"DON'T TALK TO ME ANYMORE."
...IF YOU HATE ME...
SO...
...IT MAKES ME SAD.
blink

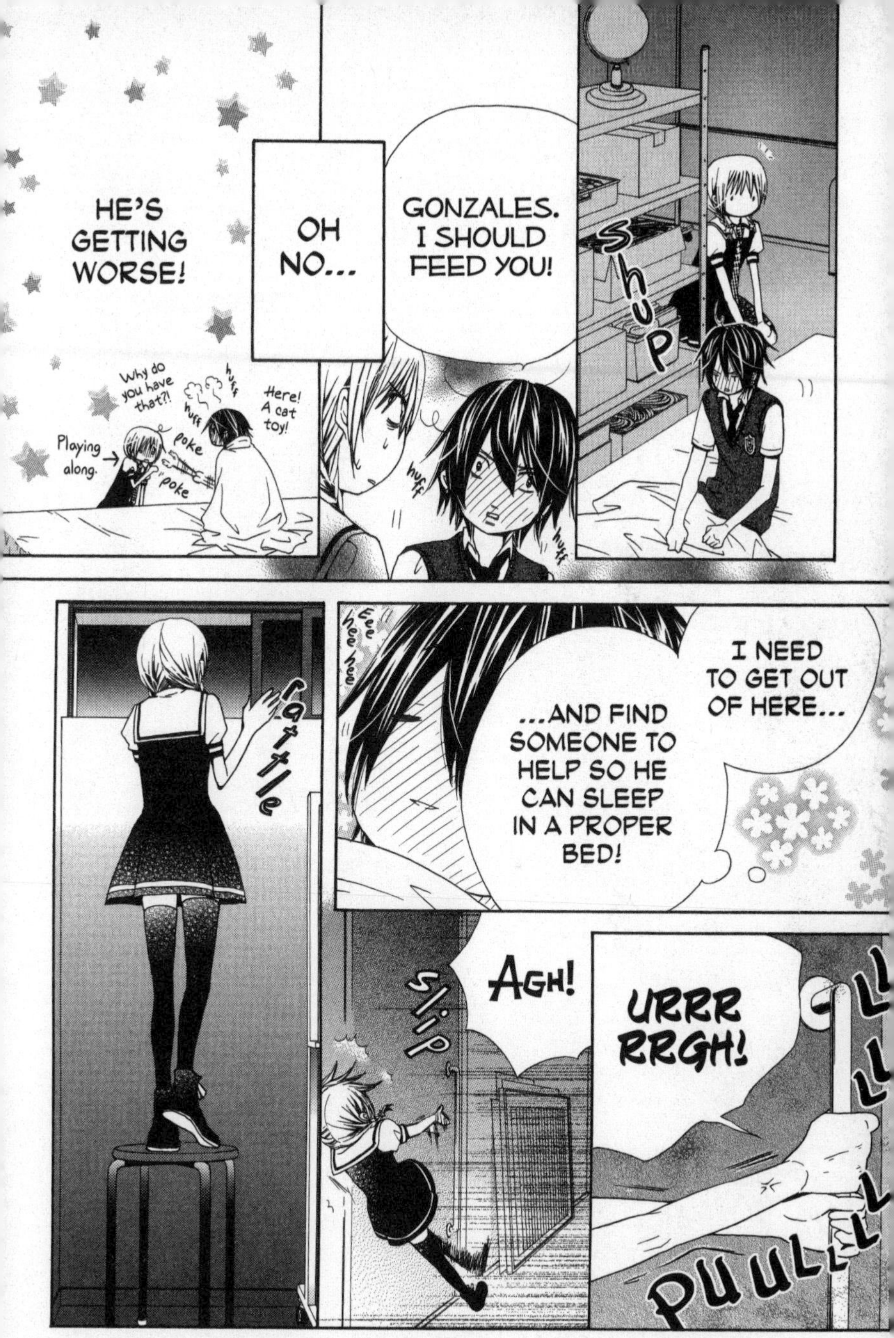
SHUP
GONZALES. I SHOULD FEED YOU!
huff
huff
OH NO...
HE'S GETTING WORSE!
Here! A cat toy!
huff
huff
Why do you have that?!
poke
poke
Playing along.
I NEED TO GET OUT OF HERE...
...AND FIND SOMEONE TO HELP SO HE CAN SLEEP IN A PROPER BED!
Eee hee hee
URRR RRGH!
PUULLLL
AGH!
slip
rattle

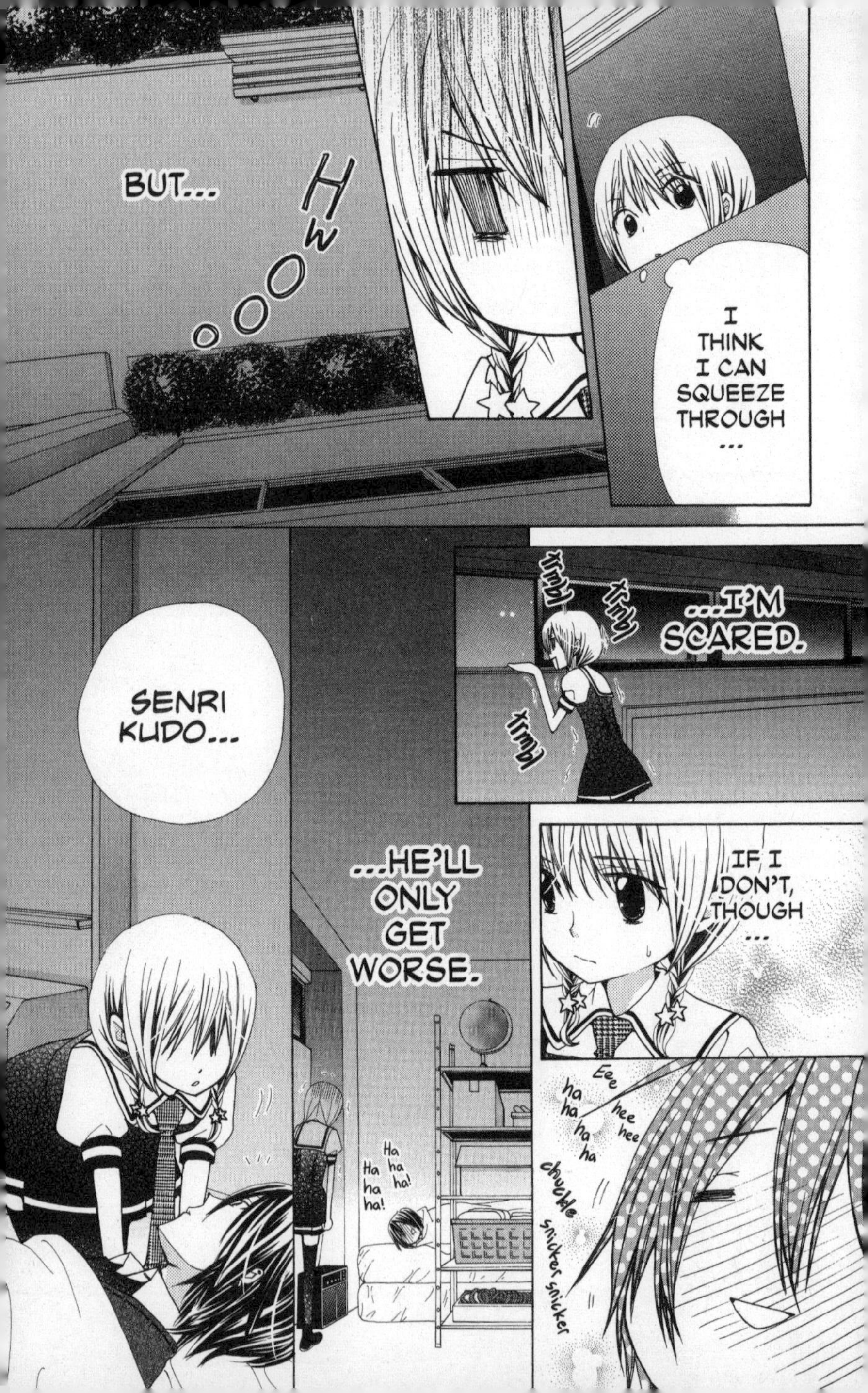
I THINK I CAN SQUEEZE THROUGH...
BUT...
HwOOo
trmbl trmbl trmbl
...I'M SCARED.
IF I DON'T, THOUGH...
Eee hee hee
ha ha ha ha
chuckle
snicker snicker
SENRI KUDO...
...HE'LL ONLY GET WORSE.
Ha ha ha! Ha ha ha!

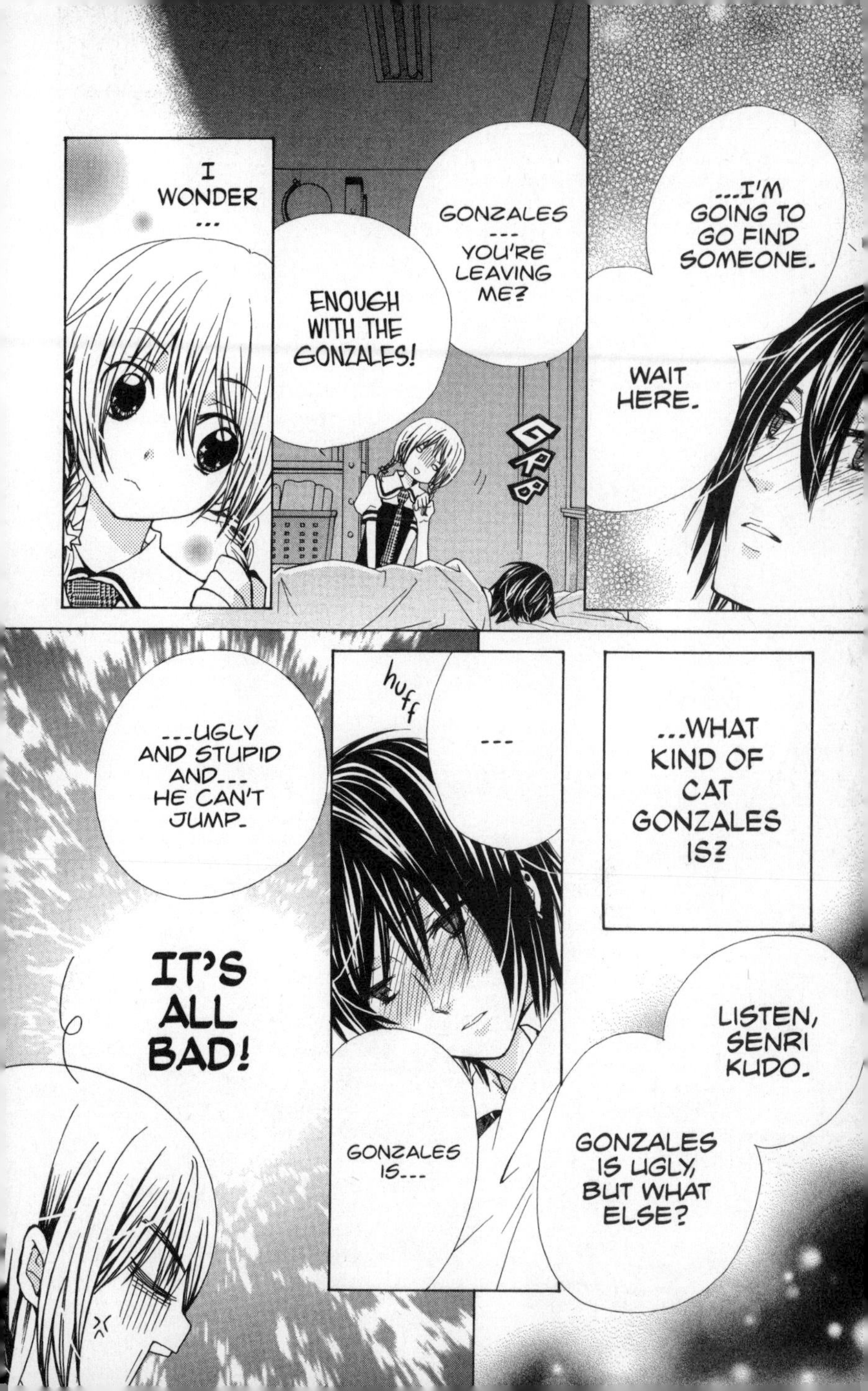
...I'M GOING TO GO FIND SOMEONE.
WAIT HERE.
GONZALES... YOU'RE LEAVING ME?
ENOUGH WITH THE GONZALES!
I WONDER...
...WHAT KIND OF CAT GONZALES IS?
LISTEN, SENRI KUDO.
GONZALES IS UGLY, BUT WHAT ELSE?
huff
...
GONZALES IS...
...UGLY AND STUPID AND... HE CAN'T JUMP.
IT'S ALL BAD!

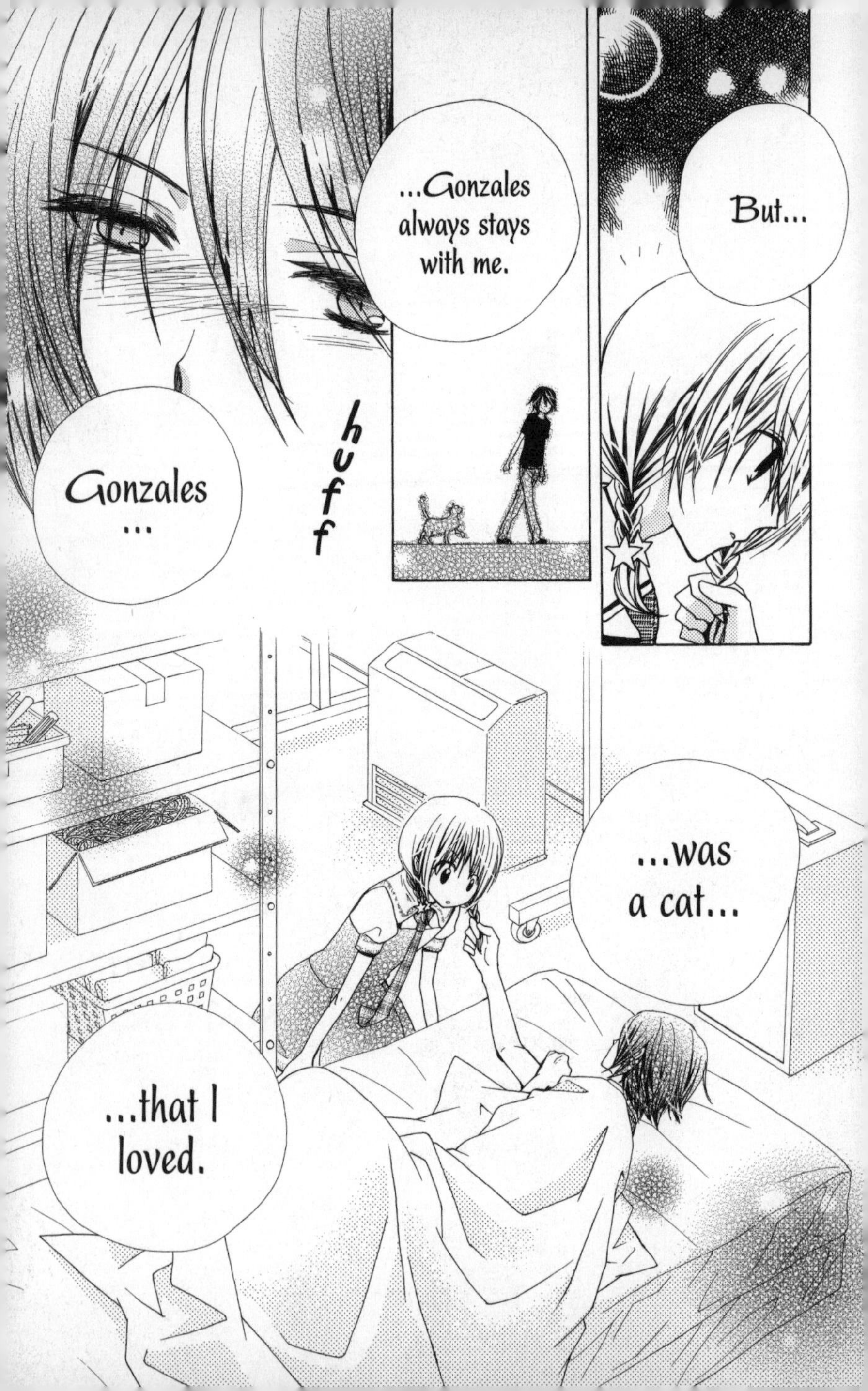
But...
...Gonzales always stays with me.
Gonzales ...
huff
...was a cat...
...that I loved.

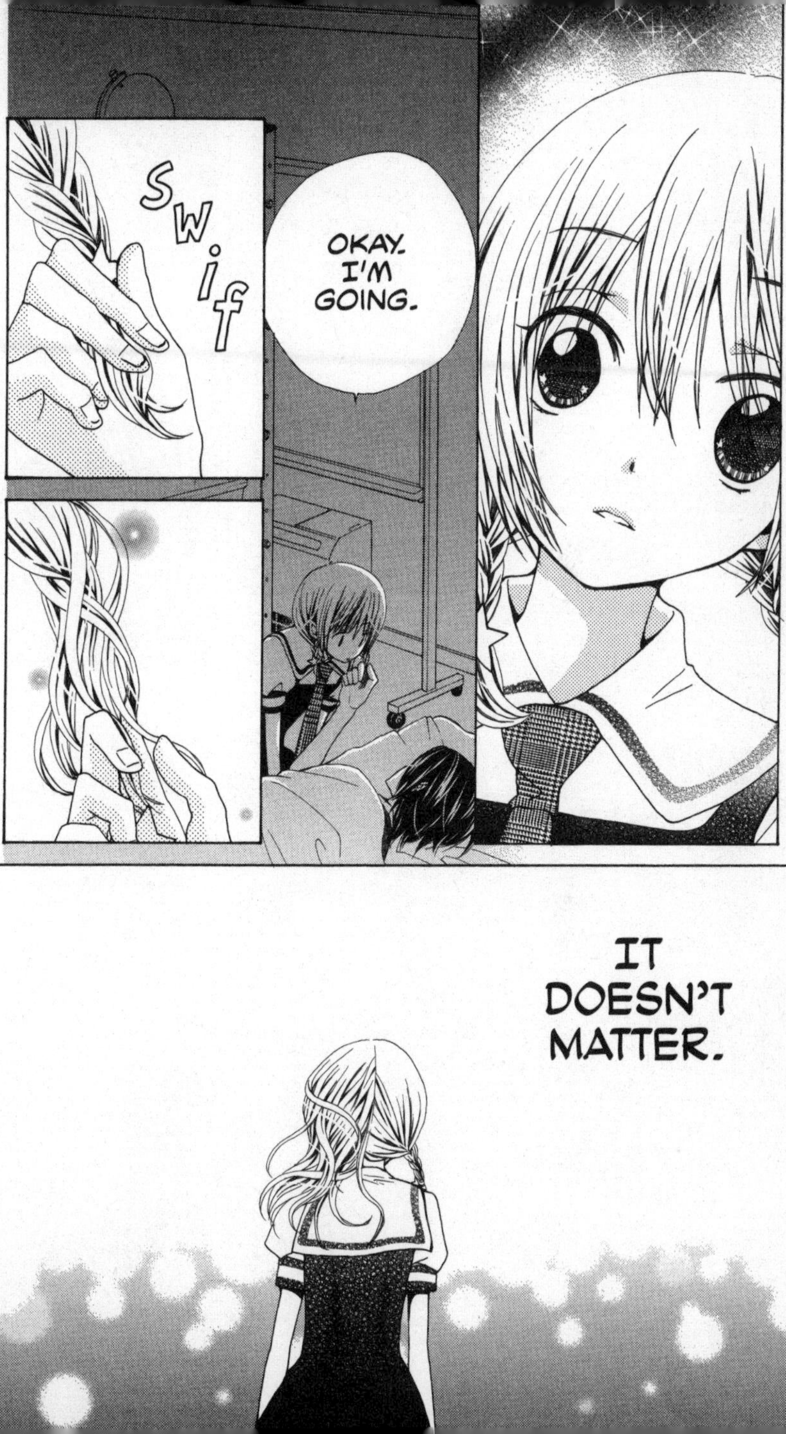
OKAY. I'M GOING.
SWIF
IT DOESN'T MATTER.

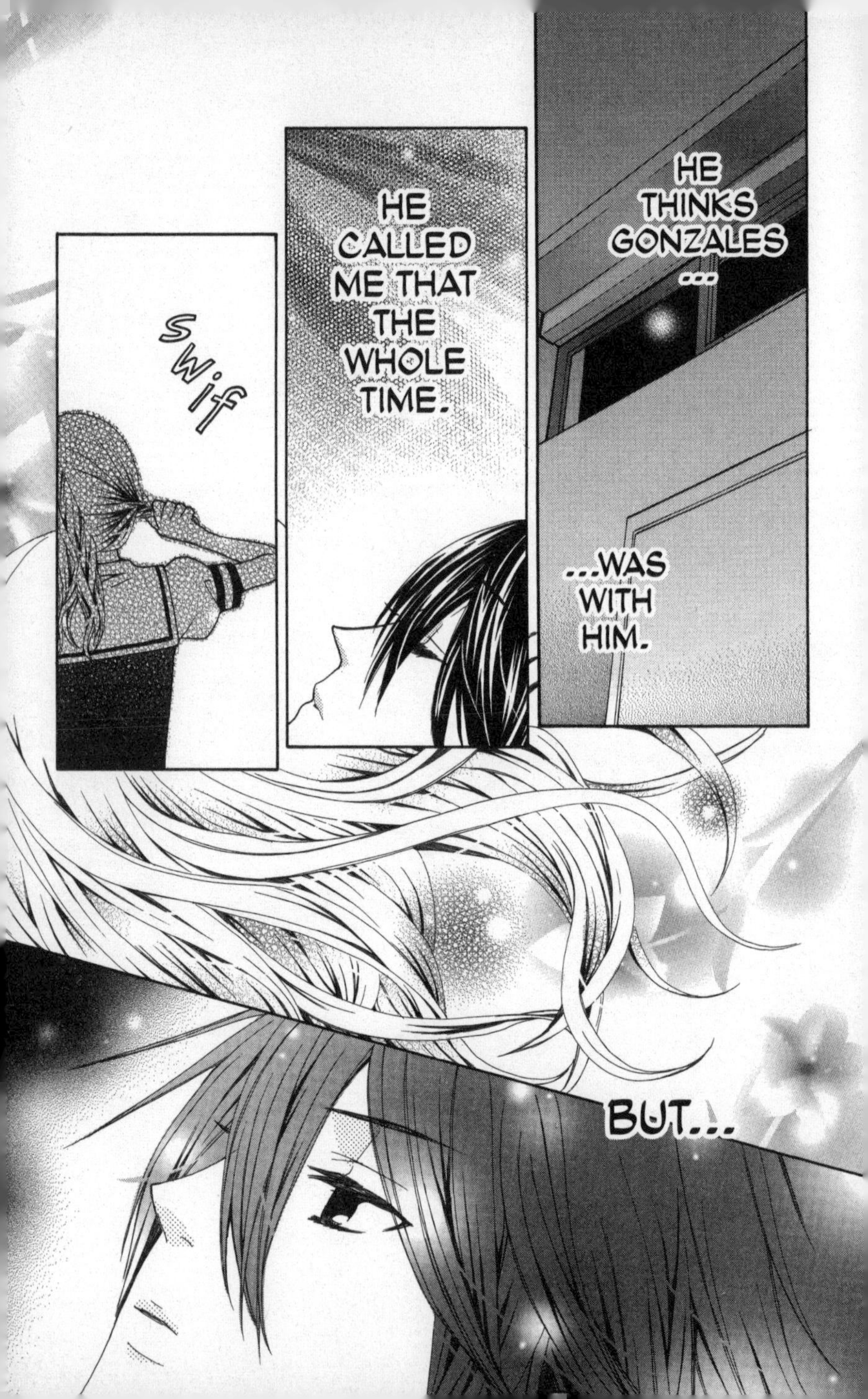
HE THINKS GONZALES...
...WAS WITH HIM.
HE CALLED ME THAT THE WHOLE TIME.
swif
BUT...

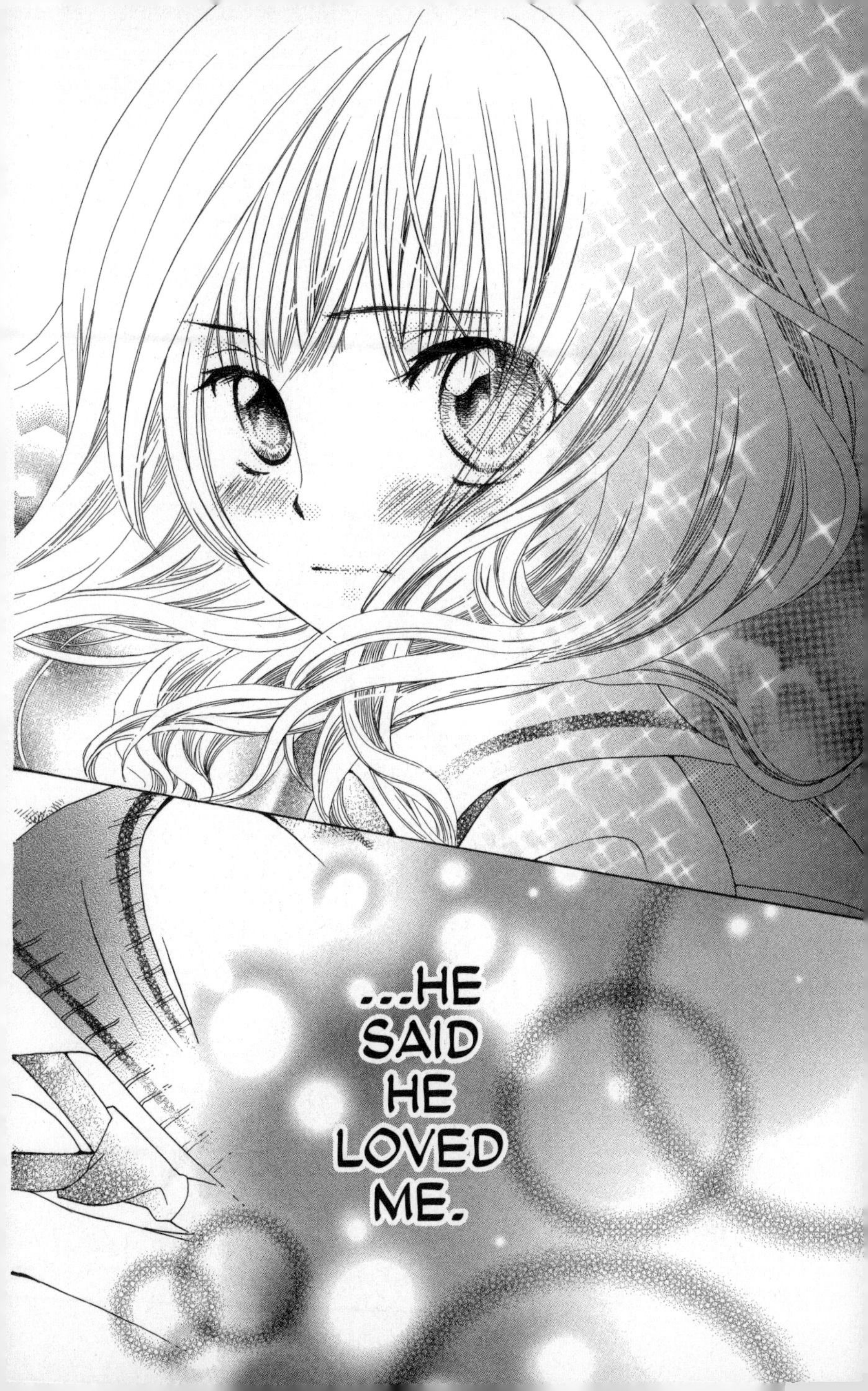
...HE SAID HE LOVED ME.

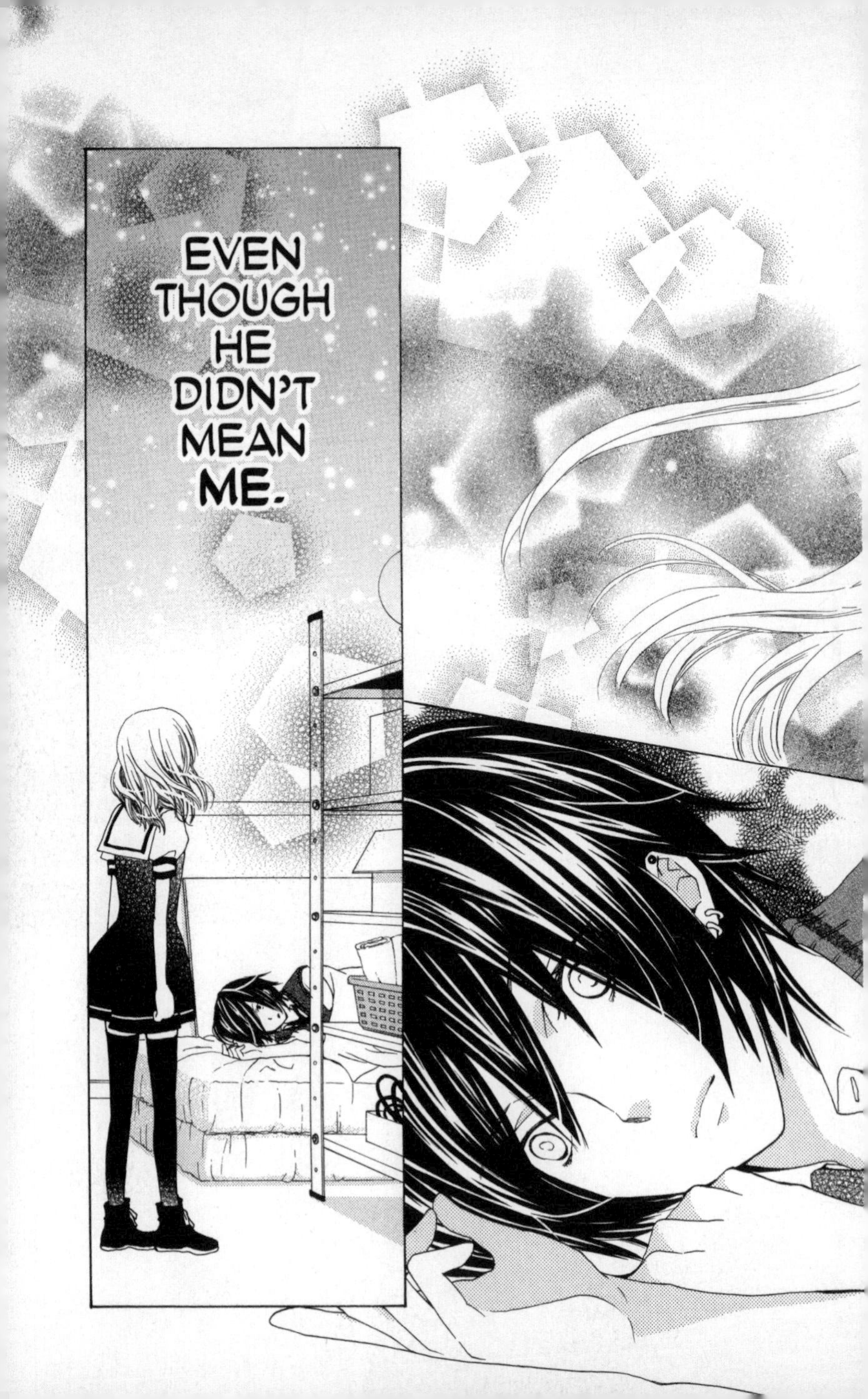
EVEN THOUGH HE DIDN'T MEAN ME.

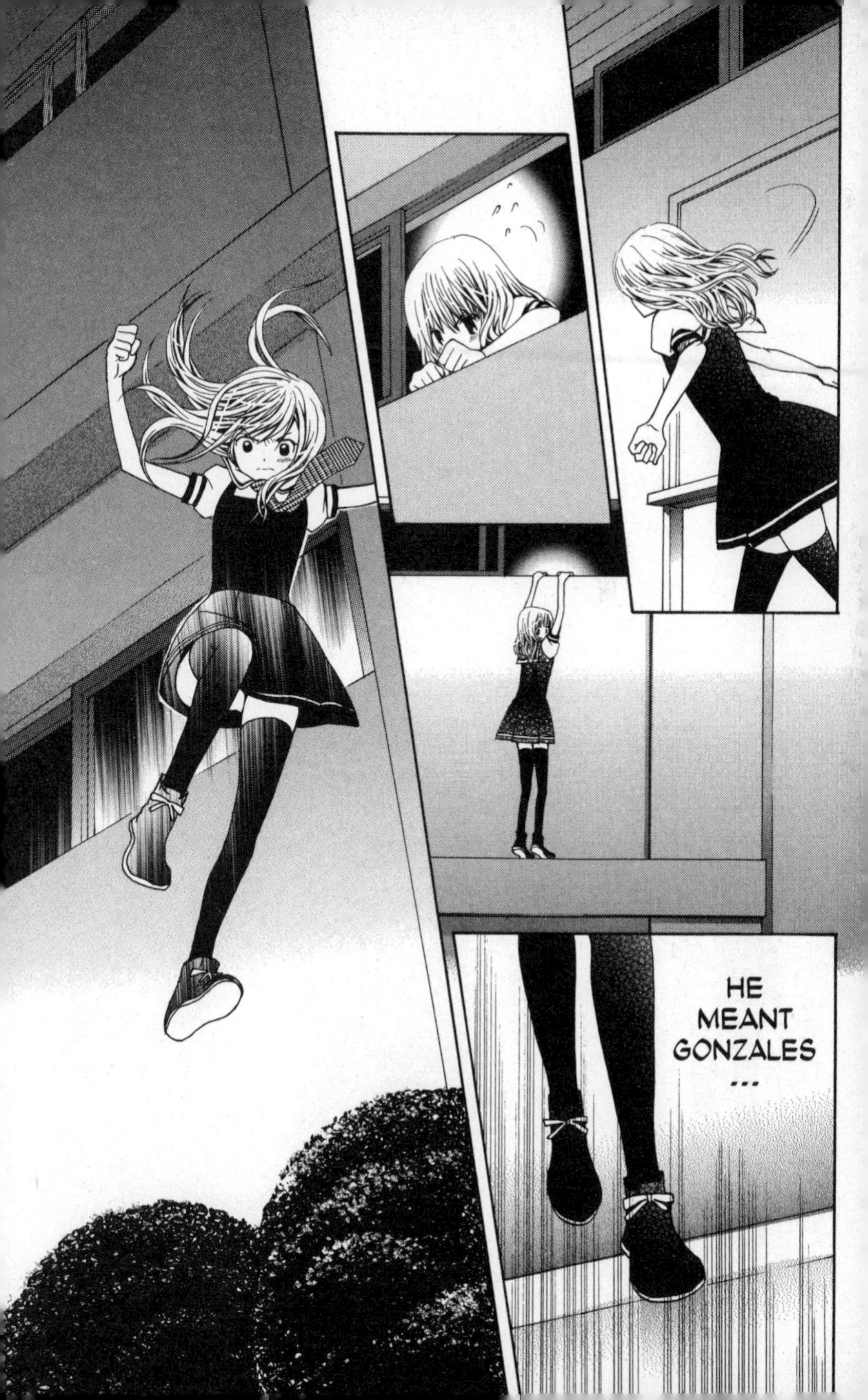
HE MEANT GONZALES ...

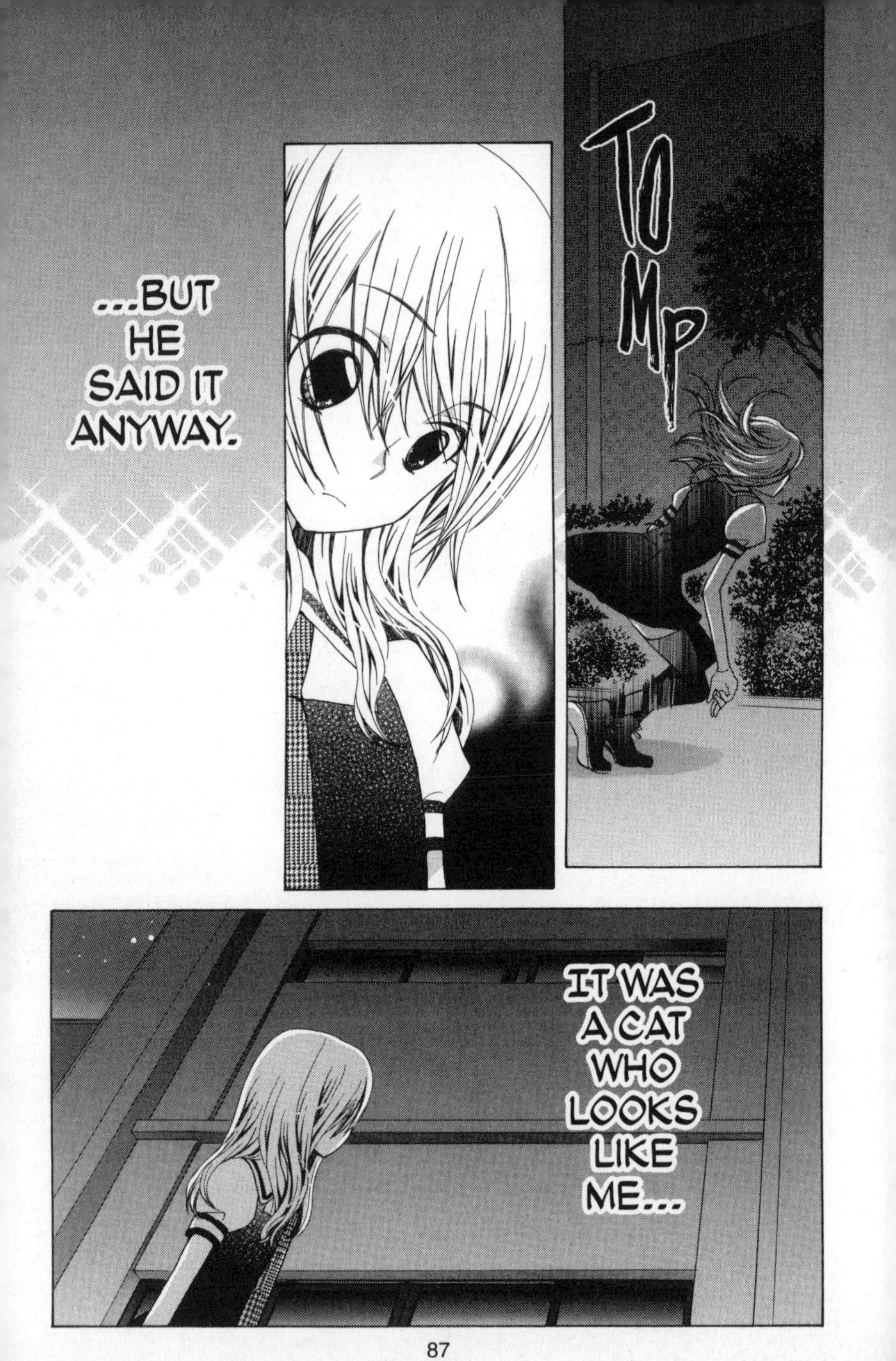
TOMP
...BUT HE SAID IT ANYWAY.
IT WAS A CAT WHO LOOKS LIKE ME...

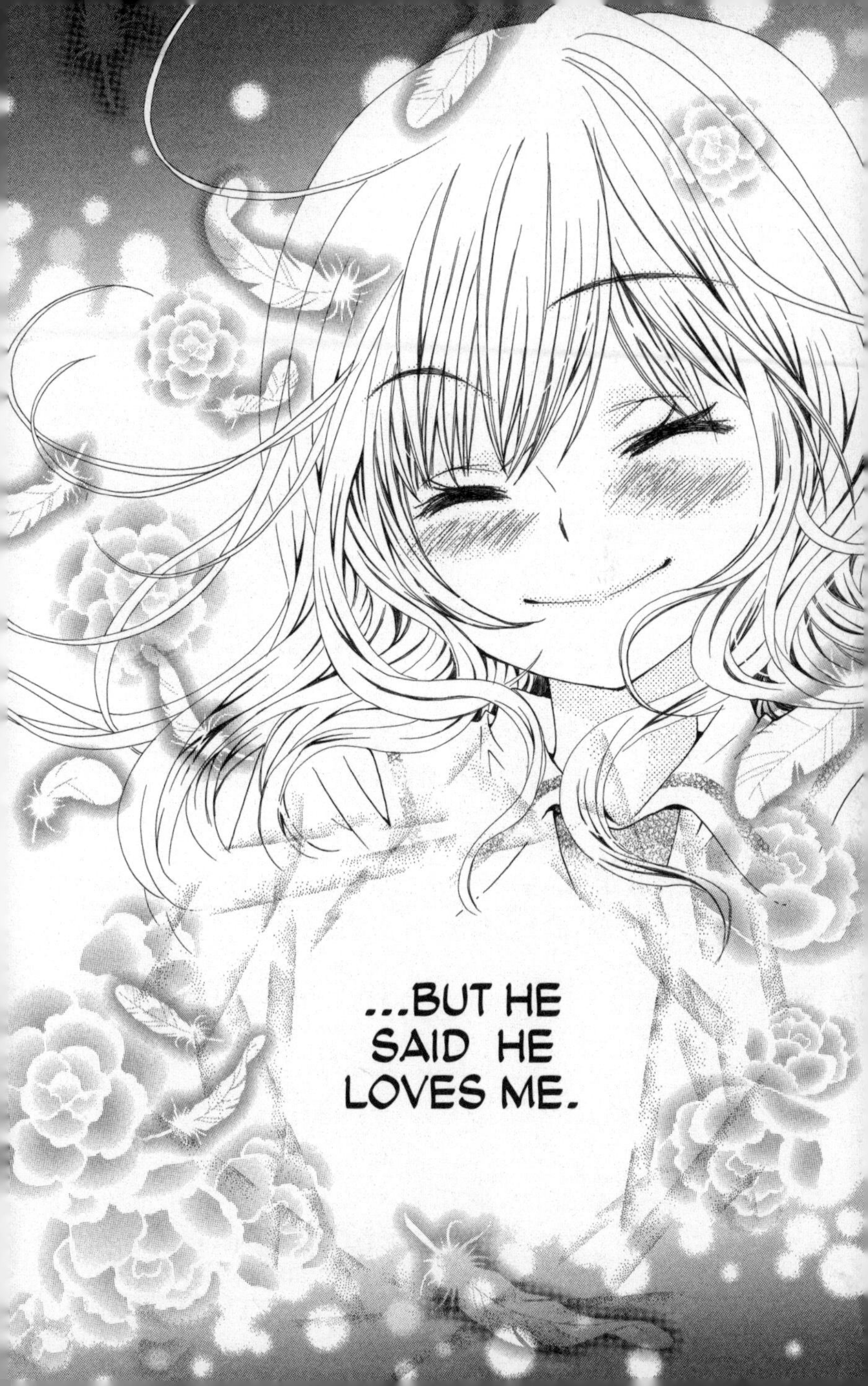
...BUT HE SAID HE LOVES ME.

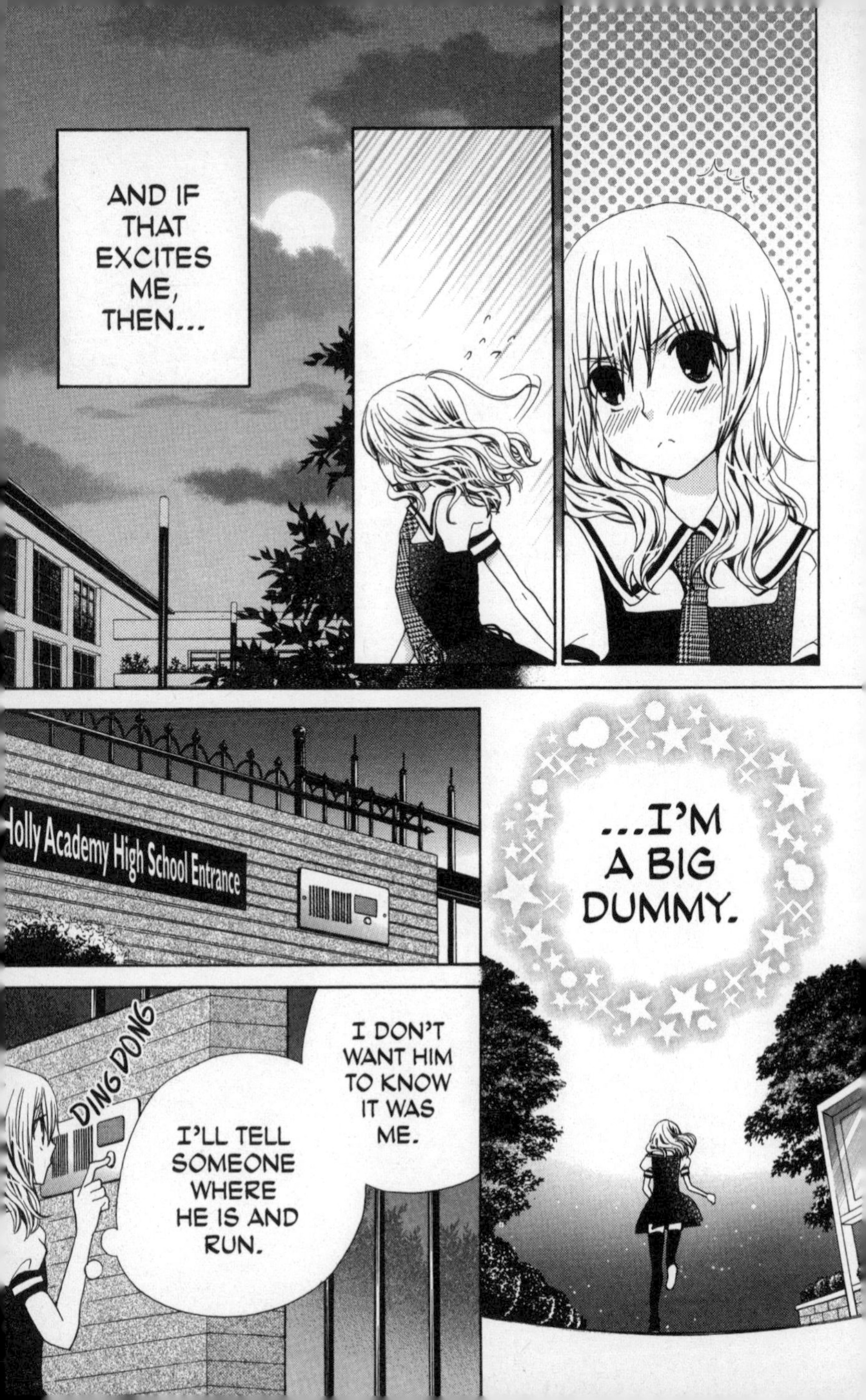
AND IF THAT EXCITES ME, THEN...
...I'M A BIG DUMMY.
Holly Academy High School Entrance
I DON'T WANT HIM TO KNOW IT WAS ME.
I'LL TELL SOMEONE WHERE HE IS AND RUN.
DING DONG

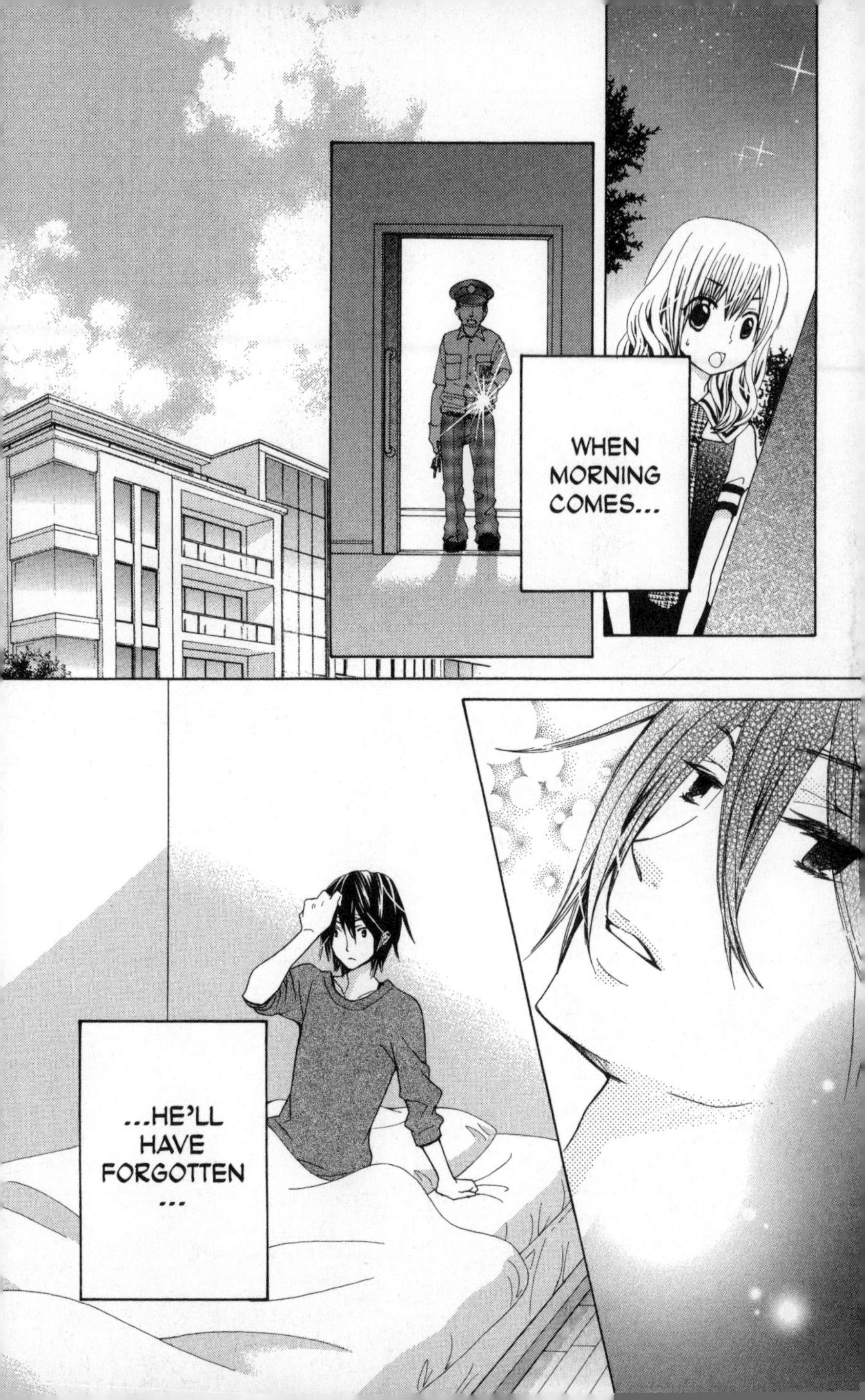
WHEN MORNING COMES...
...HE'LL HAVE FORGOTTEN ...

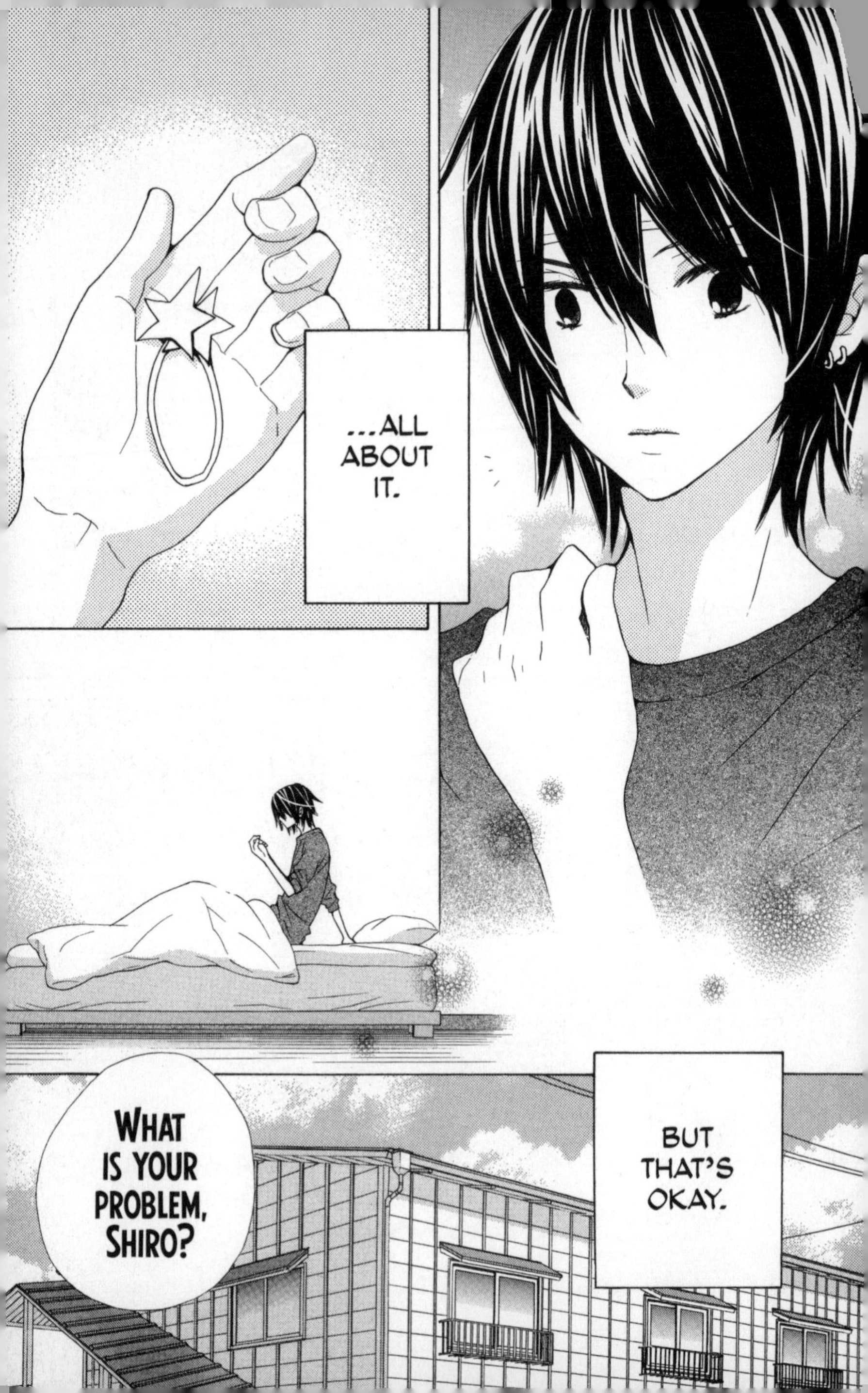
...ALL ABOUT IT.
BUT THAT'S OKAY.
WHAT IS YOUR PROBLEM, SHIRO?

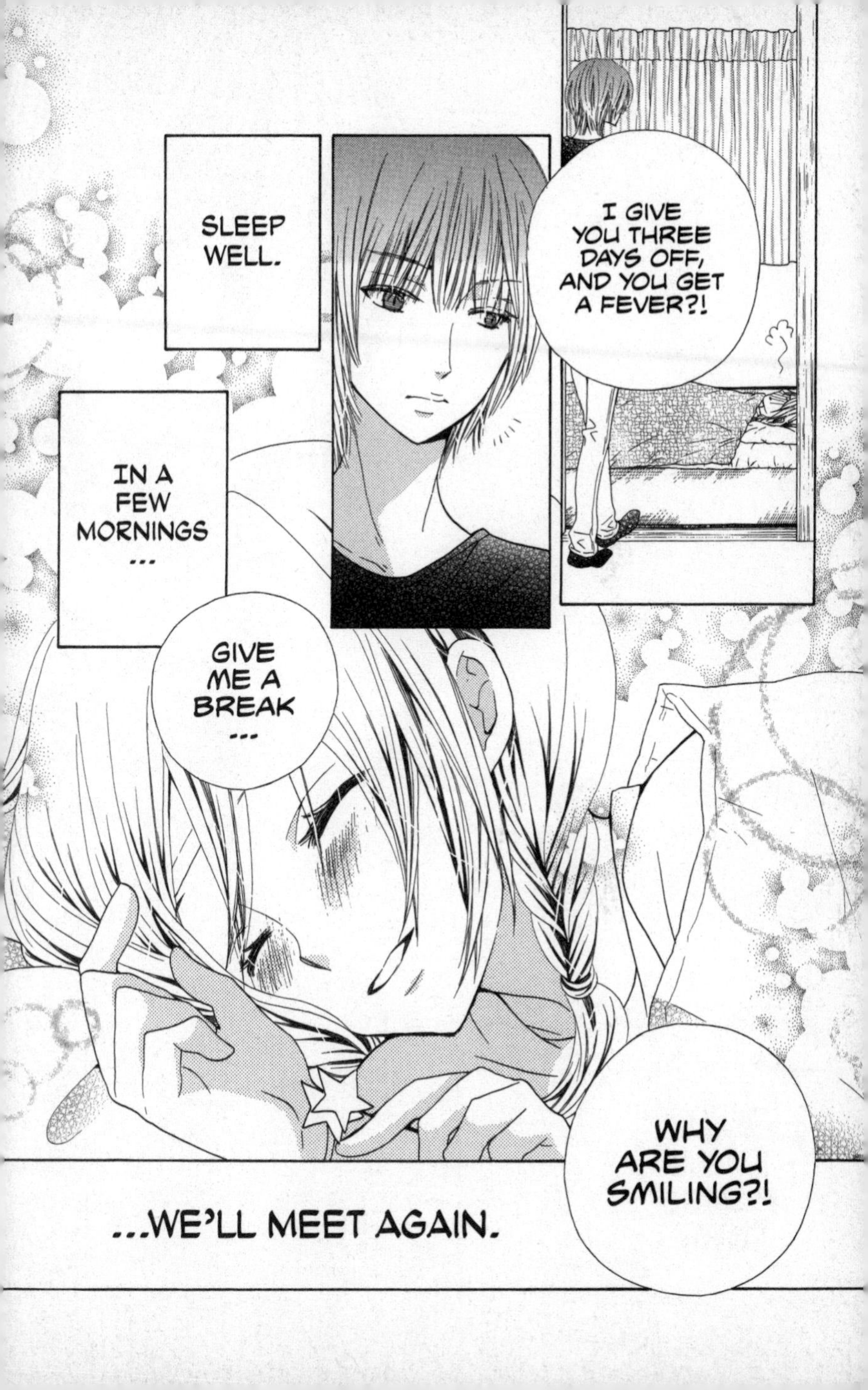
I GIVE YOU THREE DAYS OFF, AND YOU GET A FEVER?!
SLEEP WELL.
IN A FEW MORNINGS...
GIVE ME A BREAK...
WHY ARE YOU SMILING?!
...WE'LL MEET AGAIN.

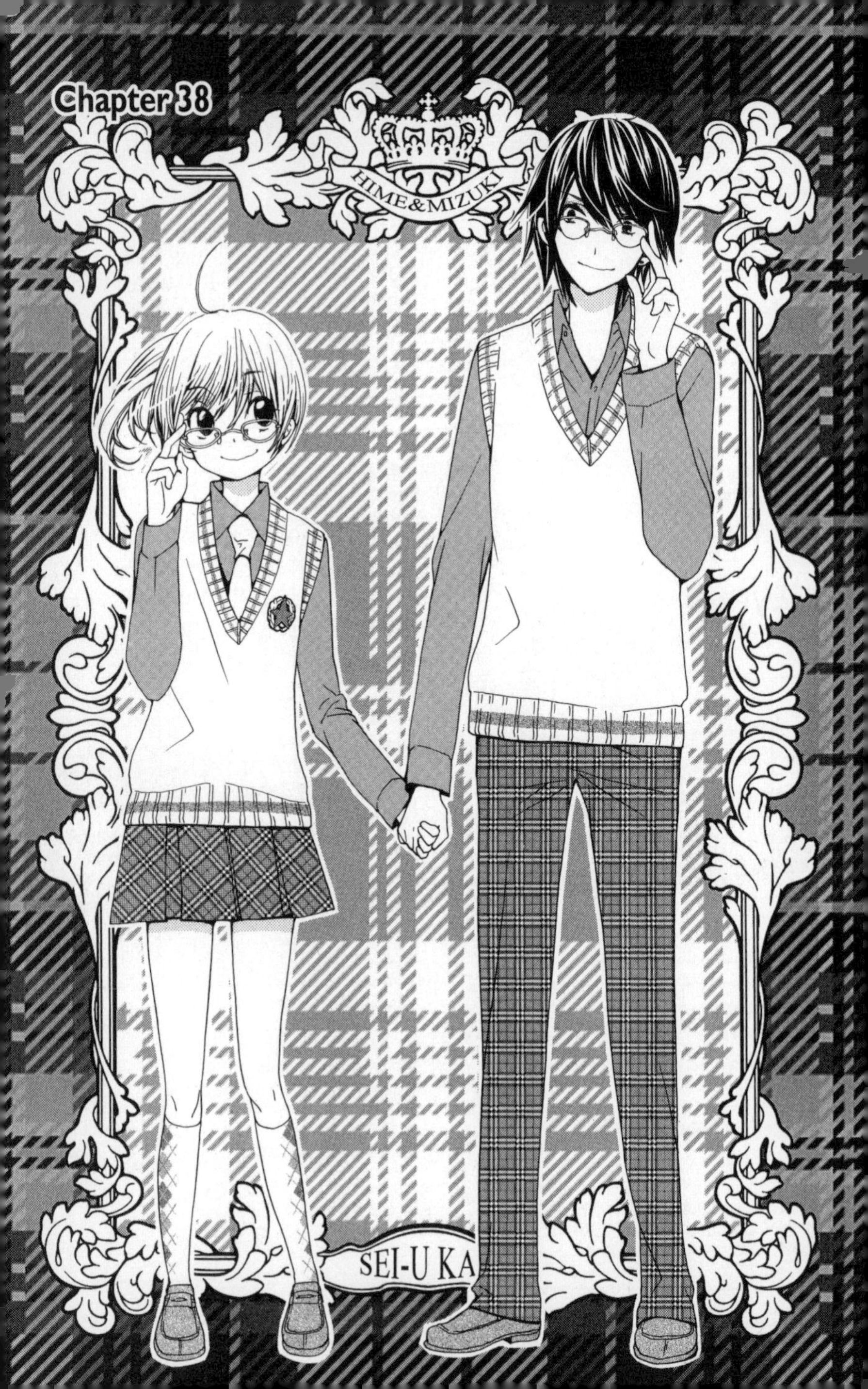
Chapter 38
HIME&MIZUKI
SEI-U KA

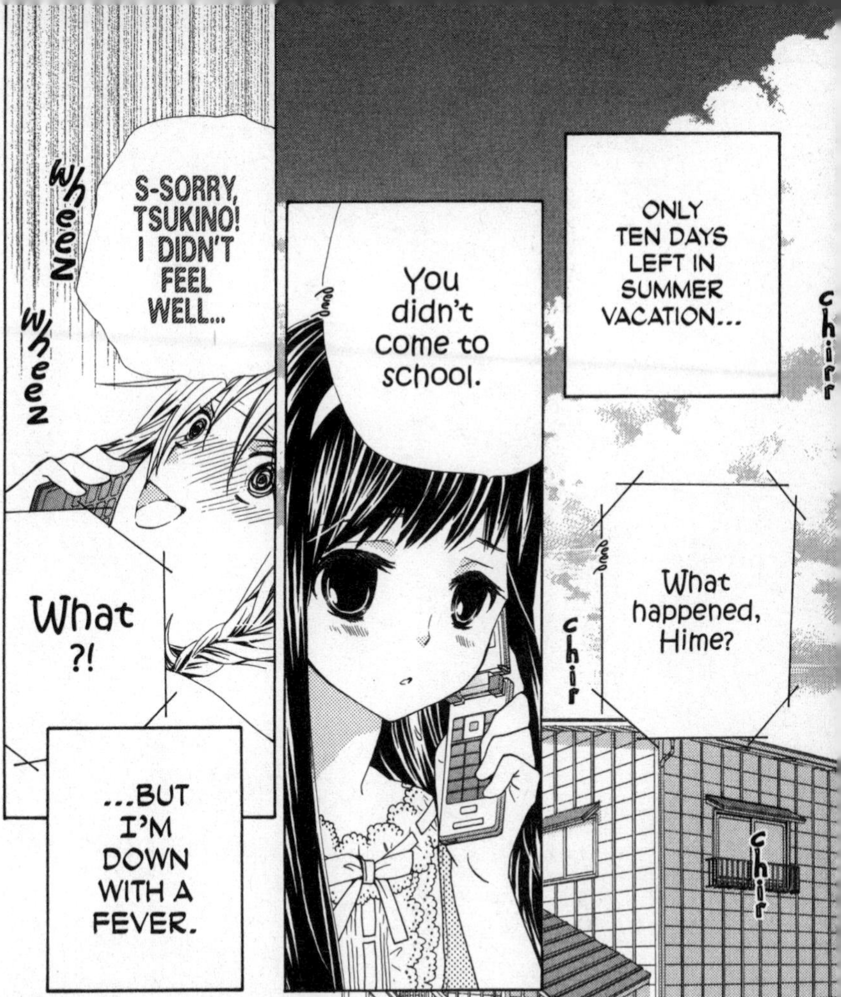
Chirr
ONLY TEN DAYS LEFT IN SUMMER VACATION...
What happened, Hime?
Chir
Chir
You didn't come to school.
S-SORRY, TSUKINO! I DIDN'T FEEL WELL...
Wheez
Wheez
What ?!
...BUT I'M DOWN WITH A FEVER.

• Autograph Signing in Taiwan Part 1 •

• When my editor suggested signing autographs in Taiwan, I was really pleased. I got to meet readers in Japan in June and readers in Taiwan in August, so I've used up about 100 years of happiness! It makes me really glad to have this job. Yaay!!

• In Taiwan, there were two events. The first one was like a Q&A. I met with a small number of readers and members of the press. The question that I remember most was "Do you like meat and do you eat lots of meat at your desk during work?" I responded, "Unfortunately no, because I don't want to dribble grease on the manuscript."

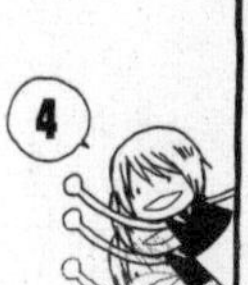
4

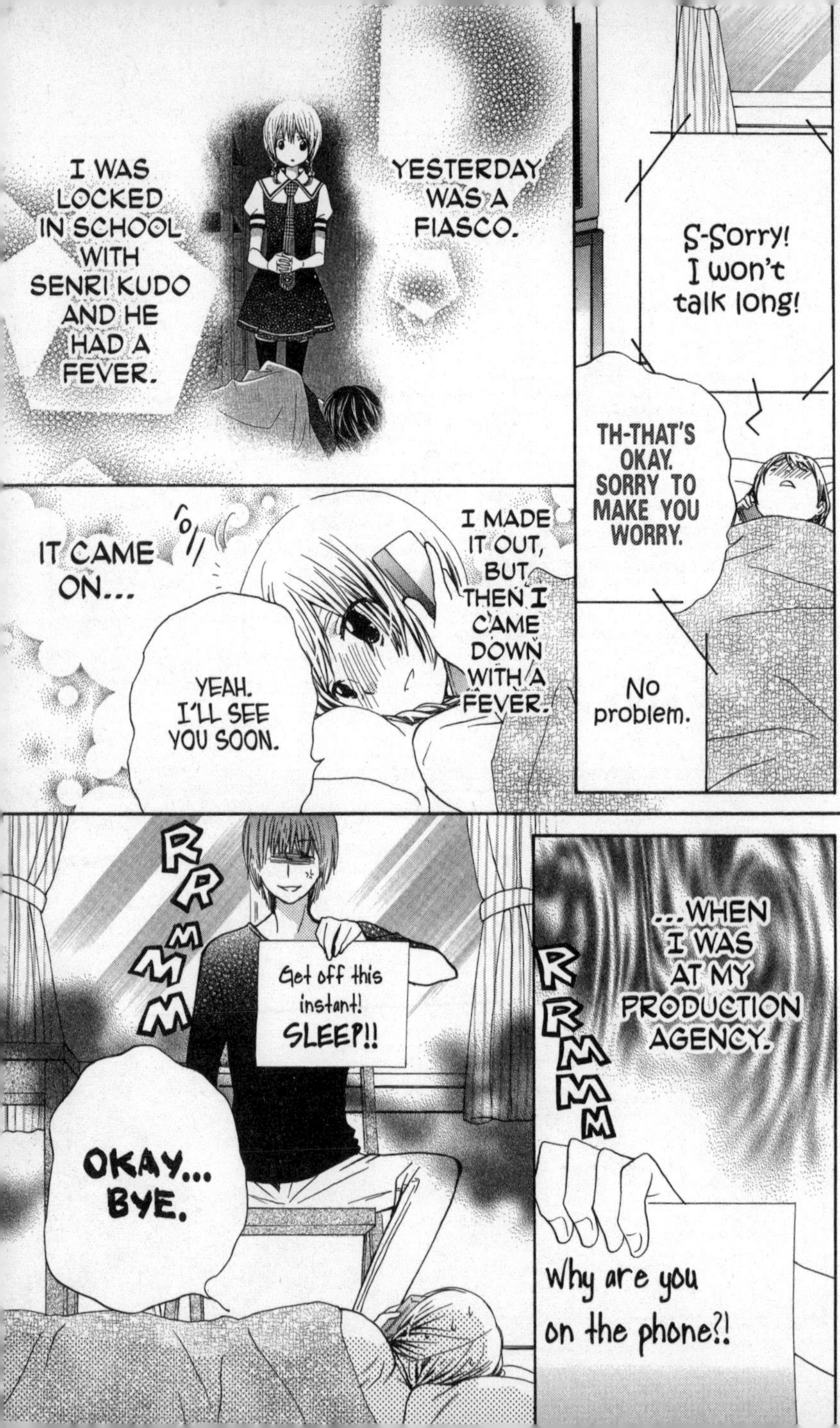
S-Sorry! I won't talk long!
TH-THAT'S OKAY. SORRY TO MAKE YOU WORRY.
No problem.
YESTERDAY WAS A FIASCO.
I WAS LOCKED IN SCHOOL WITH SENRI KUDO AND HE HAD A FEVER.
I MADE IT OUT, BUT THEN I CAME DOWN WITH A FEVER.
IT CAME ON...
roll
YEAH. I'LL SEE YOU SOON.
...WHEN I WAS AT MY PRODUCTION AGENCY.
RRMMM
Why are you on the phone?!
RRMMM
Get off this instant! SLEEP!!
OKAY... BYE.

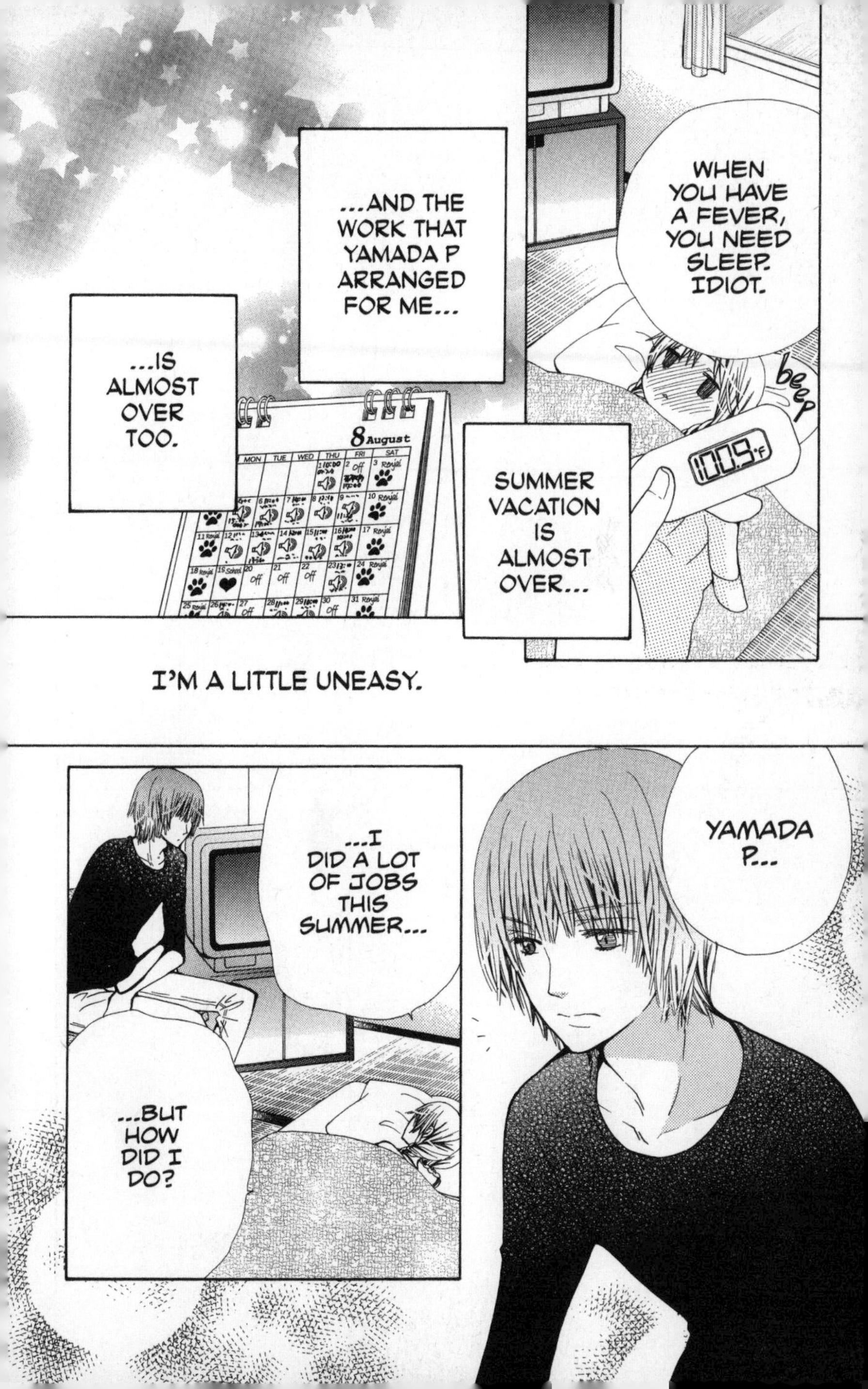
WHEN YOU HAVE A FEVER, YOU NEED SLEEP. IDIOT.
beep
100.9°F
SUMMER VACATION IS ALMOST OVER...
...AND THE WORK THAT YAMADA P ARRANGED FOR ME...
...IS ALMOST OVER TOO.
8 August
I'M A LITTLE UNEASY.
YAMADA P...
...I DID A LOT OF JOBS THIS SUMMER...
...BUT HOW DID I DO?

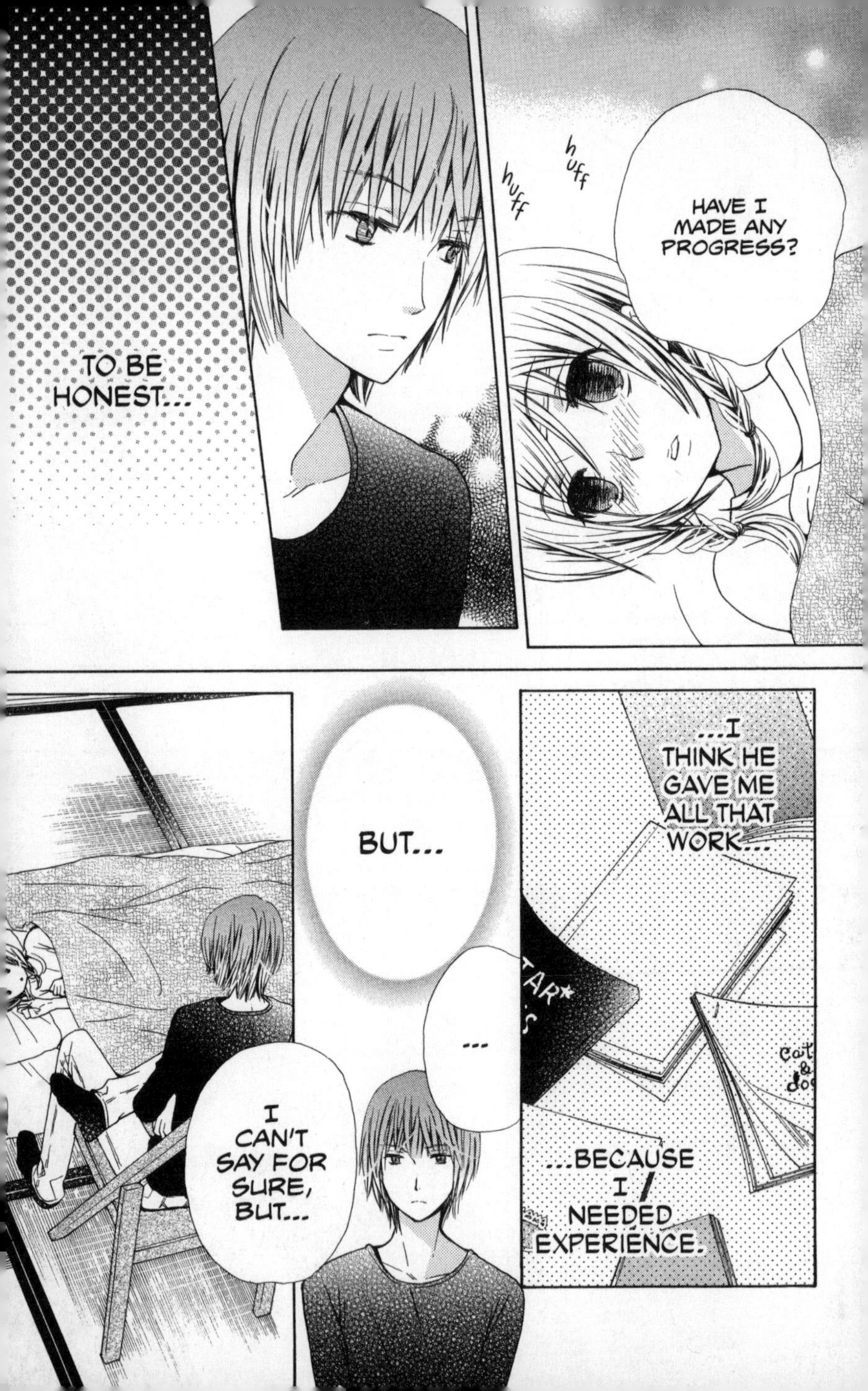
huff
huff
HAVE I MADE ANY PROGRESS?
TO BE HONEST...
...I THINK HE GAVE ME ALL THAT WORK...
...BECAUSE I NEEDED EXPERIENCE.
BUT...
...
I CAN'T SAY FOR SURE, BUT...

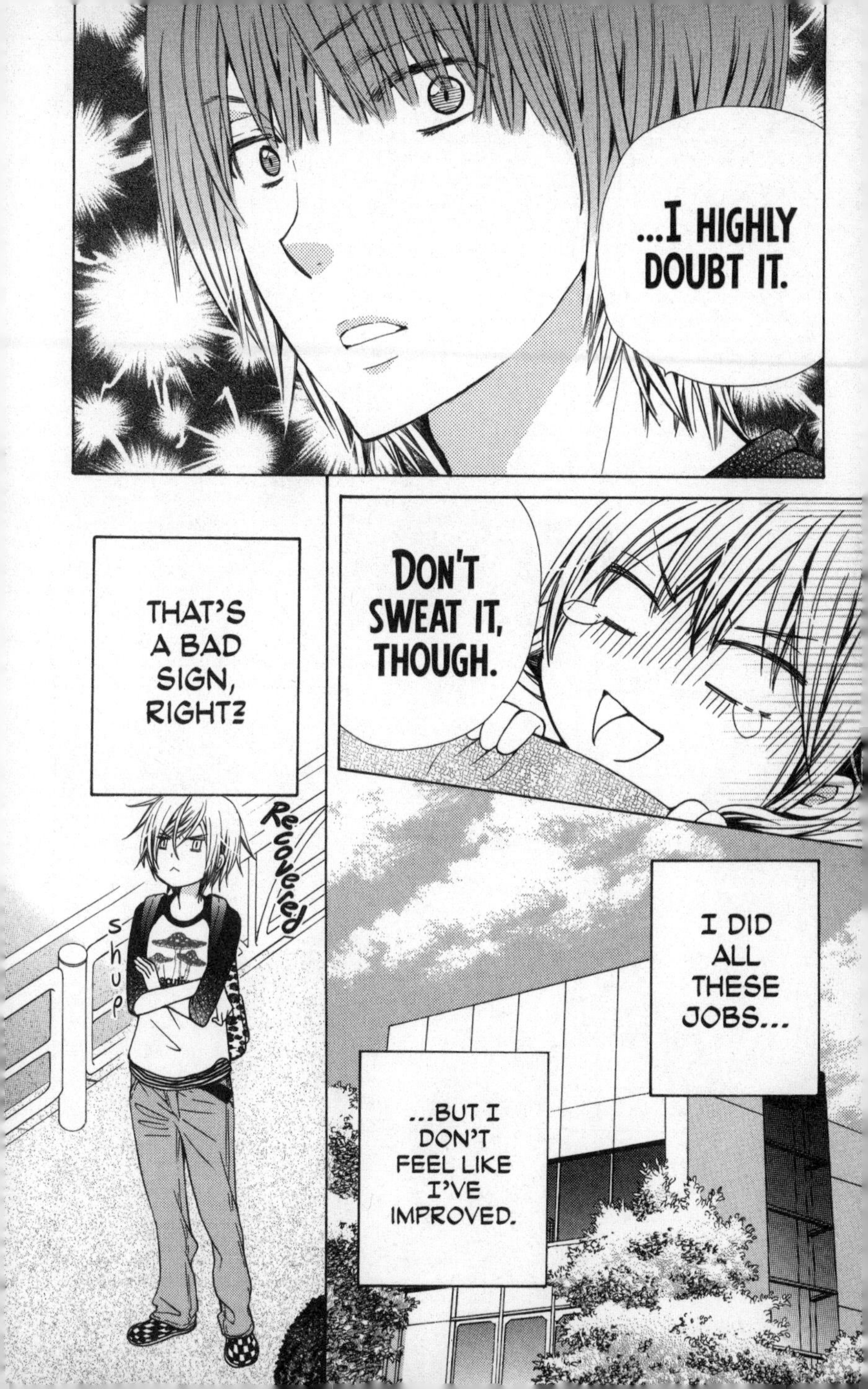
...I HIGHLY DOUBT IT.
DON'T SWEAT IT, THOUGH.
I DID ALL THESE JOBS...
...BUT I DON'T FEEL LIKE I'VE IMPROVED.
THAT'S A BAD SIGN, RIGHT?
Recovered
shup

◦ In Taiwan ◦

I was in Taiwan for the autograph session for four days and three nights.

Schedule:

Day 1: Arrival

Day 2: Autograph session

Day 3: Sightseeing

Day 4: Departure

People from the Taiwanese company Tong Li Publishing made my time there really great!

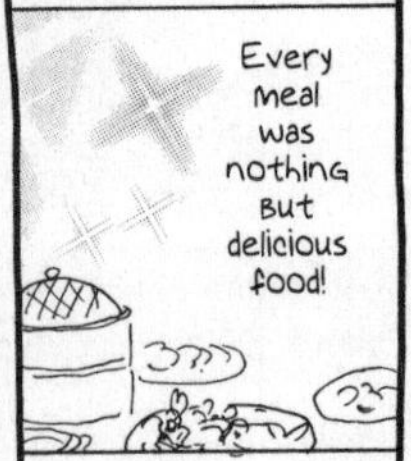
Every meal was nothing but delicious food!

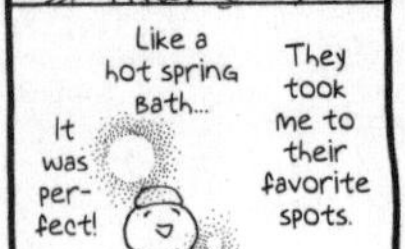
They took me to their favorite spots.
Like a hot spring bath...
It was perfect!

Thank you Chang-san, Liu-san and Kato-san for escorting me around for four days! And thank you so much to Taguchi-san, Ishizone-san, Iida-san, Shirayanagi-san and the president of Tong Li Publishing Co., Ltd. for taking care of me!

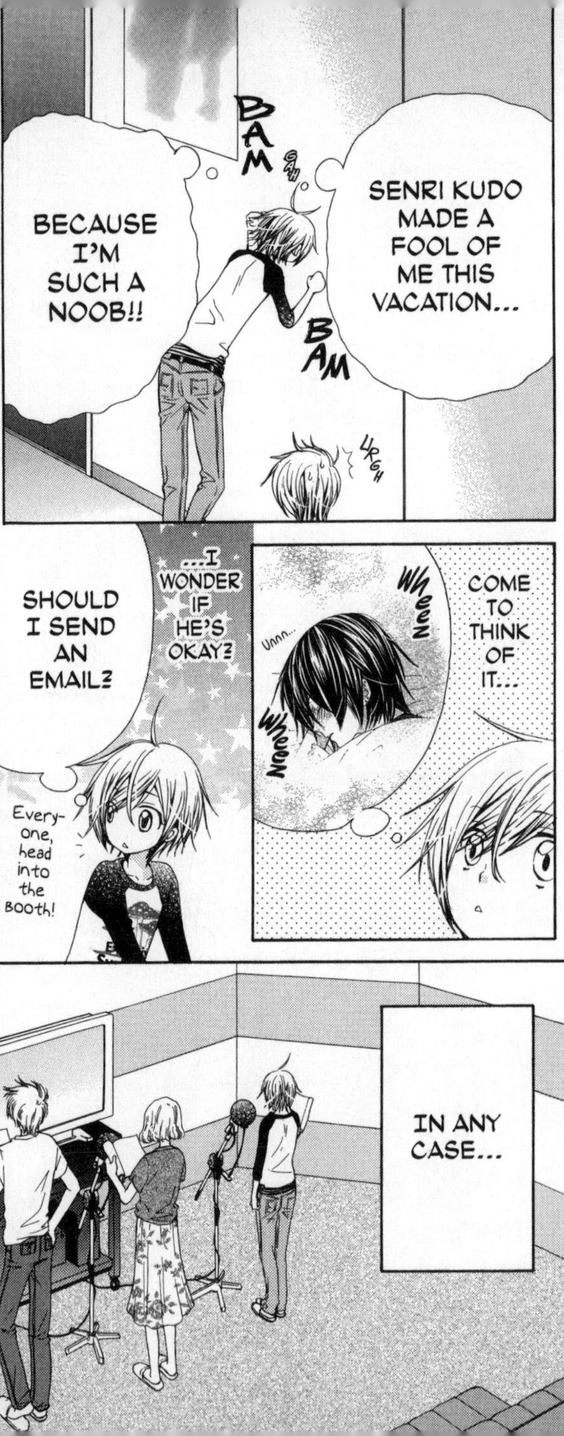
SENRI KUDO MADE A FOOL OF ME THIS VACATION...
BAM
GAH
BECAUSE I'M SUCH A NOOB!!
BAM
URGH
COME TO THINK OF IT...
WHEEN
Unnn...
WHEEN
...I WONDER IF HE'S OKAY?
SHOULD I SEND AN EMAIL?
Every-one, head into the booth!
IN ANY CASE...

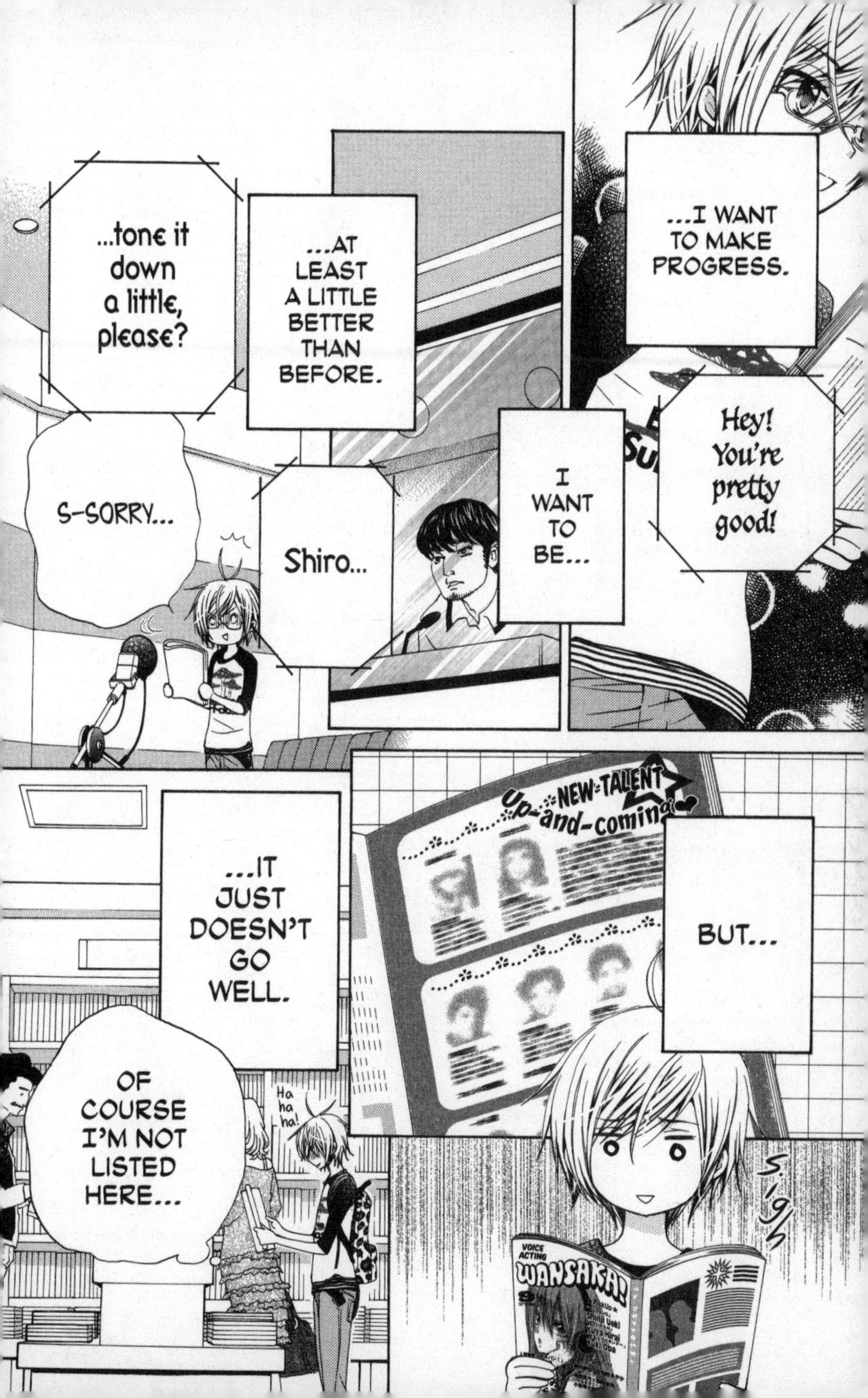
...I WANT TO MAKE PROGRESS.
Hey! You're pretty good!
I WANT TO BE...
...AT LEAST A LITTLE BETTER THAN BEFORE.
Shiro...
...tone it down a little, please?
S-SORRY...
NEW TALENT
Up-and-coming
BUT...
Sigh
VOICE ACTING
WANSAKA!
...IT JUST DOESN'T GO WELL.
OF COURSE I'M NOT LISTED HERE...
Ha ha ha!

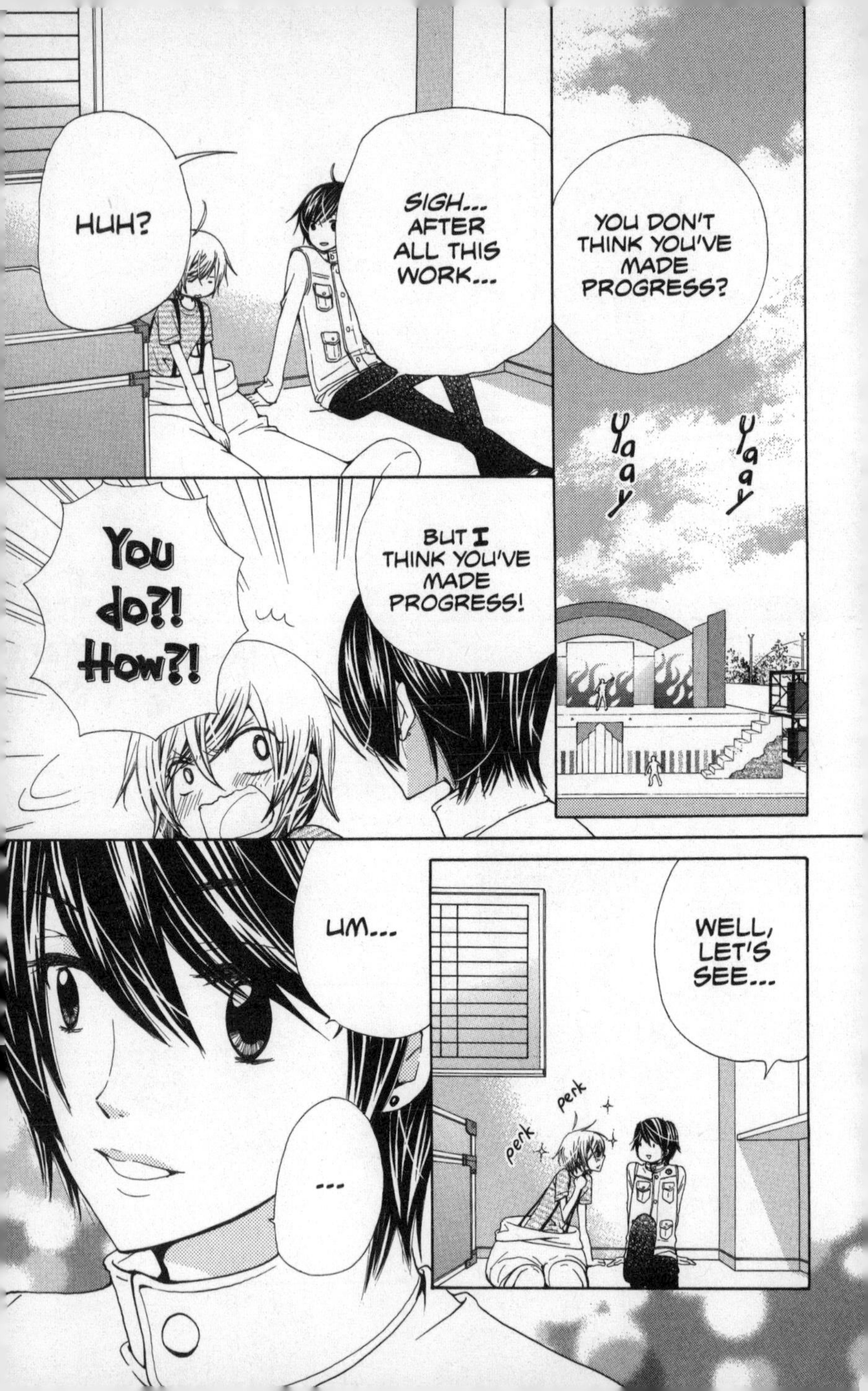
YOU DON'T THINK YOU'VE MADE PROGRESS?
Yaay
Yaay
SIGH... AFTER ALL THIS WORK...
HUH?
BUT I THINK YOU'VE MADE PROGRESS!
You do?! How?!
WELL, LET'S SEE...
perk
perk
UM...
...

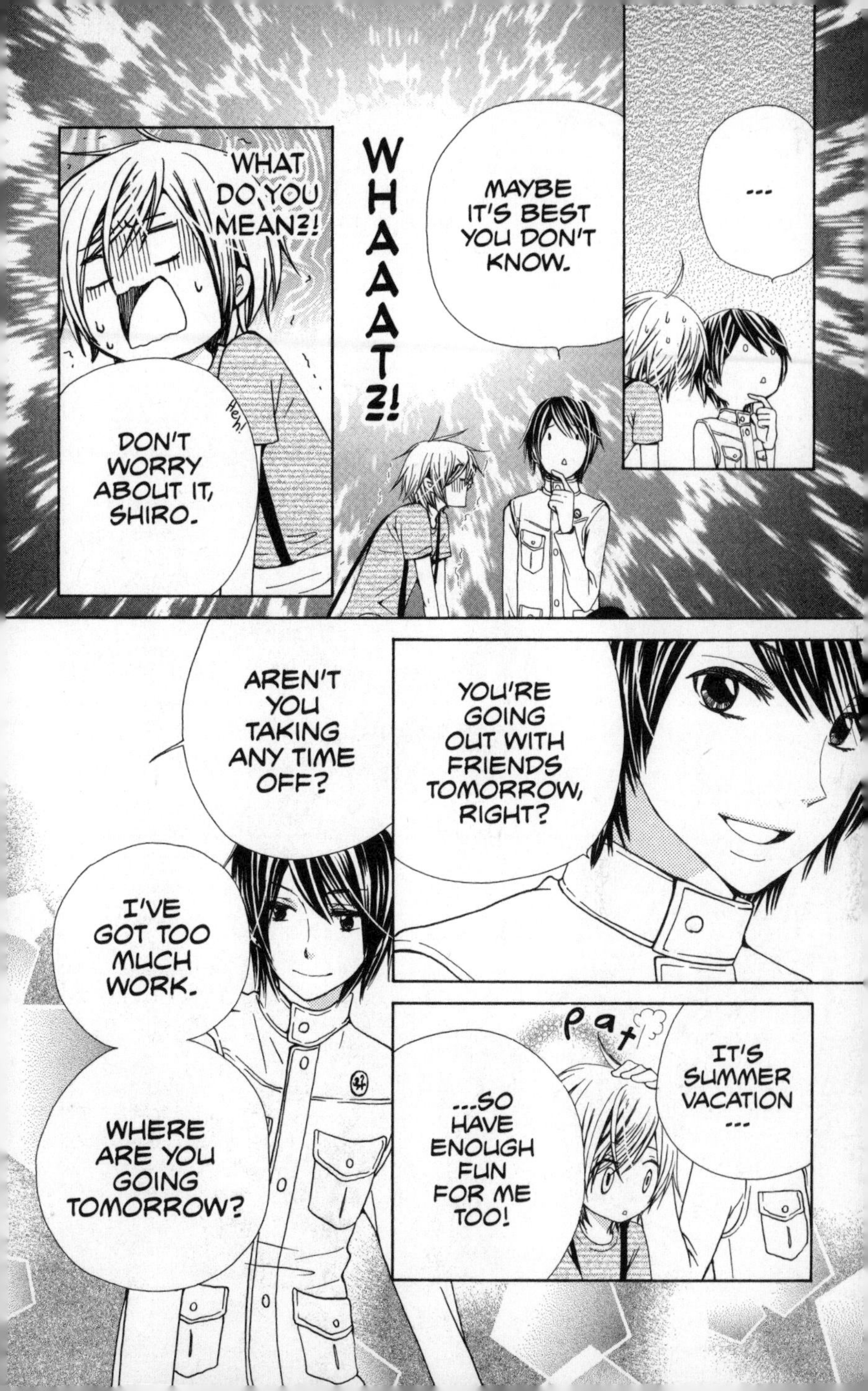
...
MAYBE IT'S BEST YOU DON'T KNOW.
WHAAAAT?!
WHAT DO YOU MEAN?!
Heh!
DON'T WORRY ABOUT IT, SHIRO.
YOU'RE GOING OUT WITH FRIENDS TOMORROW, RIGHT?
pat
IT'S SUMMER VACATION...
...SO HAVE ENOUGH FUN FOR ME TOO!
AREN'T YOU TAKING ANY TIME OFF?
I'VE GOT TOO MUCH WORK.
WHERE ARE YOU GOING TOMORROW?

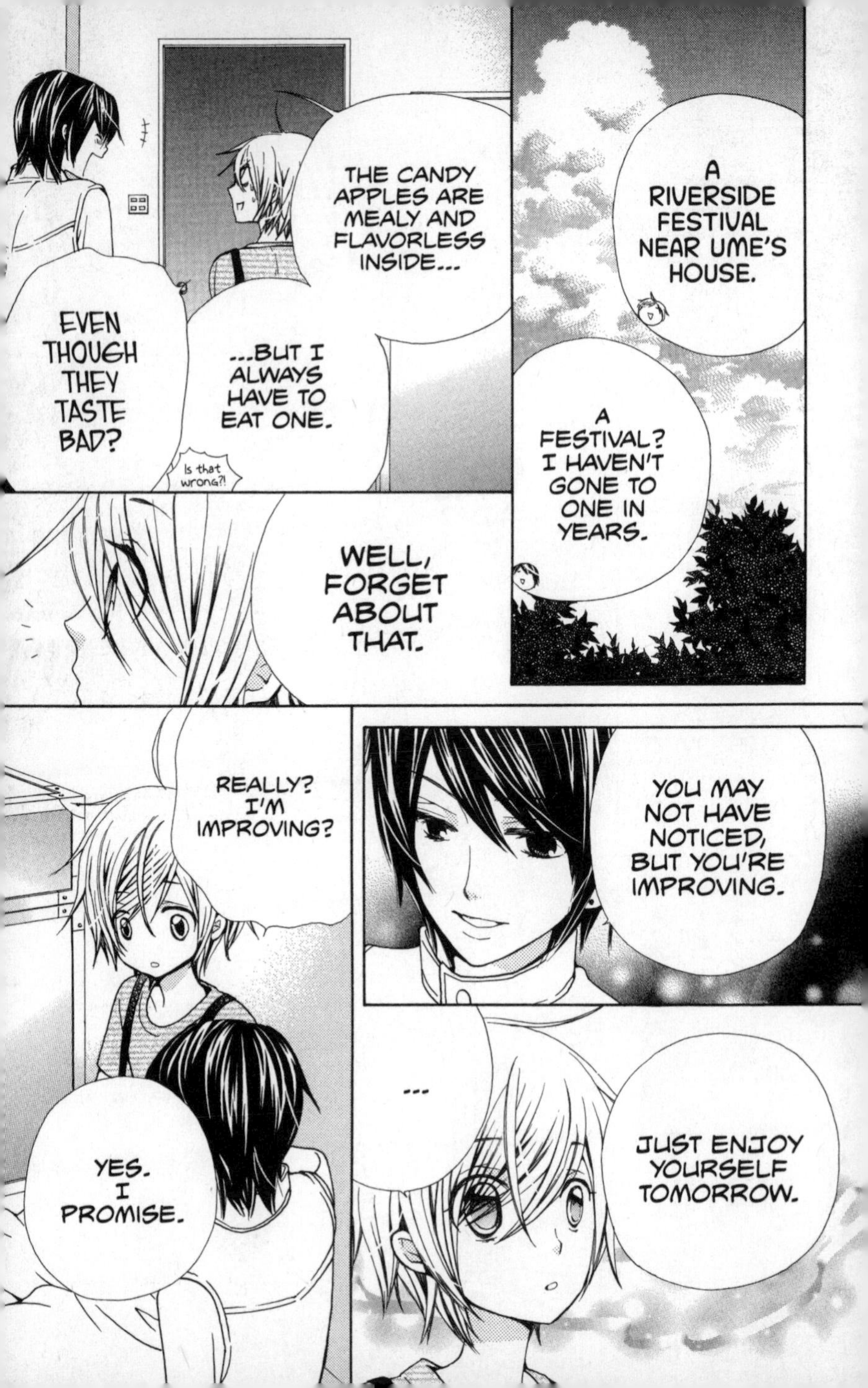
A RIVERSIDE FESTIVAL NEAR UME'S HOUSE.
A FESTIVAL? I HAVEN'T GONE TO ONE IN YEARS.
THE CANDY APPLES ARE MEALY AND FLAVORLESS INSIDE...
...BUT I ALWAYS HAVE TO EAT ONE.
Is that wrong?!
EVEN THOUGH THEY TASTE BAD?
WELL, FORGET ABOUT THAT.
YOU MAY NOT HAVE NOTICED, BUT YOU'RE IMPROVING.
JUST ENJOY YOURSELF TOMORROW.
...
REALLY? I'M IMPROVING?
YES. I PROMISE.

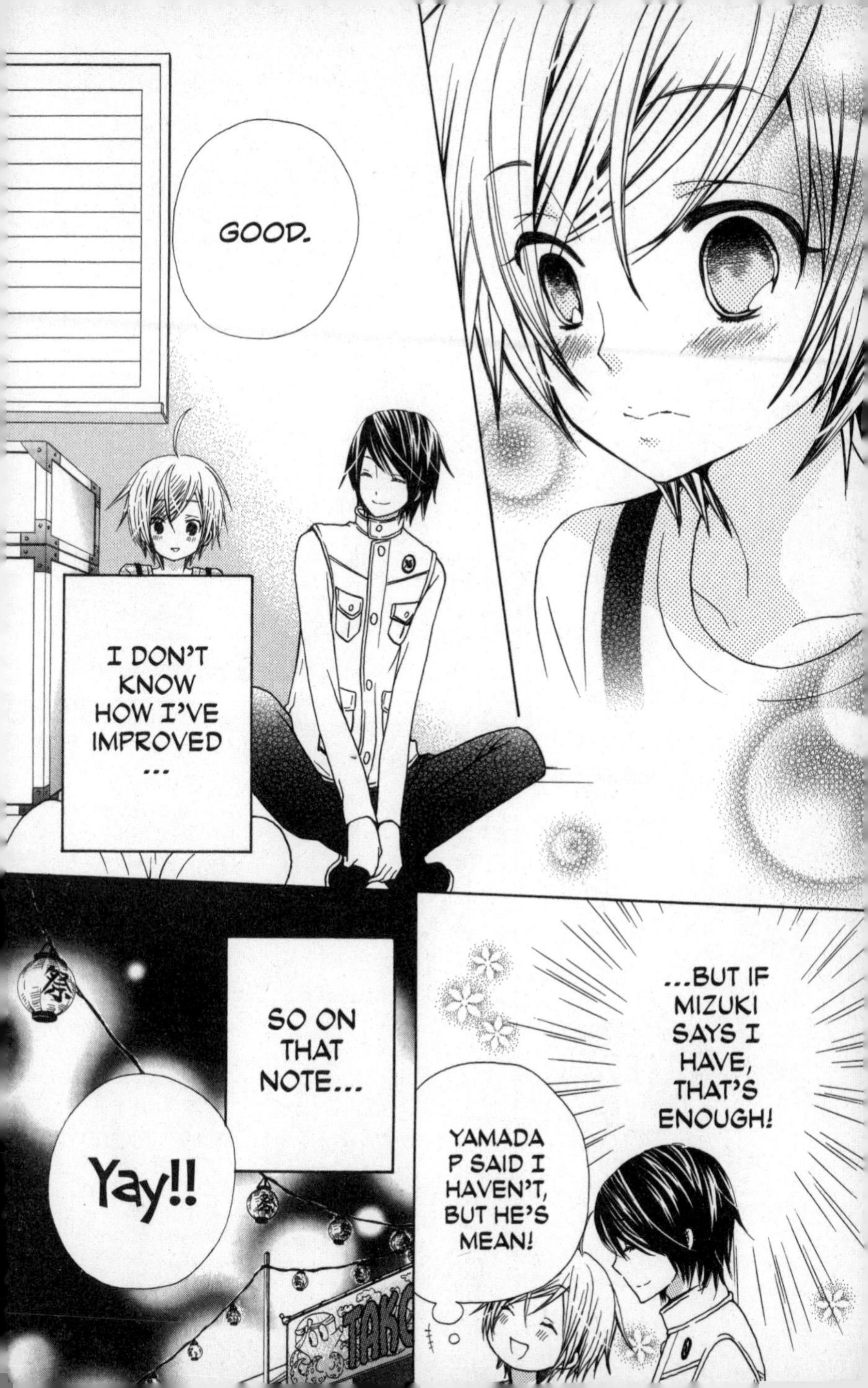
GOOD.
I DON'T KNOW HOW I'VE IMPROVED...
...BUT IF MIZUKI SAYS I HAVE, THAT'S ENOUGH!
YAMADA P SAID I HAVEN'T, BUT HE'S MEAN!
SO ON THAT NOTE...
Yay!!

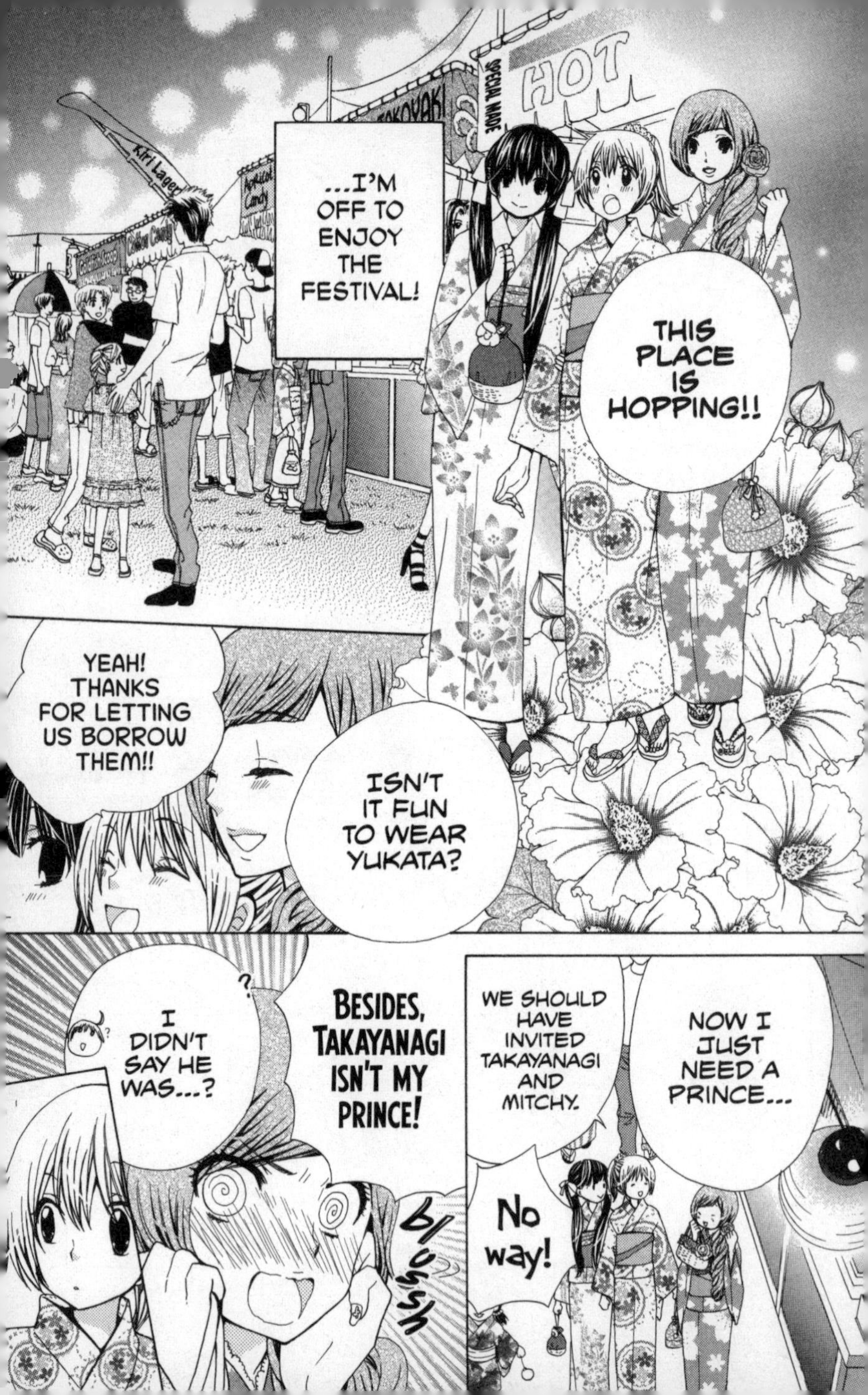
SPECIAL MADE
HOT
TAKOYAKI
...I'M OFF TO ENJOY THE FESTIVAL!
THIS PLACE IS HOPPING!!
ISN'T IT FUN TO WEAR YUKATA?
YEAH! THANKS FOR LETTING US BORROW THEM!!
NOW I JUST NEED A PRINCE...
WE SHOULD HAVE INVITED TAKAYANAGI AND MITCHY.
No way!
blussh
BESIDES, TAKAYANAGI ISN'T MY PRINCE!
I DIDN'T SAY HE WAS...?

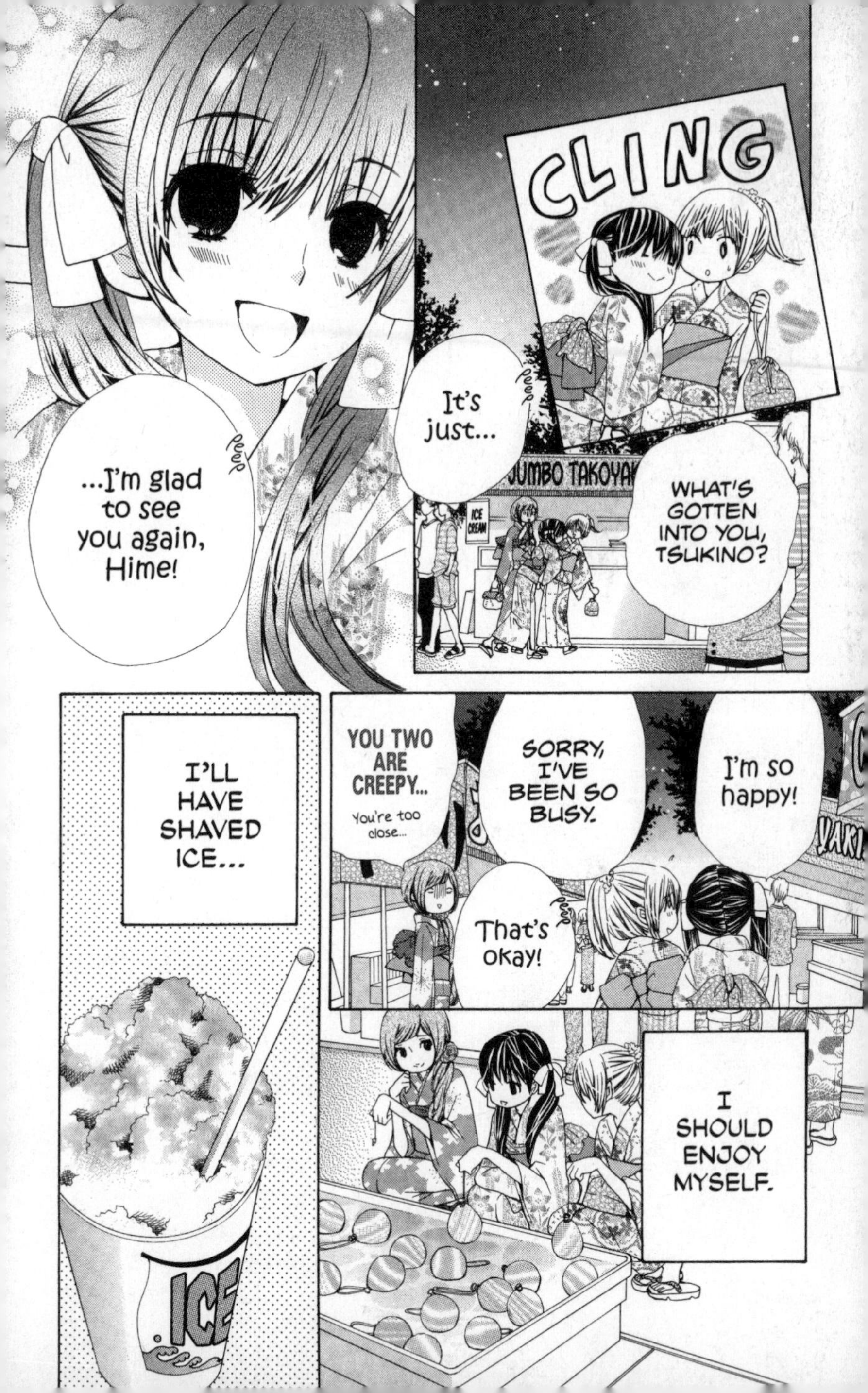
CLING
JUMBO TAKOYAK
ICE CREAM
WHAT'S GOTTEN INTO YOU, TSUKINO?
peep
It's just...
peep
...I'm glad to see you again, Hime!
I'm so happy!
SORRY, I'VE BEEN SO BUSY.
YOU TWO ARE CREEPY...
You're too close...
YAKI
peep
That's okay!
I SHOULD ENJOY MYSELF.
I'LL HAVE SHAVED ICE...
ICE

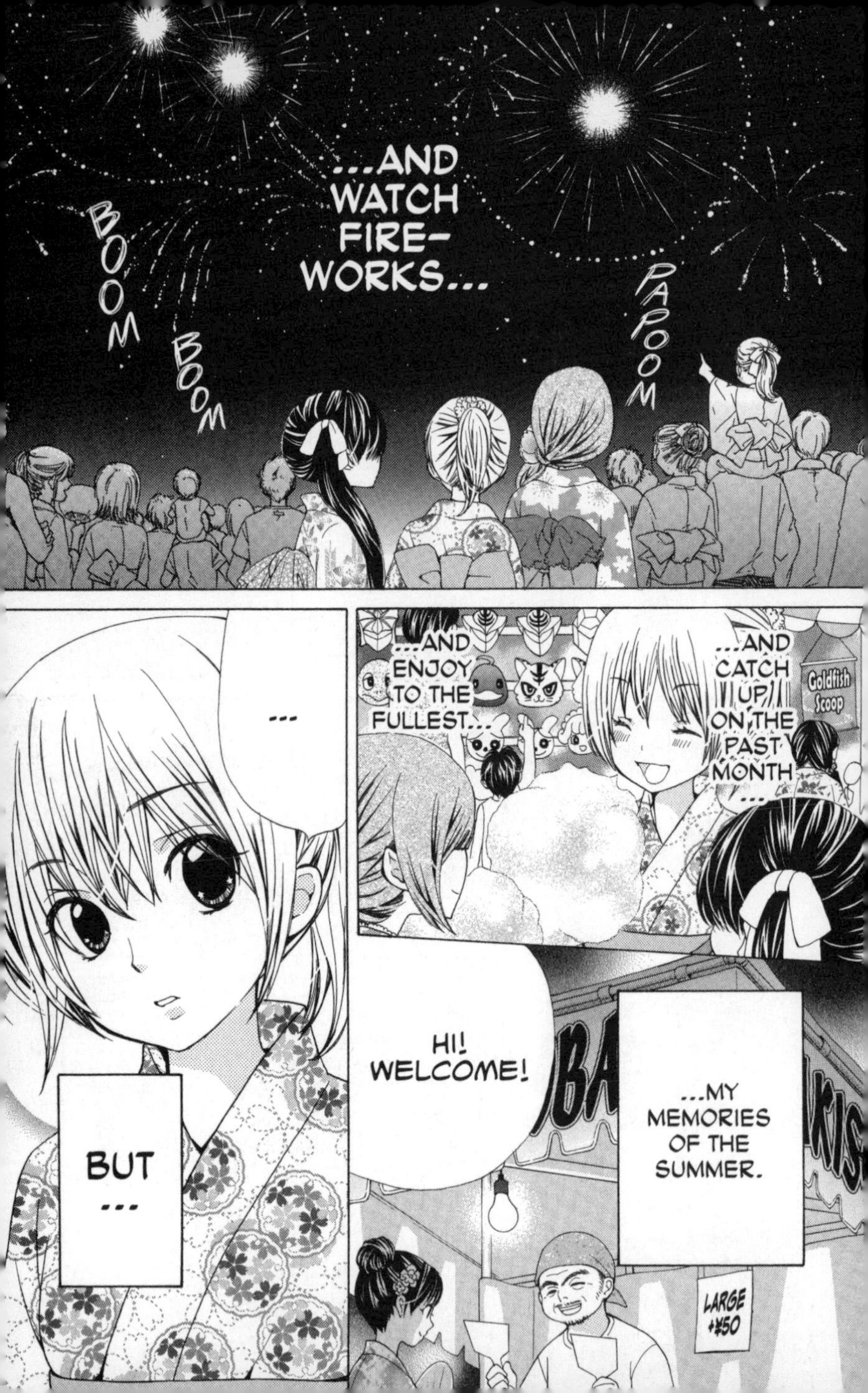
PAPOOM
...AND WATCH FIRE-WORKS...
BOOM
BOOM
...AND CATCH UP ON THE PAST MONTH...
Goldfish Scoop
...AND ENJOY TO THE FULLEST...
...MY MEMORIES OF THE SUMMER.
HI! WELCOME!
LARGE +¥50
...
BUT ...

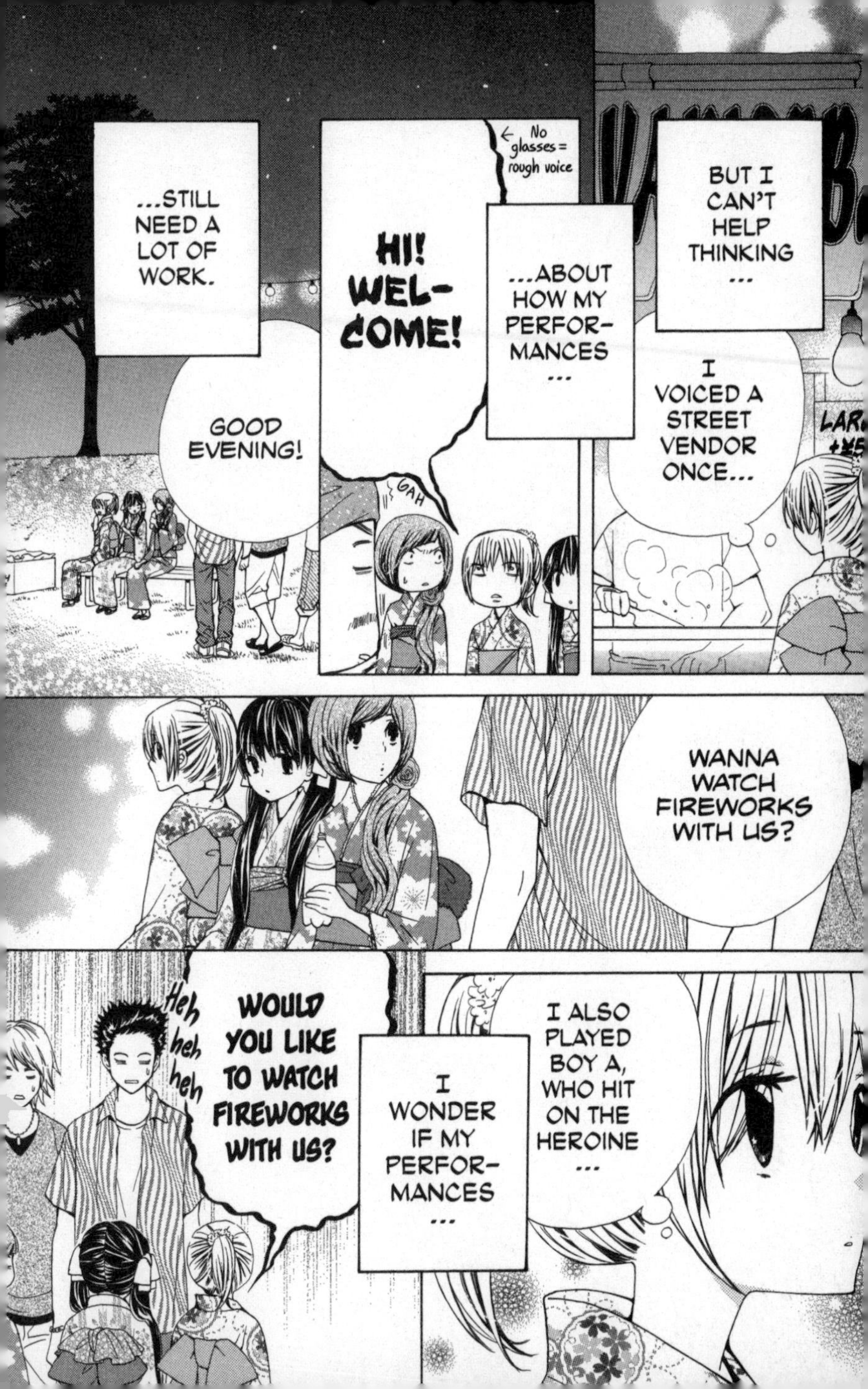
BUT I CAN'T HELP THINKING...
I VOICED A STREET VENDOR ONCE...
...ABOUT HOW MY PERFORMANCES...
← No glasses = rough voice
HI! WELCOME!
GAH
...STILL NEED A LOT OF WORK.
GOOD EVENING!
WANNA WATCH FIREWORKS WITH US?
I ALSO PLAYED BOY A, WHO HIT ON THE HEROINE...
I WONDER IF MY PERFORMANCES...
WOULD YOU LIKE TO WATCH FIREWORKS WITH US?
Heh heh heh

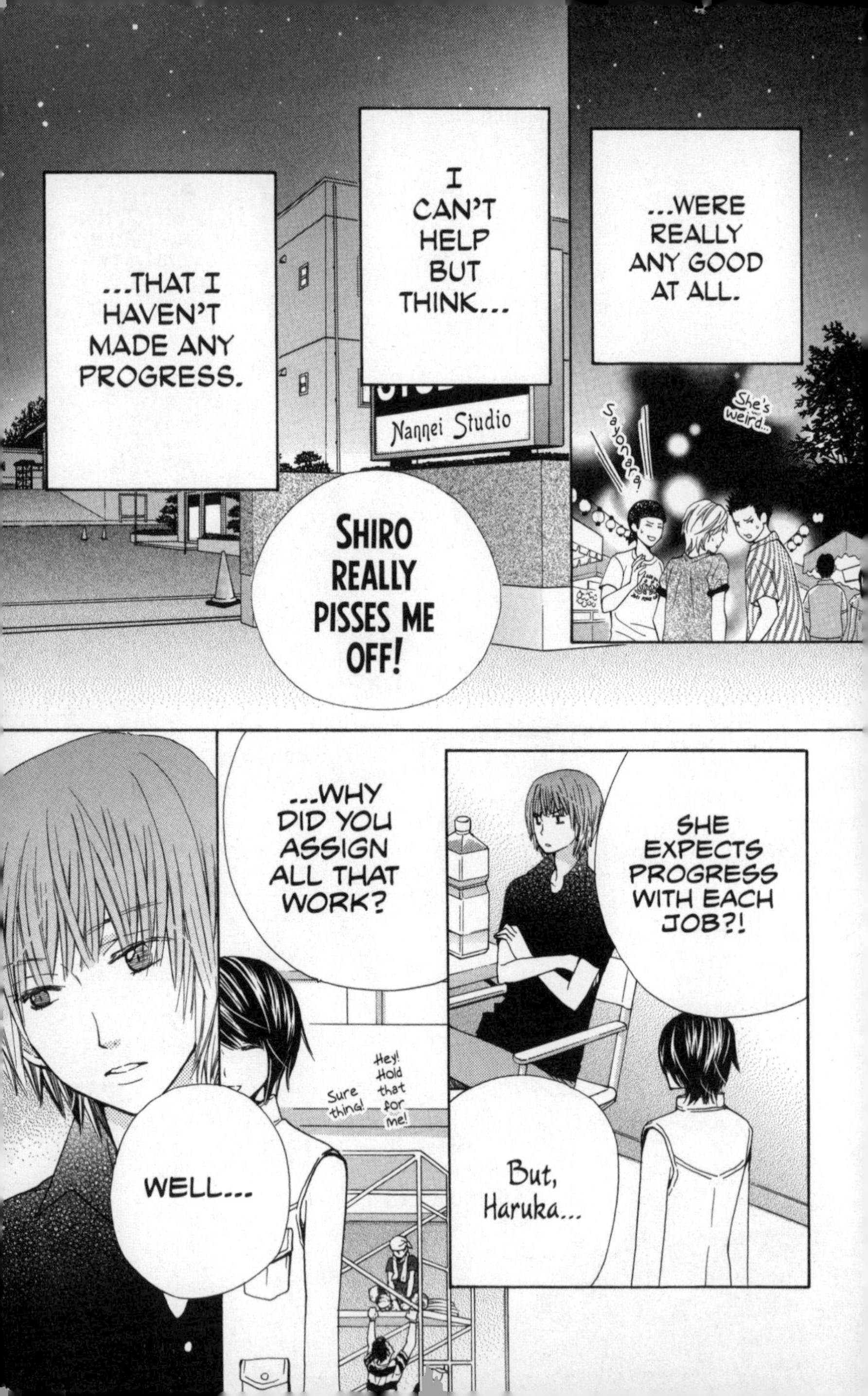
...WERE REALLY ANY GOOD AT ALL.
She's weird...
Sayonara!
I CAN'T HELP BUT THINK...
...THAT I HAVEN'T MADE ANY PROGRESS.
Nannei Studio
SHIRO REALLY PISSES ME OFF!
SHE EXPECTS PROGRESS WITH EACH JOB?!
But, Haruka...
...WHY DID YOU ASSIGN ALL THAT WORK?
Hey! Hold that for me!
Sure thing!
WELL...

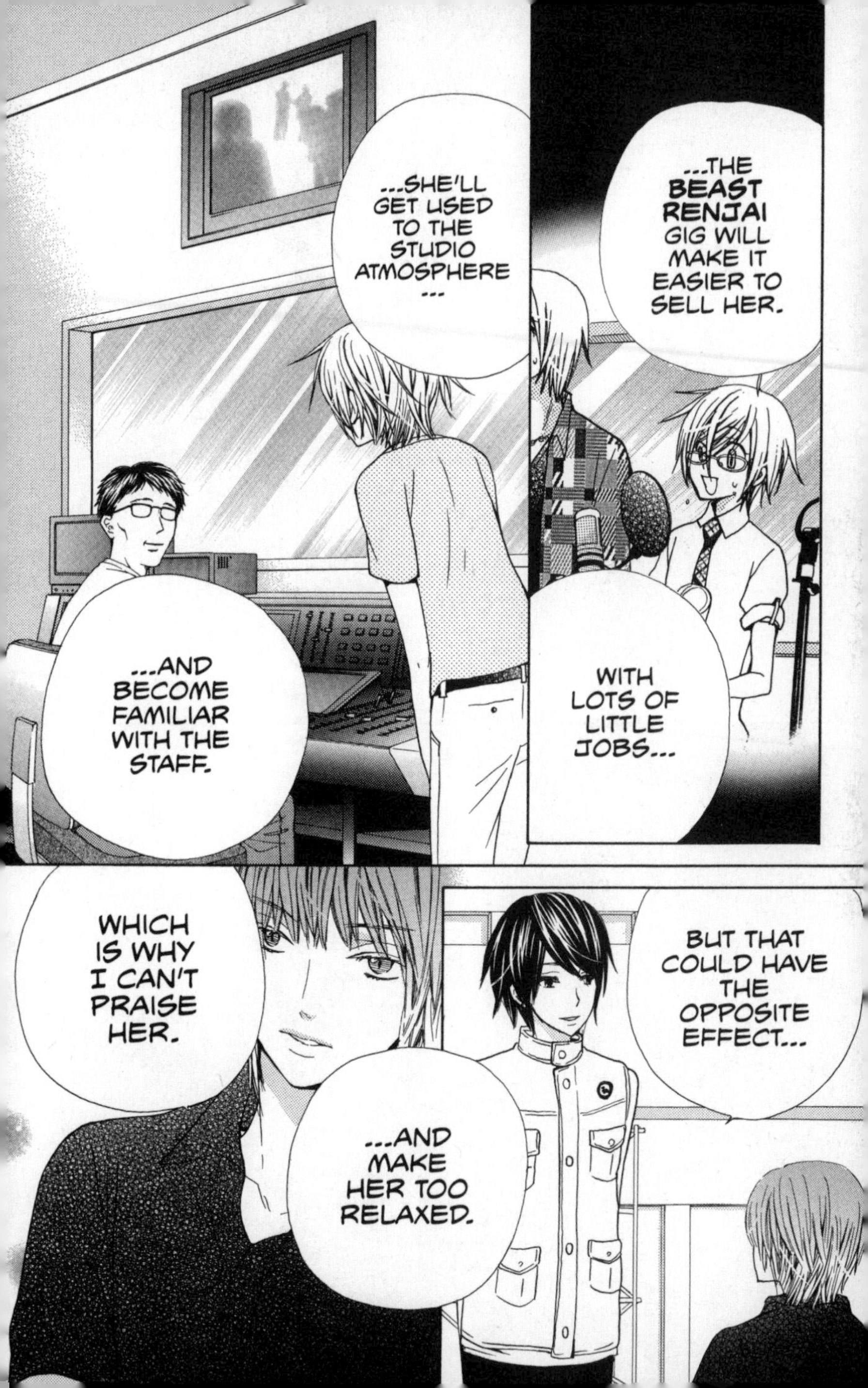
...THE BEAST RENJAI GIG WILL MAKE IT EASIER TO SELL HER.
WITH LOTS OF LITTLE JOBS...
...SHE'LL GET USED TO THE STUDIO ATMOSPHERE...
...AND BECOME FAMILIAR WITH THE STAFF.
BUT THAT COULD HAVE THE OPPOSITE EFFECT...
...AND MAKE HER TOO RELAXED.
WHICH IS WHY I CAN'T PRAISE HER.

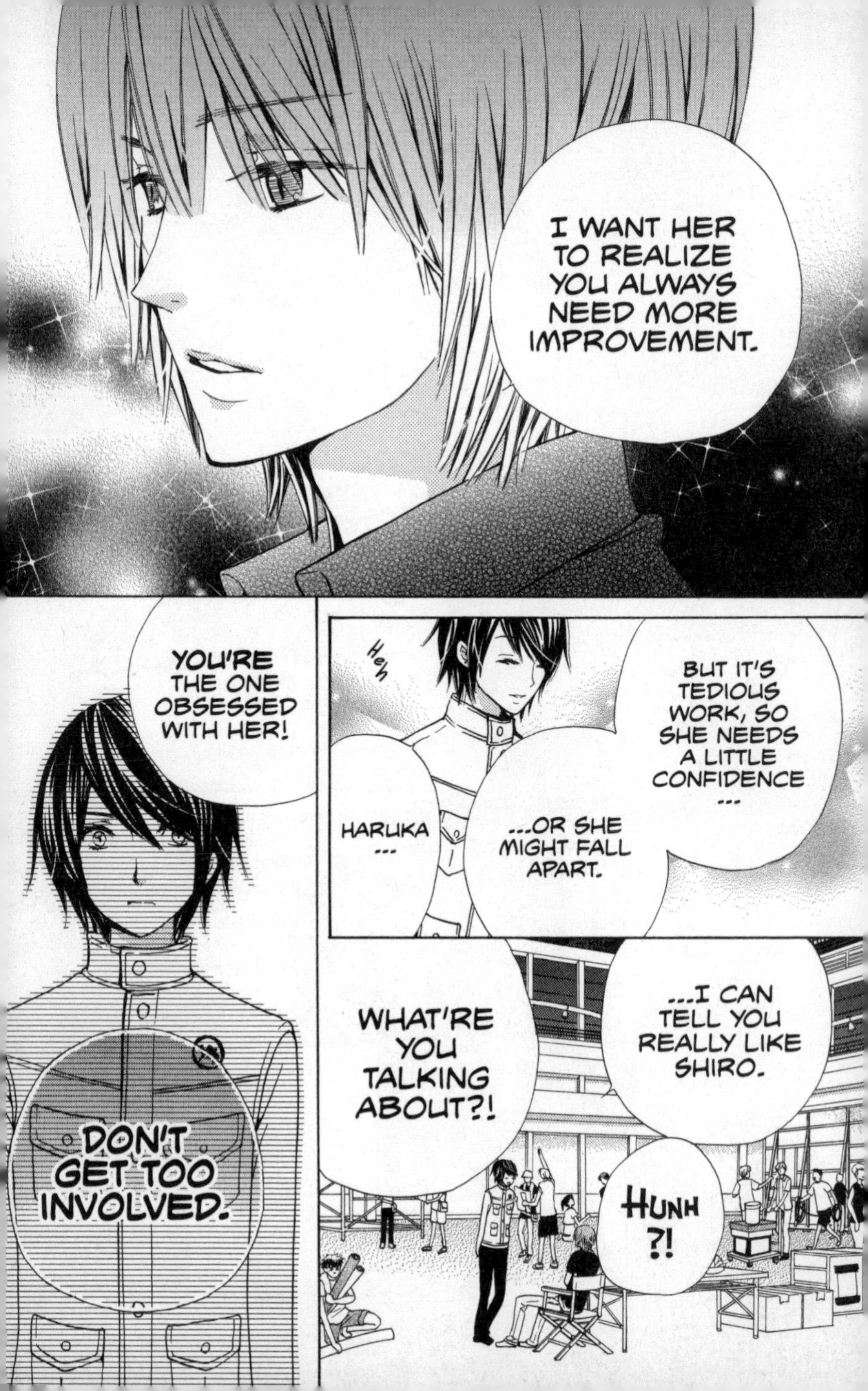
I WANT HER TO REALIZE YOU ALWAYS NEED MORE IMPROVEMENT.
Heh
BUT IT'S TEDIOUS WORK, SO SHE NEEDS A LITTLE CONFIDENCE ---
...OR SHE MIGHT FALL APART.
HARUKA ---
...I CAN TELL YOU REALLY LIKE SHIRO.
WHAT'RE YOU TALKING ABOUT?!
HUNH ?!
YOU'RE THE ONE OBSESSED WITH HER!
DON'T GET TOO INVOLVED.

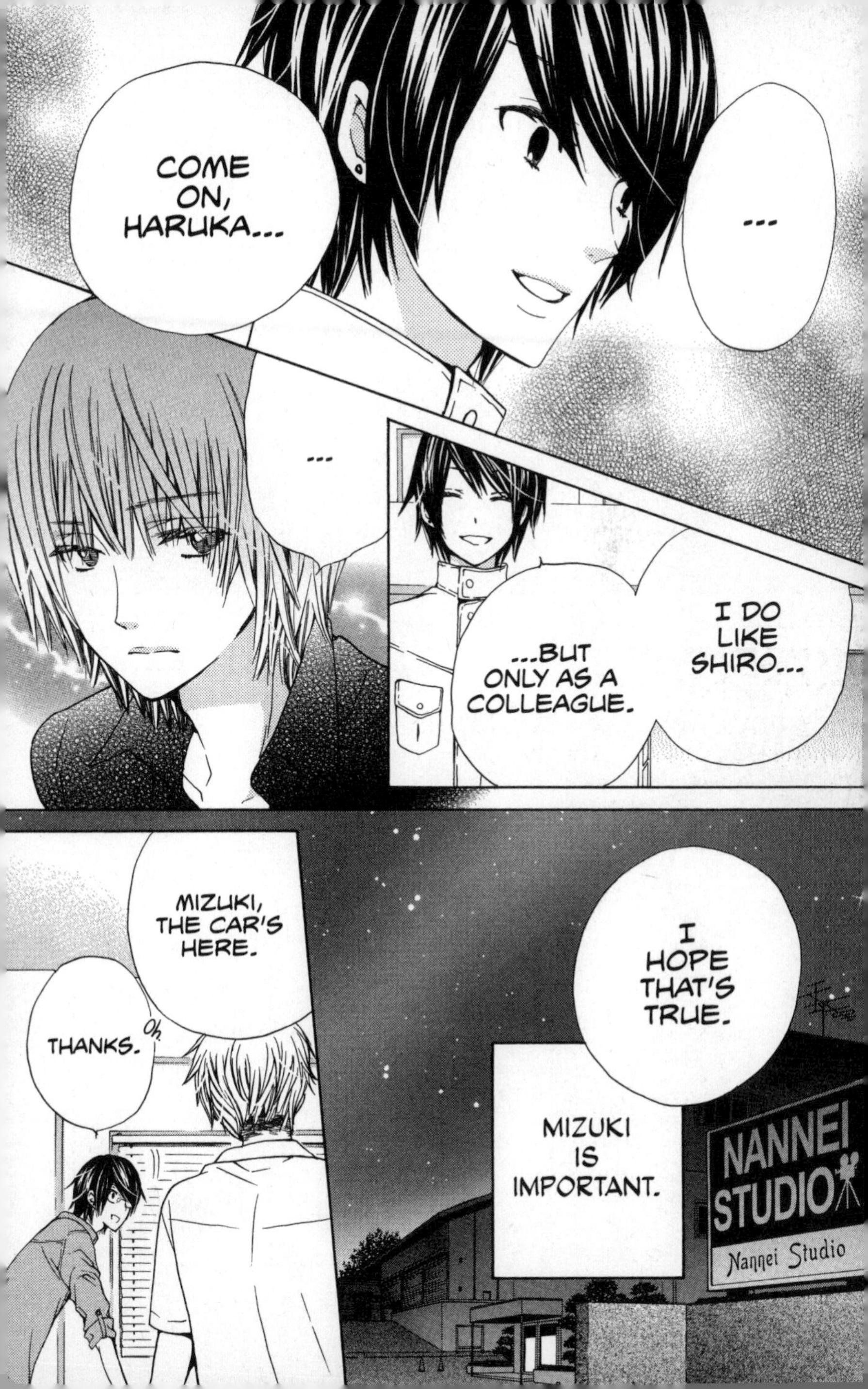
...
COME ON, HARUKA...
I DO LIKE SHIRO...
...BUT ONLY AS A COLLEAGUE.
...
I HOPE THAT'S TRUE.
MIZUKI IS IMPORTANT.
NANNEI STUDIO
Nannei Studio
MIZUKI, THE CAR'S HERE.
Oh.
THANKS.

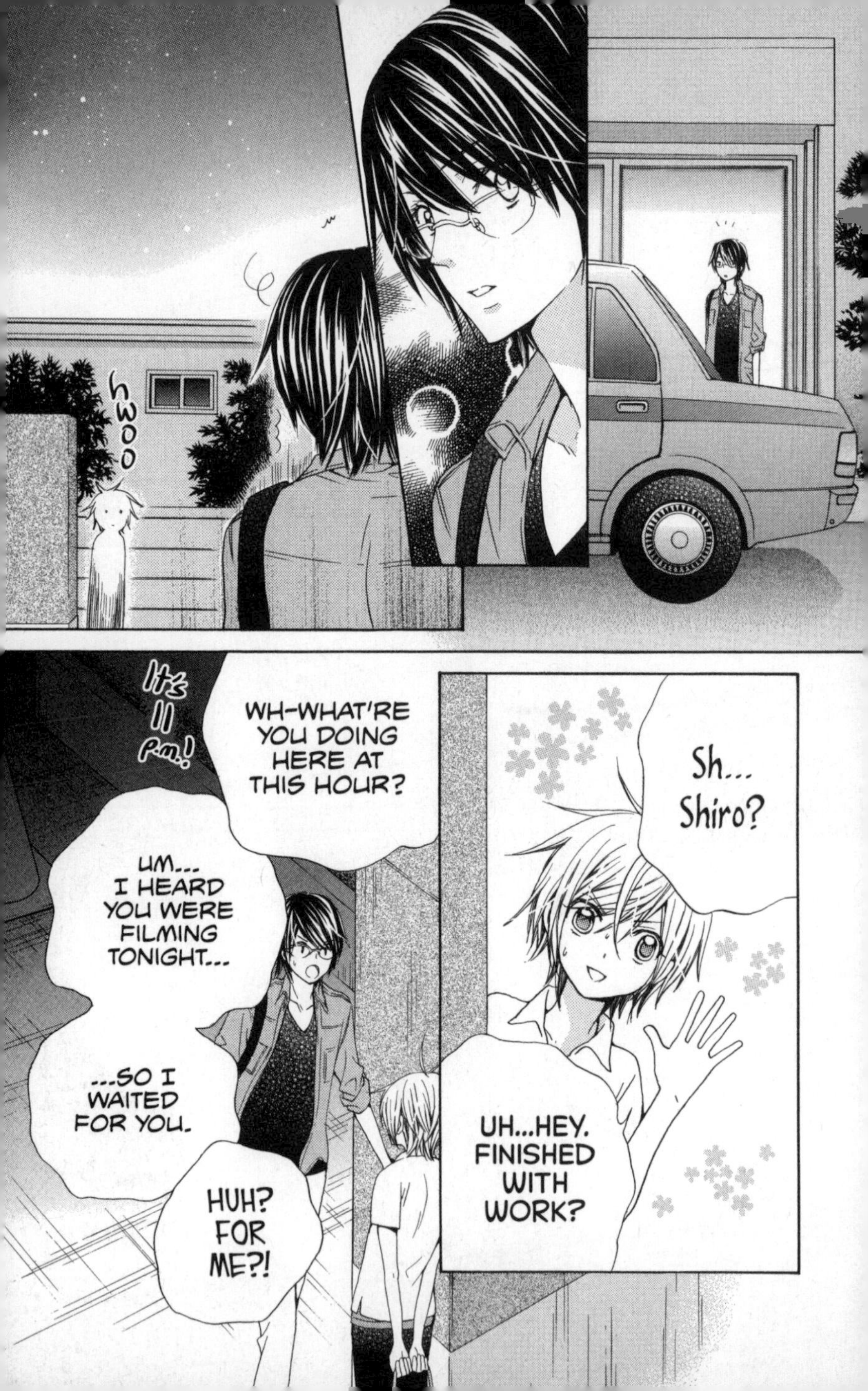
hwoo
Sh... Shiro?
UH...HEY. FINISHED WITH WORK?
WH-WHAT'RE YOU DOING HERE AT THIS HOUR?
It's 11 p.m.!
UM... I HEARD YOU WERE FILMING TONIGHT...
...SO I WAITED FOR YOU.
HUH? FOR ME?!

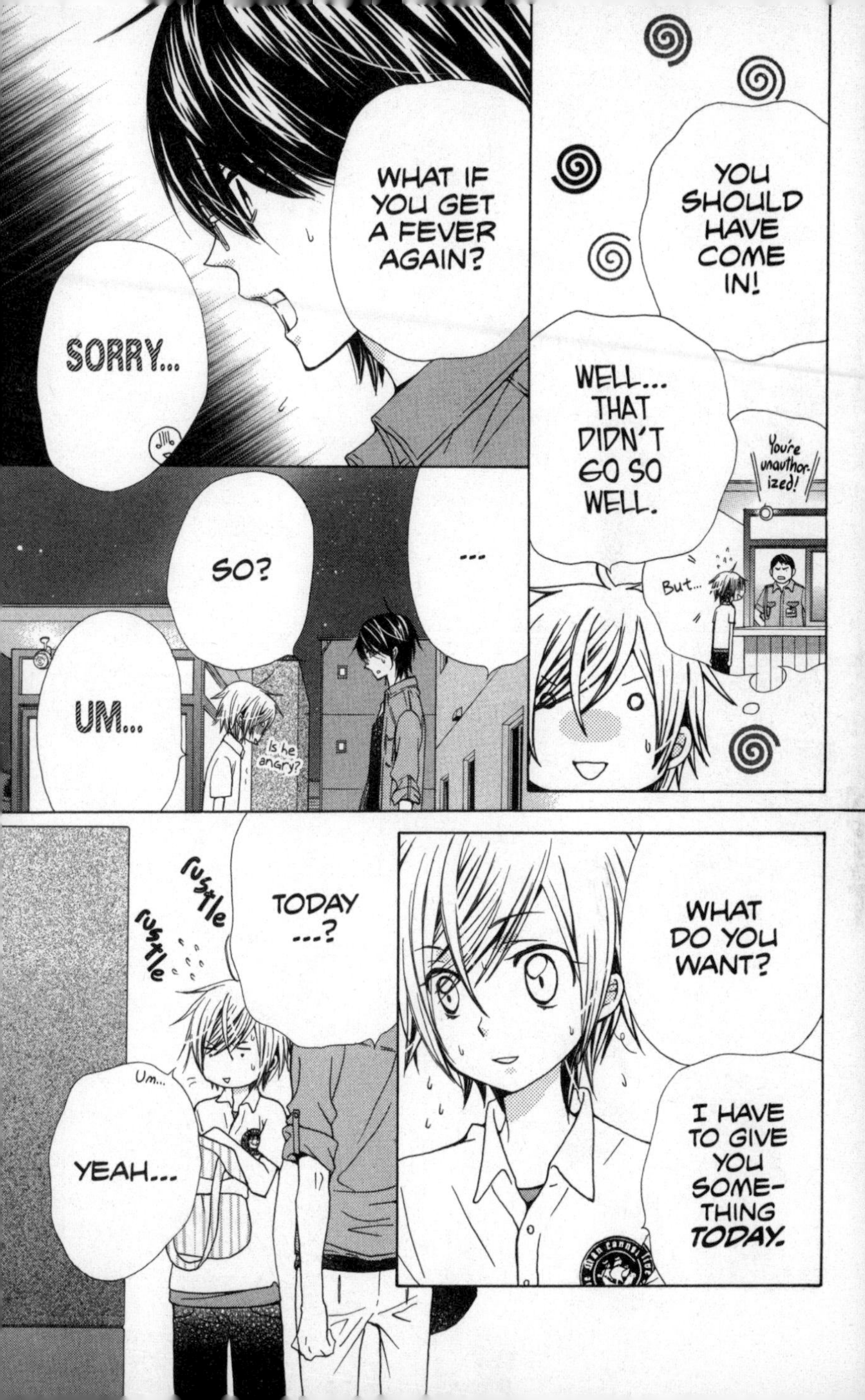
YOU SHOULD HAVE COME IN!
WELL... THAT DIDN'T GO SO WELL.
You're unauthorized!
But...
WHAT IF YOU GET A FEVER AGAIN?
SORRY...
...
SO?
UM...
Is he angry?
WHAT DO YOU WANT?
I HAVE TO GIVE YOU SOMETHING TODAY.
TODAY...?
rustle
rustle
Um...
YEAH...

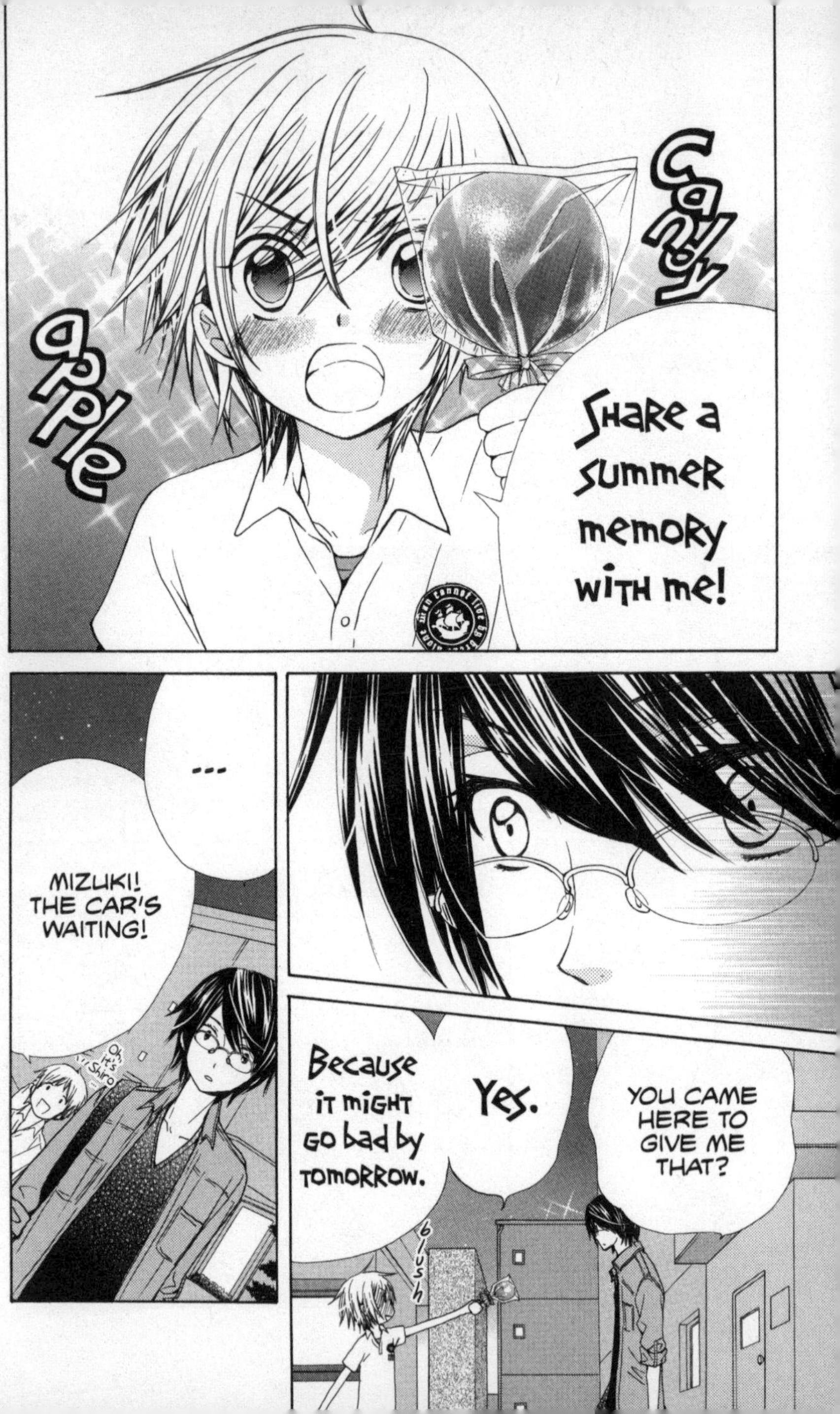
Candy
apple
Share a summer memory with me!
YOU CAME HERE TO GIVE ME THAT?
Yes.
Because it might go bad by tomorrow.
blush
...
MIZUKI! THE CAR'S WAITING!
Oh, it's Shiro

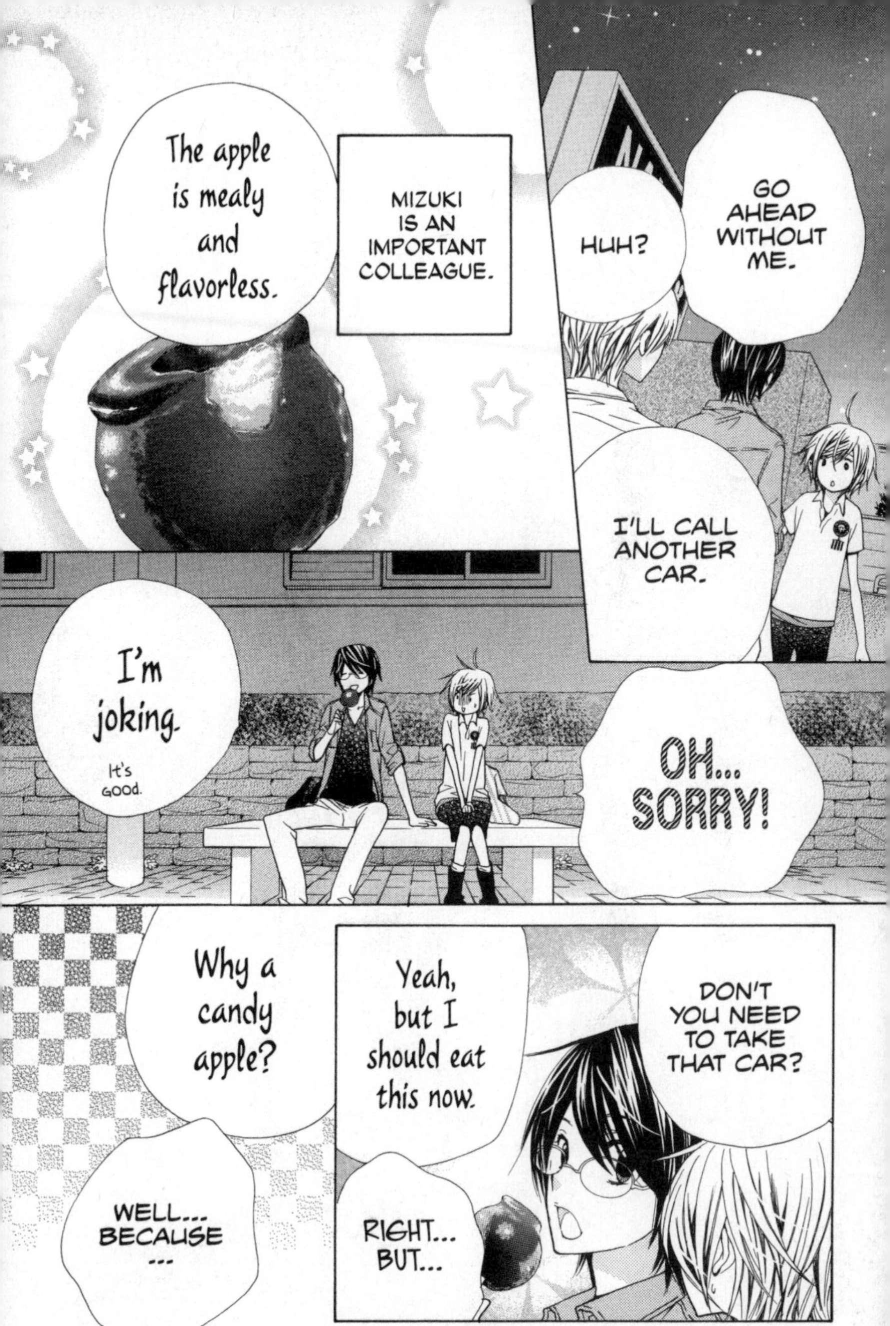

GO AHEAD WITHOUT ME.
HUH?
I'LL CALL ANOTHER CAR.
MIZUKI IS AN IMPORTANT COLLEAGUE.
The apple is mealy and flavorless.
OH... SORRY!
I'm joking.
It's good.
DON'T YOU NEED TO TAKE THAT CAR?
Yeah, but I should eat this now.
RIGHT... BUT...
Why a candy apple?
WELL... BECAUSE ...

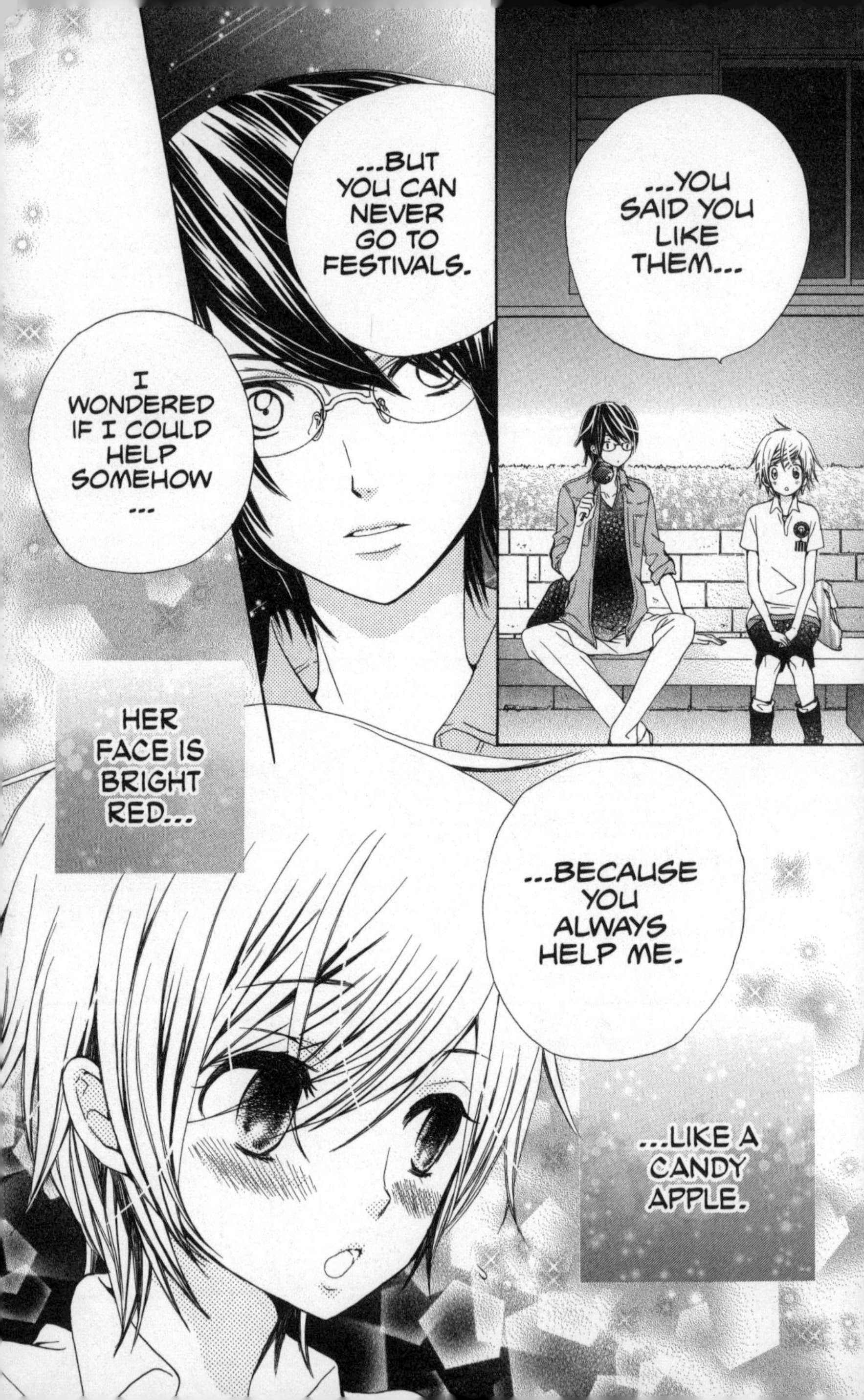
...YOU SAID YOU LIKE THEM...
...BUT YOU CAN NEVER GO TO FESTIVALS.
I WONDERED IF I COULD HELP SOMEHOW...
...BECAUSE YOU ALWAYS HELP ME.
HER FACE IS BRIGHT RED...
...LIKE A CANDY APPLE.

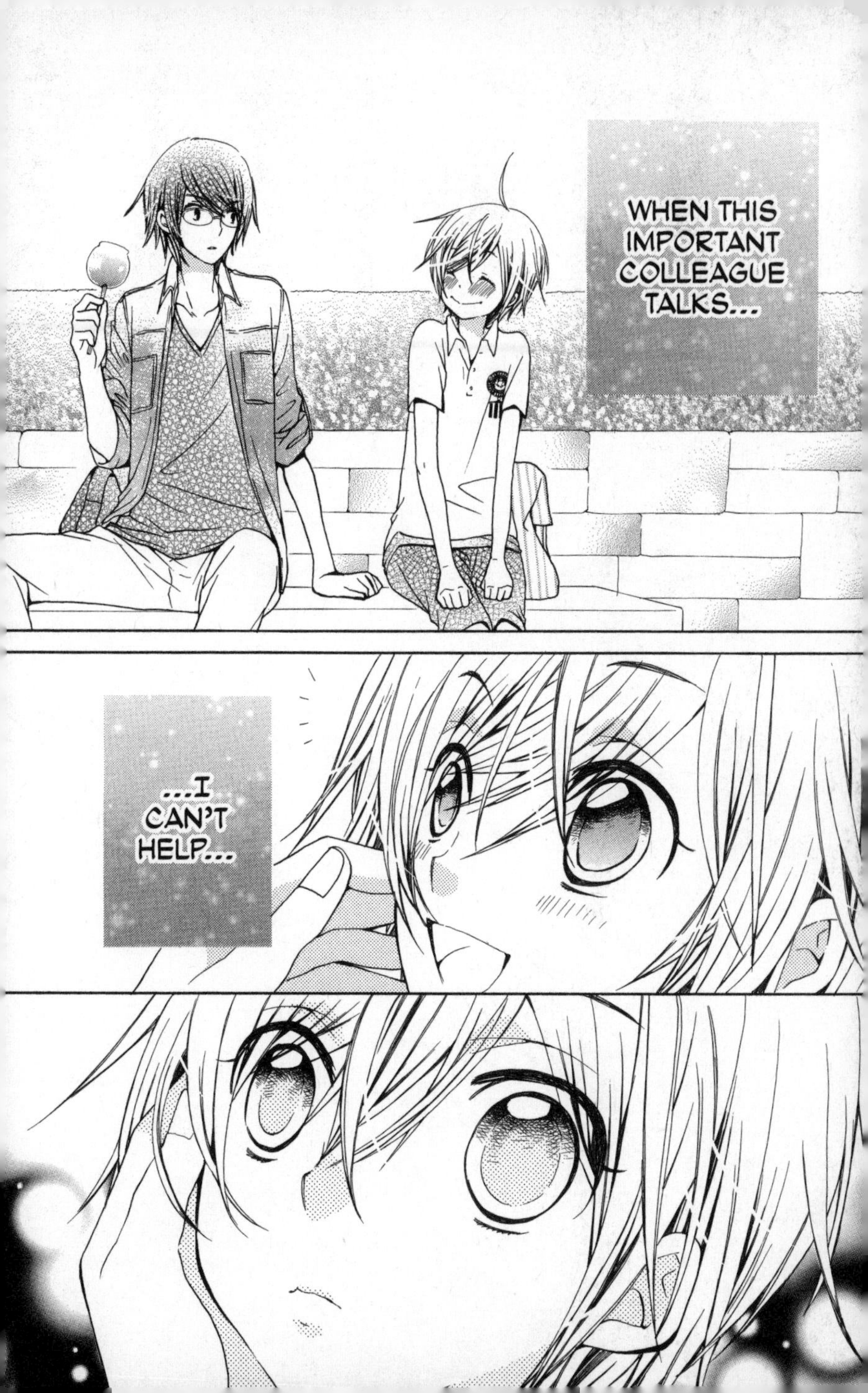
WHEN THIS IMPORTANT COLLEAGUE TALKS...
...I CAN'T HELP...

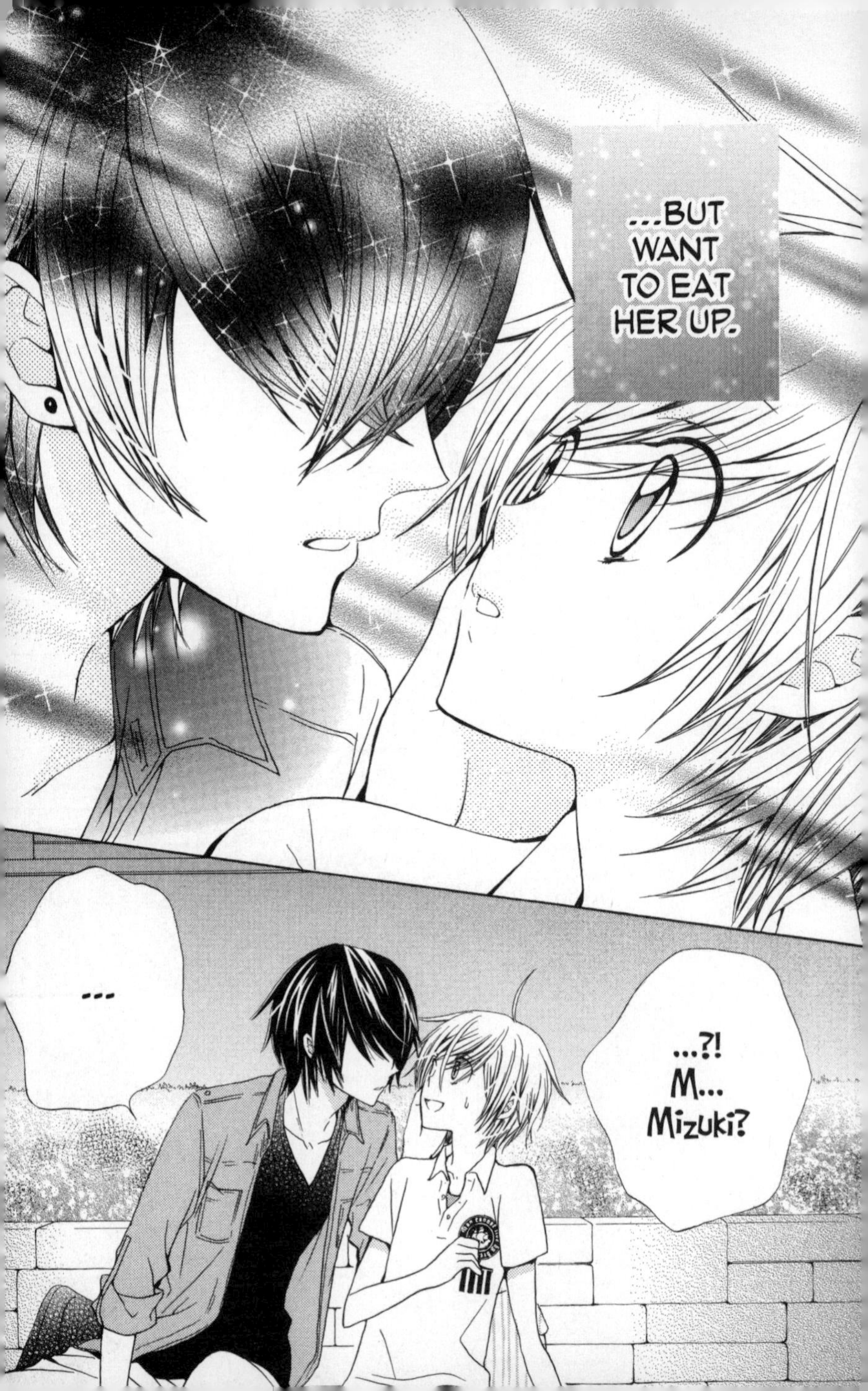
...BUT WANT TO EAT HER UP.
...?! M... Mizuki?
...

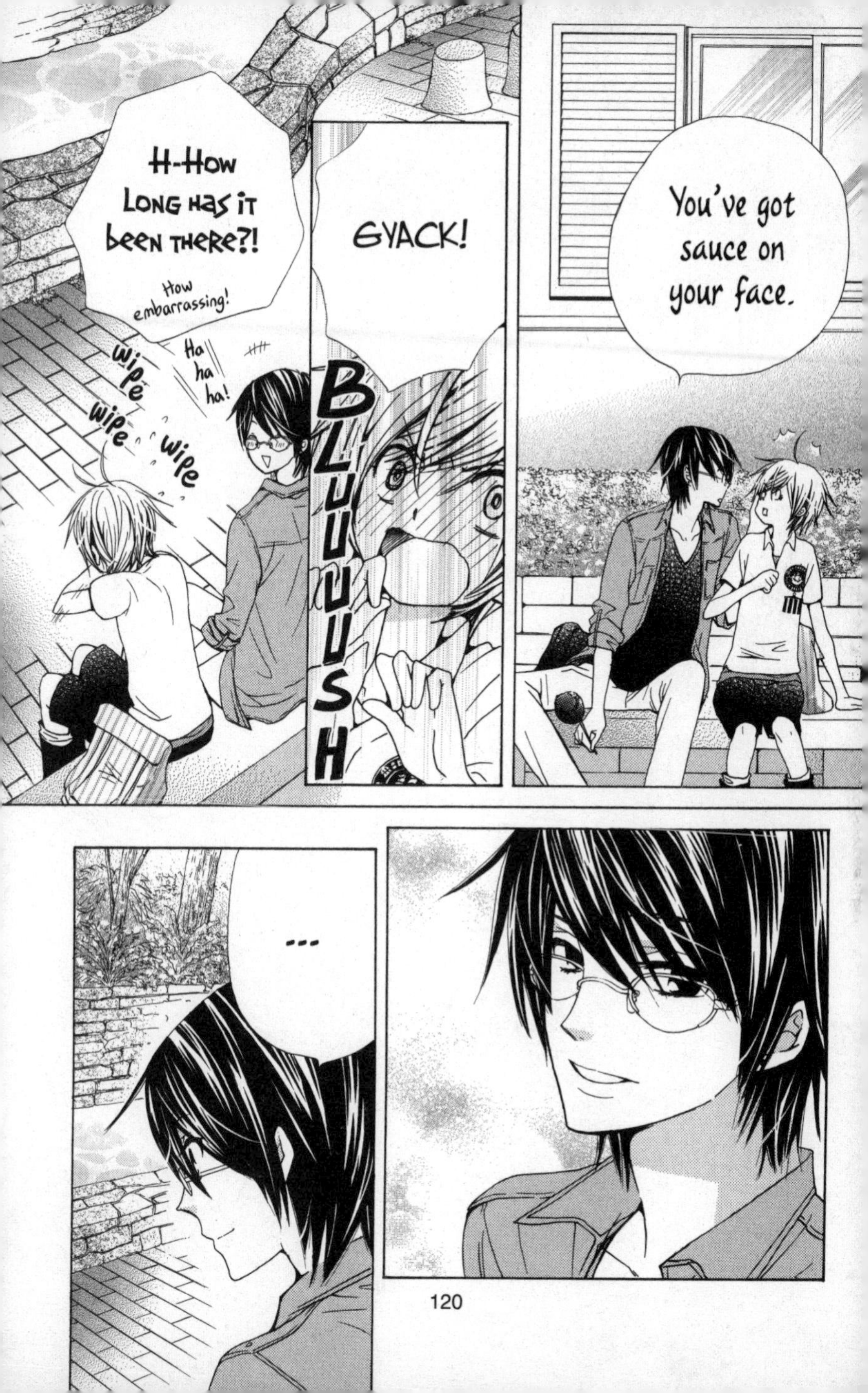
You've got sauce on your face.
GYACK!
BLUUUUUSH
H-How long has it been there?!
How embarrassing!
Ha ha ha!
wipe
wipe
wipe
...

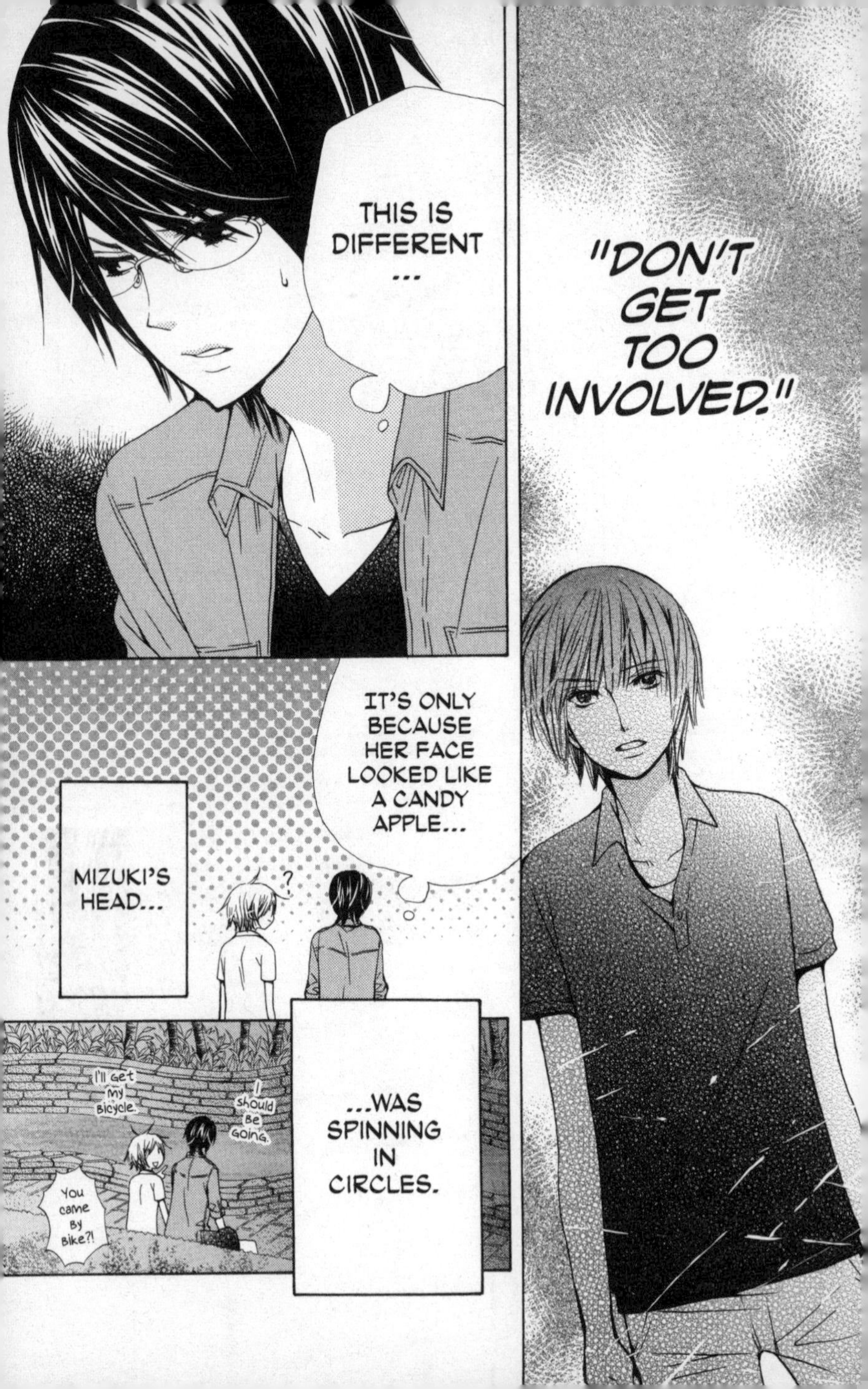
"DON'T GET TOO INVOLVED."
THIS IS DIFFERENT ...
IT'S ONLY BECAUSE HER FACE LOOKED LIKE A CANDY APPLE...
MIZUKI'S HEAD...
?
...WAS SPINNING IN CIRCLES.
I should be going.
I'll get my bicycle.
You came by bike?!

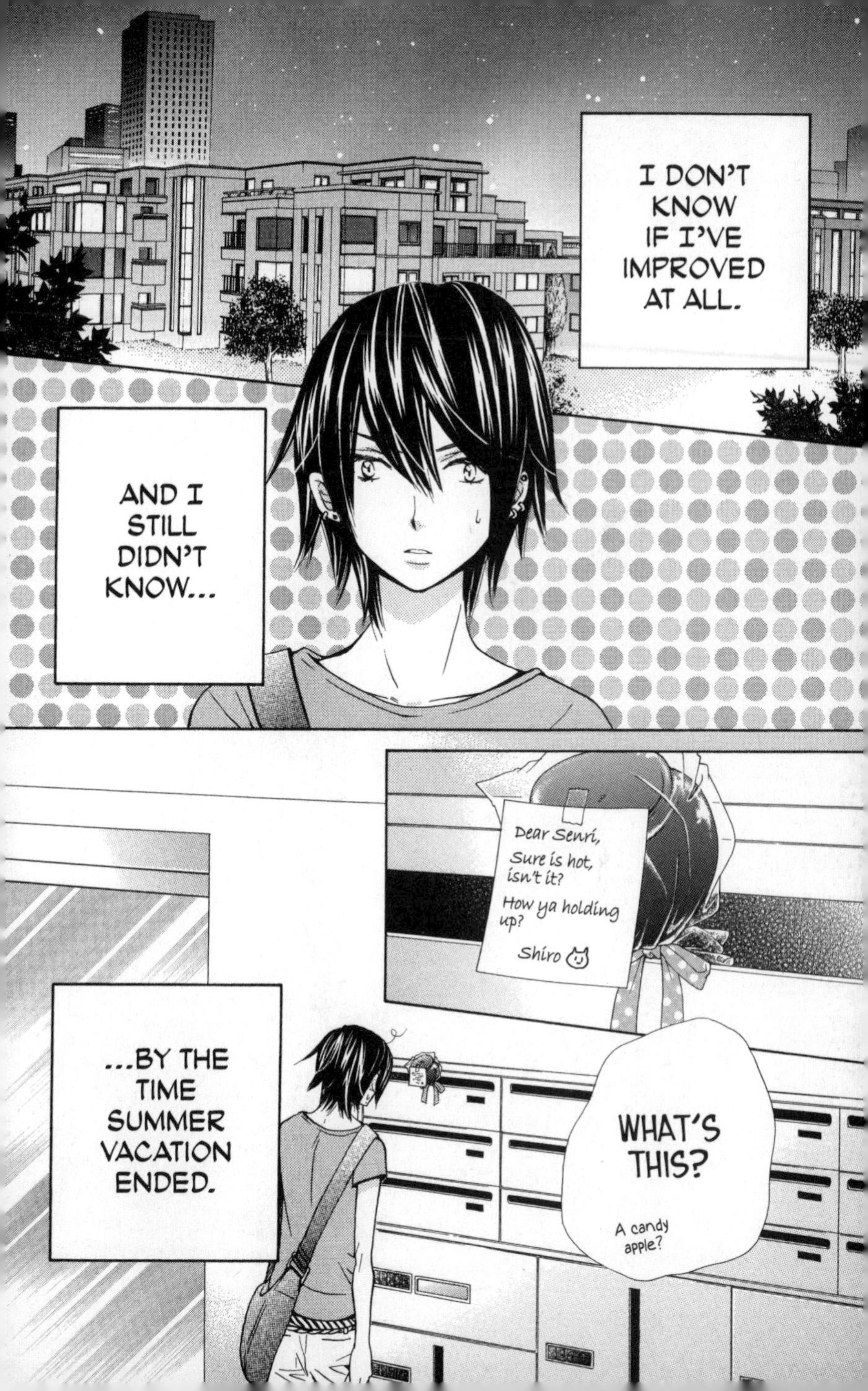
I DON'T KNOW IF I'VE IMPROVED AT ALL.
AND I STILL DIDN'T KNOW...
Dear Senri,
Sure is hot, isn't it?
How ya holding up?
Shiro
WHAT'S THIS?
A candy apple?
...BY THE TIME SUMMER VACATION ENDED.

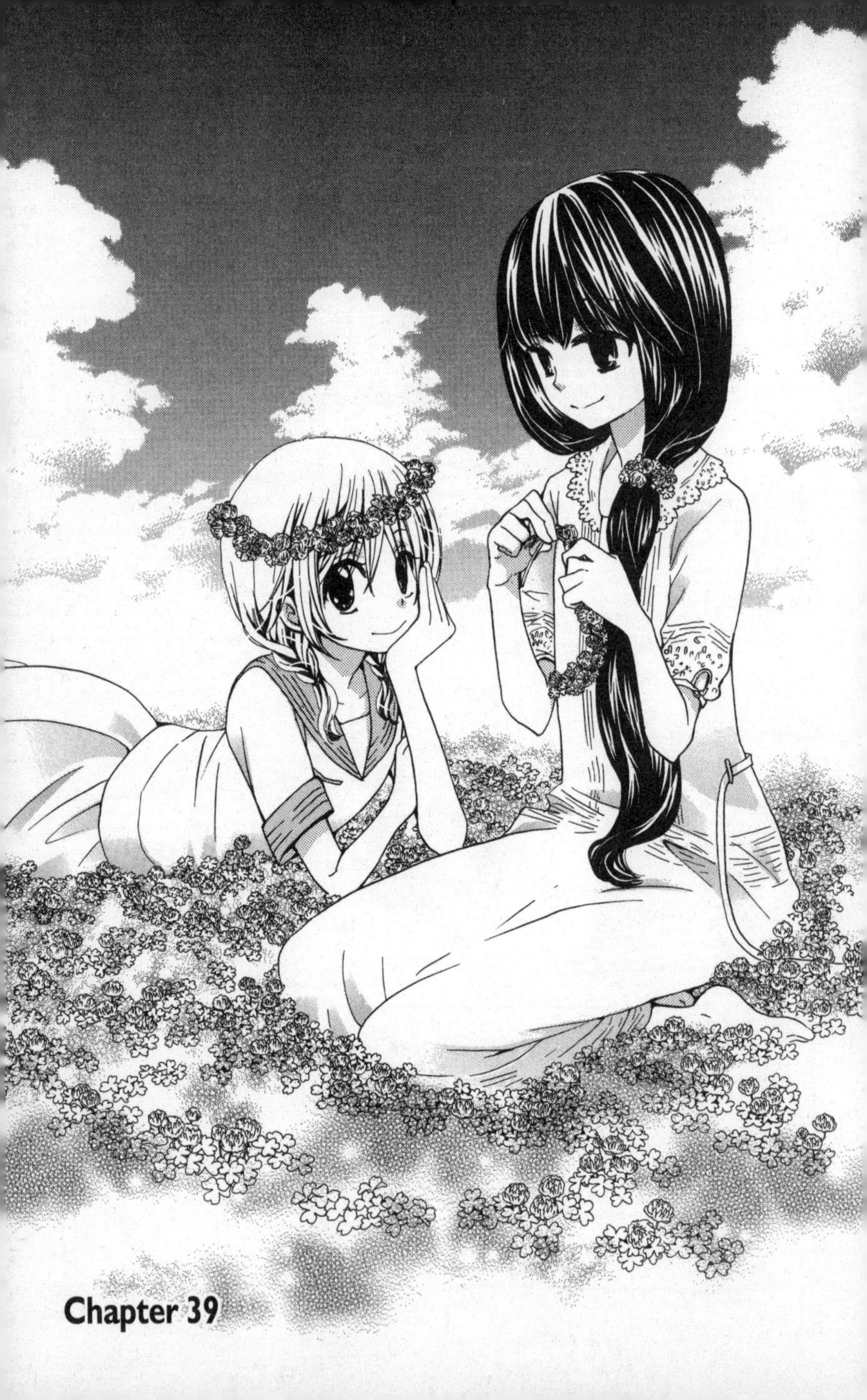

Chapter 39

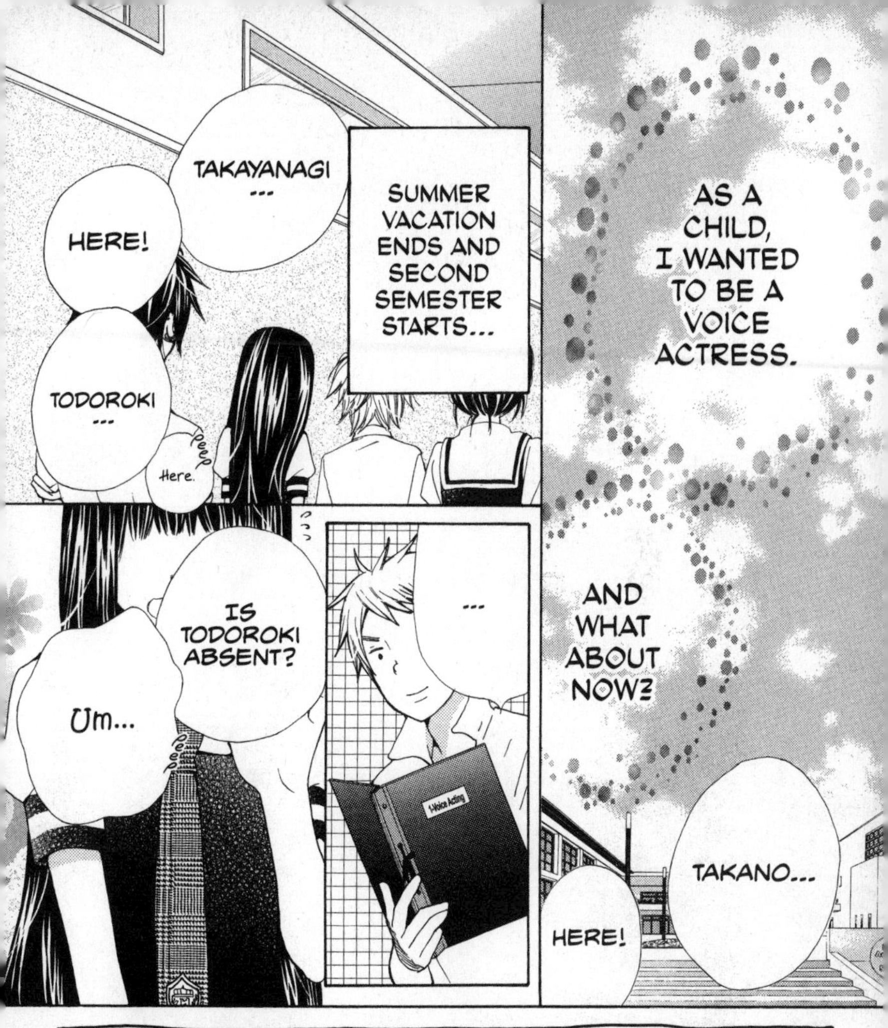
AS A CHILD, I WANTED TO BE A VOICE ACTRESS.
AND WHAT ABOUT NOW?
TAKANO...
HERE!
SUMMER VACATION ENDS AND SECOND SEMESTER STARTS...
TAKAYANAGI ...
HERE!
TODOROKI ...
peep
Here.
...
1-Voice Acting
IS TODOROKI ABSENT?
Um...
peep

• Autograph Signing in Taiwan •

- The second event in Taiwan was held in a big hall like for a manga convention. Lots of readers were there and cheering in response to the calls of the lady presiding over the events, so it was quite lively!! Tons of people!
- And a friend of the Taiwanese reader in Tokyo also came!
- Thank you to everyone who made giant versions of panels from the manga and other stuff!!
- And many thanks to everyone at Tong Li Publishing who cooperated and was so kind to me. I love Taiwan even more now!
- And everyone who did cosplay was incredibly cute!! Like Shiro from the cover of Volume 3, Hime in summer clothes and Senri and Hime in winter clothes!!

5

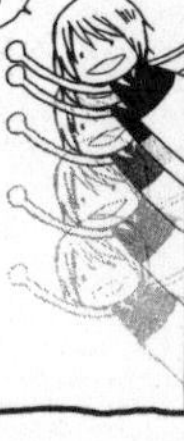

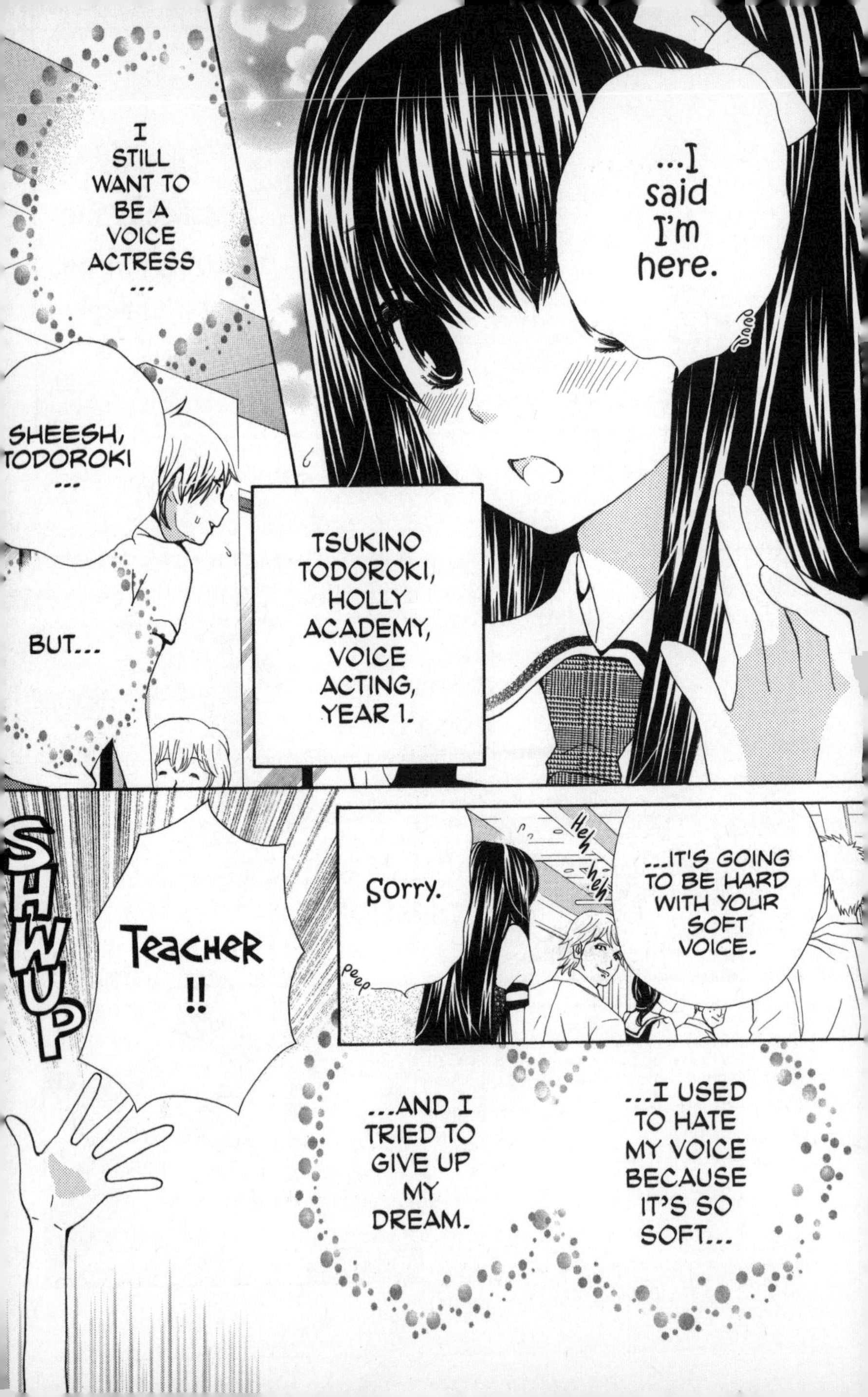
...I said I'm here.
peep
TSUKINO TODOROKI, HOLLY ACADEMY, VOICE ACTING, YEAR 1.
I STILL WANT TO BE A VOICE ACTRESS...
SHEESH, TODOROKI...
BUT...
...IT'S GOING TO BE HARD WITH YOUR SOFT VOICE.
Heh heh
Sorry.
peep
...I USED TO HATE MY VOICE BECAUSE IT'S SO SOFT...
...AND I TRIED TO GIVE UP MY DREAM.
SHWUP
Teacher !!

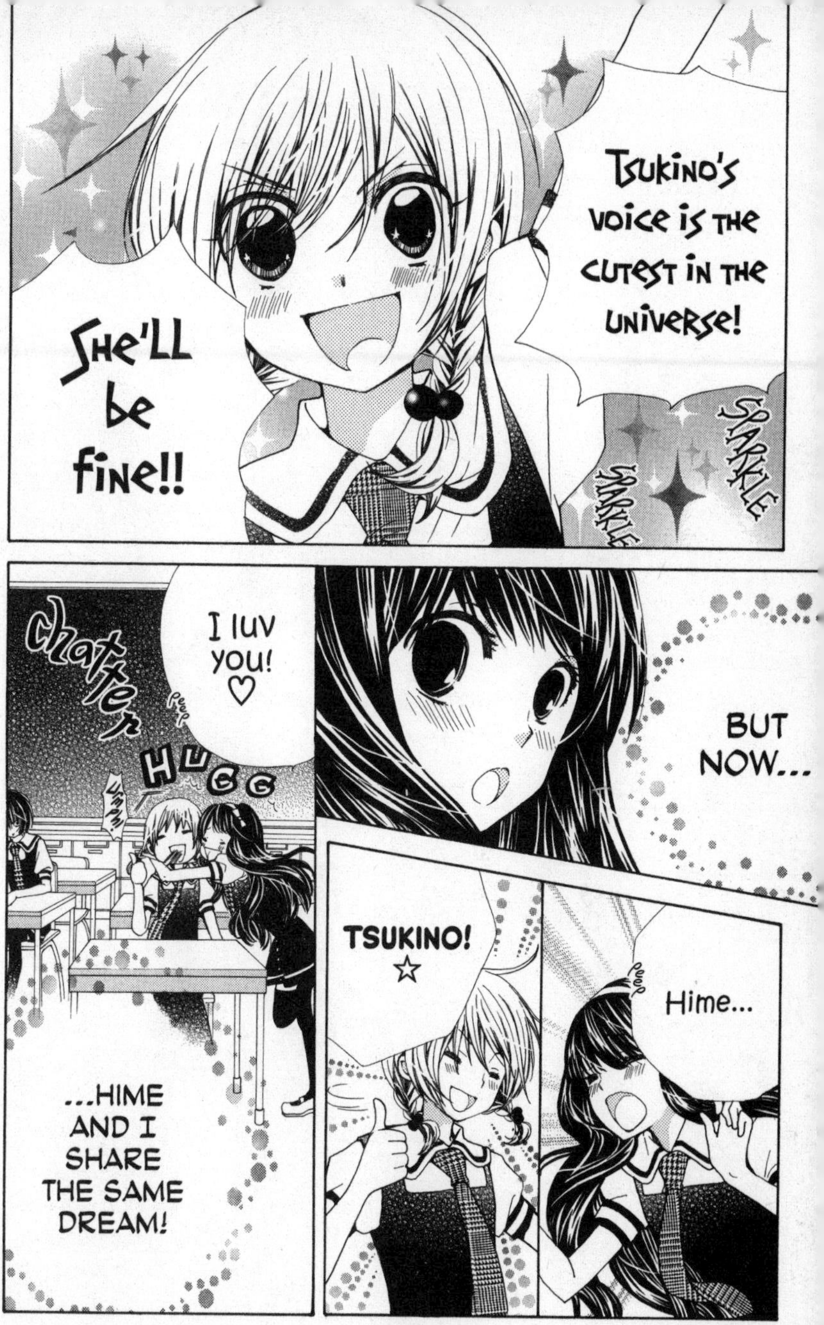
Tsukino's voice is the cutest in the universe!
She'll be fine!!
SPARKLE
SPARKLE
BUT NOW...
peep
Hime...
TSUKINO! ☆
I luv you! ♡
chatter
peep
HUGG
...HIME AND I SHARE THE SAME DREAM!

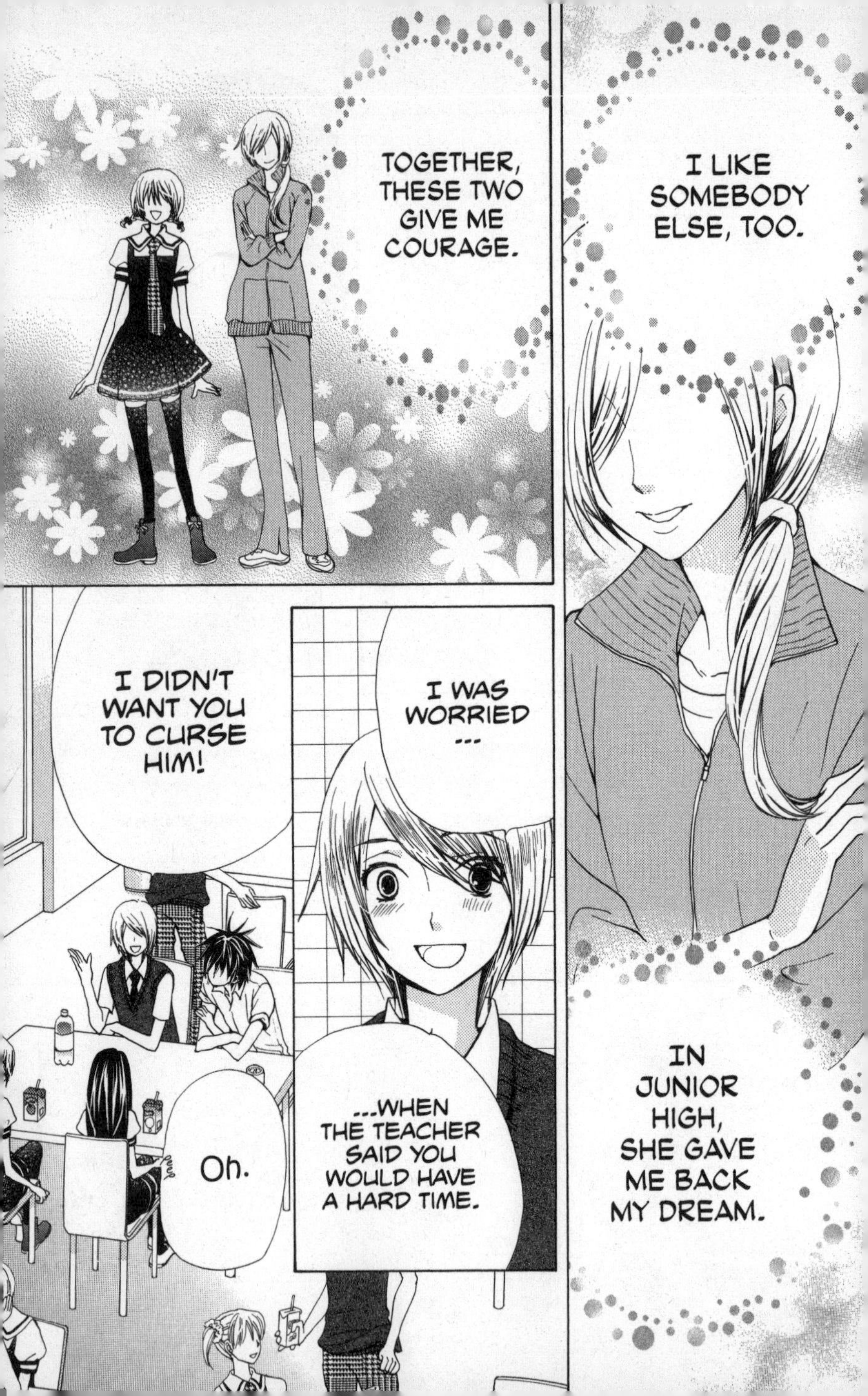
I LIKE SOMEBODY ELSE, TOO.
IN JUNIOR HIGH, SHE GAVE ME BACK MY DREAM.
TOGETHER, THESE TWO GIVE ME COURAGE.
I WAS WORRIED...
...WHEN THE TEACHER SAID YOU WOULD HAVE A HARD TIME.
I DIDN'T WANT YOU TO CURSE HIM!
Oh.

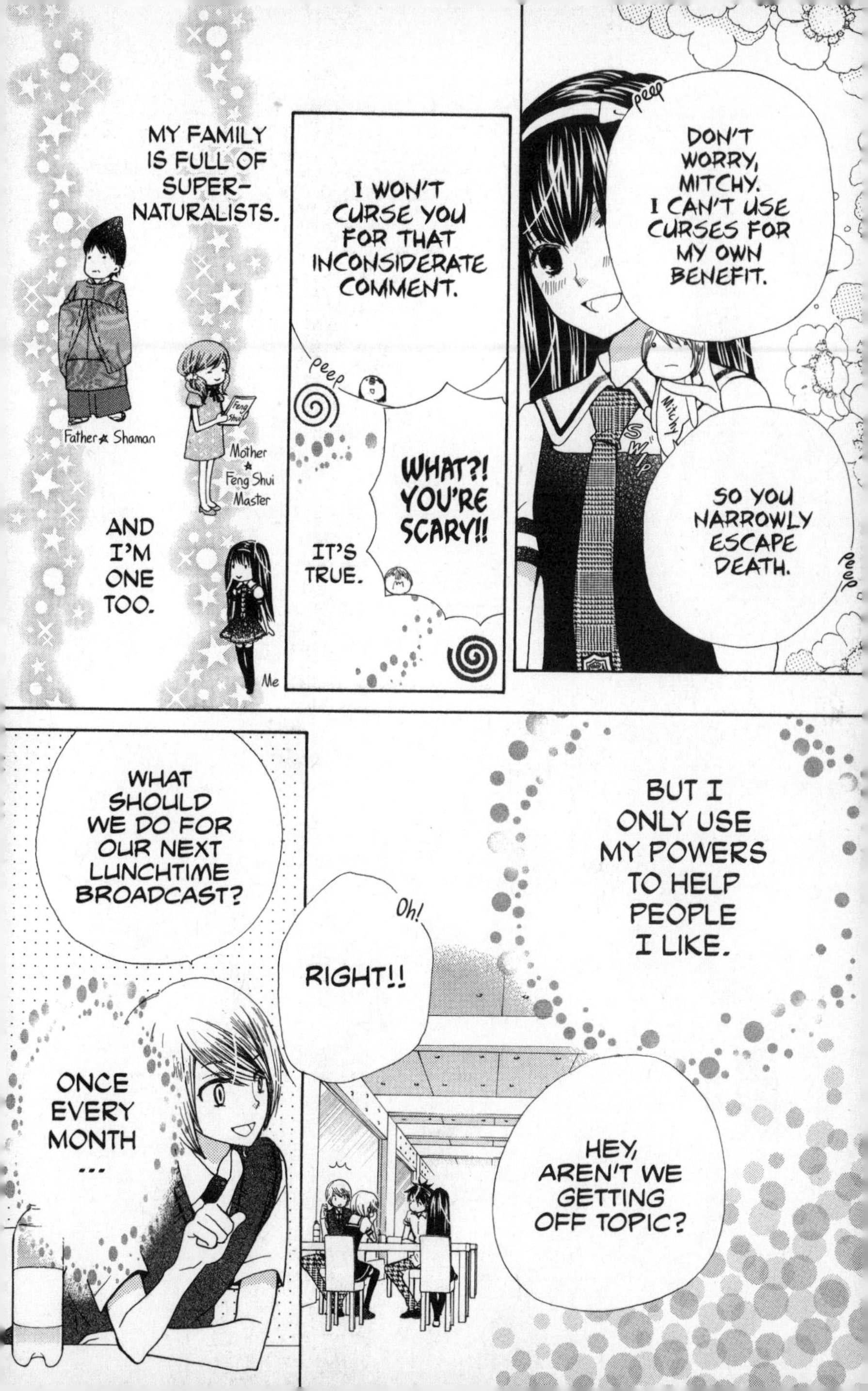
peep
DON'T WORRY, MITCHY. I CAN'T USE CURSES FOR MY OWN BENEFIT.
Mitchy
SWIP
SO YOU NARROWLY ESCAPE DEATH.
peep
I WON'T CURSE YOU FOR THAT INCONSIDERATE COMMENT.
peep
WHAT?! YOU'RE SCARY!!
IT'S TRUE.
MY FAMILY IS FULL OF SUPER-NATURALISTS.
Feng Shui
Father ★ Shaman
Mother ★ Feng Shui Master
AND I'M ONE TOO.
Me
BUT I ONLY USE MY POWERS TO HELP PEOPLE I LIKE.
HEY, AREN'T WE GETTING OFF TOPIC?
Oh!
RIGHT!!
WHAT SHOULD WE DO FOR OUR NEXT LUNCHTIME BROADCAST?
ONCE EVERY MONTH ...

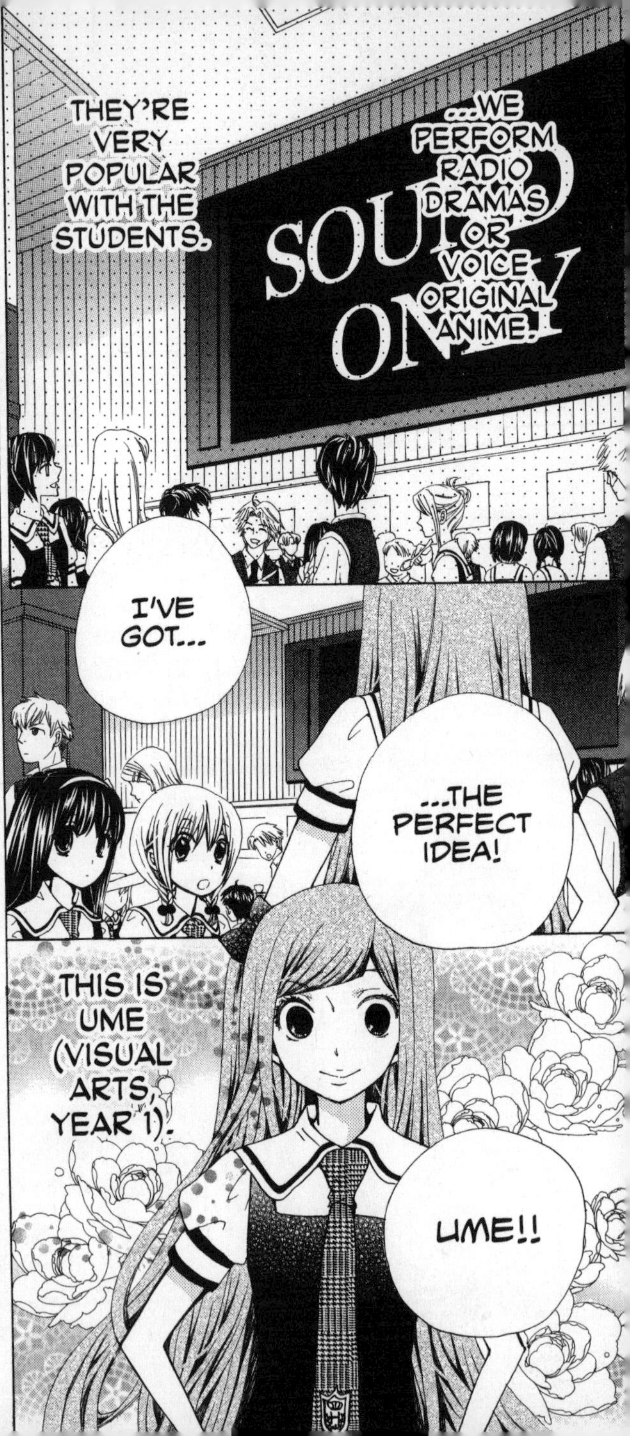
...WE PERFORM RADIO DRAMAS OR VOICE ORIGINAL ANIME.
THEY'RE VERY POPULAR WITH THE STUDENTS.
I'VE GOT...
...THE PERFECT IDEA!
UME!!
THIS IS UME (VISUAL ARTS, YEAR 1).

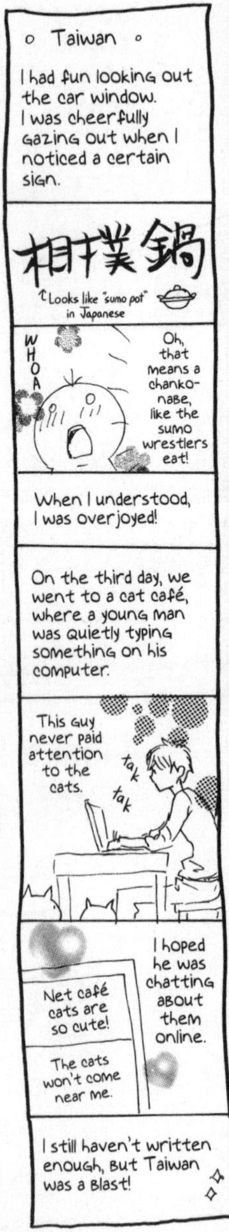
○ Taiwan ○
I had fun looking out the car window. I was cheerfully gazing out when I noticed a certain sign.
相撲鍋
↑Looks like "sumo pot" in Japanese
WHOA
Oh, that means a chanko-nabe, like the sumo wrestlers eat!
When I understood, I was overjoyed!
On the third day, we went to a cat café, where a young man was quietly typing something on his computer.
This guy never paid attention to the cats.
tak tak
I hoped he was chatting about them online.
Net café cats are so cute!
The cats won't come near me.
I still haven't written enough, but Taiwan was a blast!

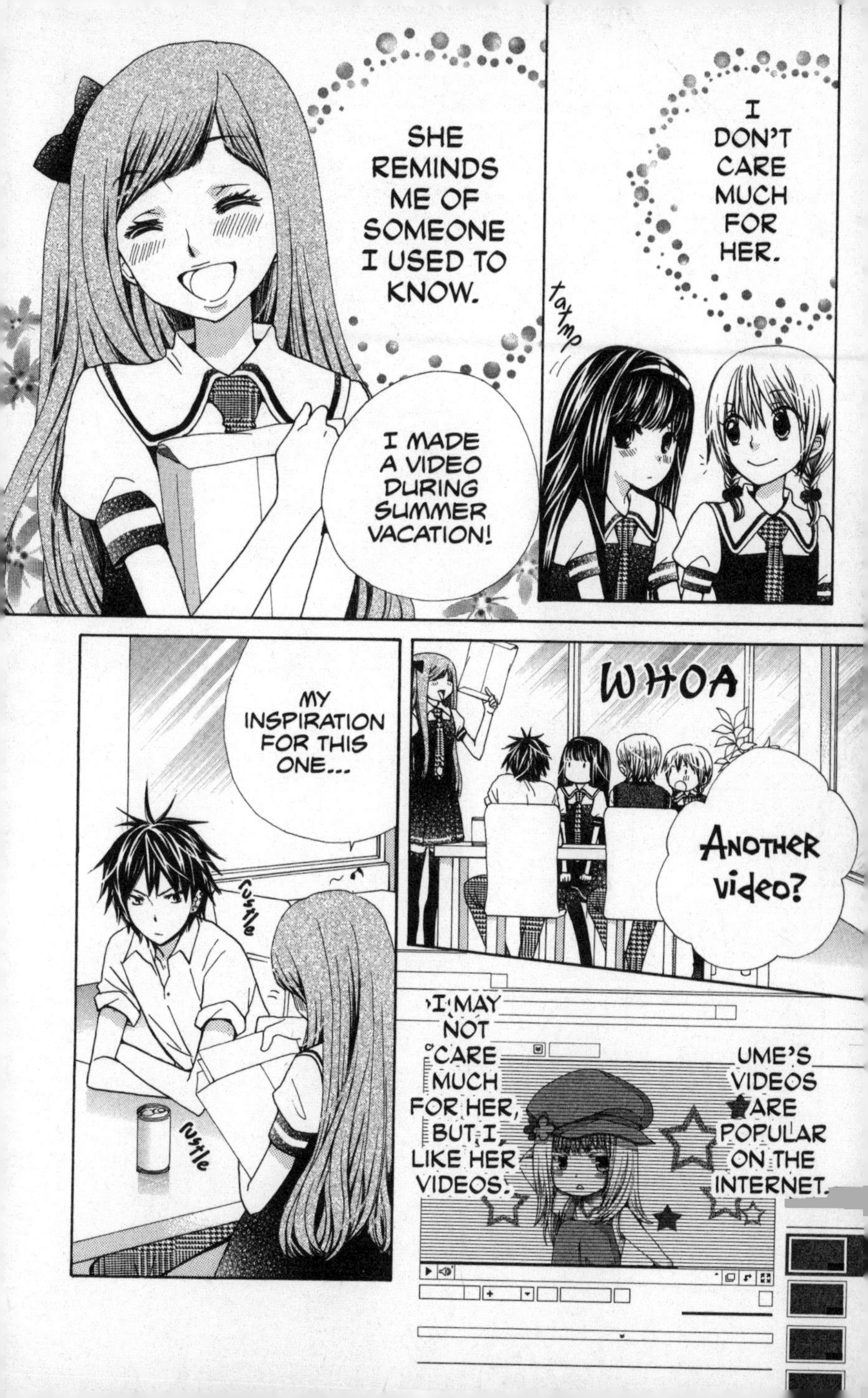
I DON'T CARE MUCH FOR HER.
tatmp
SHE REMINDS ME OF SOMEONE I USED TO KNOW.
I MADE A VIDEO DURING SUMMER VACATION!
WHOA
Another video?
UME'S VIDEOS ARE POPULAR ON THE INTERNET.
I MAY NOT CARE MUCH FOR HER, BUT I LIKE HER VIDEOS.
MY INSPIRATION FOR THIS ONE...
rustle
rustle

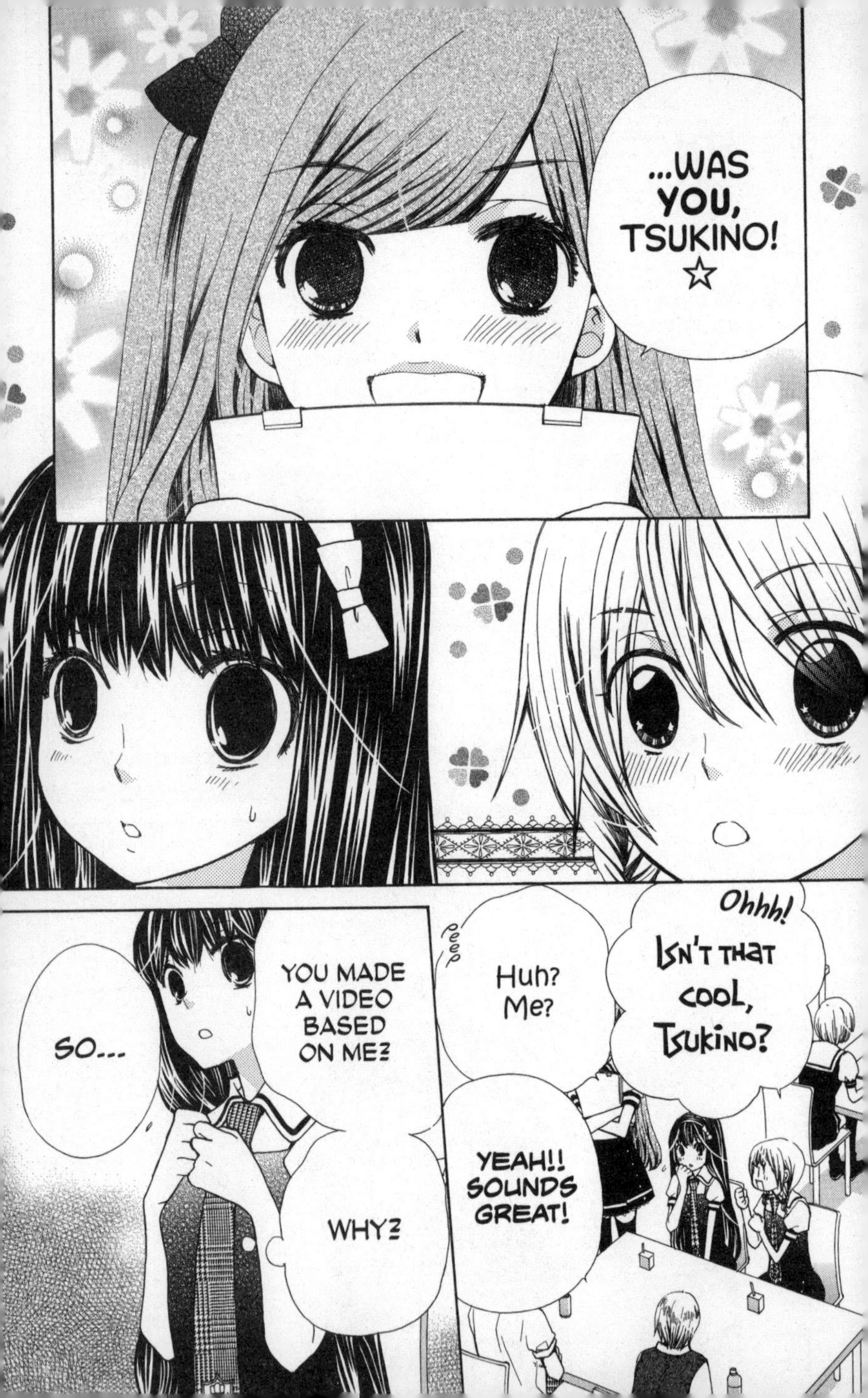
...WAS YOU, TSUKINO! ☆
Ohhh!
ISN'T THAT COOL, TSUKINO?
Huh? Me?
Peep
YEAH!! SOUNDS GREAT!
YOU MADE A VIDEO BASED ON ME?
SO...
WHY?

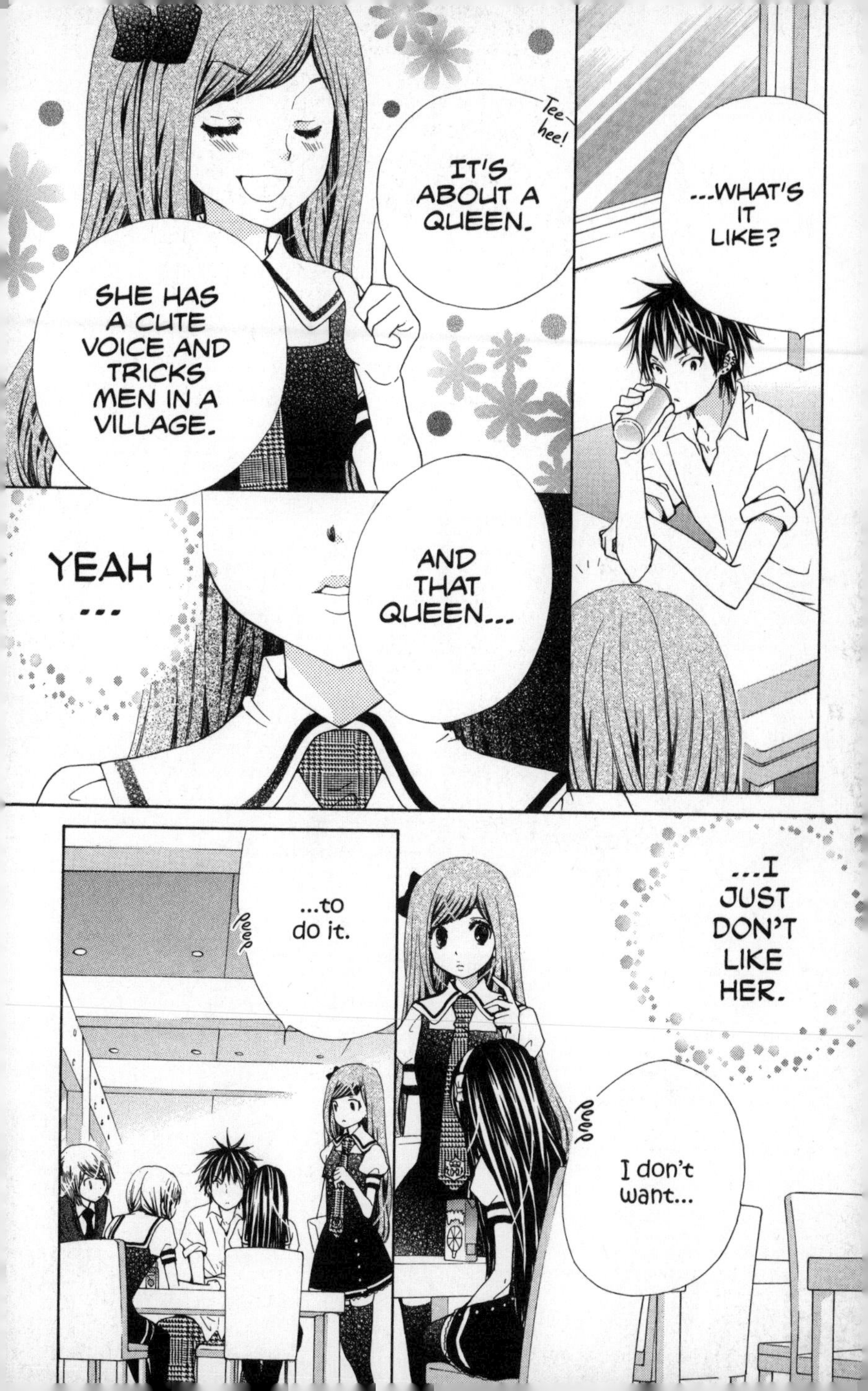
...WHAT'S IT LIKE?
Tee-hee!
IT'S ABOUT A QUEEN.
SHE HAS A CUTE VOICE AND TRICKS MEN IN A VILLAGE.
AND THAT QUEEN...
YEAH ...
...I JUST DON'T LIKE HER.
Peep
I don't want...
Peep
...to do it.

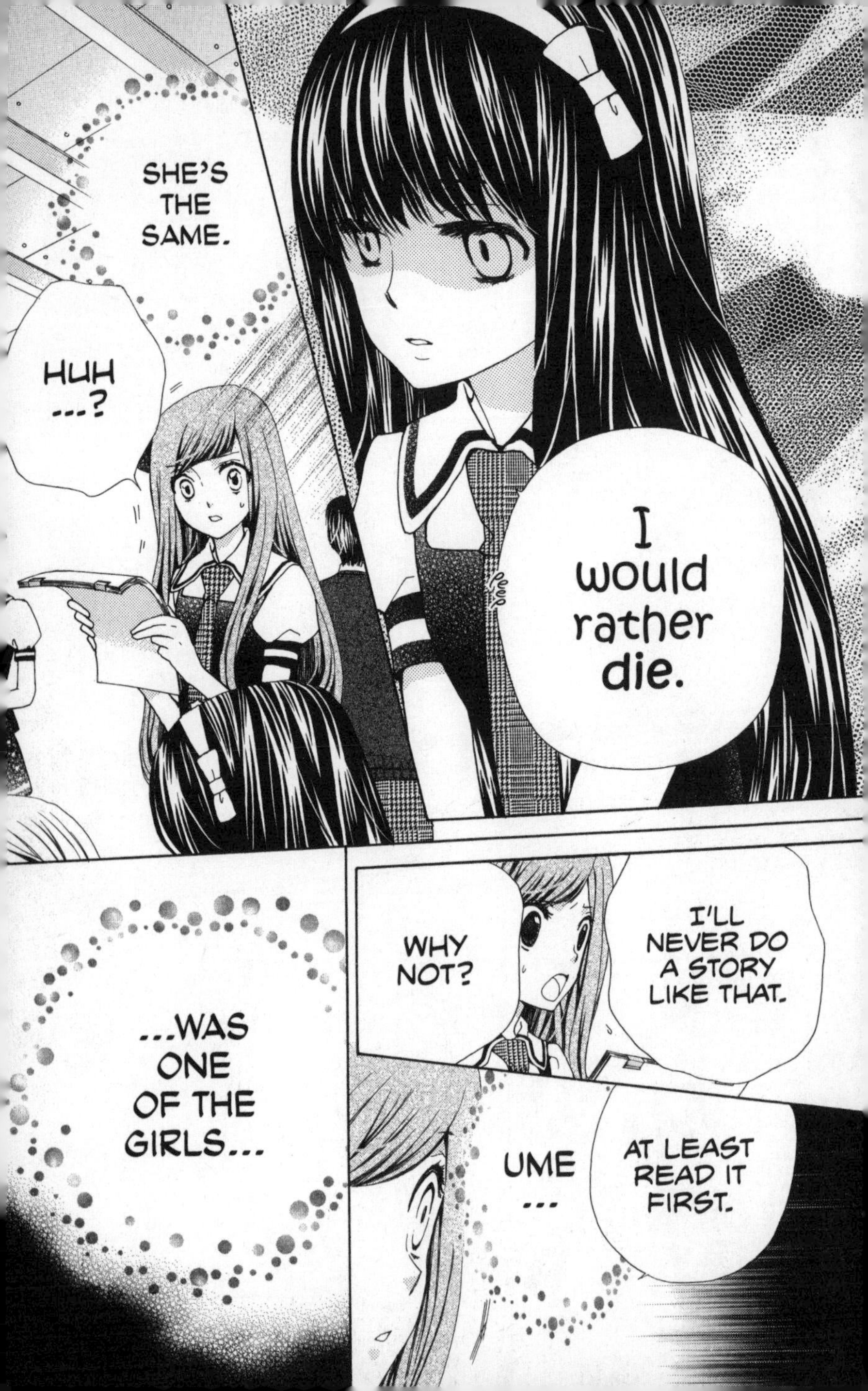
I would rather die.
SHE'S THE SAME.
HUH...?
I'LL NEVER DO A STORY LIKE THAT.
WHY NOT?
AT LEAST READ IT FIRST.
UME...
...WAS ONE OF THE GIRLS...

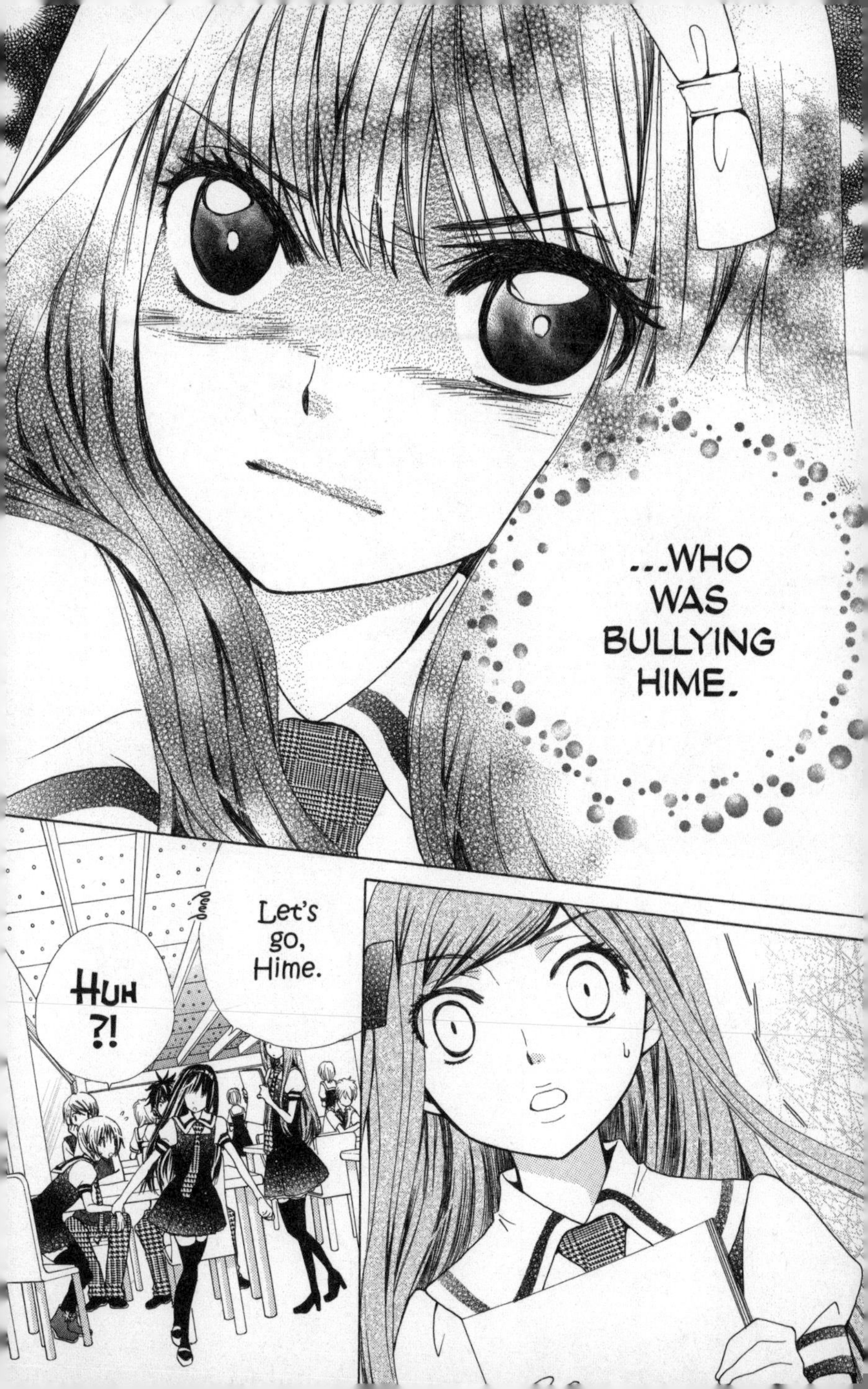
...WHO WAS BULLYING HIME.
Let's go, Hime.
HUH?!

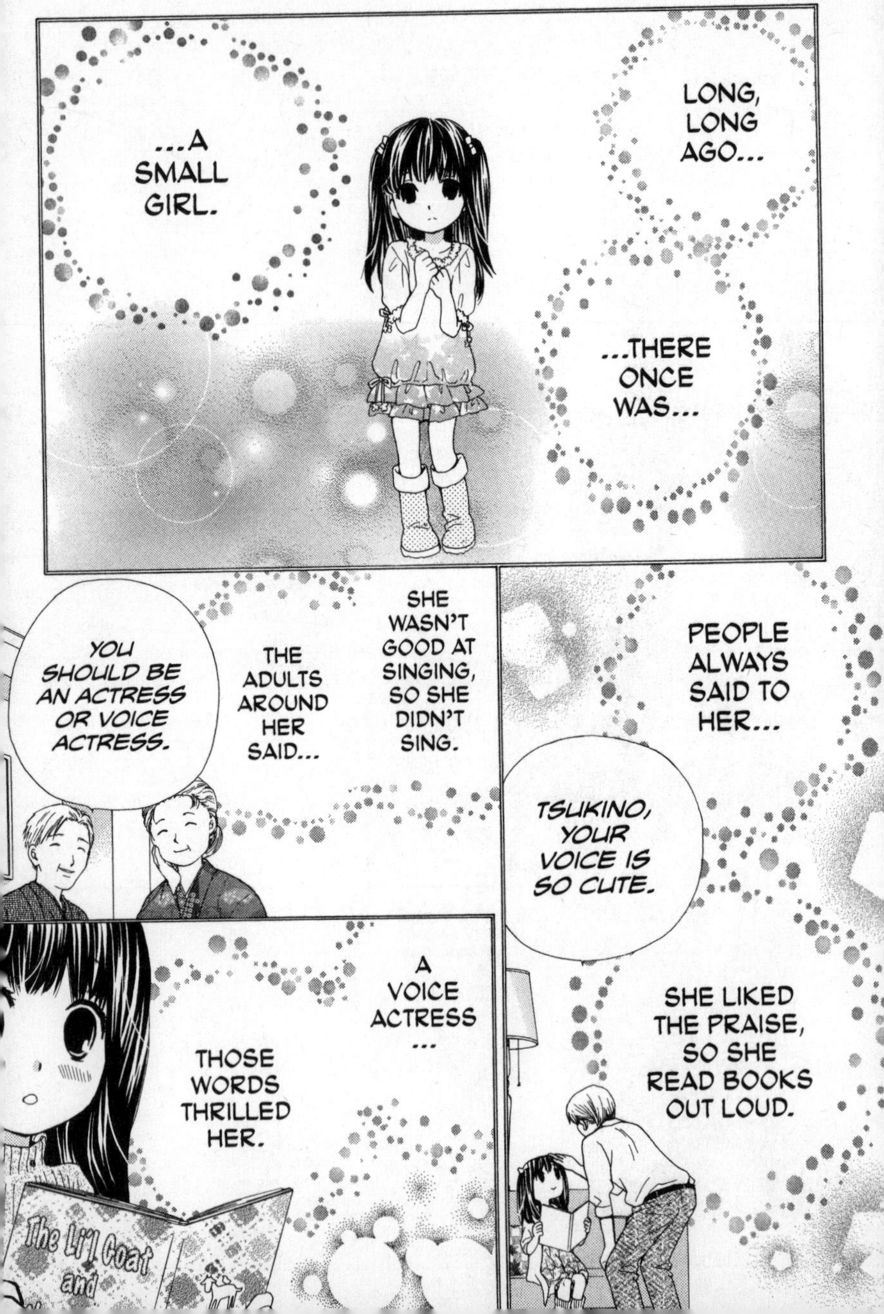
LONG, LONG AGO...
...THERE ONCE WAS...
...A SMALL GIRL.
PEOPLE ALWAYS SAID TO HER...
TSUKINO, YOUR VOICE IS SO CUTE.
SHE LIKED THE PRAISE, SO SHE READ BOOKS OUT LOUD.
SHE WASN'T GOOD AT SINGING, SO SHE DIDN'T SING.
THE ADULTS AROUND HER SAID...
YOU SHOULD BE AN ACTRESS OR VOICE ACTRESS.
A VOICE ACTRESS...
THOSE WORDS THRILLED HER.
The Li'l Goat and

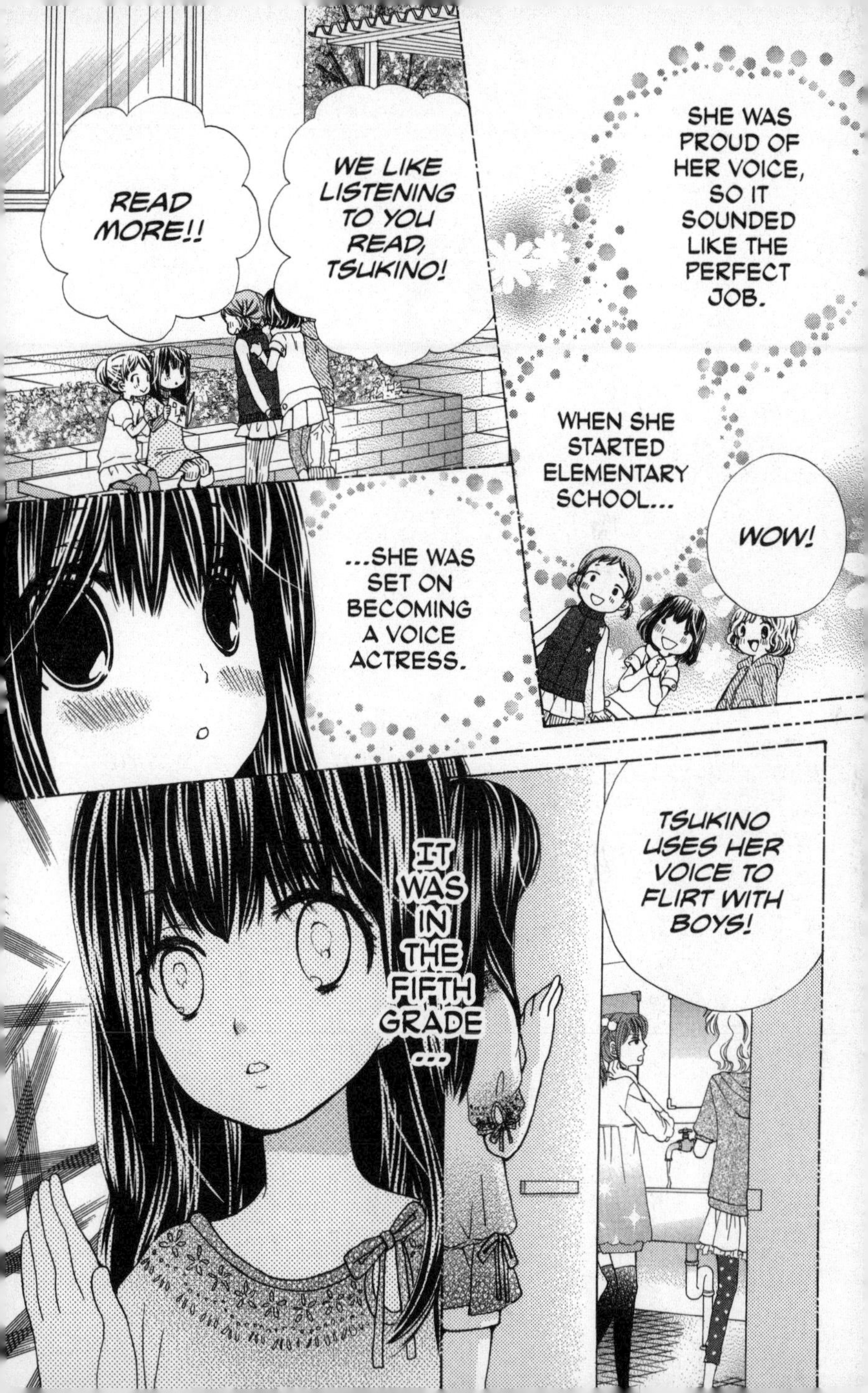
SHE WAS PROUD OF HER VOICE, SO IT SOUNDED LIKE THE PERFECT JOB.
WE LIKE LISTENING TO YOU READ, TSUKINO!
READ MORE!!
WHEN SHE STARTED ELEMENTARY SCHOOL...
WOW!
...SHE WAS SET ON BECOMING A VOICE ACTRESS.
TSUKINO USES HER VOICE TO FLIRT WITH BOYS!
IT WAS IN THE FIFTH GRADE...

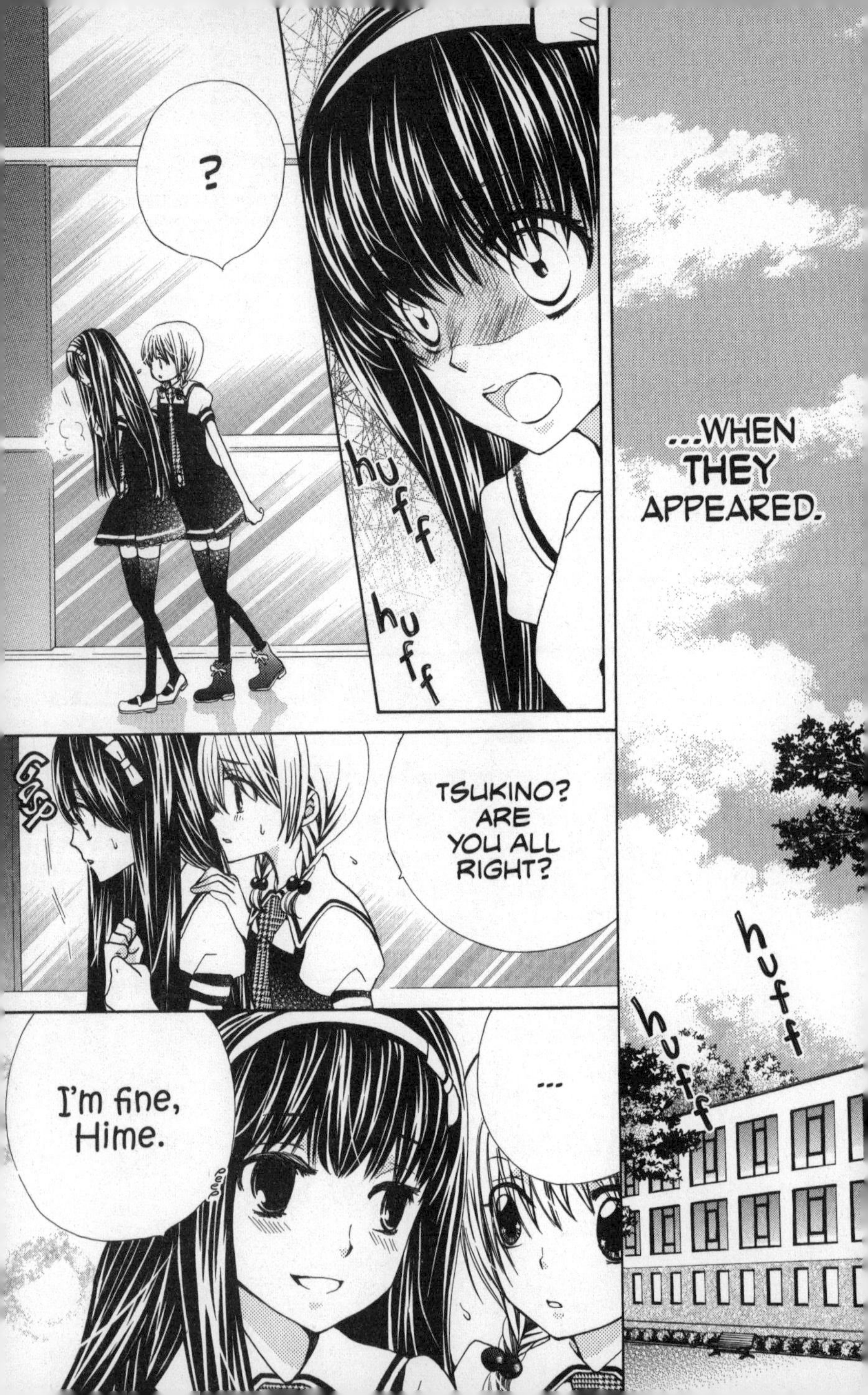
...WHEN THEY APPEARED.
huff
huff
huff
huff
huff
huff
?
TSUKINO? ARE YOU ALL RIGHT?
Gasp
...
I'm fine, Hime.

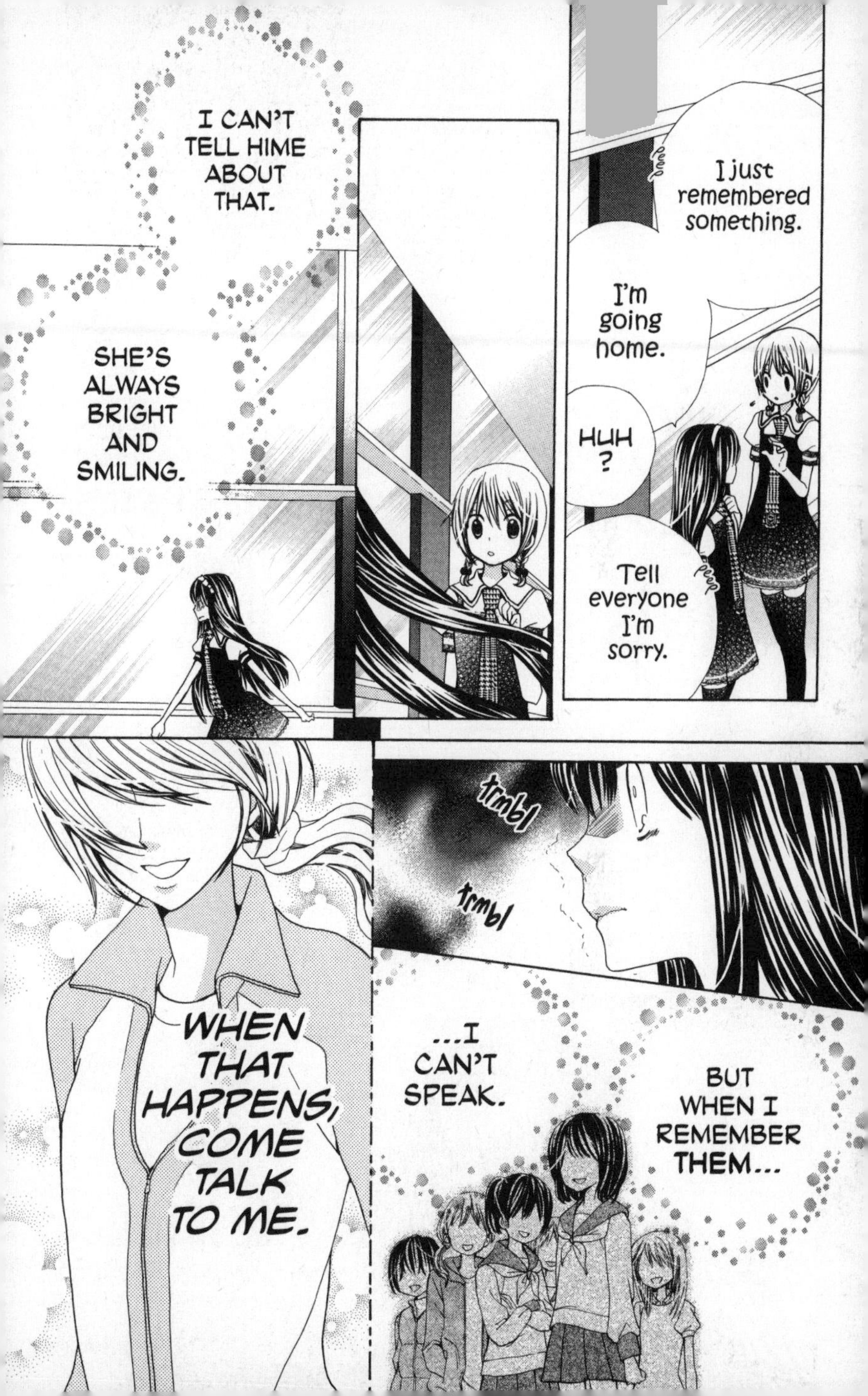
I just remembered something.
I'm going home.
HUH?
Tell everyone I'm sorry.
I CAN'T TELL HIME ABOUT THAT.
SHE'S ALWAYS BRIGHT AND SMILING.
trmbl
trmbl
BUT WHEN I REMEMBER THEM...
...I CAN'T SPEAK.
WHEN THAT HAPPENS, COME TALK TO ME.

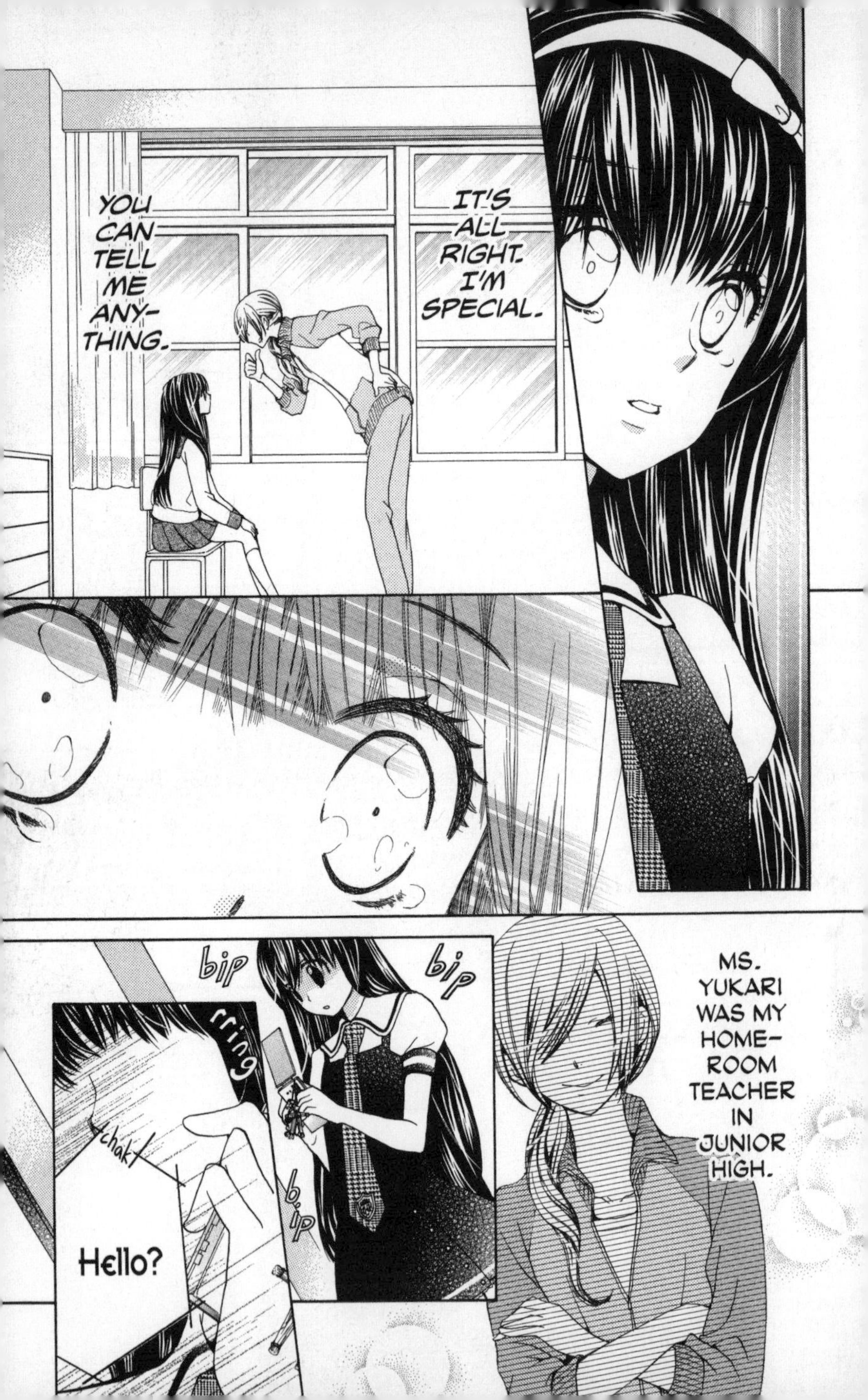

IT'S ALL RIGHT. I'M SPECIAL.
YOU CAN TELL ME ANYTHING.
MS. YUKARI WAS MY HOMEROOM TEACHER IN JUNIOR HIGH.
bip
bip
rring
chak
bip
Hello?

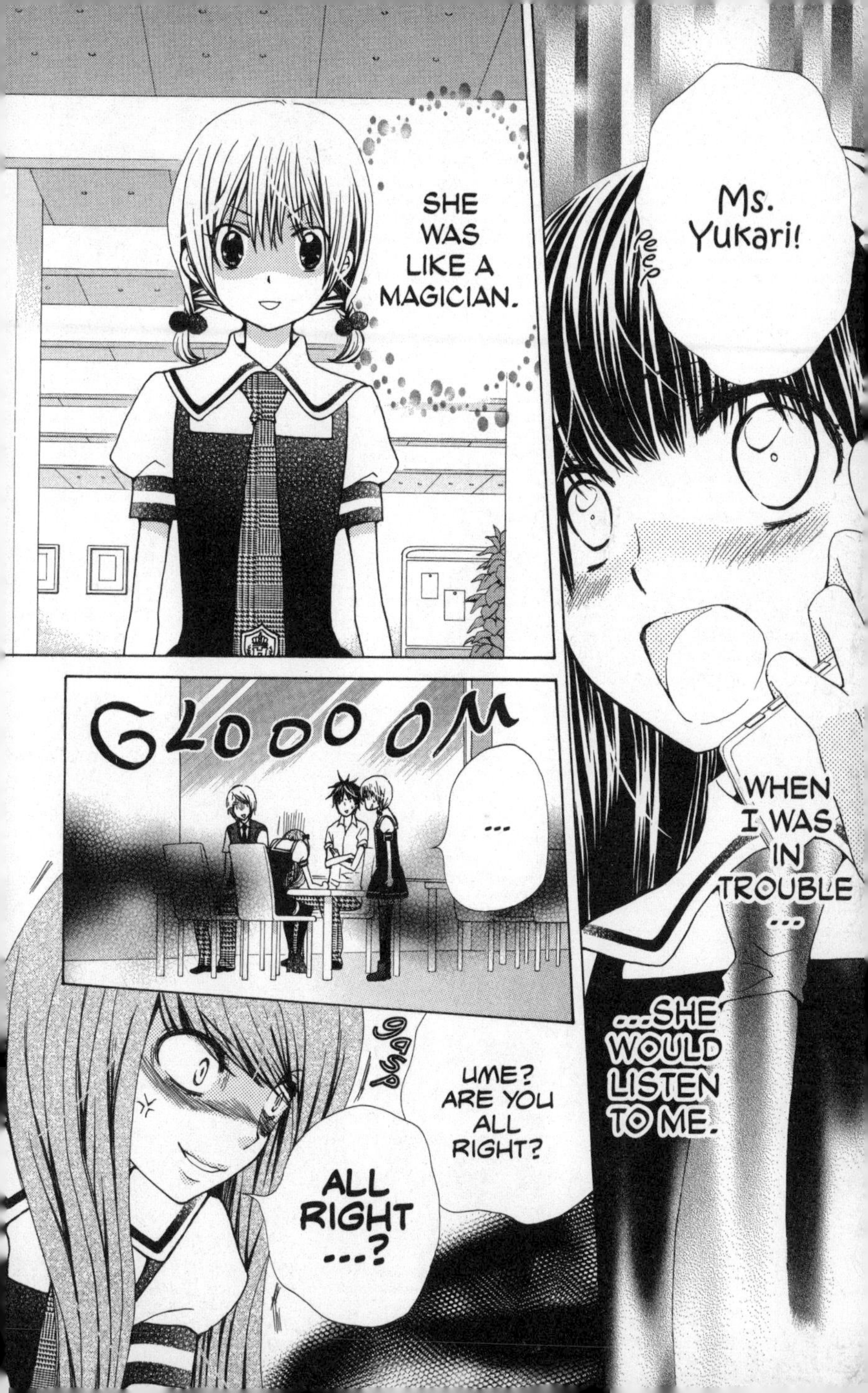
Ms. Yukari!
peep
WHEN I WAS IN TROUBLE...
...SHE WOULD LISTEN TO ME.
SHE WAS LIKE A MAGICIAN.
GLOOOOM
...
gasp
UME? ARE YOU ALL RIGHT?
ALL RIGHT...?

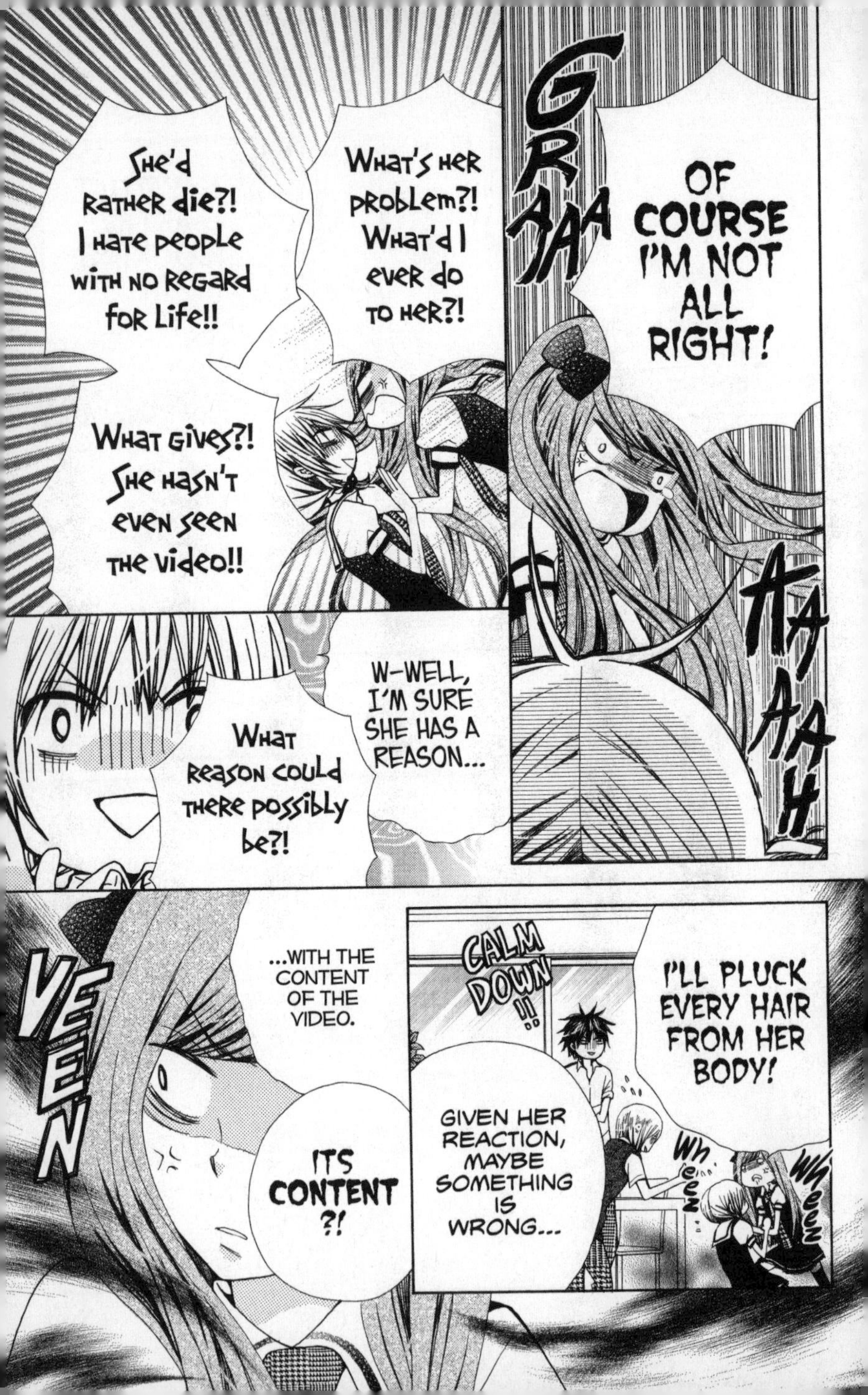
GRAAA
OF COURSE I'M NOT ALL RIGHT!
AAAAH
What's her problem?! What'd I ever do to her?!
She'd rather die?! I hate people with no regard for life!!
What gives?! She hasn't even seen the video!!
W-WELL, I'M SURE SHE HAS A REASON...
What reason could there possibly be?!
I'LL PLUCK EVERY HAIR FROM HER BODY!
CALM DOWN!!
GIVEN HER REACTION, MAYBE SOMETHING IS WRONG...
...WITH THE CONTENT OF THE VIDEO.
VEEEN
ITS CONTENT?!

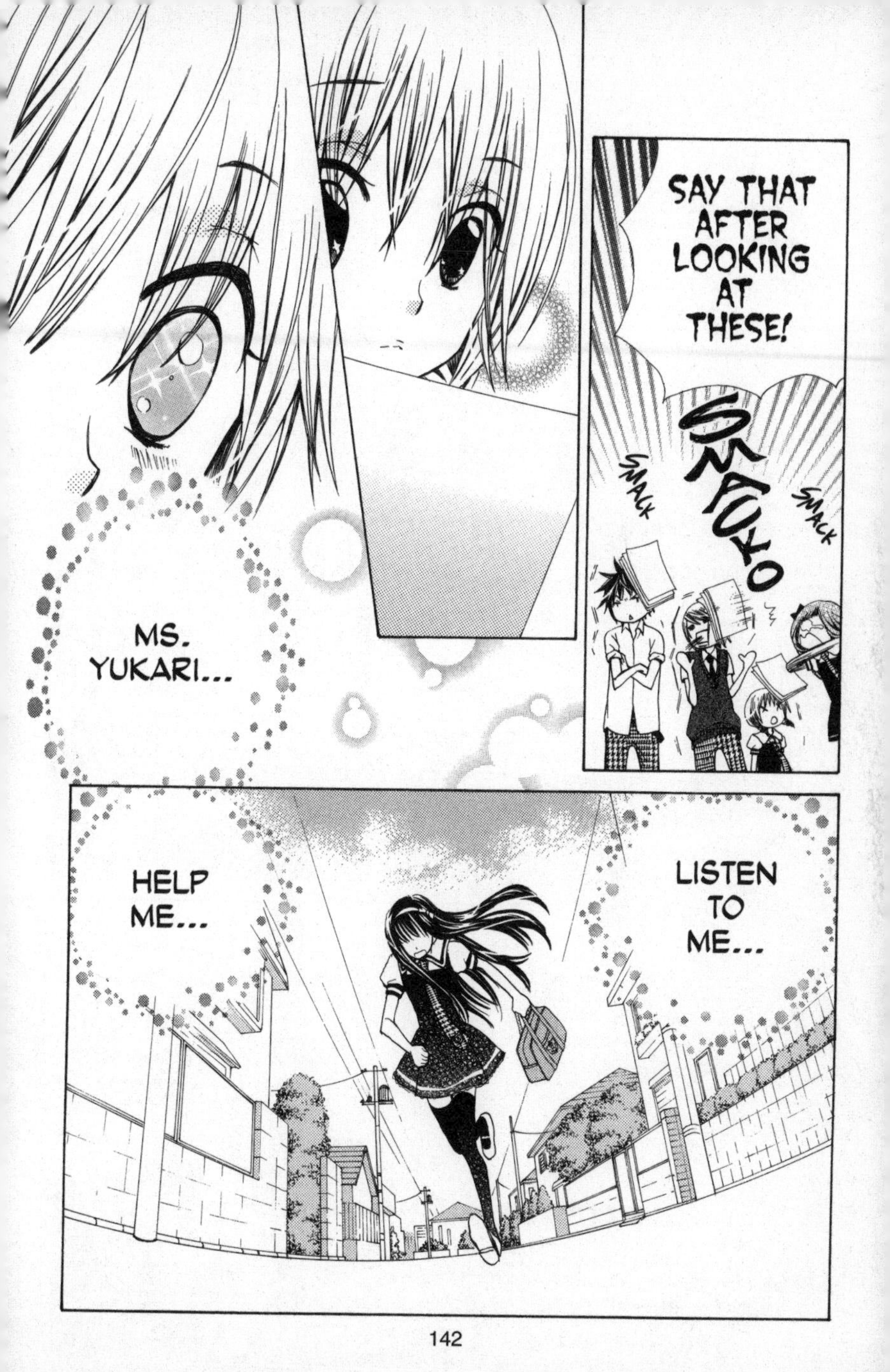
SAY THAT AFTER LOOKING AT THESE!
SMACK
SMACKO
SMACK
MS. YUKARI...
LISTEN TO ME...
HELP ME...

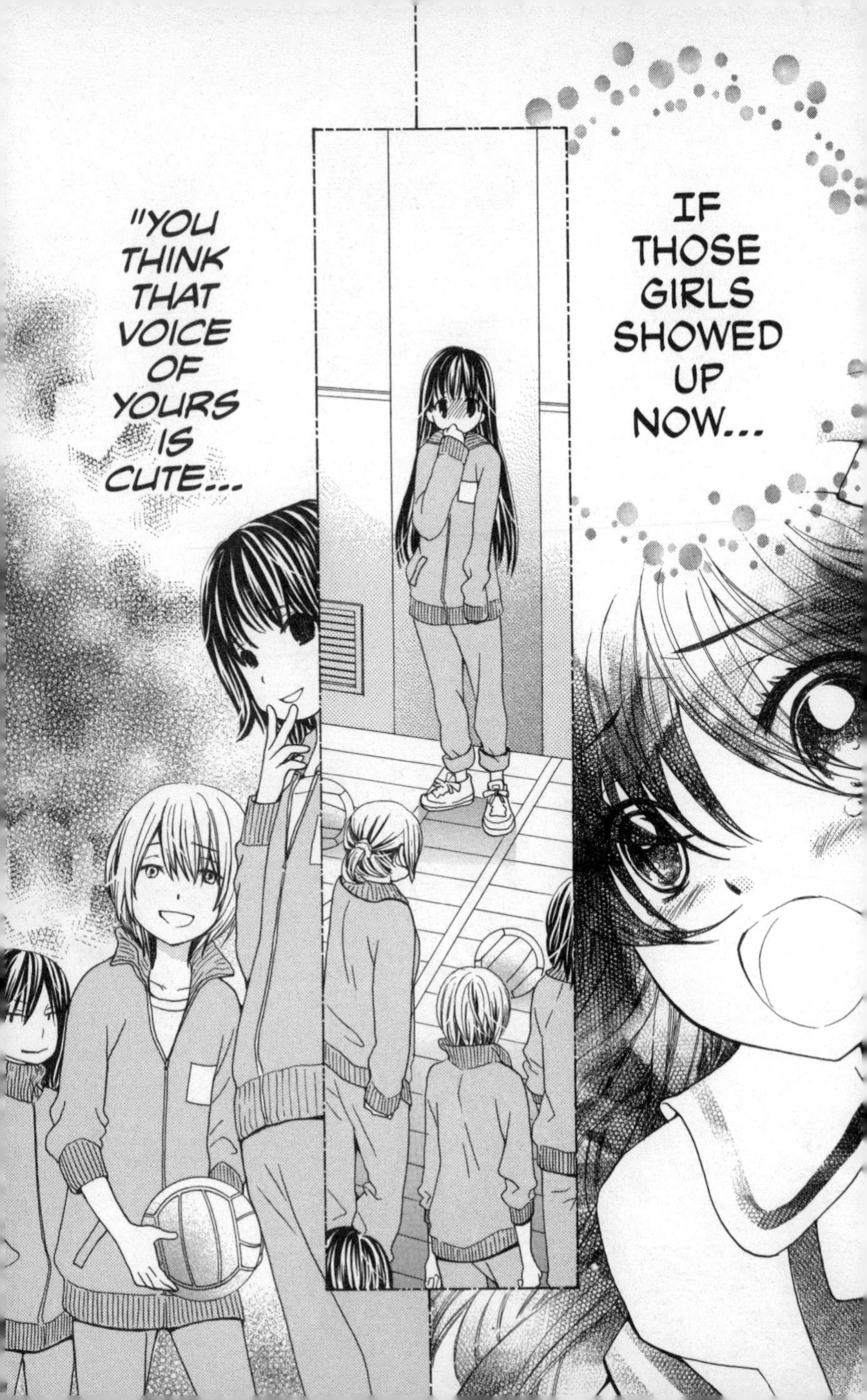
IF THOSE GIRLS SHOWED UP NOW...
"YOU THINK THAT VOICE OF YOURS IS CUTE...

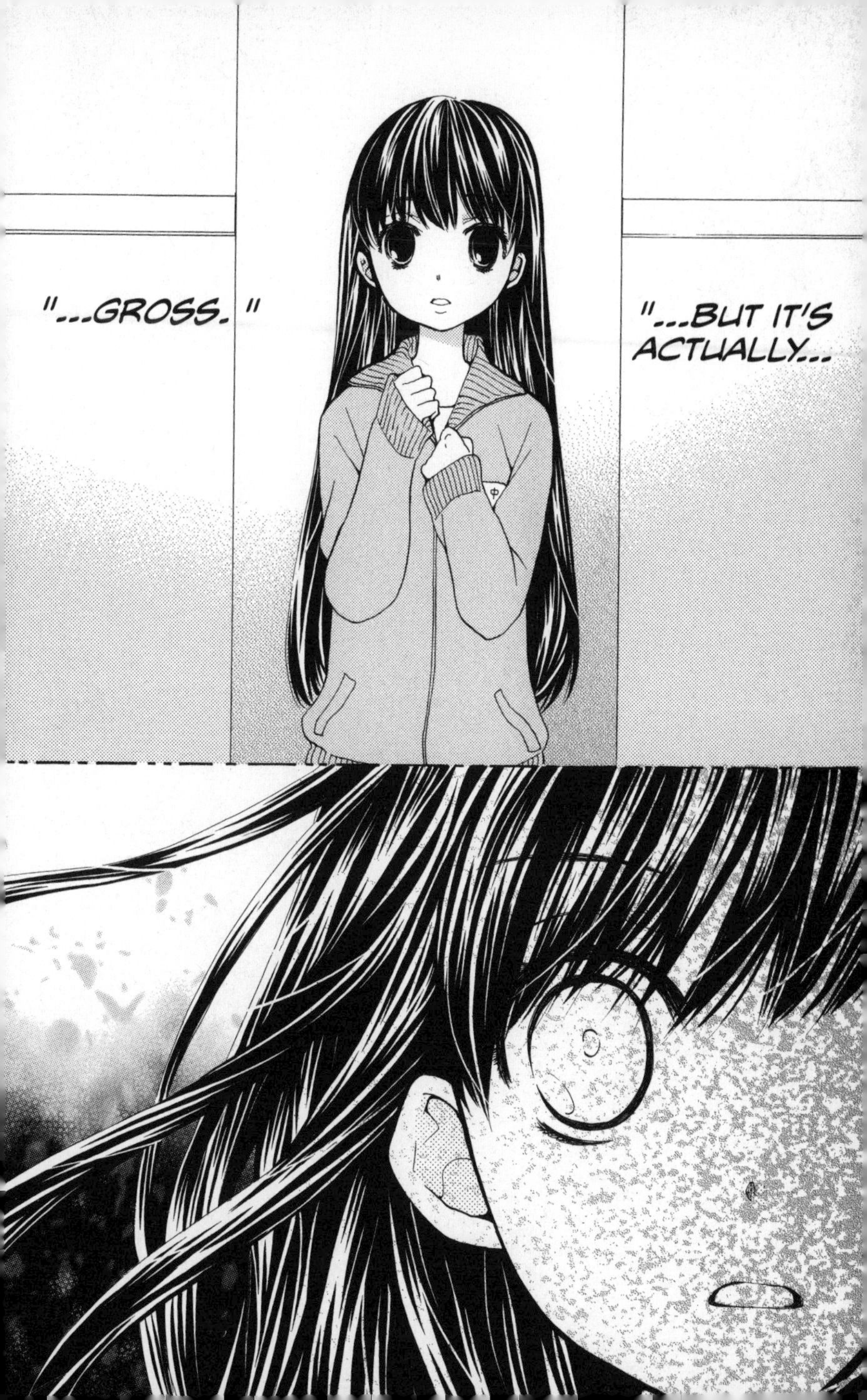
"...BUT IT'S ACTUALLY...
"...GROSS."

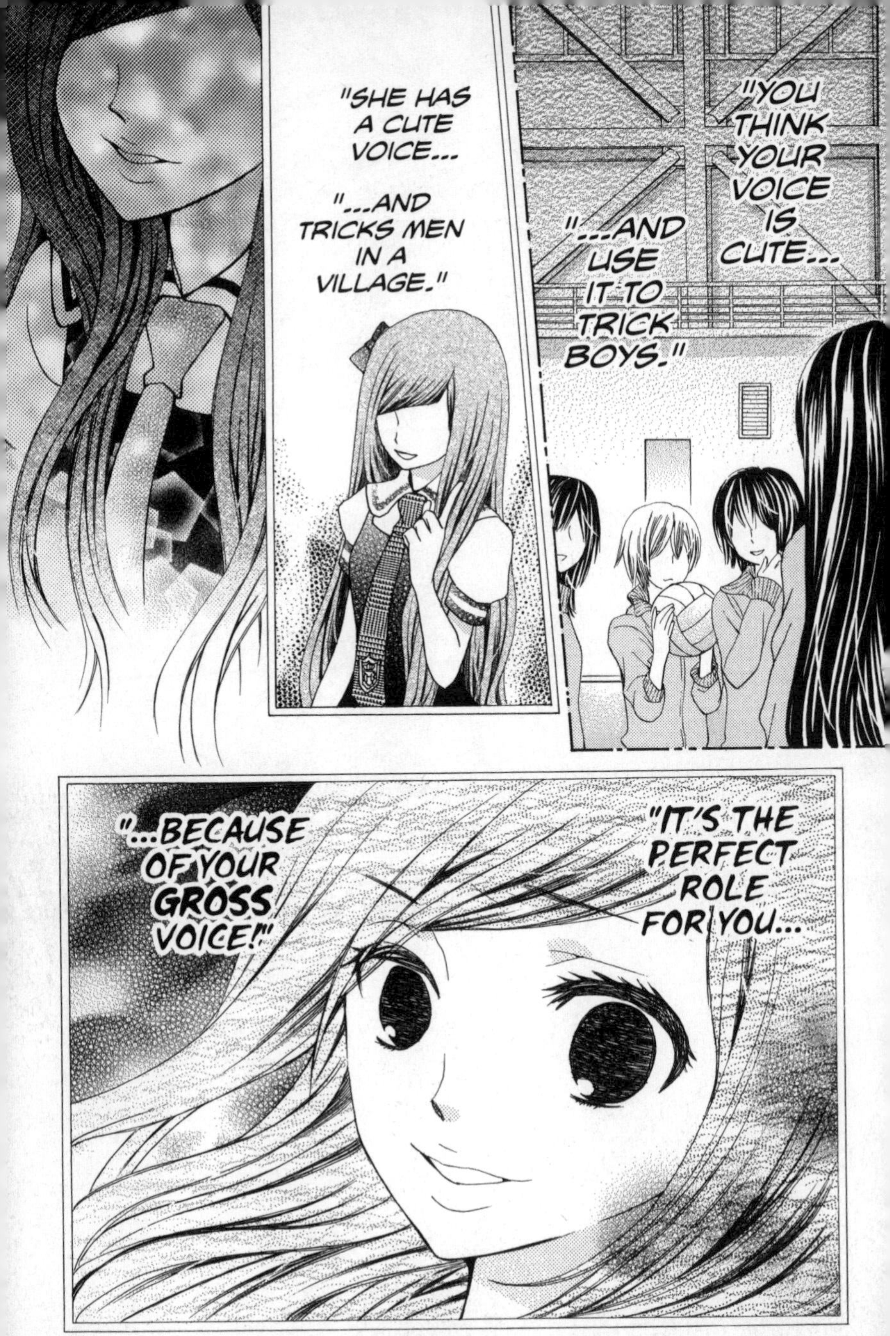
"YOU THINK YOUR VOICE IS CUTE...
"...AND USE IT TO TRICK BOYS."
"SHE HAS A CUTE VOICE...
"...AND TRICKS MEN IN A VILLAGE."
"IT'S THE PERFECT ROLE FOR YOU...
"...BECAUSE OF YOUR GROSS VOICE!"

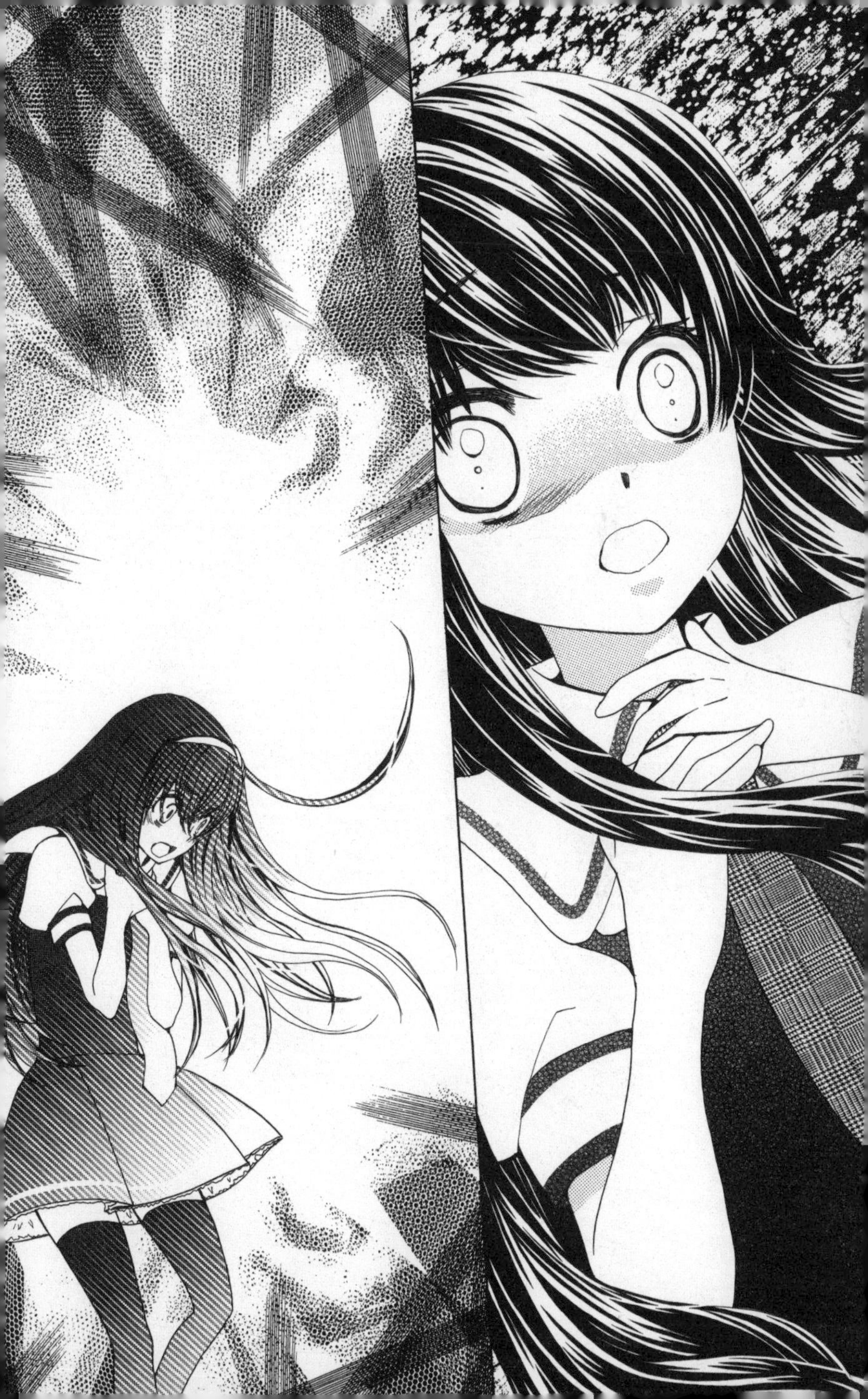

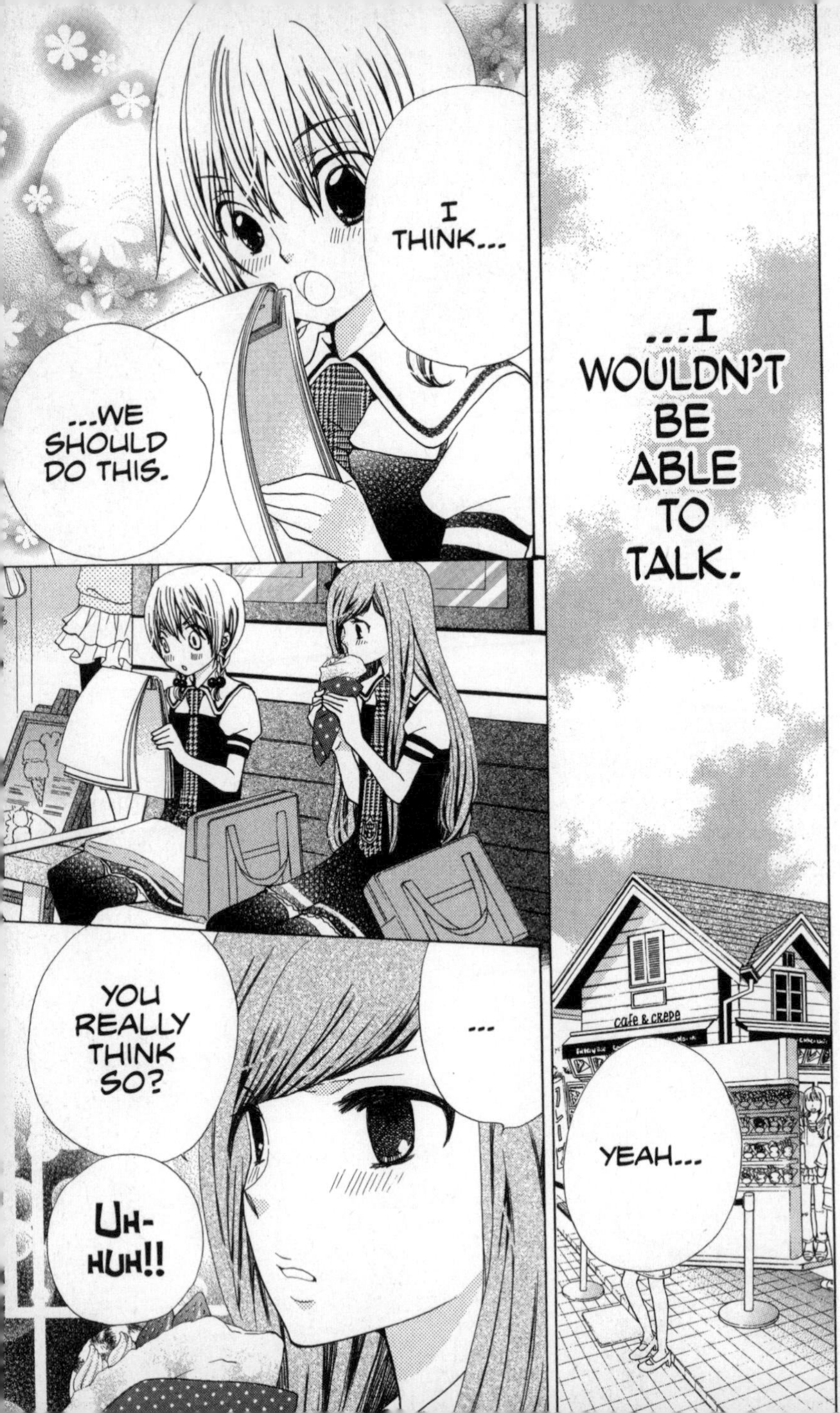
...I WOULDN'T BE ABLE TO TALK.
cafe & crepe
YEAH...
I THINK...
...WE SHOULD DO THIS.
...
YOU REALLY THINK SO?
UH-HUH!!

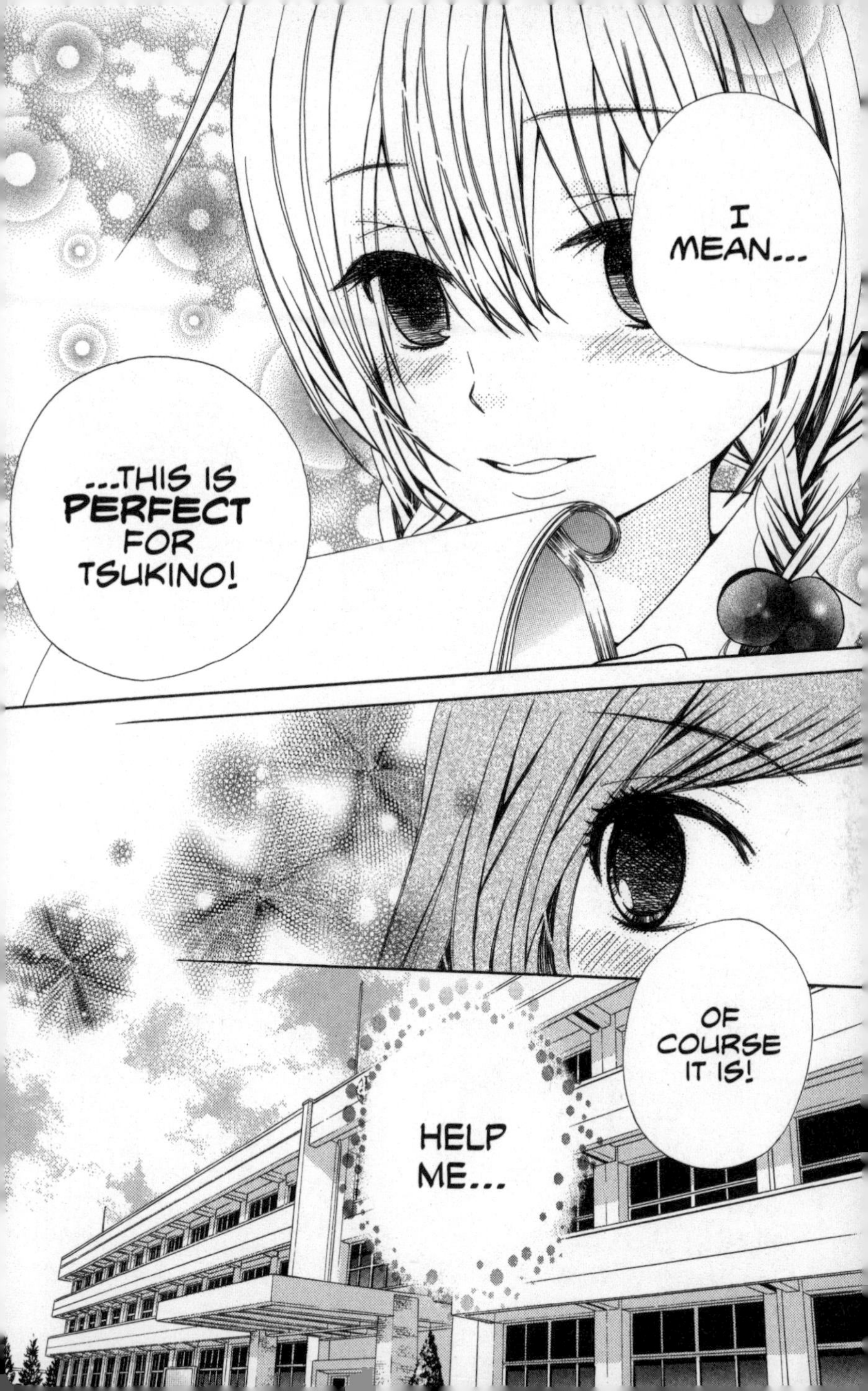
I MEAN...
...THIS IS **PERFECT** FOR TSUKINO!
OF COURSE IT IS!
HELP ME...

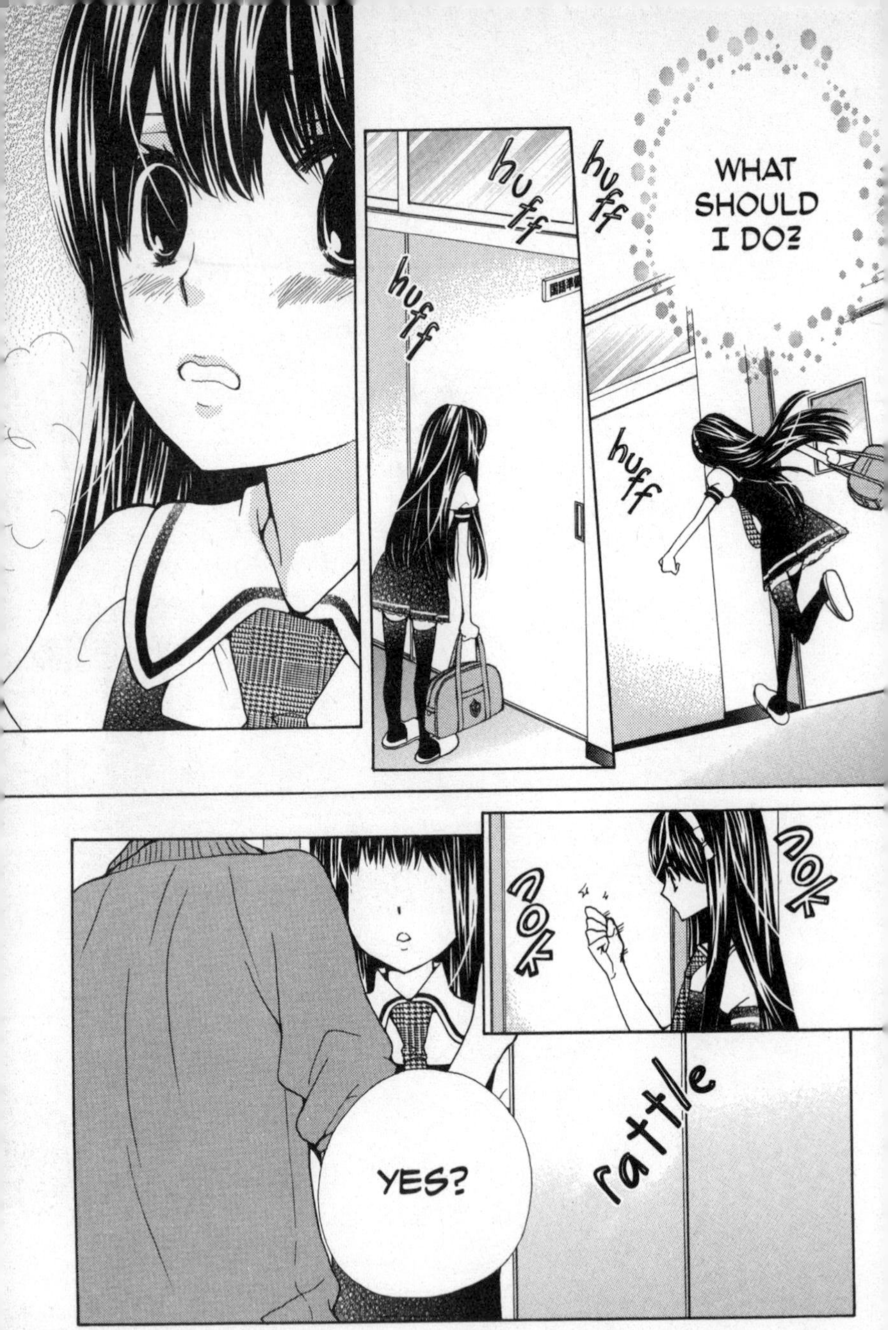
WHAT SHOULD I DO?
huff
huff
huff
huff
nok
nok
rattle
YES?

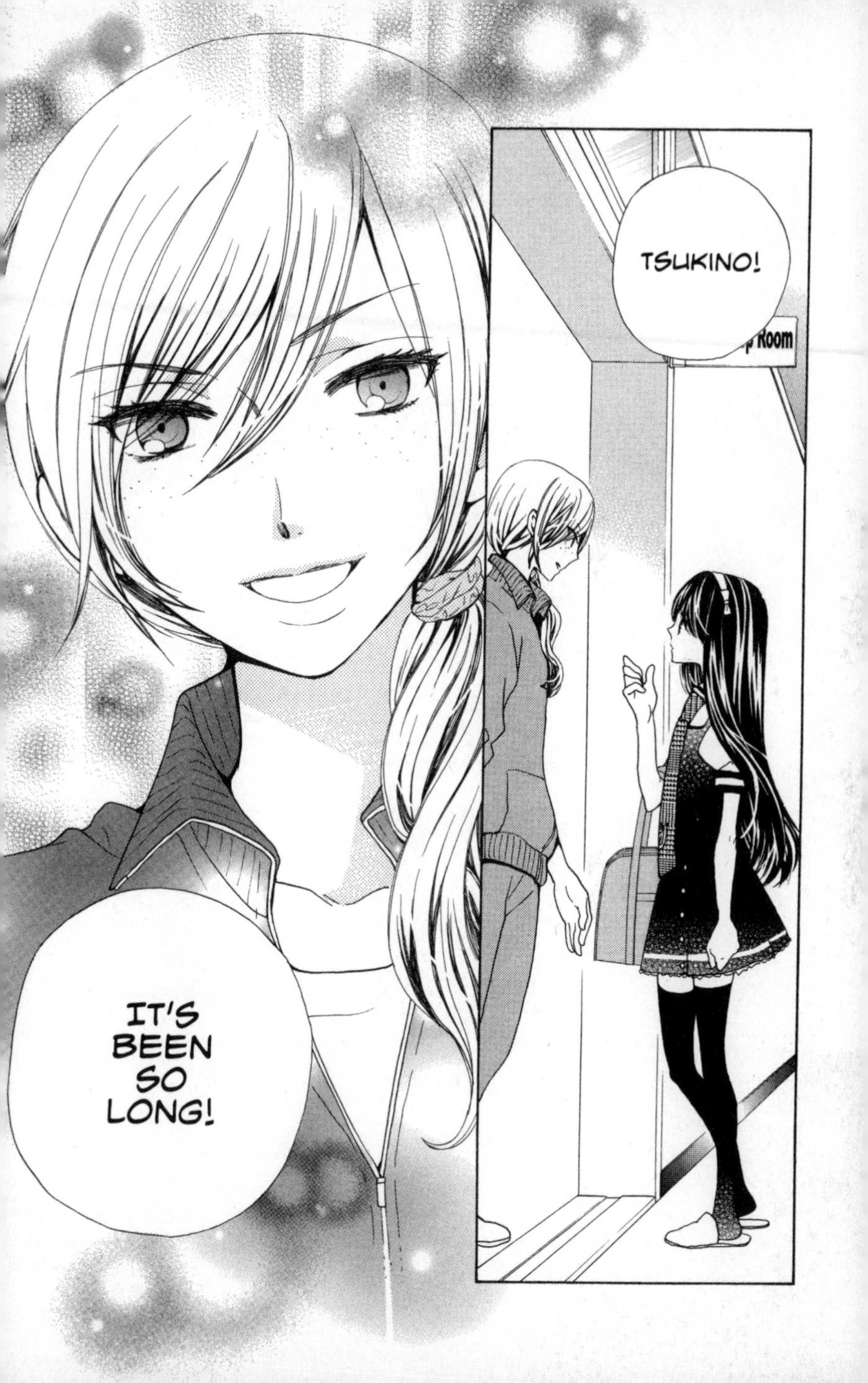
TSUKINO!
Room
IT'S BEEN SO LONG!

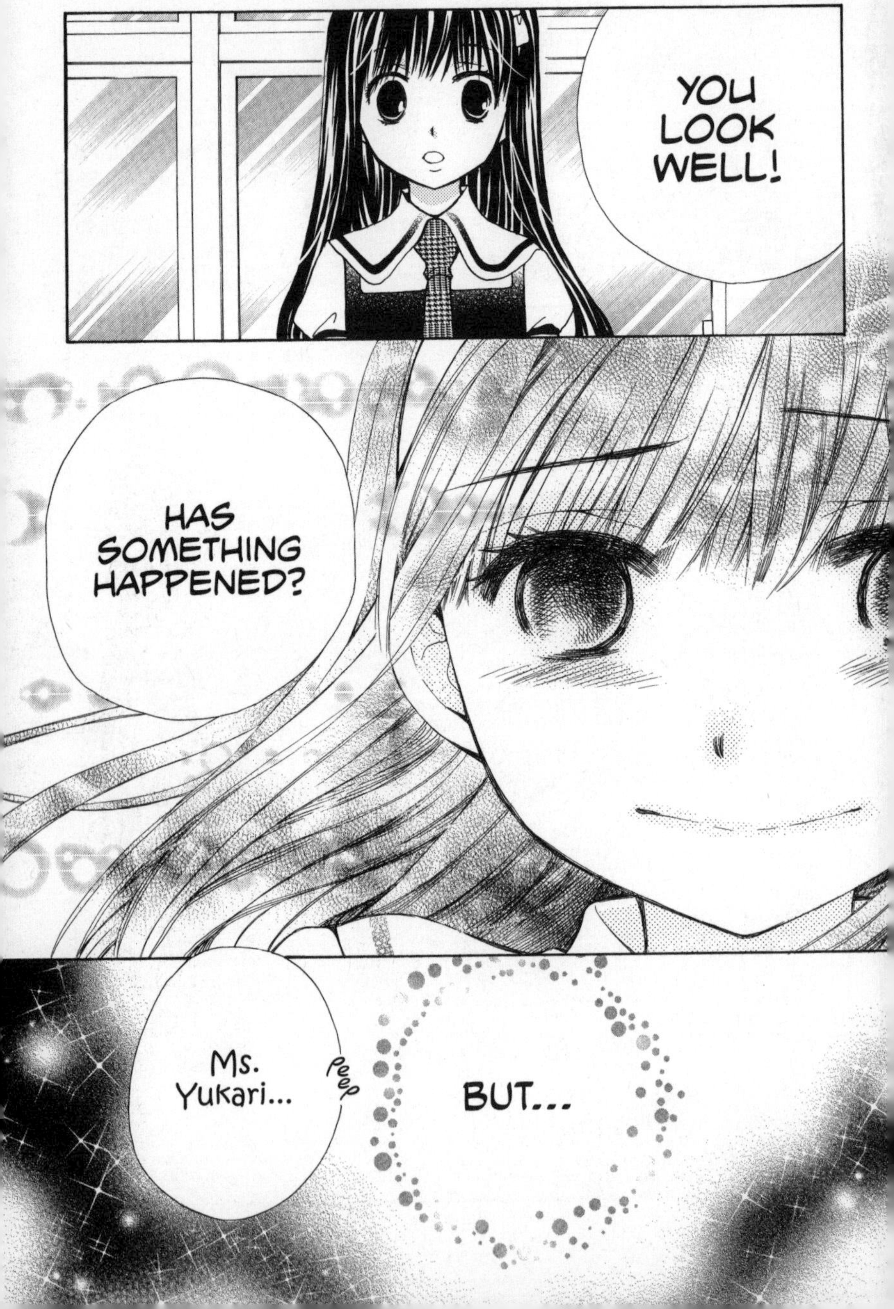
YOU LOOK WELL!
HAS SOMETHING HAPPENED?
BUT...
Ms. Yukari...
peep

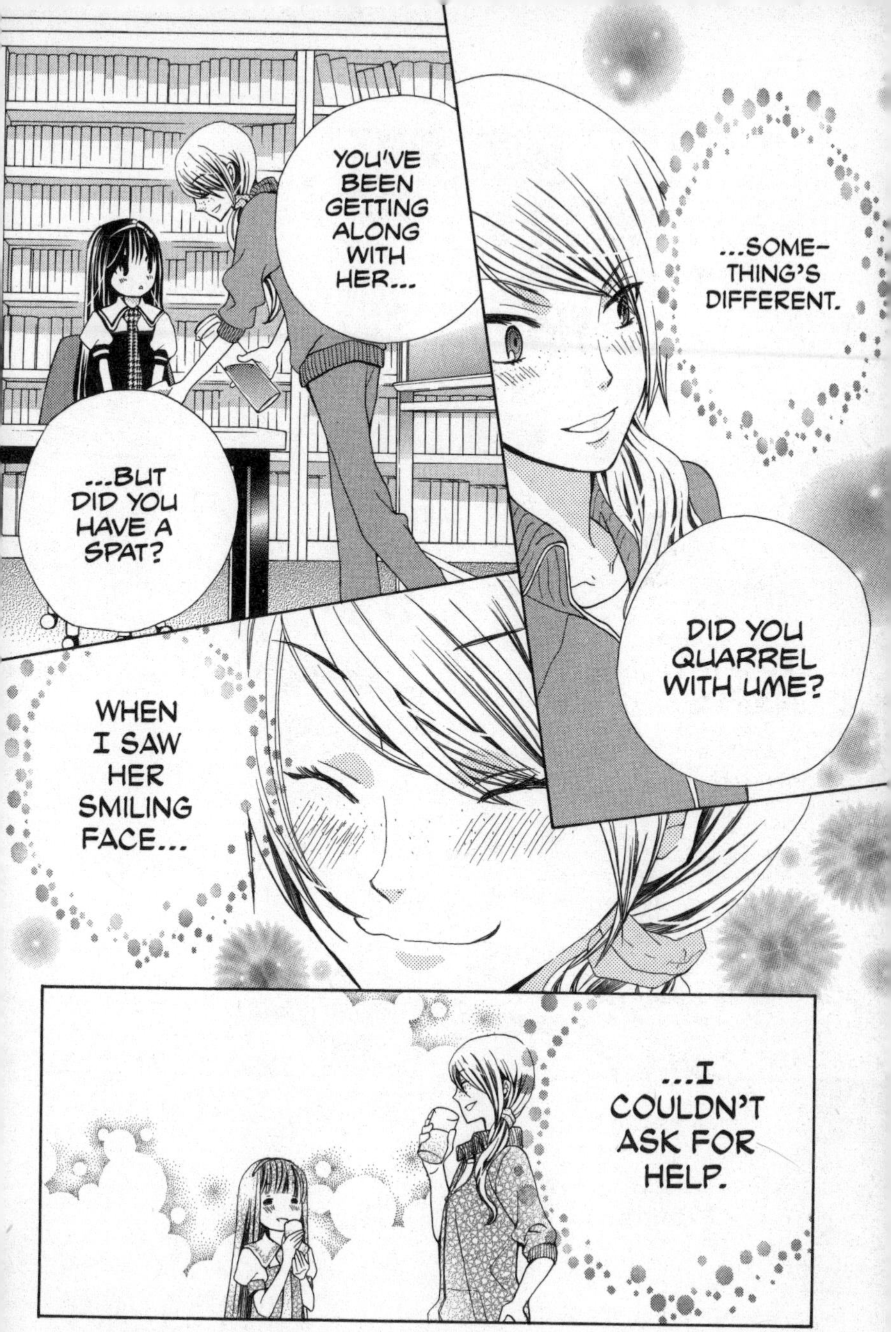
...SOME-THING'S DIFFERENT.
DID YOU QUARREL WITH UME?
YOU'VE BEEN GETTING ALONG WITH HER...
...BUT DID YOU HAVE A SPAT?
WHEN I SAW HER SMILING FACE...
...I COULDN'T ASK FOR HELP.

Chapter 40

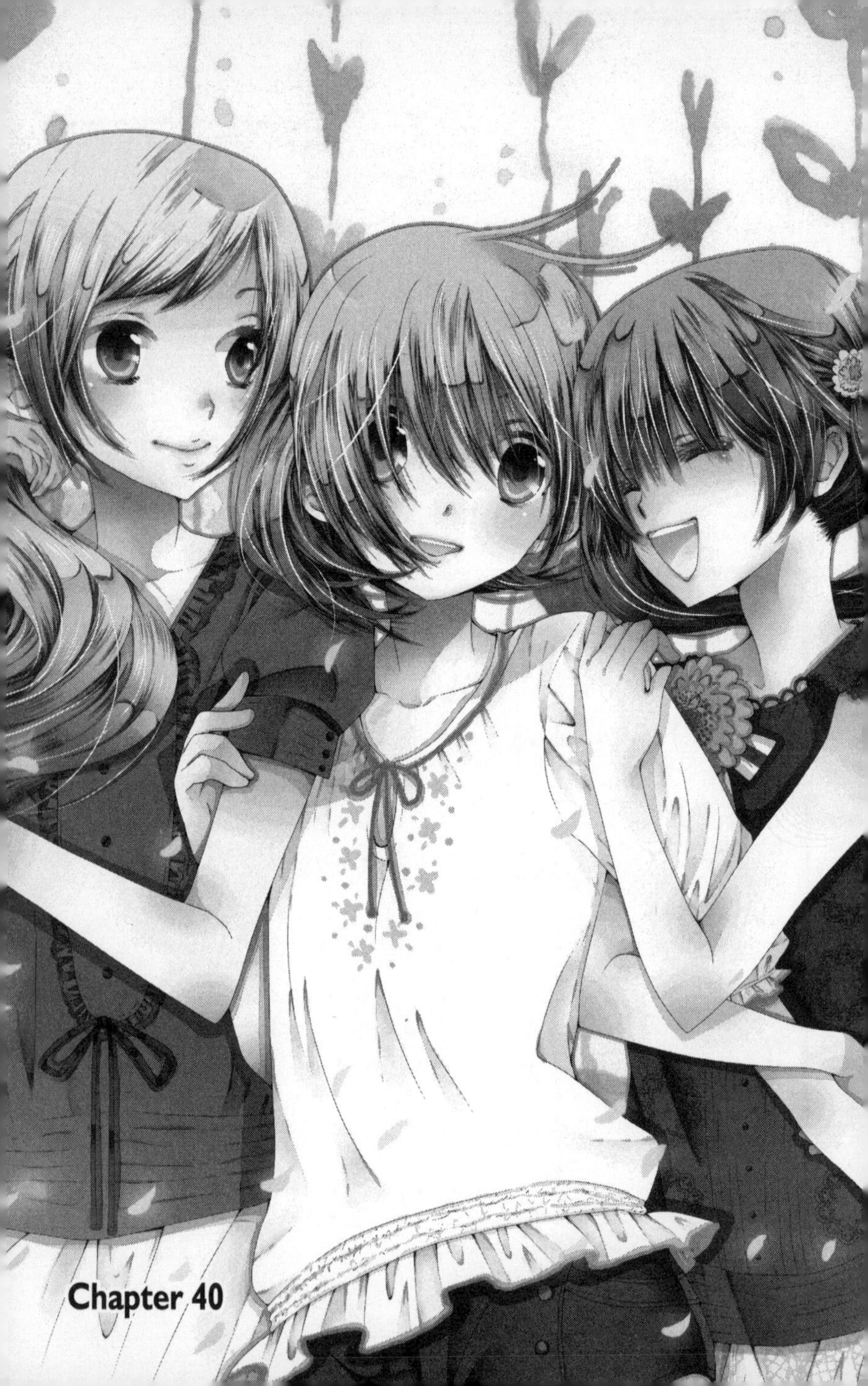

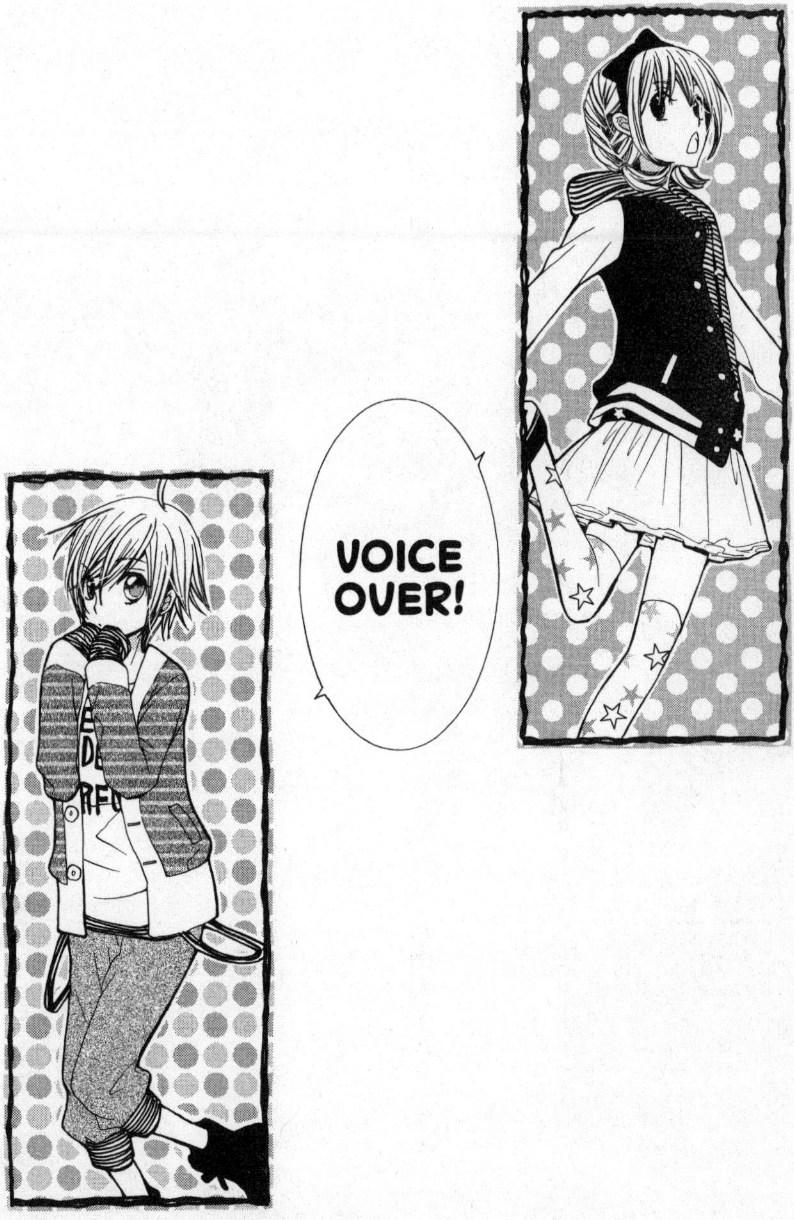
VOICE OVER!

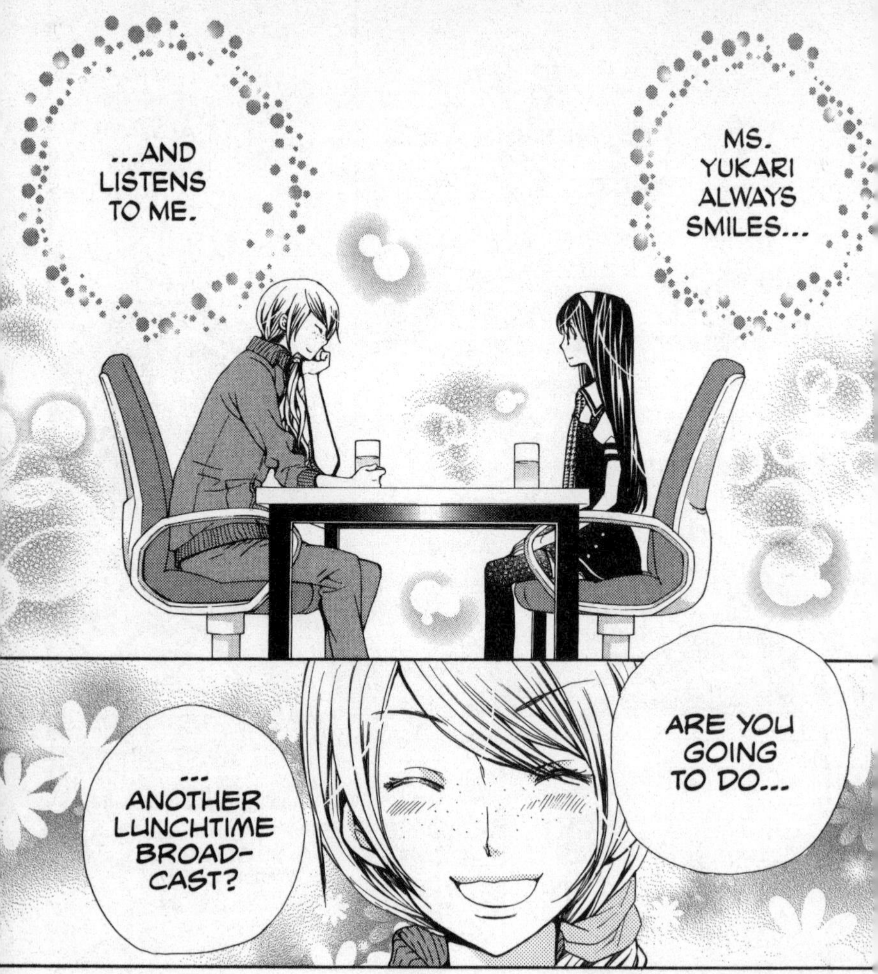
MS. YUKARI ALWAYS SMILES...
...AND LISTENS TO ME.
ARE YOU GOING TO DO...
...ANOTHER LUNCHTIME BROAD-CAST?

○ Various Things ○

○ Guests drew bonus content this time!! I'd like to use this space to thank them.

• Kazumi Mitsuki •
Thank you for drawing such a cute Tsukino!! She's so lovely. I want to take her home with me! huff huff She really is lovely!!!!! So important I said it twice!

• Yu Ito •
Westerns!!! Fantasy!!!! Super cool! In an email, I said he drew Shiro perfectly. Very handsome! And Senri, too! Hime was so handsome I wanted to take her home. Handsome?

Thank you to both for agreeing to do this! I'll treasure your contributions forever!

My assistant M-yama-san made the rising Mitchy!!

6

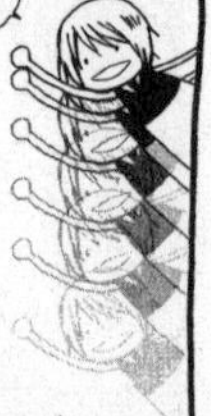

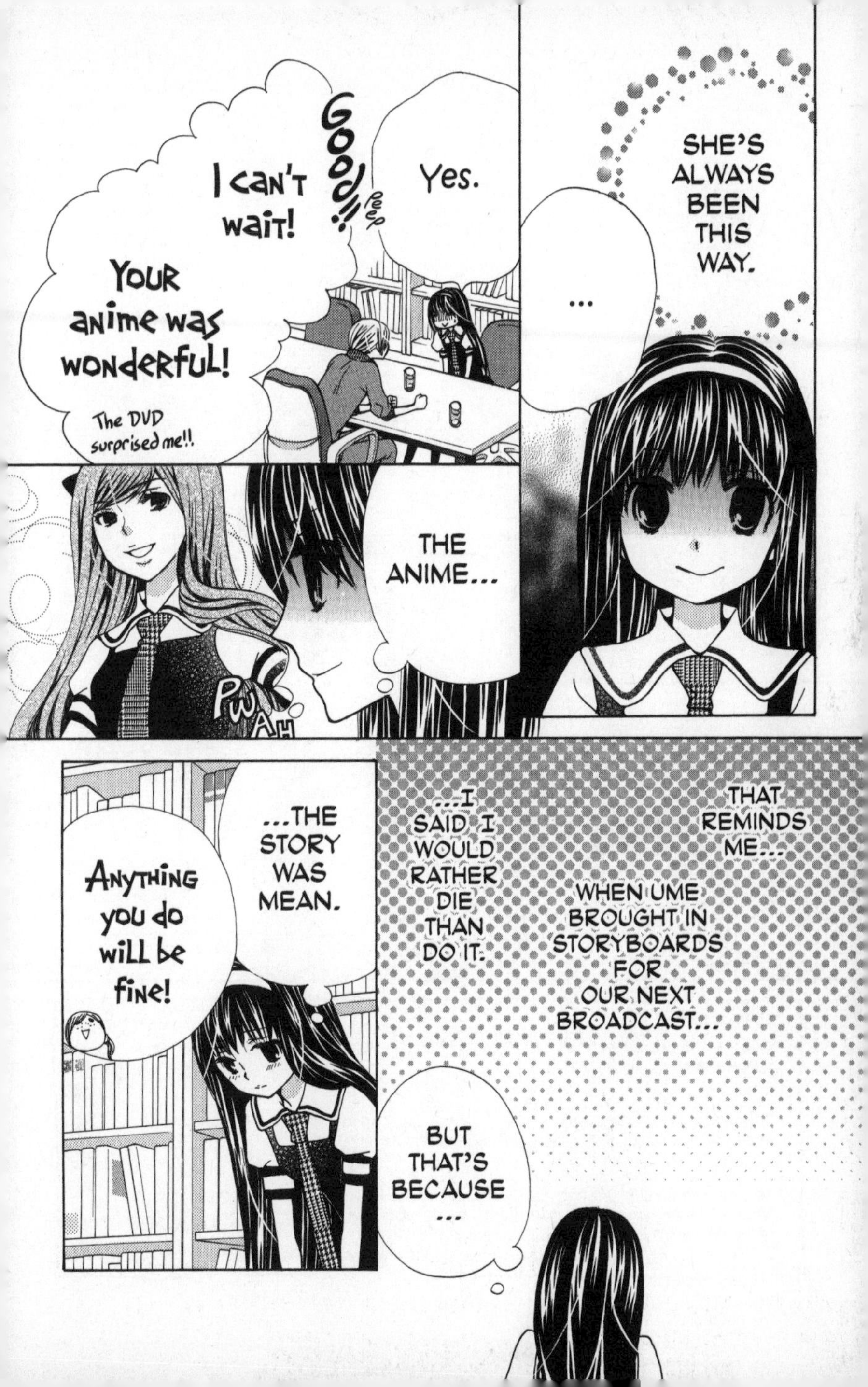
SHE'S ALWAYS BEEN THIS WAY.
...
Yes.
GOOD!!
PEEP
I can't wait!
YOUR anime was wonderful!
The DVD surprised me!!
THE ANIME...
PWAH
THAT REMINDS ME...
WHEN UME BROUGHT IN STORYBOARDS FOR OUR NEXT BROADCAST...
...I SAID I WOULD RATHER DIE THAN DO IT.
BUT THAT'S BECAUSE ...
...THE STORY WAS MEAN.
Anything you do will be fine!

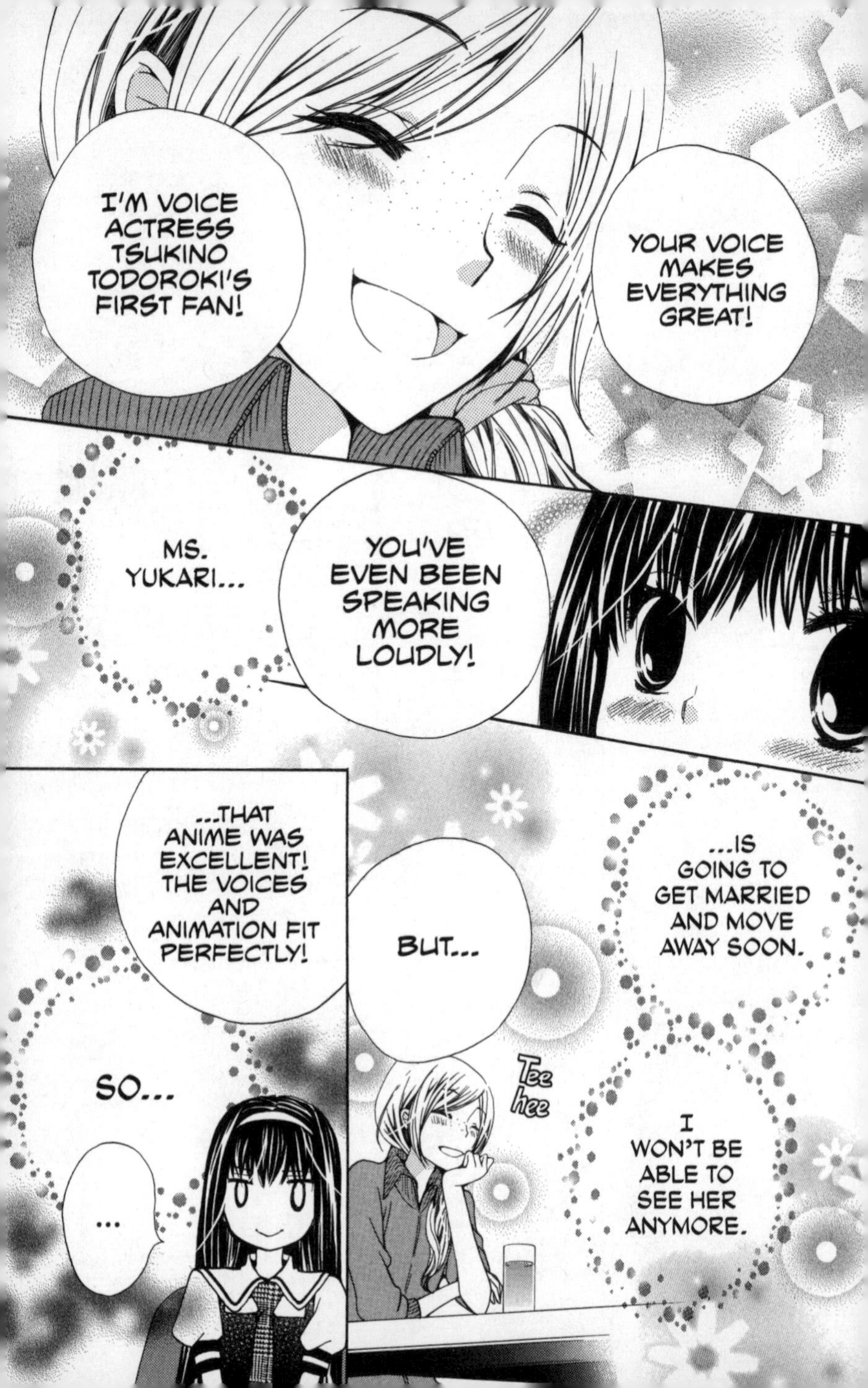
YOUR VOICE MAKES EVERYTHING GREAT!
I'M VOICE ACTRESS TSUKINO TODOROKI'S FIRST FAN!
YOU'VE EVEN BEEN SPEAKING MORE LOUDLY!
MS. YUKARI...
...IS GOING TO GET MARRIED AND MOVE AWAY SOON.
BUT...
Tee hee
I WON'T BE ABLE TO SEE HER ANYMORE.
...THAT ANIME WAS EXCELLENT! THE VOICES AND ANIMATION FIT PERFECTLY!
SO...
...

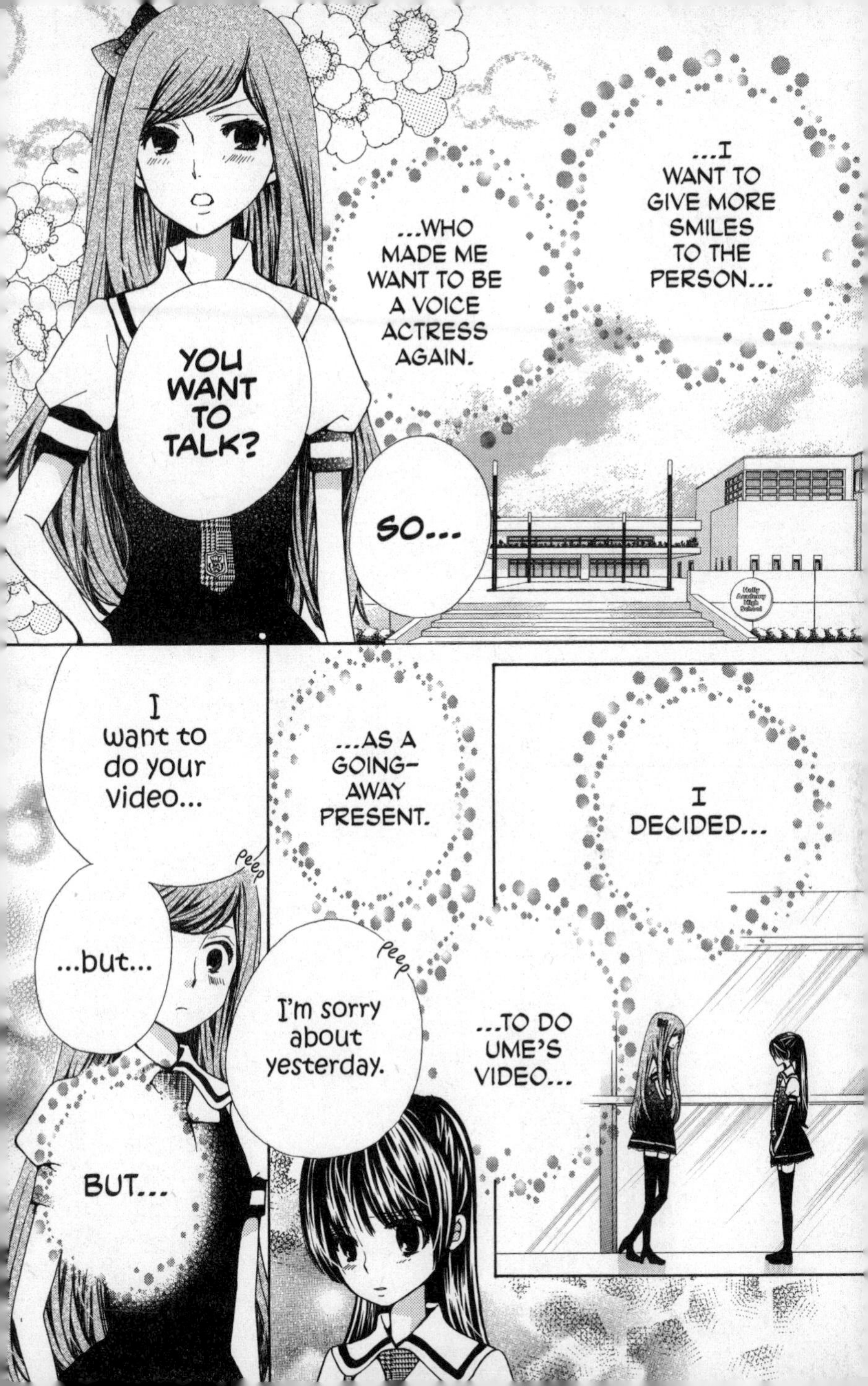
...I WANT TO GIVE MORE SMILES TO THE PERSON...
...WHO MADE ME WANT TO BE A VOICE ACTRESS AGAIN.
SO...
YOU WANT TO TALK?
I DECIDED...
...TO DO UME'S VIDEO...
...AS A GOING-AWAY PRESENT.
Peep
I'm sorry about yesterday.
I want to do your video...
Peep
...but...
BUT...

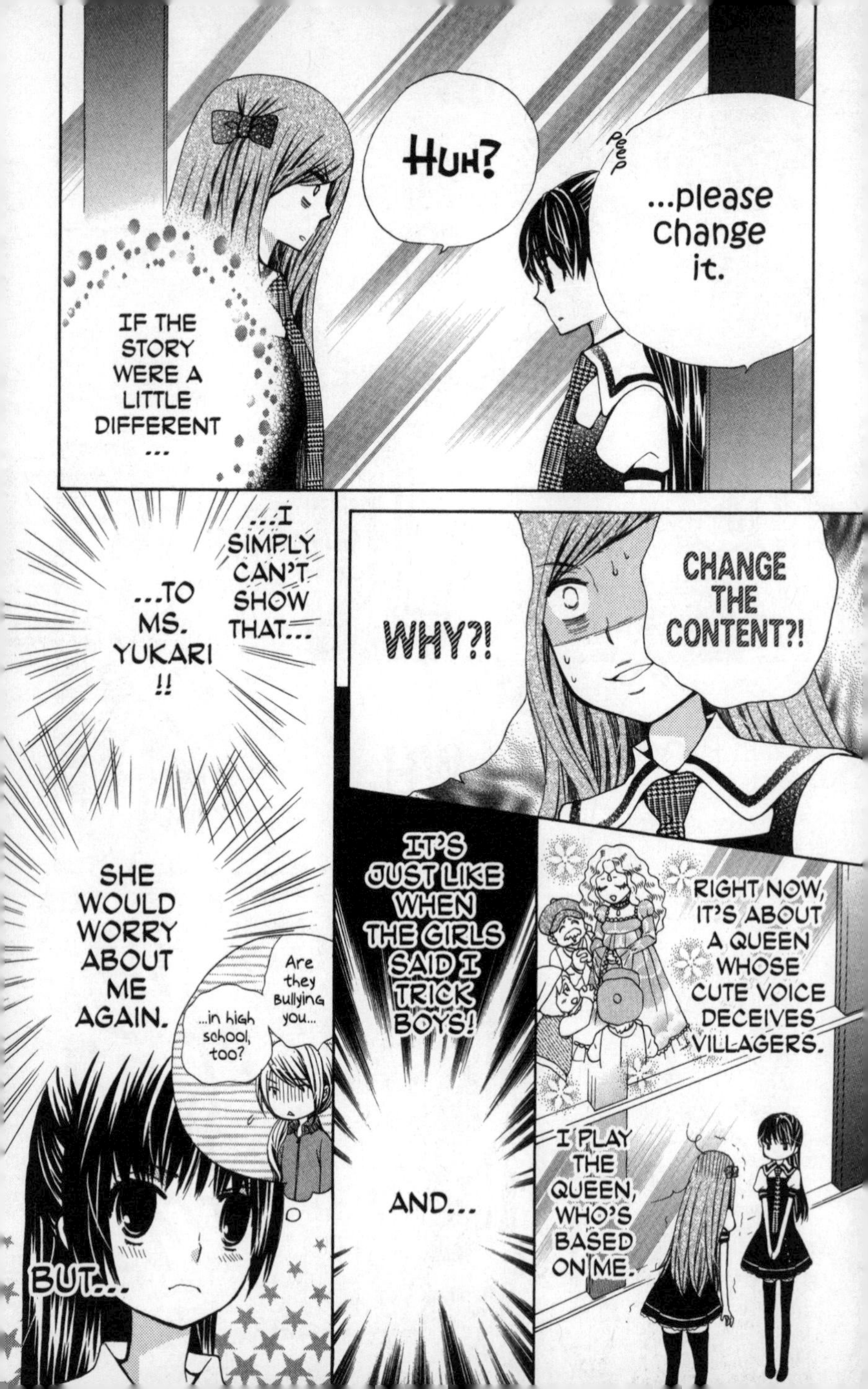
PEEP
...please change it.
HUH?
IF THE STORY WERE A LITTLE DIFFERENT...
CHANGE THE CONTENT?!
WHY?!
...I SIMPLY CAN'T SHOW THAT...
...TO MS. YUKARI!!
RIGHT NOW, IT'S ABOUT A QUEEN WHOSE CUTE VOICE DECEIVES VILLAGERS.
I PLAY THE QUEEN, WHO'S BASED ON ME.
IT'S JUST LIKE WHEN THE GIRLS SAID I TRICK BOYS!
AND...
SHE WOULD WORRY ABOUT ME AGAIN.
Are they bullying you...
...in high school, too?
BUT...

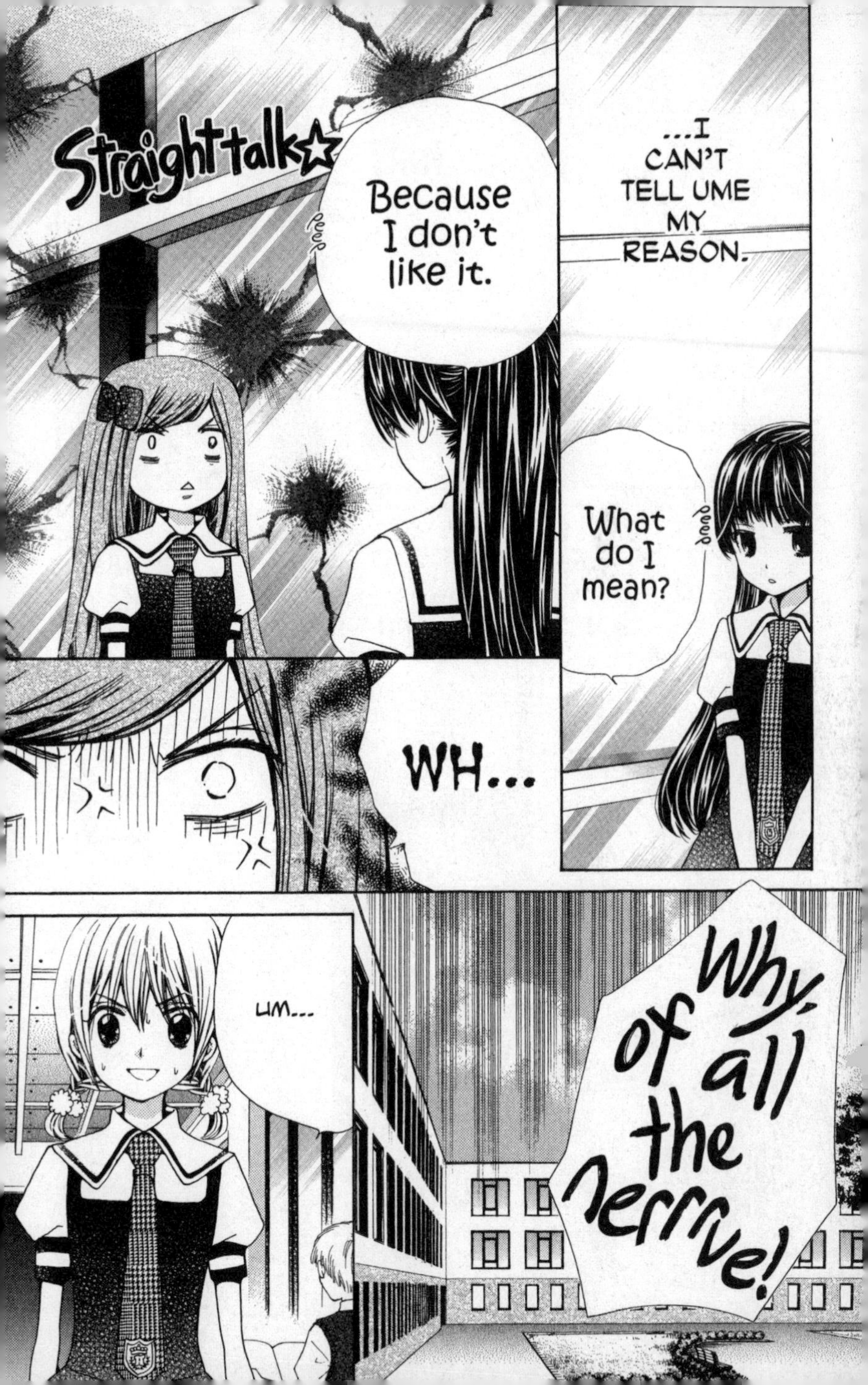
...I CAN'T TELL UME MY REASON.
What do I mean?
Straight talk☆
Because I don't like it.
peep
WH...
Why, of all the nerrrve!
um...

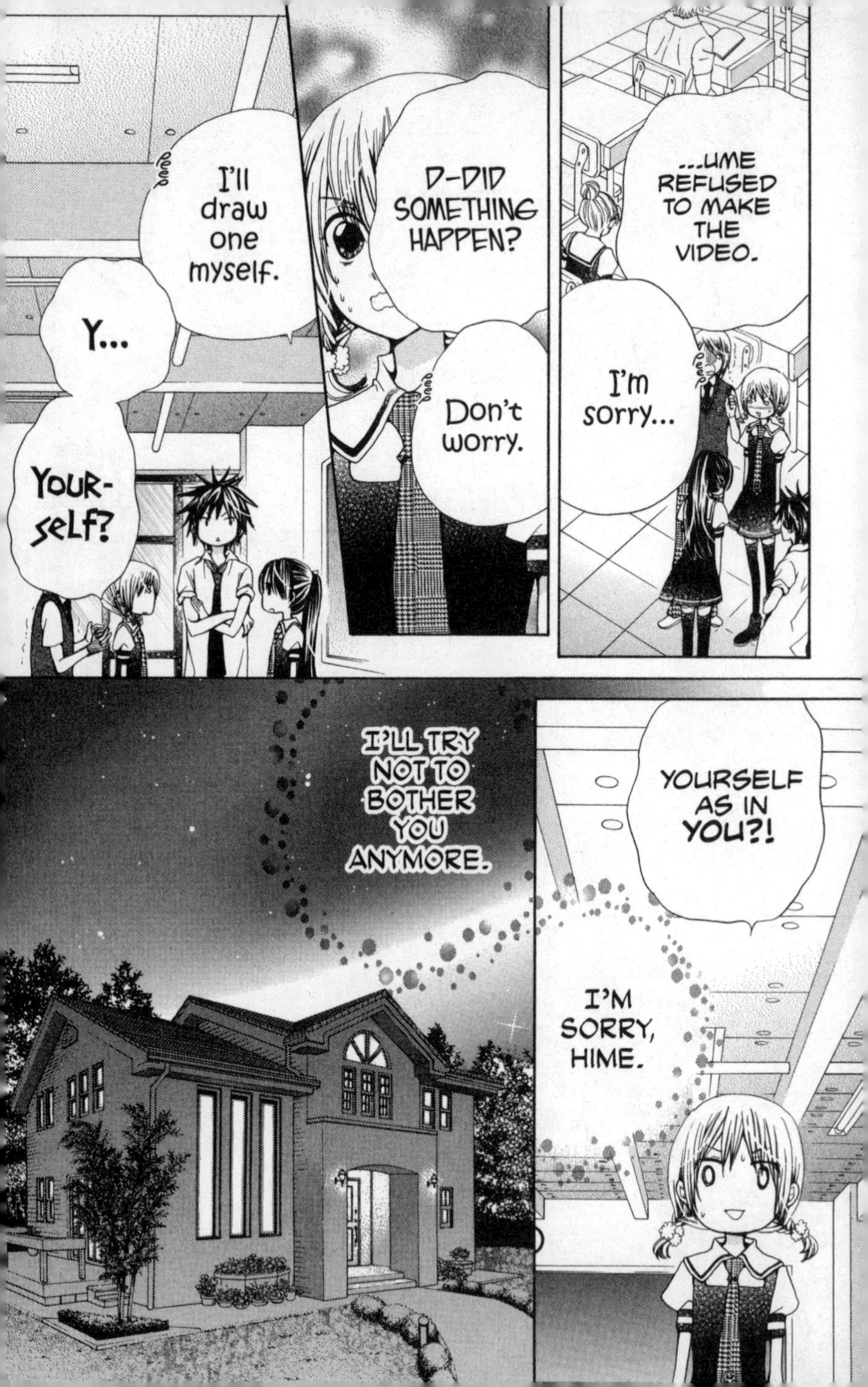
...UME REFUSED TO MAKE THE VIDEO.
I'm sorry...
D-DID SOMETHING HAPPEN?
Don't worry.
I'll draw one myself.
Y...
YOUR-self?
YOURSELF AS IN YOU?!
I'M SORRY, HIME.
I'LL TRY NOT TO BOTHER YOU ANYMORE.

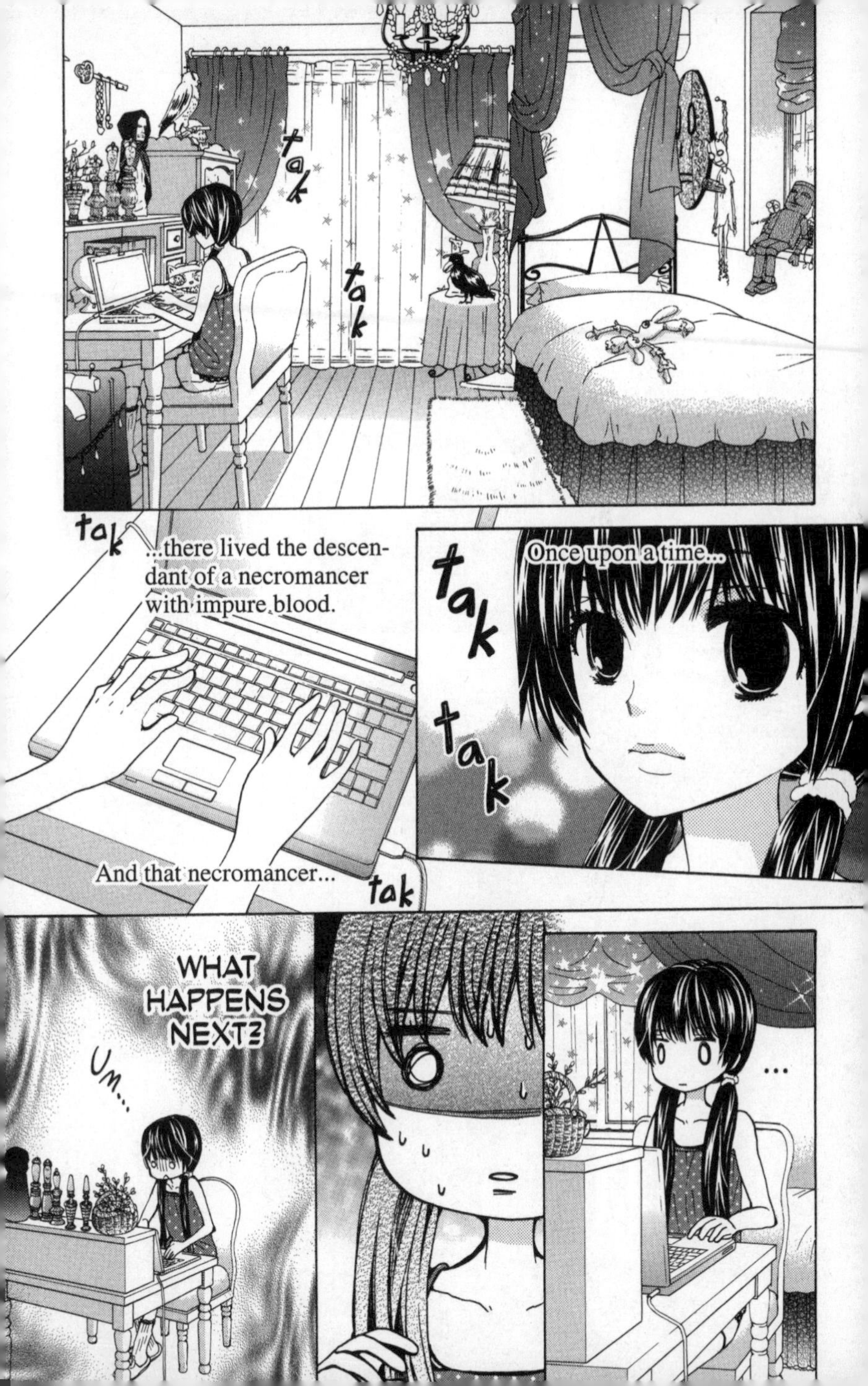
tak
tak
Once upon a time...
tak
tak
tak
...there lived the descendant of a necromancer with impure blood.
And that necromancer...
tak
...
WHAT HAPPENS NEXT?
Um...

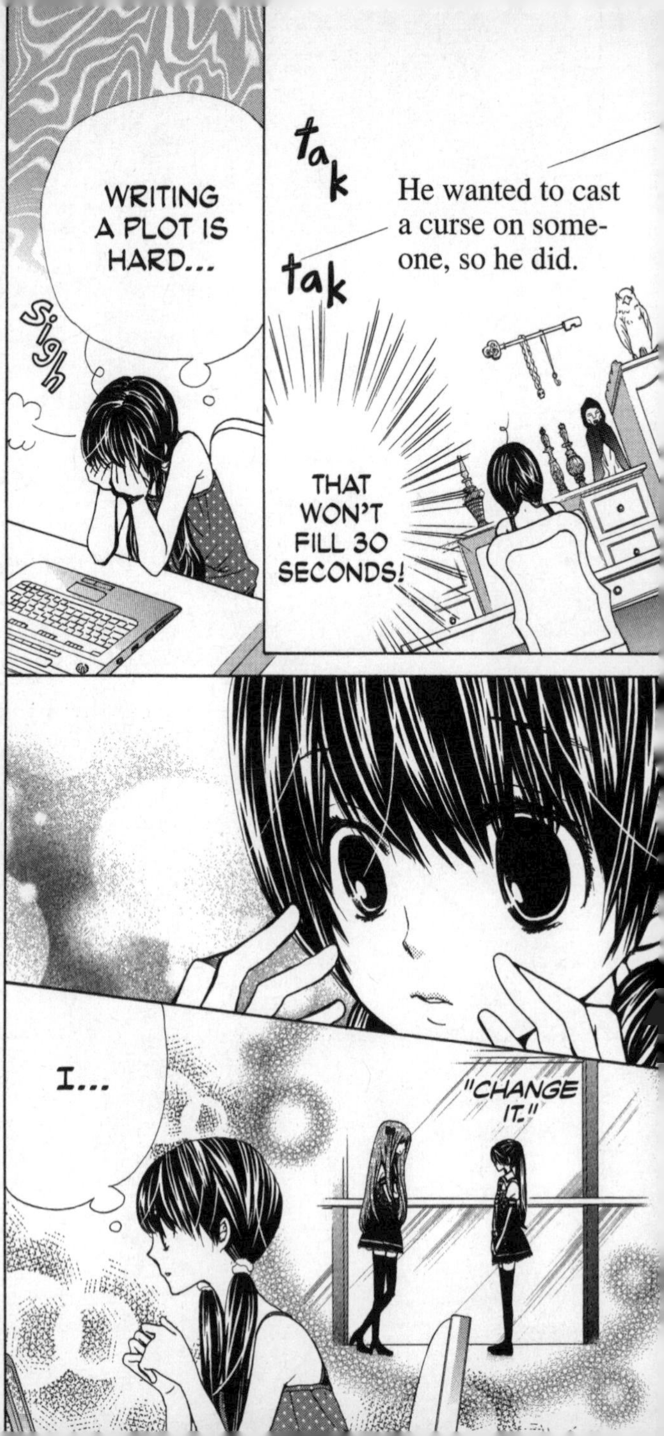
tak
tak
He wanted to cast a curse on some-one, so he did.
THAT WON'T FILL 30 SECONDS!
WRITING A PLOT IS HARD...
Sigh
"CHANGE IT."
I...

◦ End ◦

This is the end of the sidebars. Thank you for reading!!

I'm still drawing black-and-white manuscripts the old-fashioned way, so the amount of screentones is increasing, and I'm holding my head wondering what to do. I like it when new patterns come out, but in recent years, the number of places coming out with them has been decreasing...

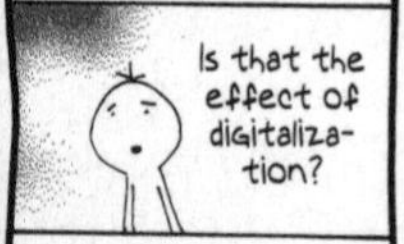
Is that the effect of digitalization?

And a heartfelt thanks to everyone who read this, everyone who helped with research, the graphic novel editor, my editor, my assistants, my friends and my family!!!!!!

♡ If you want, let me hear your thoughts! ♡

Maki Minami c/o
Shojo Beat
P.O. Box 77010
San Francisco, CA
94107

Maki Minami

南マキ

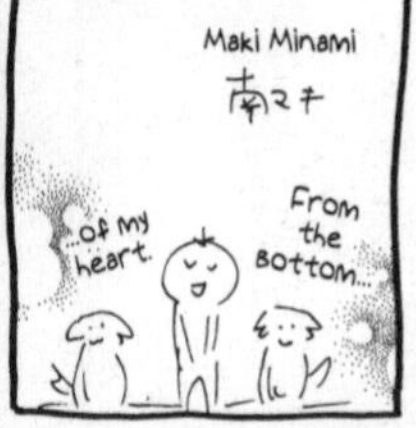
From the bottom...
...of my heart.

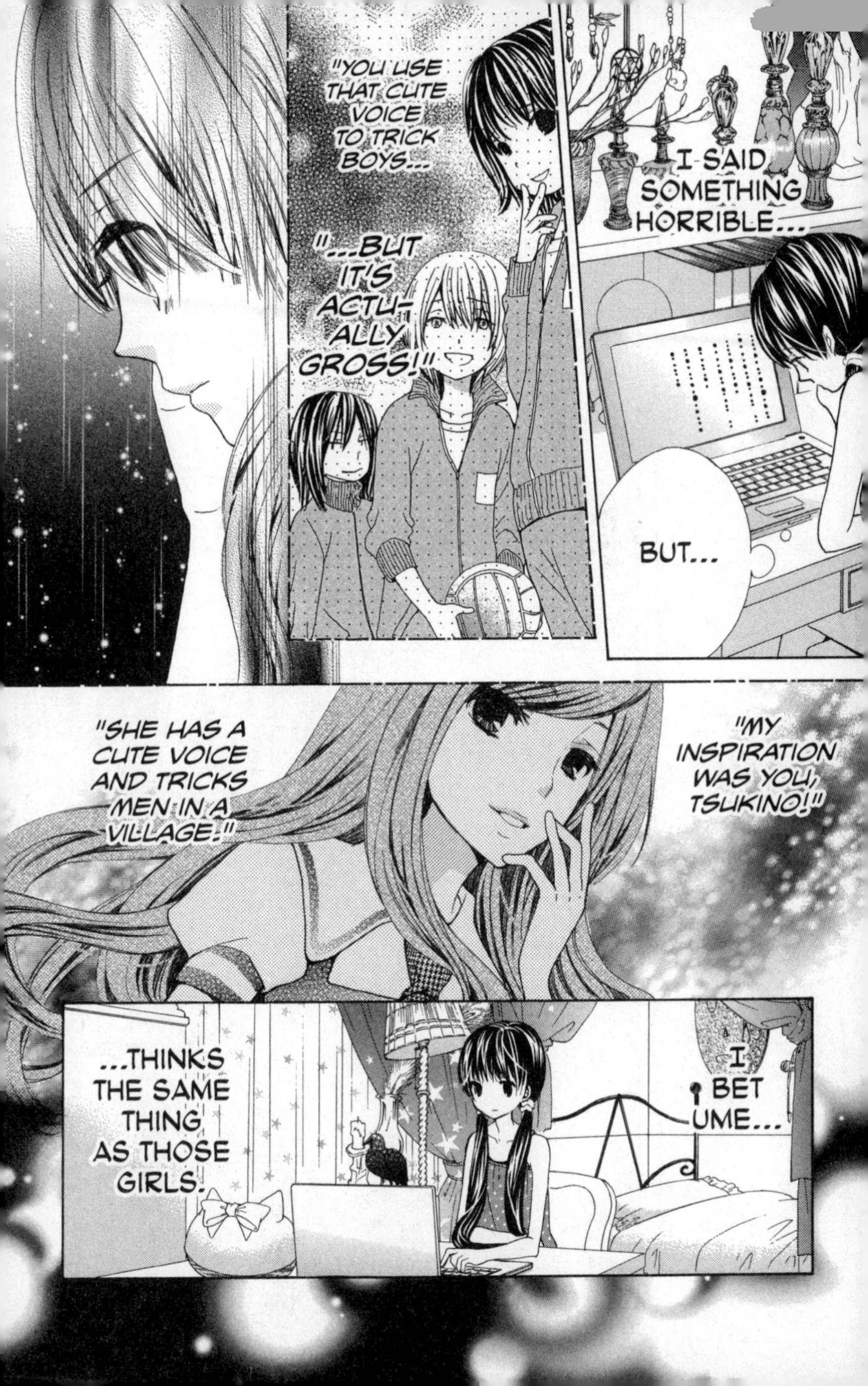
I SAID SOMETHING HORRIBLE...
BUT...
"YOU USE THAT CUTE VOICE TO TRICK BOYS...
"...BUT IT'S ACTU-ALLY GROSS!"
"MY INSPIRATION WAS YOU, TSUKINO!"
"SHE HAS A CUTE VOICE AND TRICKS MEN IN A VILLAGE."
I BET UME...
...THINKS THE SAME THING AS THOSE GIRLS.

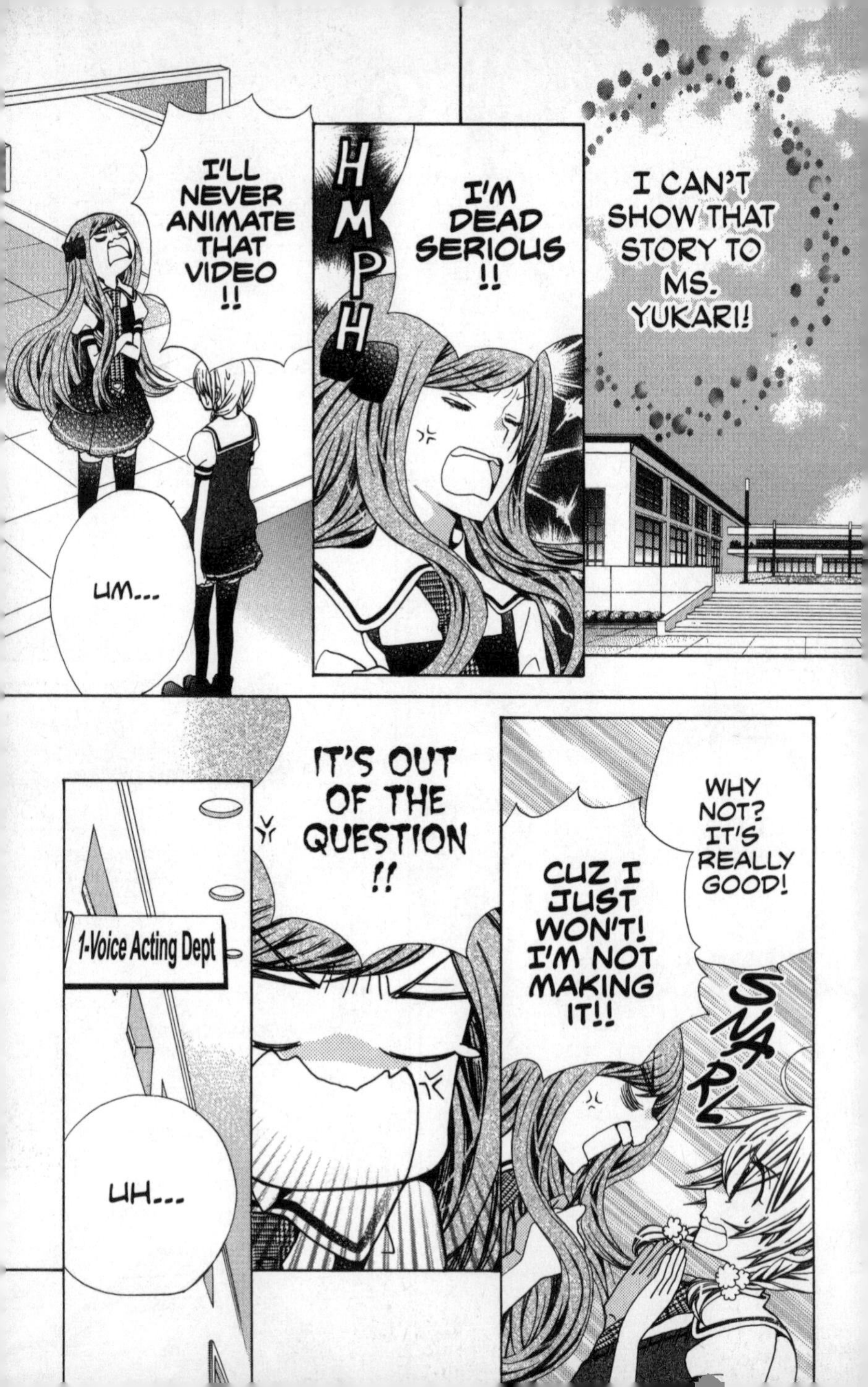
I CAN'T SHOW THAT STORY TO MS. YUKARI!
HMPH
I'M DEAD SERIOUS!!
I'LL NEVER ANIMATE THAT VIDEO!!
UM...
WHY NOT? IT'S REALLY GOOD!
SNARL
CUZ I JUST WON'T! I'M NOT MAKING IT!!
IT'S OUT OF THE QUESTION!!
1-Voice Acting Dept
UH...

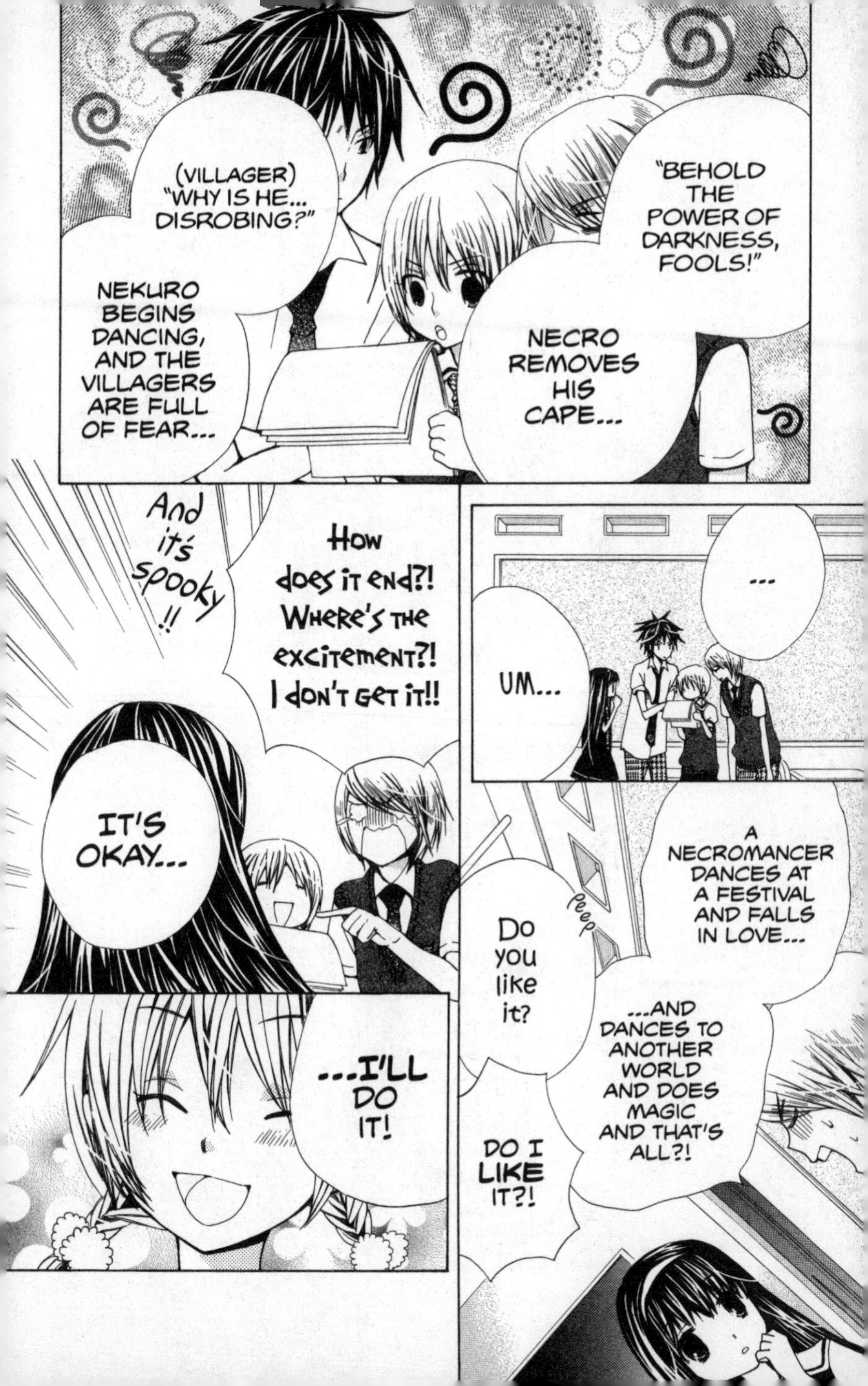
"BEHOLD THE POWER OF DARKNESS, FOOLS!"
NECRO REMOVES HIS CAPE...
(VILLAGER) "WHY IS HE... DISROBING?"
NEKURO BEGINS DANCING, AND THE VILLAGERS ARE FULL OF FEAR...
...
UM...
A NECROMANCER DANCES AT A FESTIVAL AND FALLS IN LOVE...
Peep
Do you like it?
...AND DANCES TO ANOTHER WORLD AND DOES MAGIC AND THAT'S ALL?!
DO I LIKE IT?!
How does it end?! Where's the excitement?! I don't get it!!
And it's spooky!!
IT'S OKAY...
...I'LL DO IT!

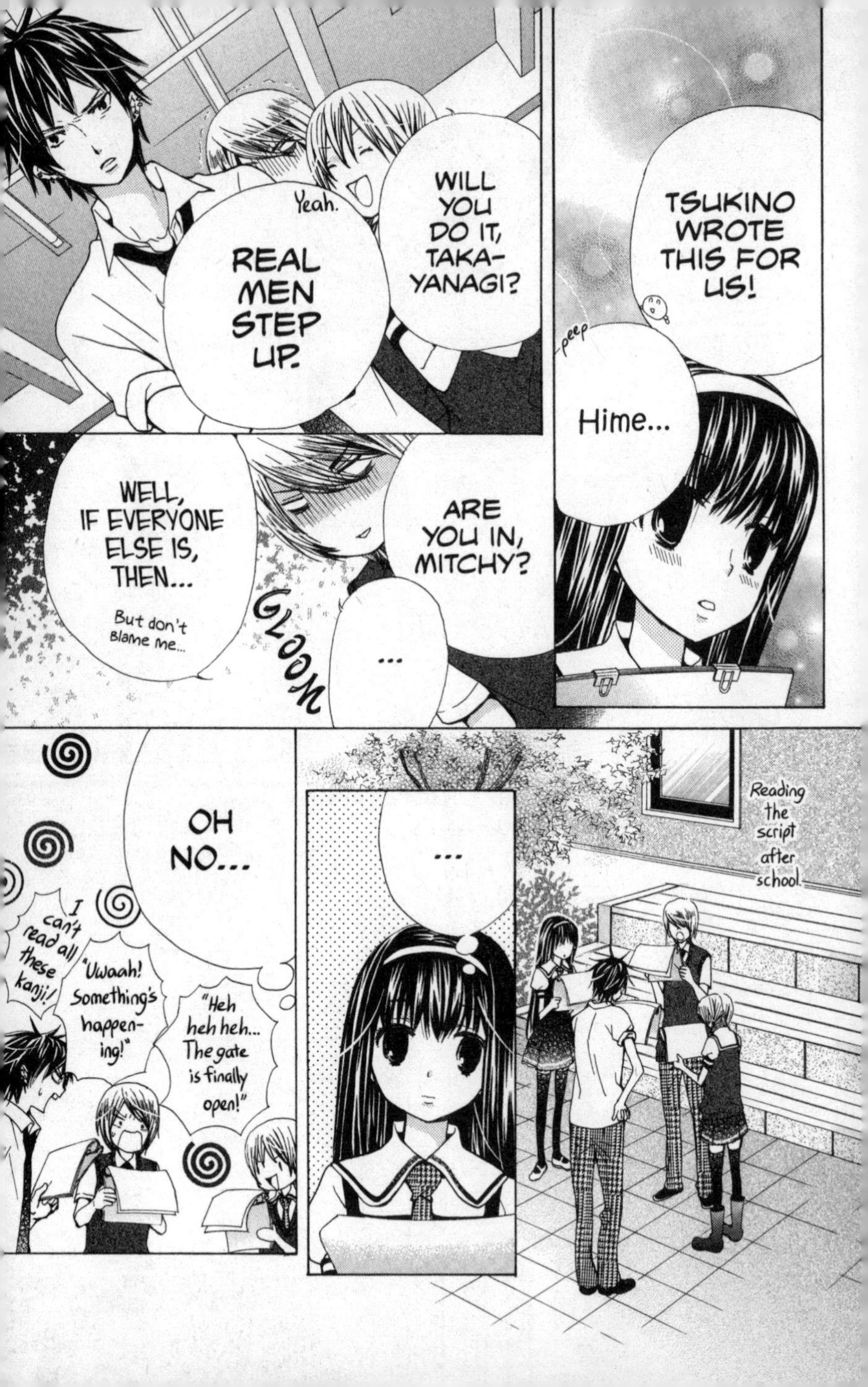
TSUKINO WROTE THIS FOR US!
peep
Hime...
WILL YOU DO IT, TAKA-YANAGI?
Yeah.
REAL MEN STEP UP.
ARE YOU IN, MITCHY?
...
WELL, IF EVERYONE ELSE IS, THEN...
But don't blame me...
GLOOOM
Reading the script after school.
...
OH NO...
"Heh heh heh... The gate is finally open!"
"Uwaah! Something's happen-ing!"
I can't read all these kanji!

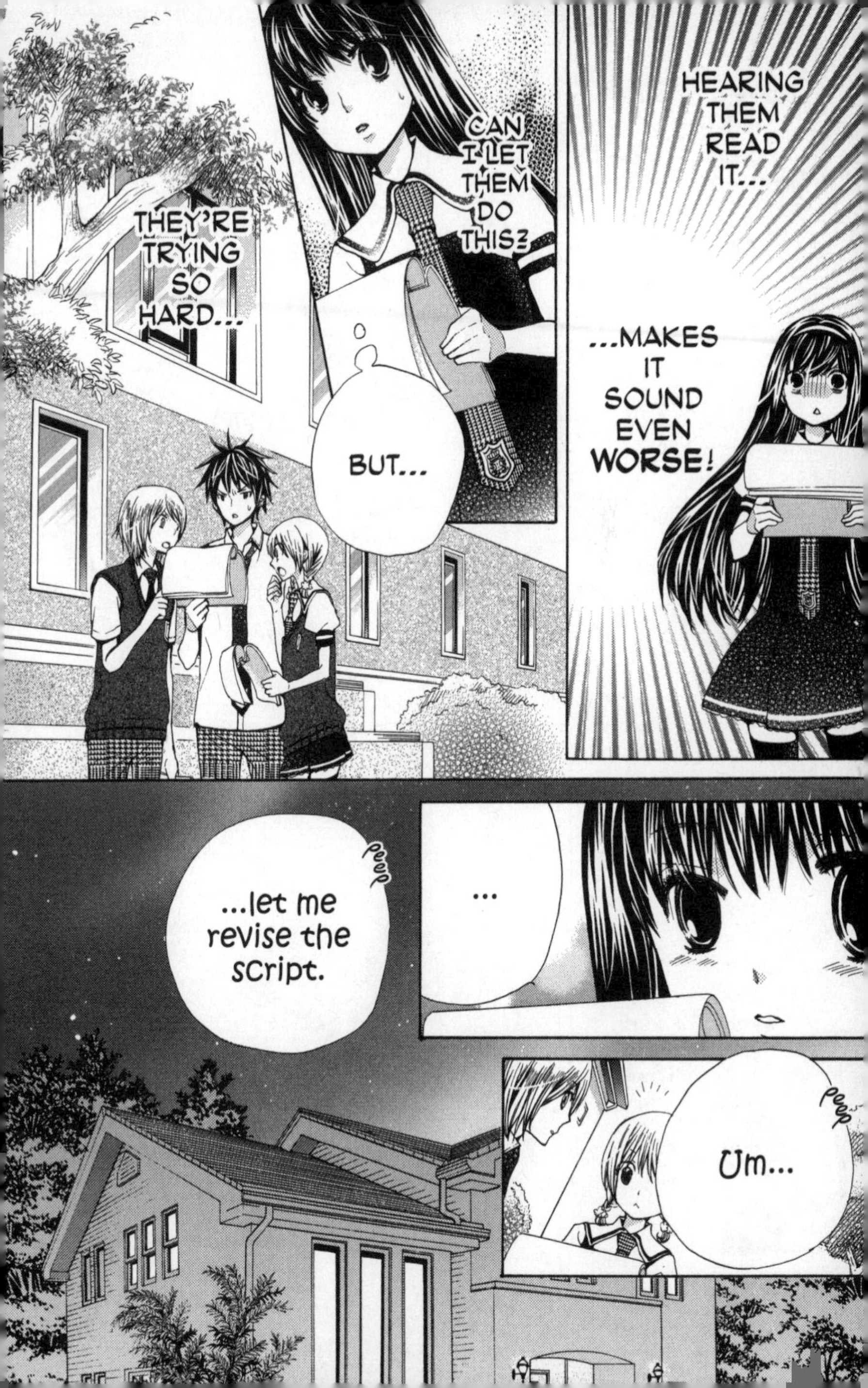

HEARING THEM READ IT...
...MAKES IT SOUND EVEN WORSE!
CAN I LET THEM DO THIS?
THEY'RE TRYING SO HARD...
BUT...
...
peep
Um...
peep
...let me revise the script.

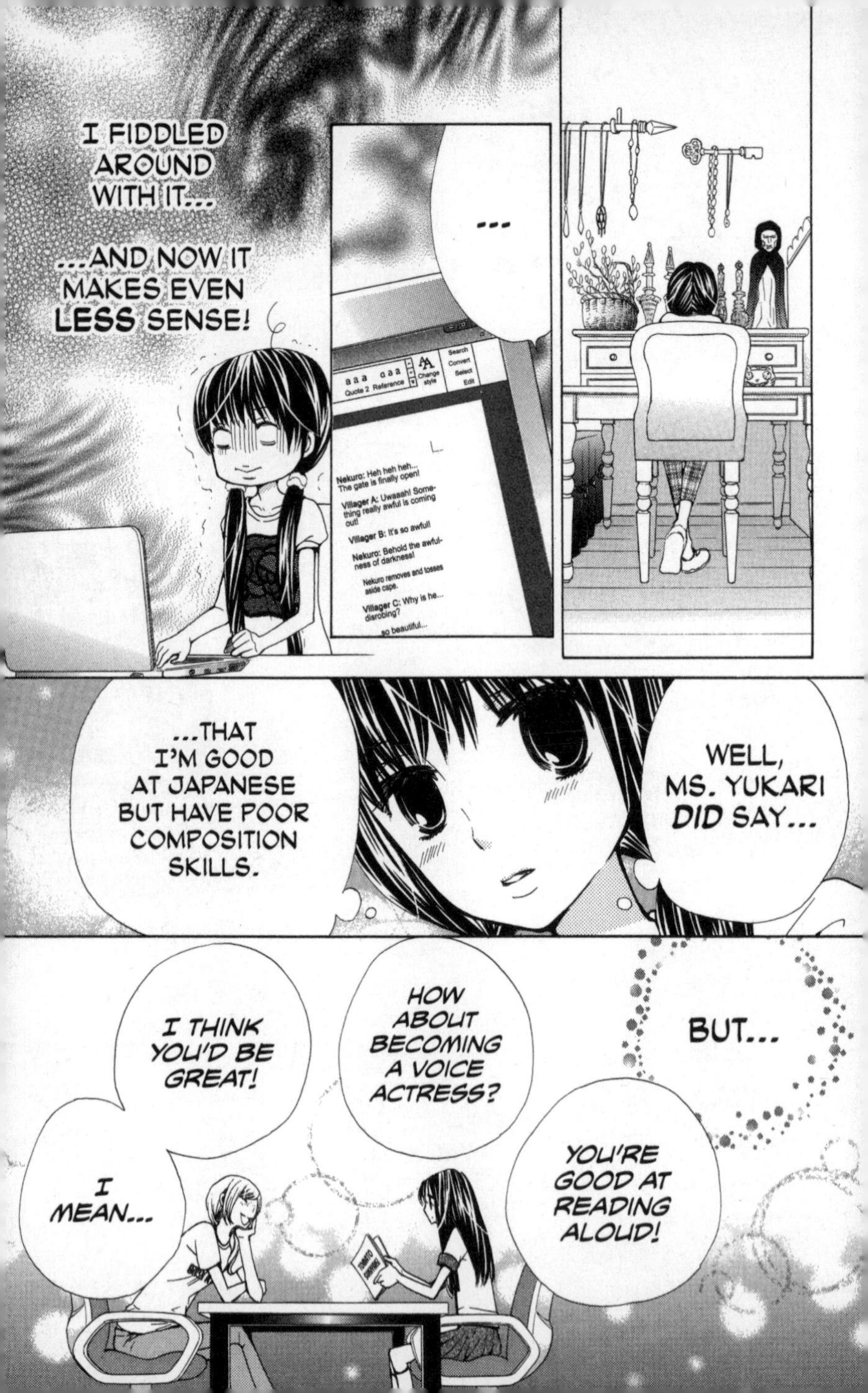
...
aaa aaa Quote 2 Reference
Change style
Search
Convert
Select
Edit
Nekuro: Heh heh heh... The gate is finally open!
Villager A: Uwaaah! Something really awful is coming out!
Villager B: It's so awful!
Nekuro: Behold the awfulness of darkness!
Nekuro removes and tosses aside cape.
Villager C: Why is he... disrobing?
so beautiful...
I FIDDLED AROUND WITH IT...
...AND NOW IT MAKES EVEN LESS SENSE!
WELL, MS. YUKARI DID SAY...
...THAT I'M GOOD AT JAPANESE BUT HAVE POOR COMPOSITION SKILLS.
BUT...
HOW ABOUT BECOMING A VOICE ACTRESS?
I THINK YOU'D BE GREAT!
YOU'RE GOOD AT READING ALOUD!
I MEAN...

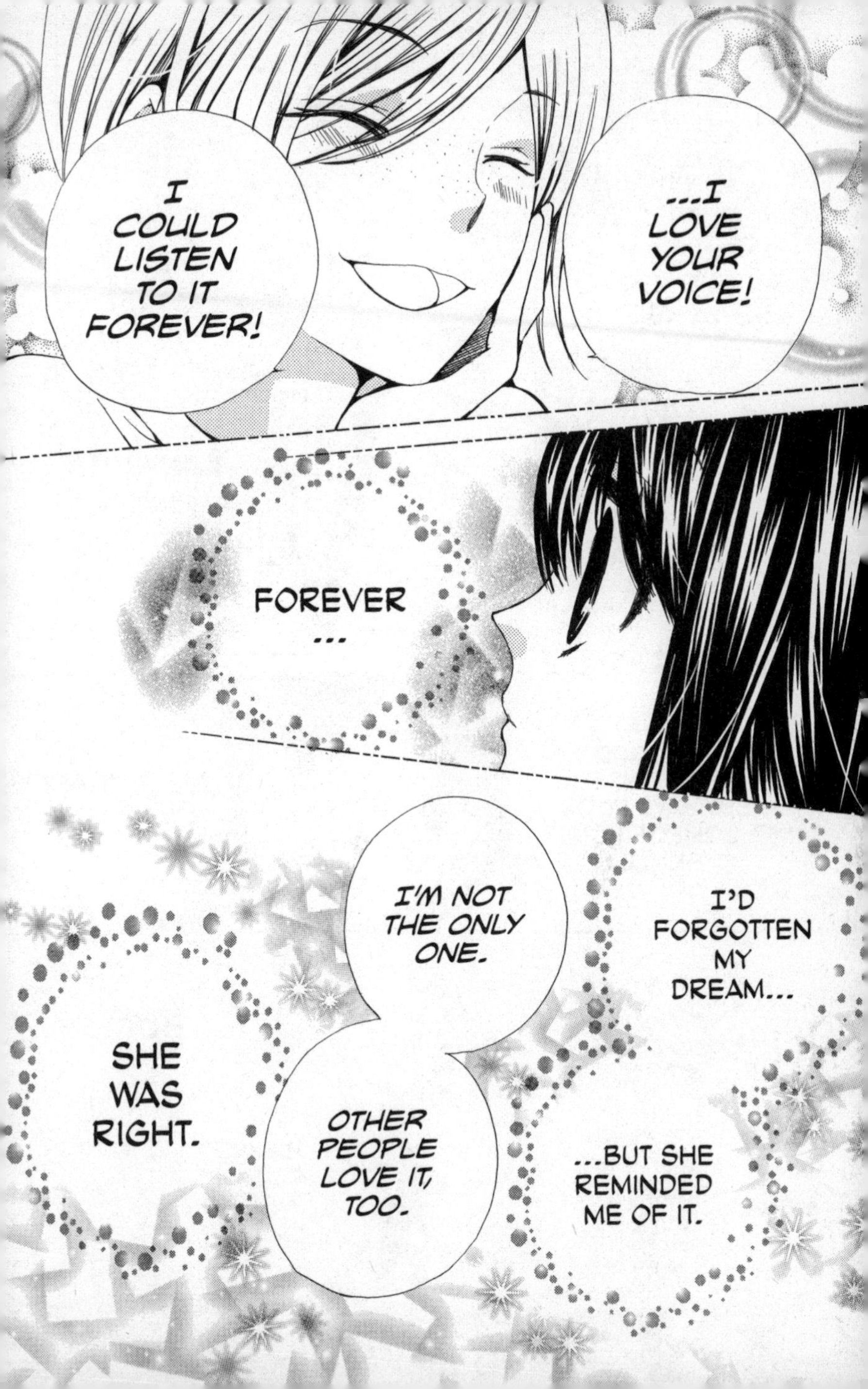
...I LOVE YOUR VOICE!
I COULD LISTEN TO IT FOREVER!
FOREVER ...
I'D FORGOTTEN MY DREAM...
...BUT SHE REMINDED ME OF IT.
I'M NOT THE ONLY ONE.
OTHER PEOPLE LOVE IT, TOO.
SHE WAS RIGHT.

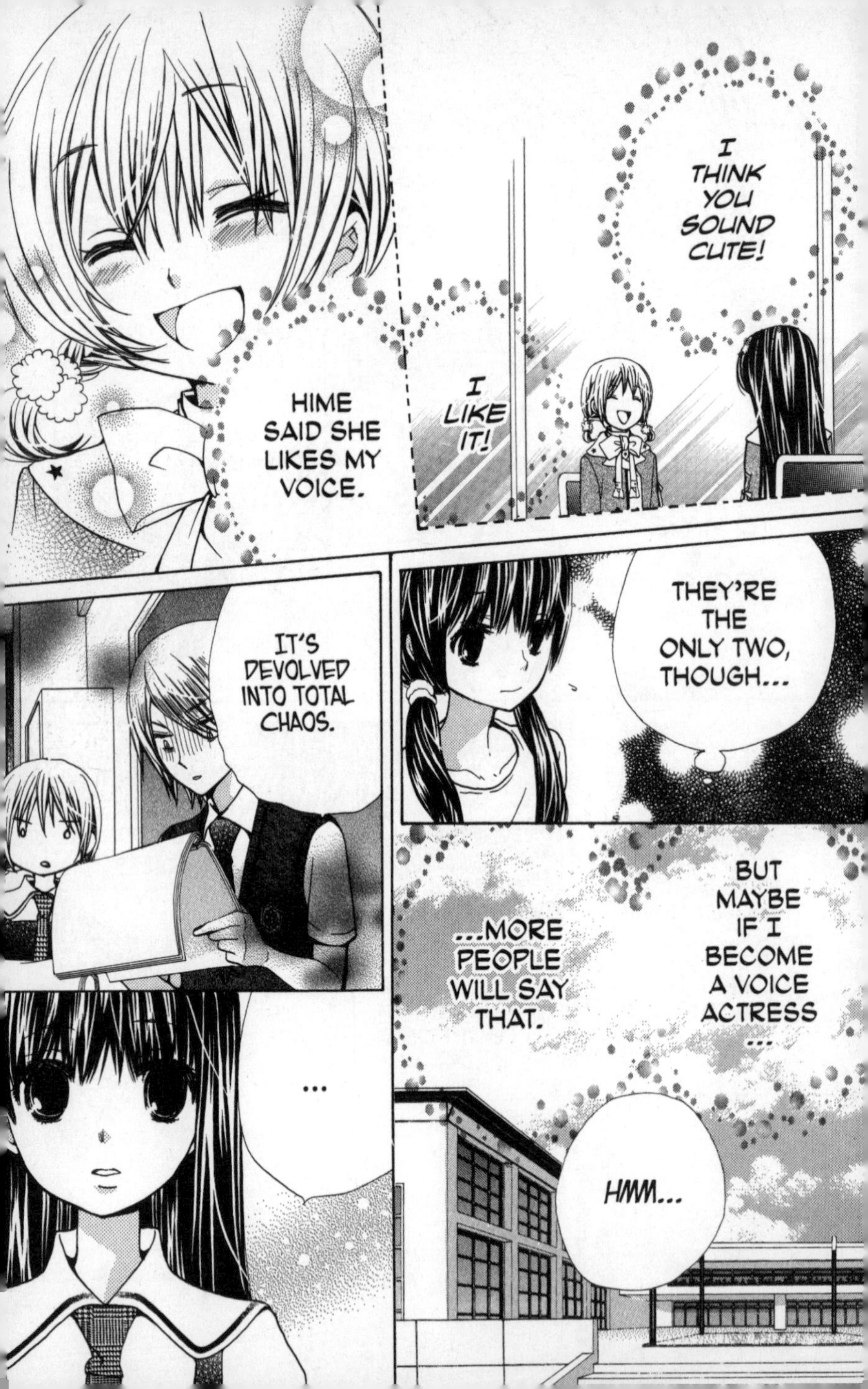
I THINK YOU SOUND CUTE!
I LIKE IT!
HIME SAID SHE LIKES MY VOICE.
THEY'RE THE ONLY TWO, THOUGH...
IT'S DEVOLVED INTO TOTAL CHAOS.
BUT MAYBE IF I BECOME A VOICE ACTRESS...
...MORE PEOPLE WILL SAY THAT.
HMM...
...

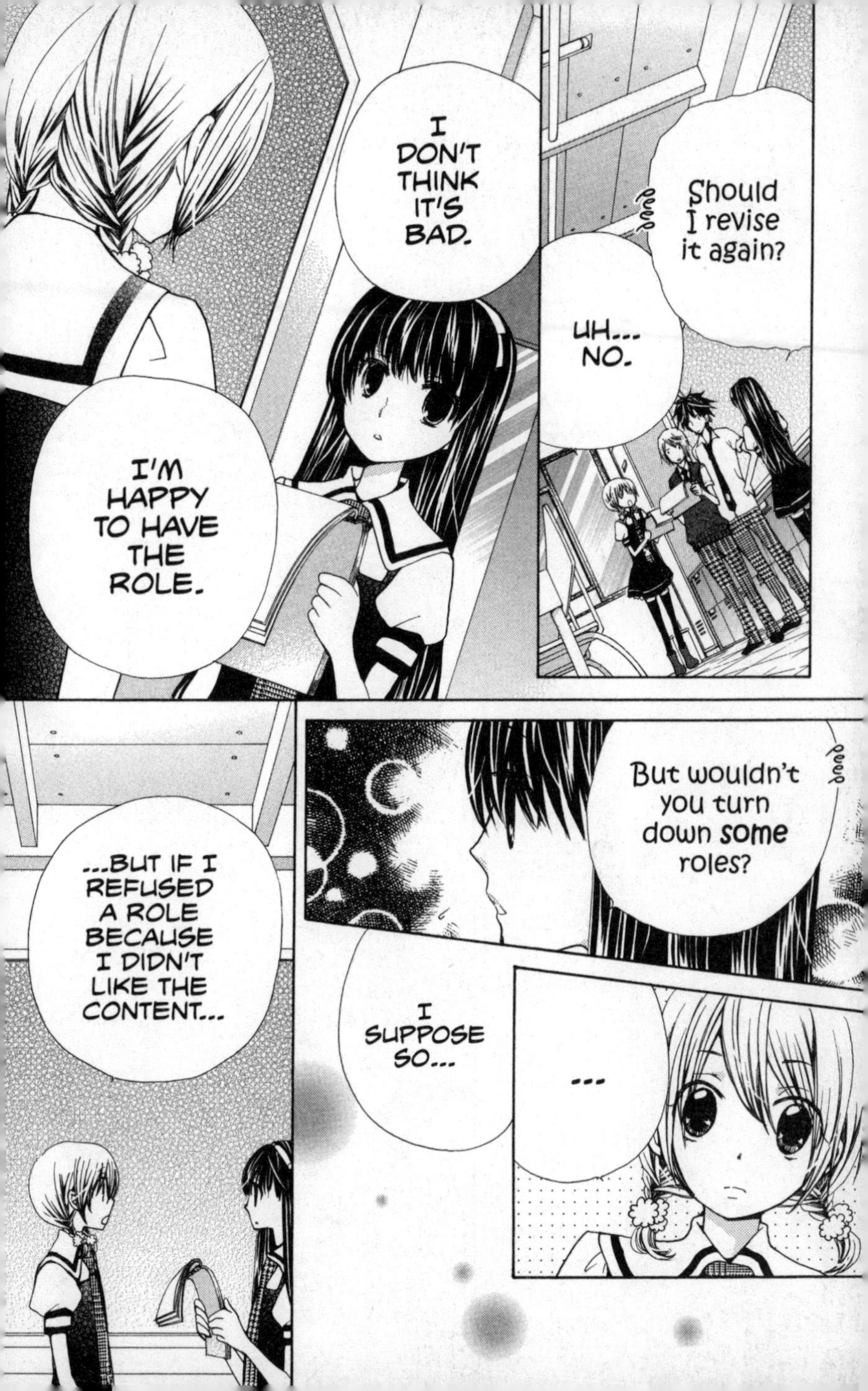
Should I revise it again?
UH... NO.
I DON'T THINK IT'S BAD.
I'M HAPPY TO HAVE THE ROLE.
But wouldn't you turn down some roles?
I SUPPOSE SO...
...
...BUT IF I REFUSED A ROLE BECAUSE I DIDN'T LIKE THE CONTENT...

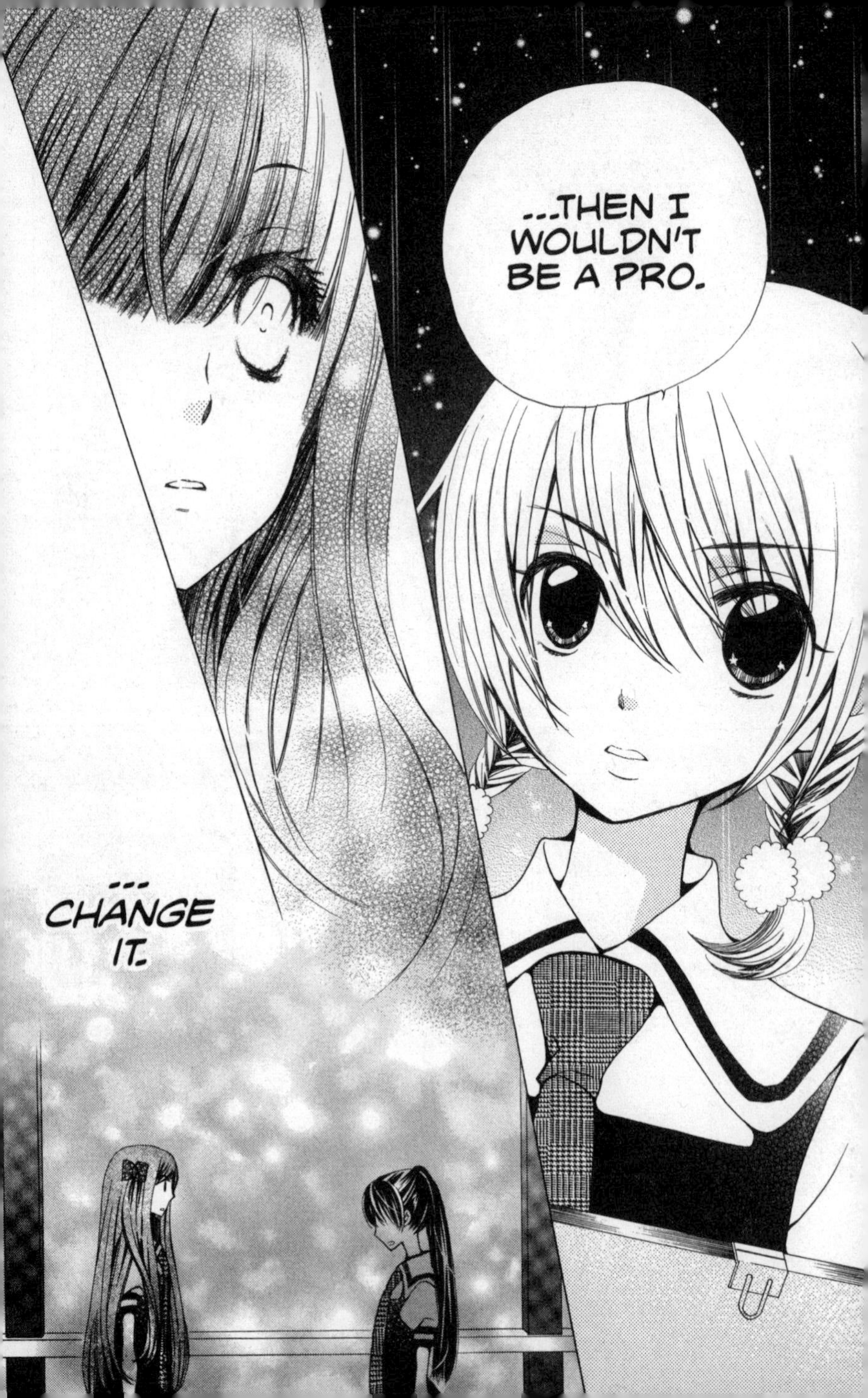
...THEN I WOULDN'T BE A PRO.
...CHANGE IT.

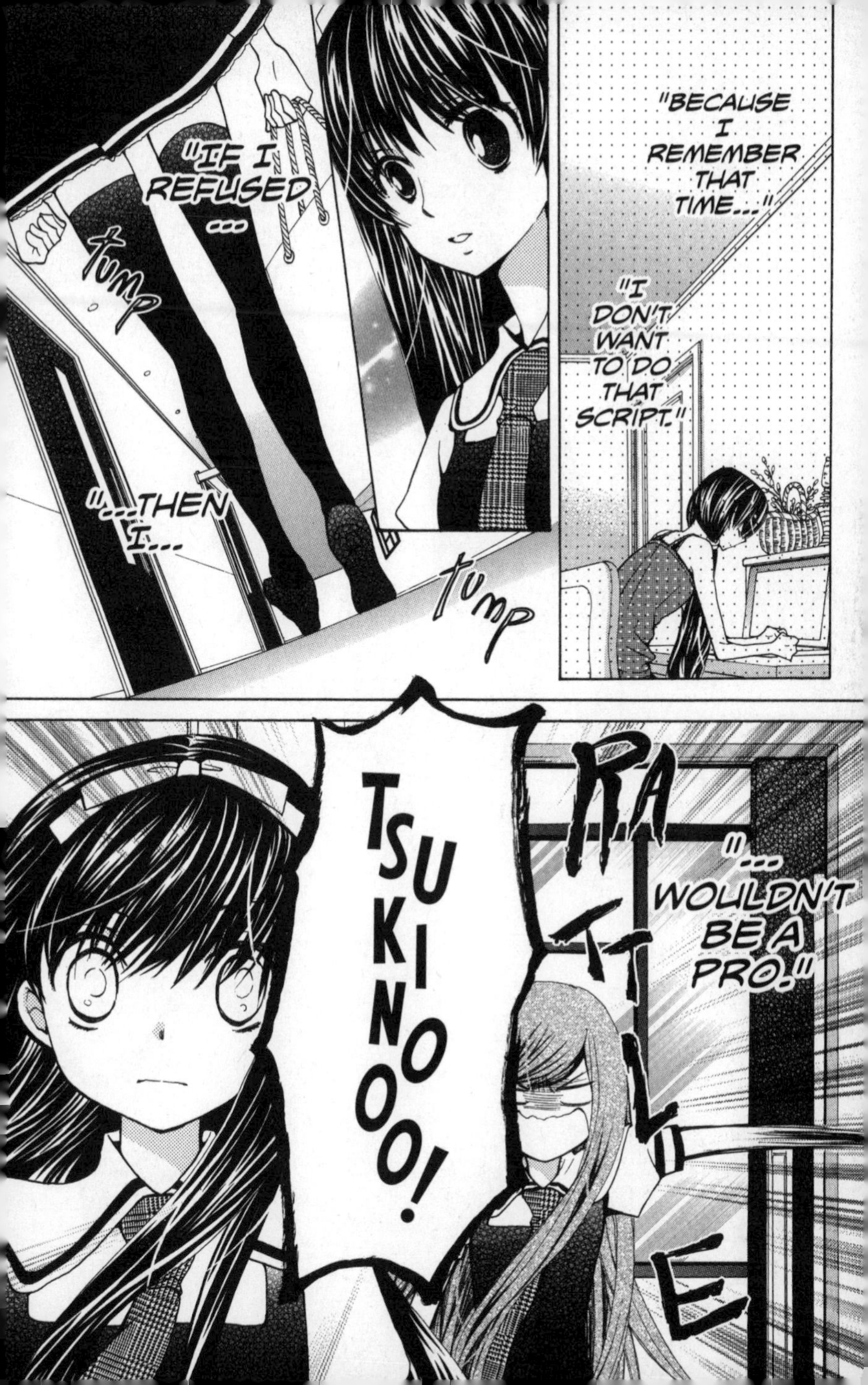
"BECAUSE I REMEMBER THAT TIME..."
"I DON'T WANT TO DO THAT SCRIPT."
"IF I REFUSED ..."
TUMP
"...THEN I...
TUMP
"...WOULDN'T BE A PRO."
RATTLE
TSUKINOOOO!

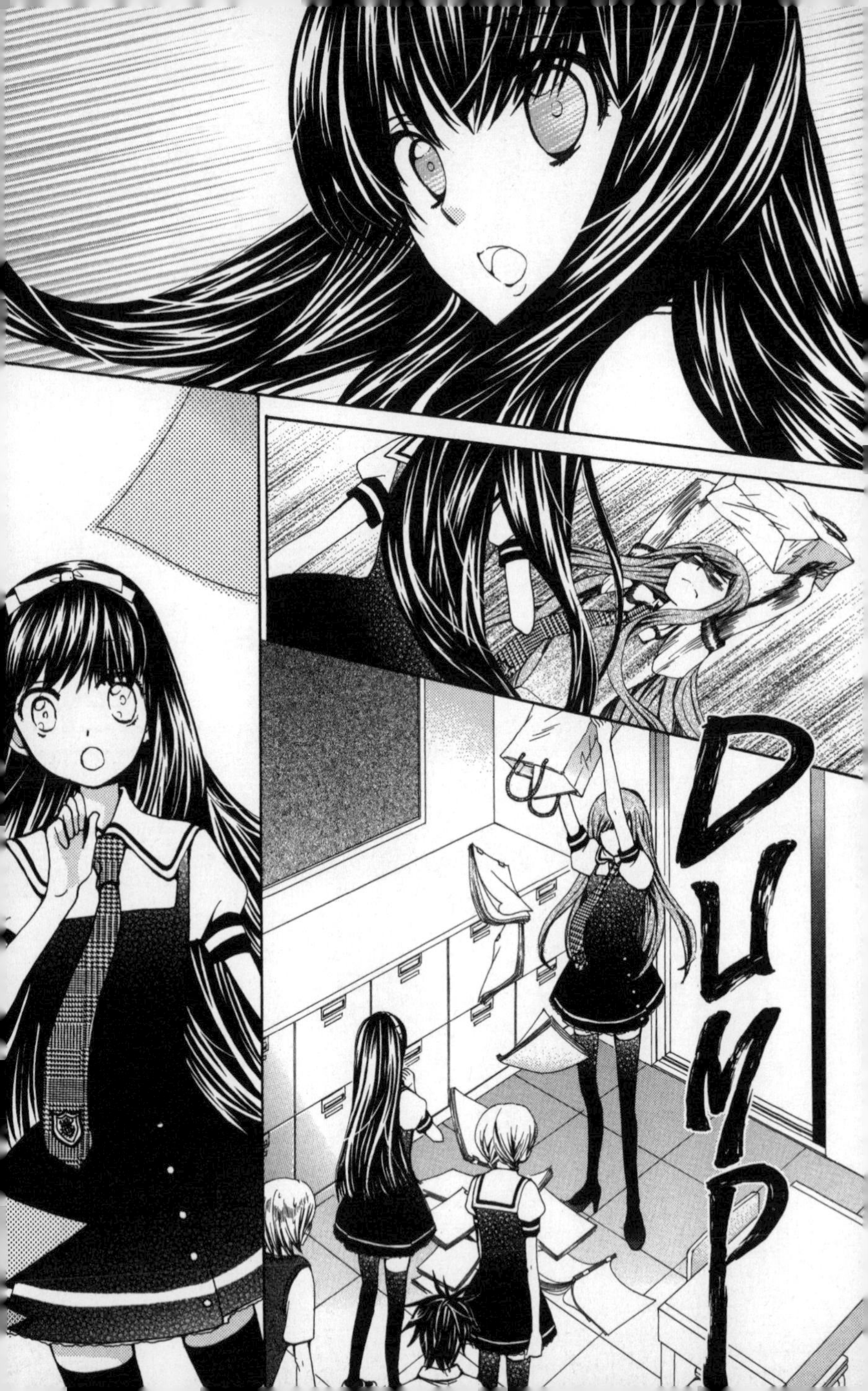
DUMP

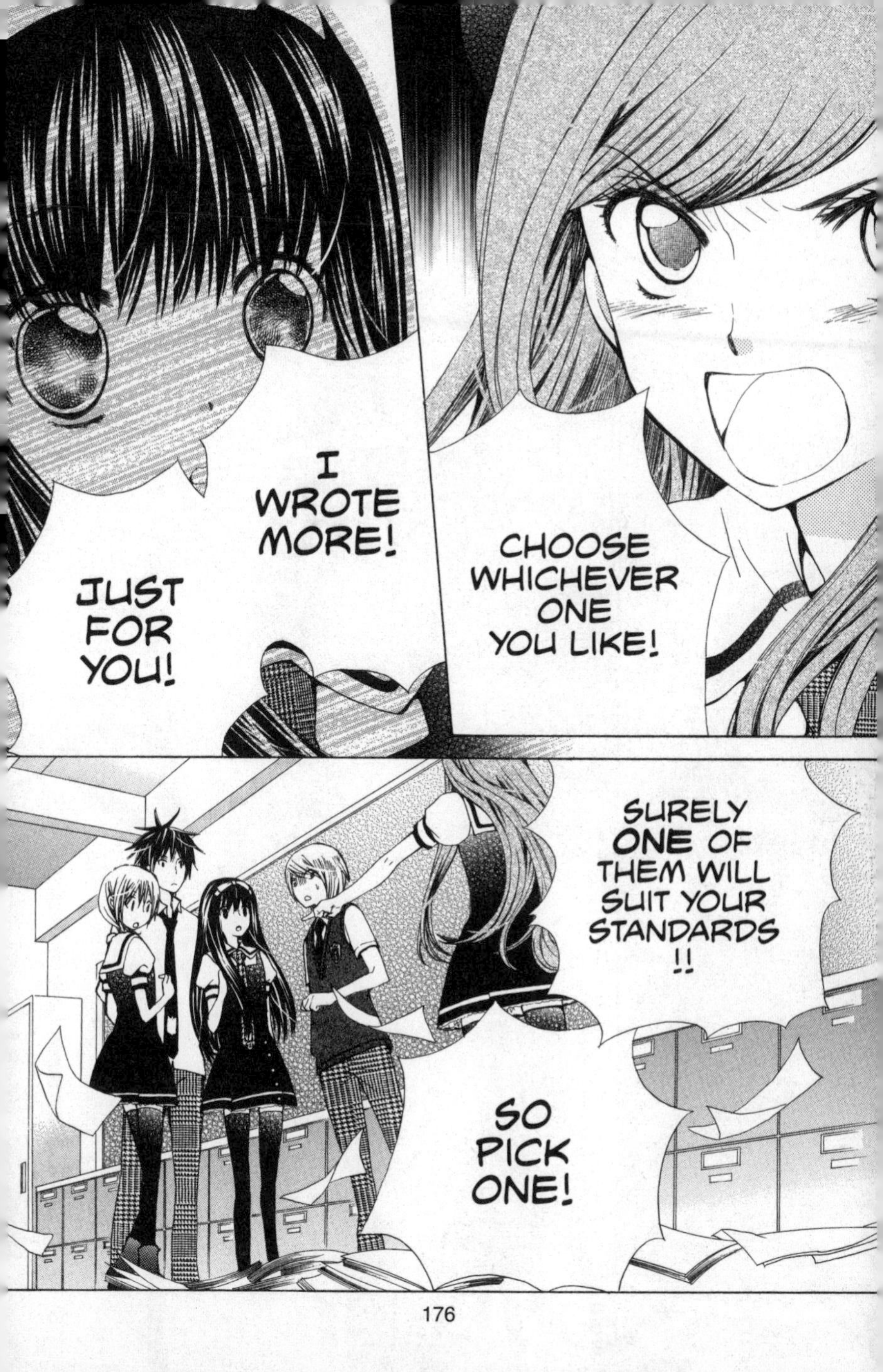
CHOOSE WHICHEVER ONE YOU LIKE!
I WROTE MORE!
JUST FOR YOU!
SURELY ONE OF THEM WILL SUIT YOUR STANDARDS!!
SO PICK ONE!

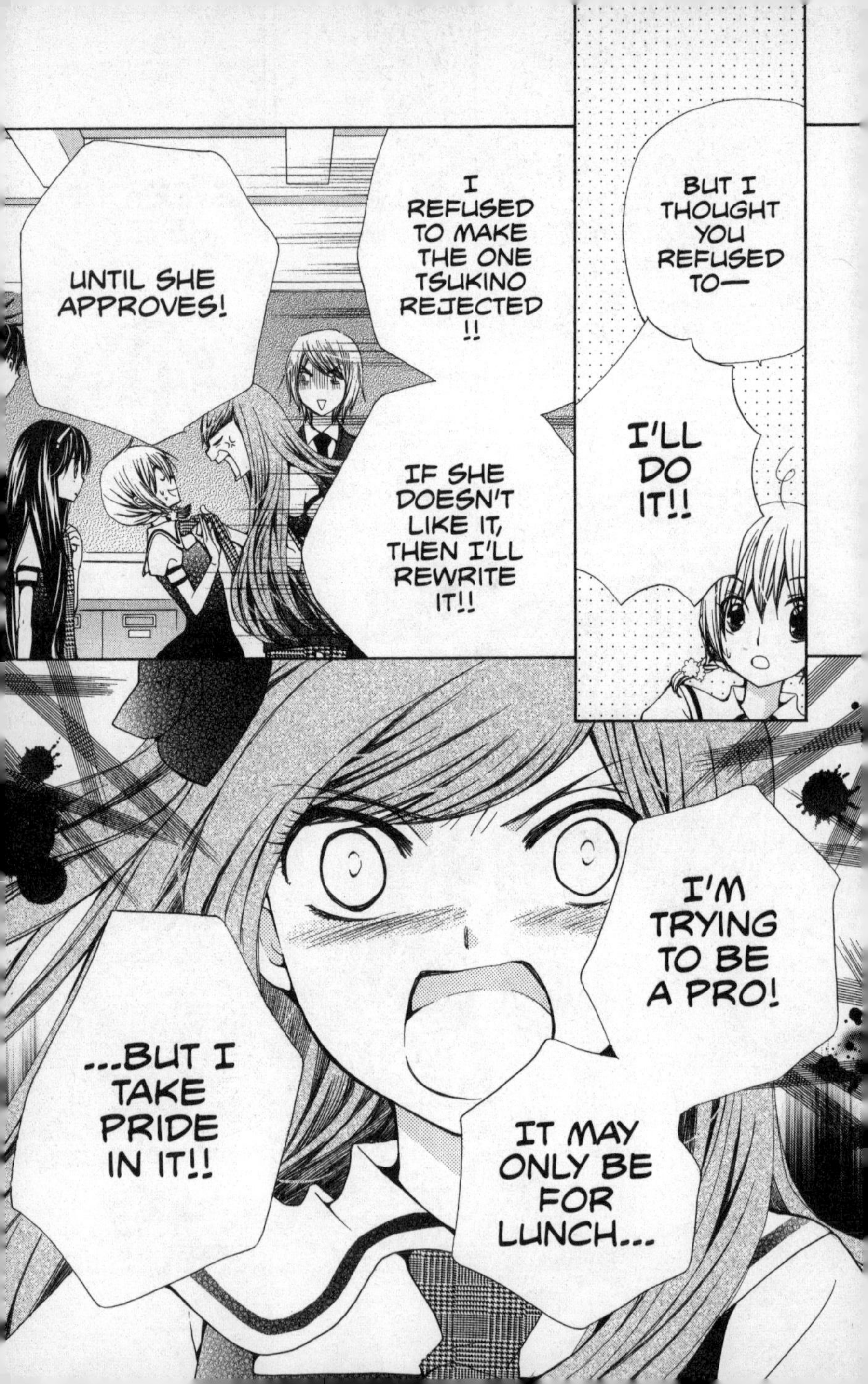
BUT I THOUGHT YOU REFUSED TO—
I'LL DO IT!!
I REFUSED TO MAKE THE ONE TSUKINO REJECTED!!
IF SHE DOESN'T LIKE IT, THEN I'LL REWRITE IT!!
UNTIL SHE APPROVES!
I'M TRYING TO BE A PRO!
IT MAY ONLY BE FOR LUNCH...
...BUT I TAKE PRIDE IN IT!!

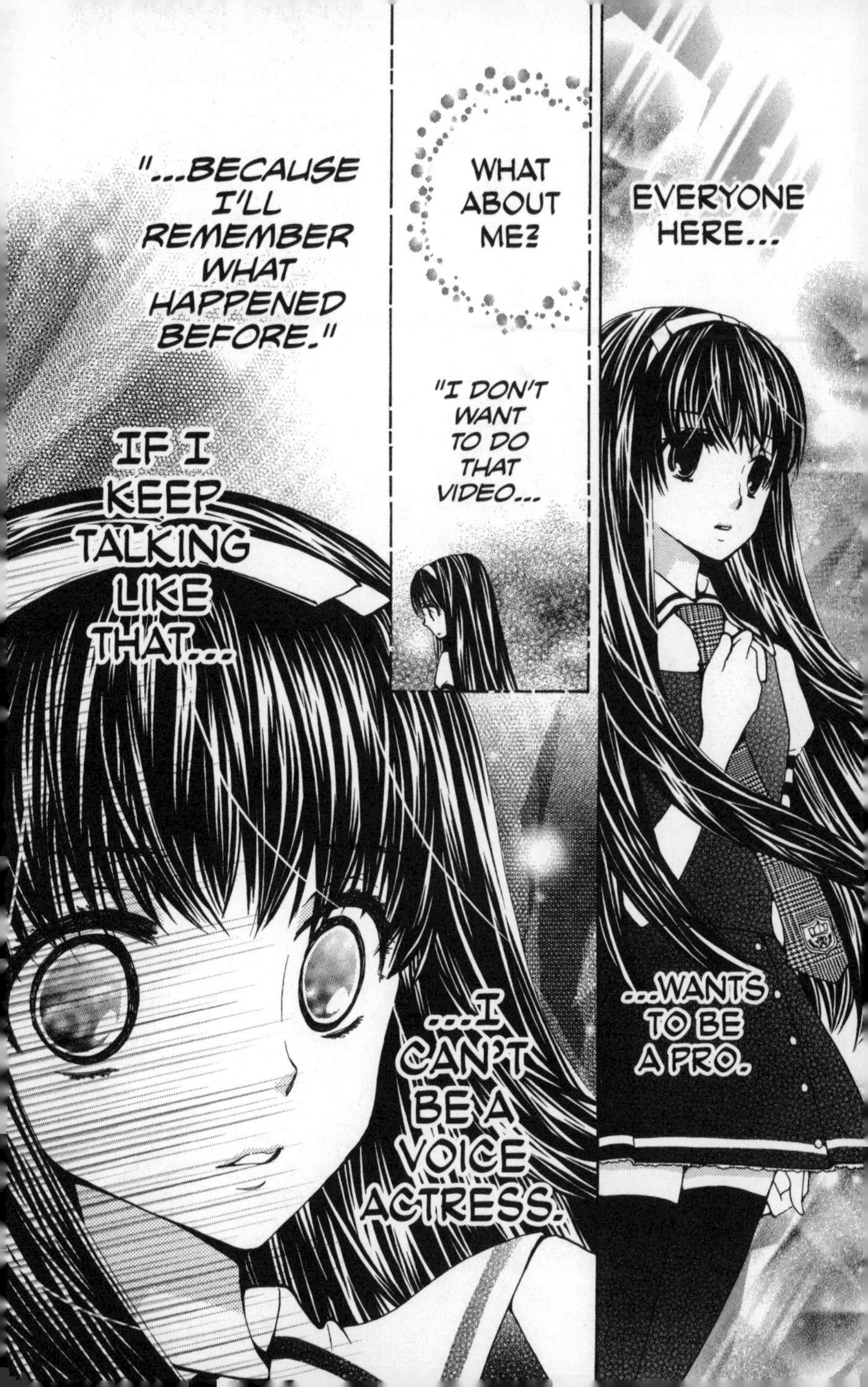
EVERYONE HERE...
...WANTS TO BE A PRO.
WHAT ABOUT ME?
"I DON'T WANT TO DO THAT VIDEO...
"...BECAUSE I'LL REMEMBER WHAT HAPPENED BEFORE."
IF I KEEP TALKING LIKE THAT...
...I CAN'T BE A VOICE ACTRESS.

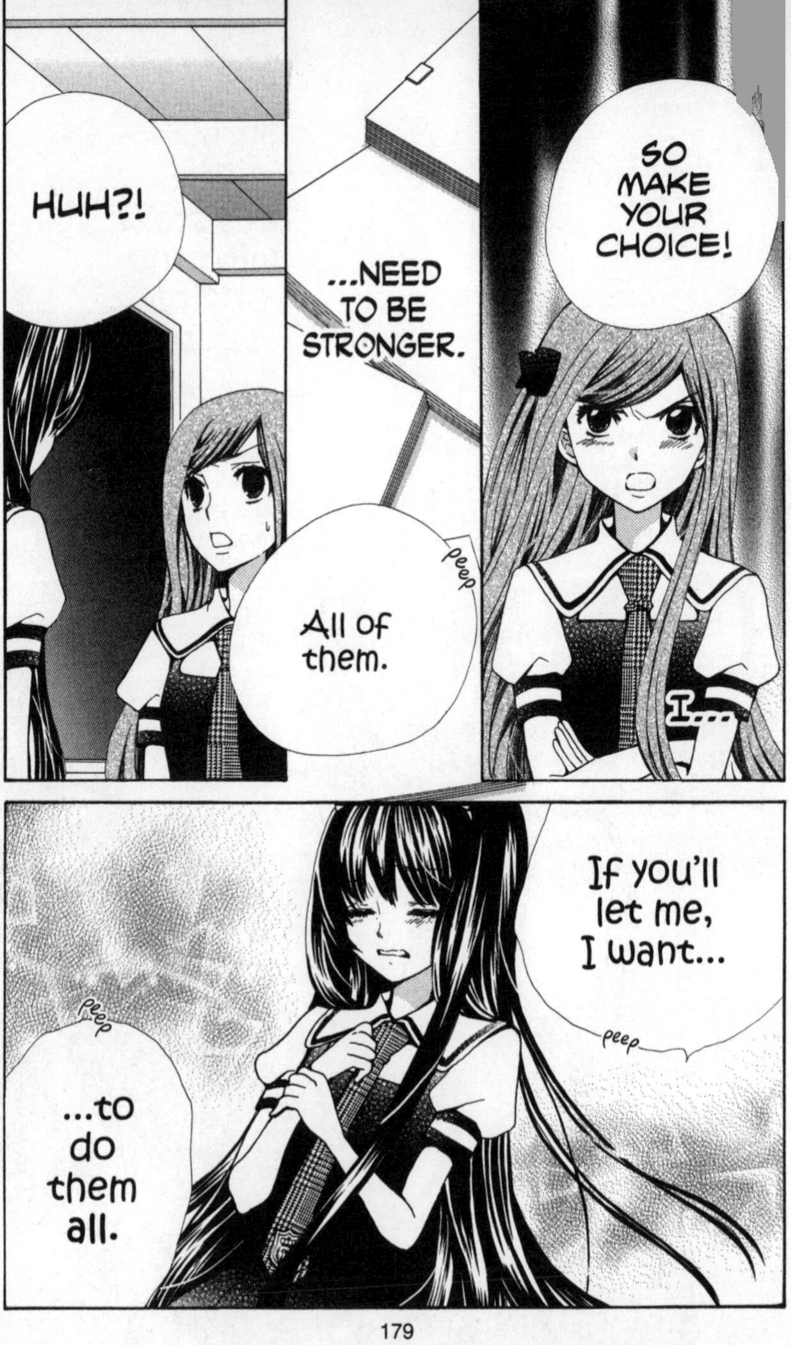
SO MAKE YOUR CHOICE!
I...
...NEED TO BE STRONGER.
peep
All of them.
HUH?!
If you'll let me, I want...
peep
peep
...to do them all.

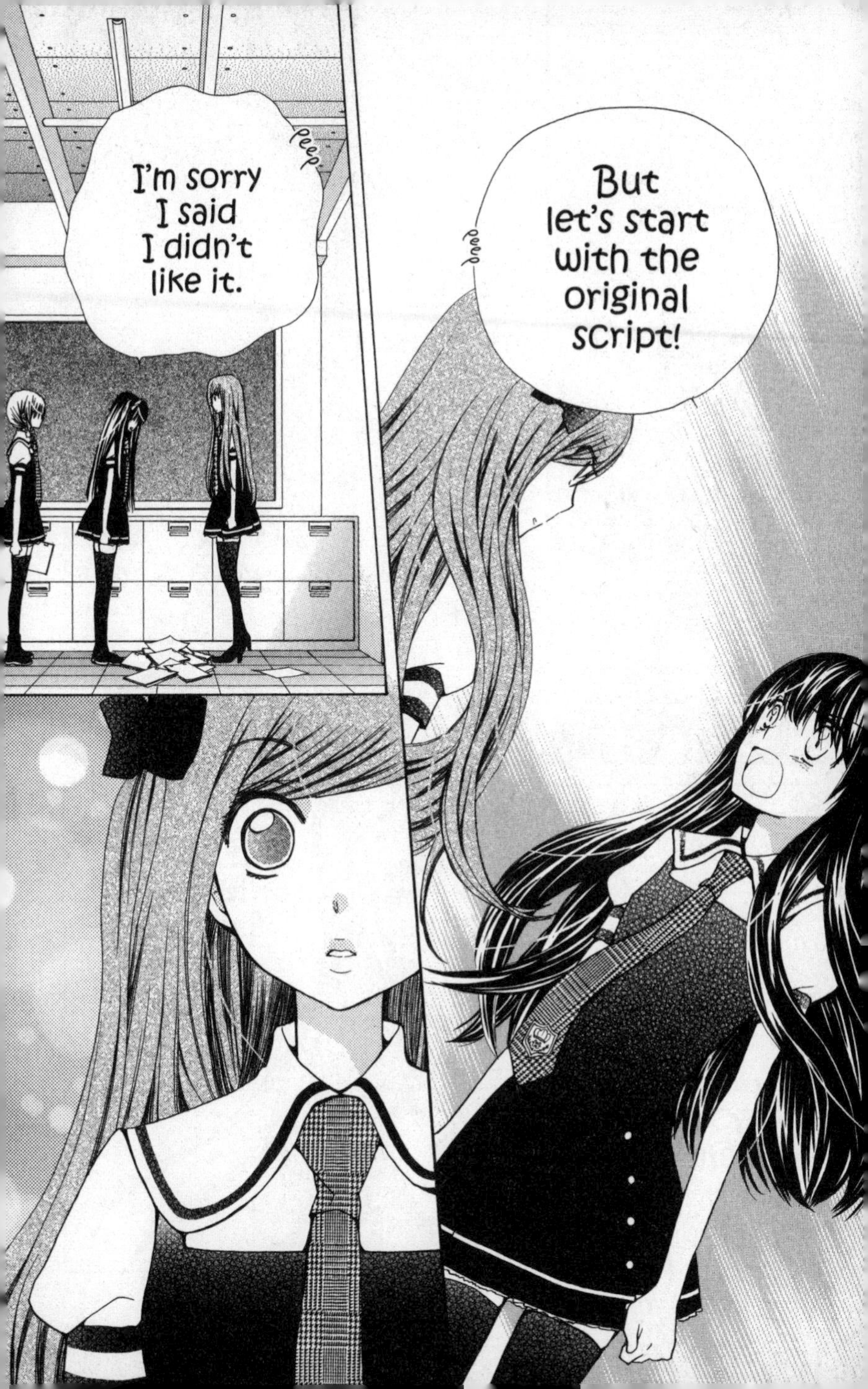
peep
I'm sorry I said I didn't like it.
peep
But let's start with the original script!

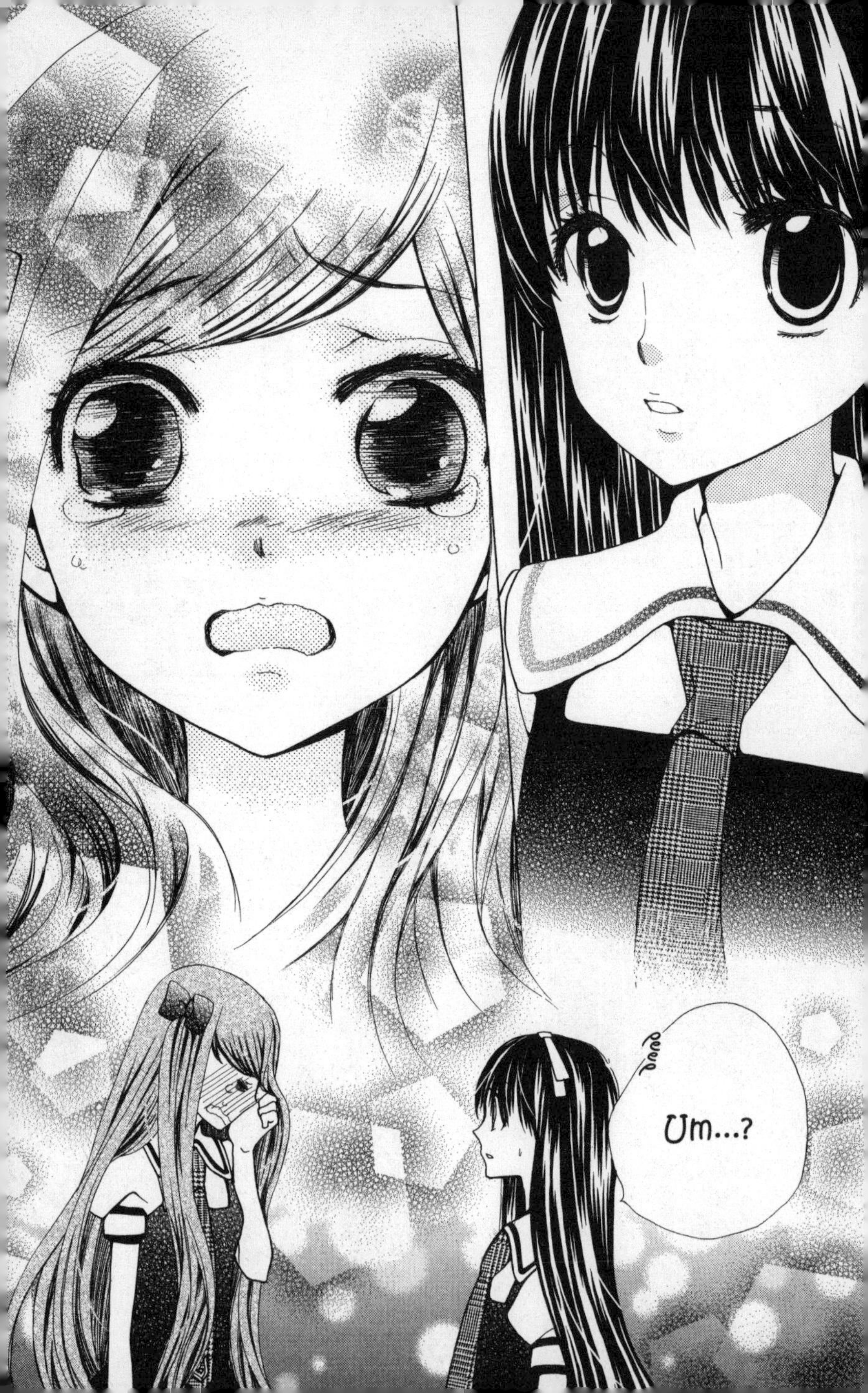
Um...?

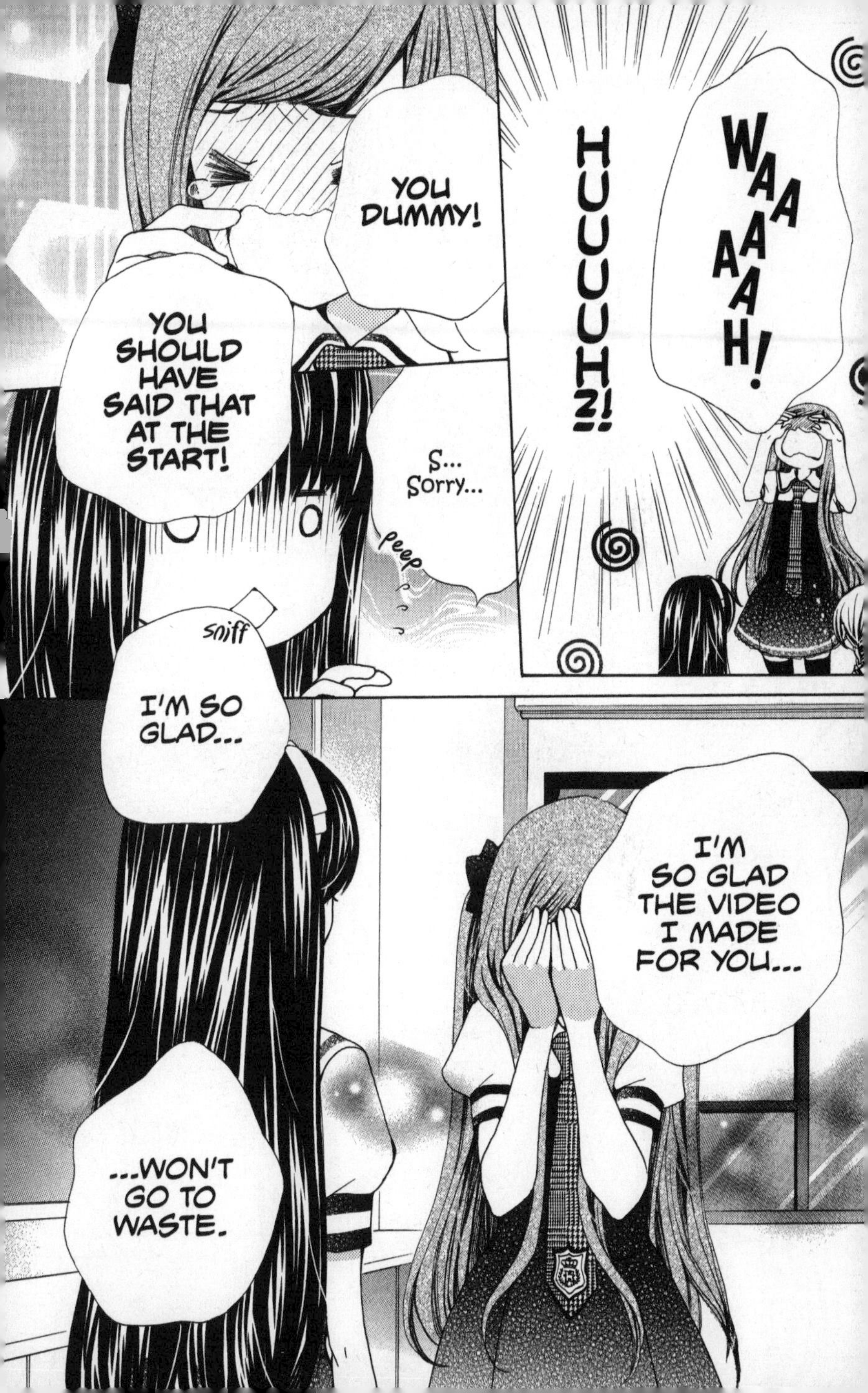
WAAAAAH!
HUUUUH?!
YOU DUMMY!
YOU SHOULD HAVE SAID THAT AT THE START!
S... Sorry...
peep
sniff
I'M SO GLAD...
I'M SO GLAD THE VIDEO I MADE FOR YOU...
...WON'T GO TO WASTE.

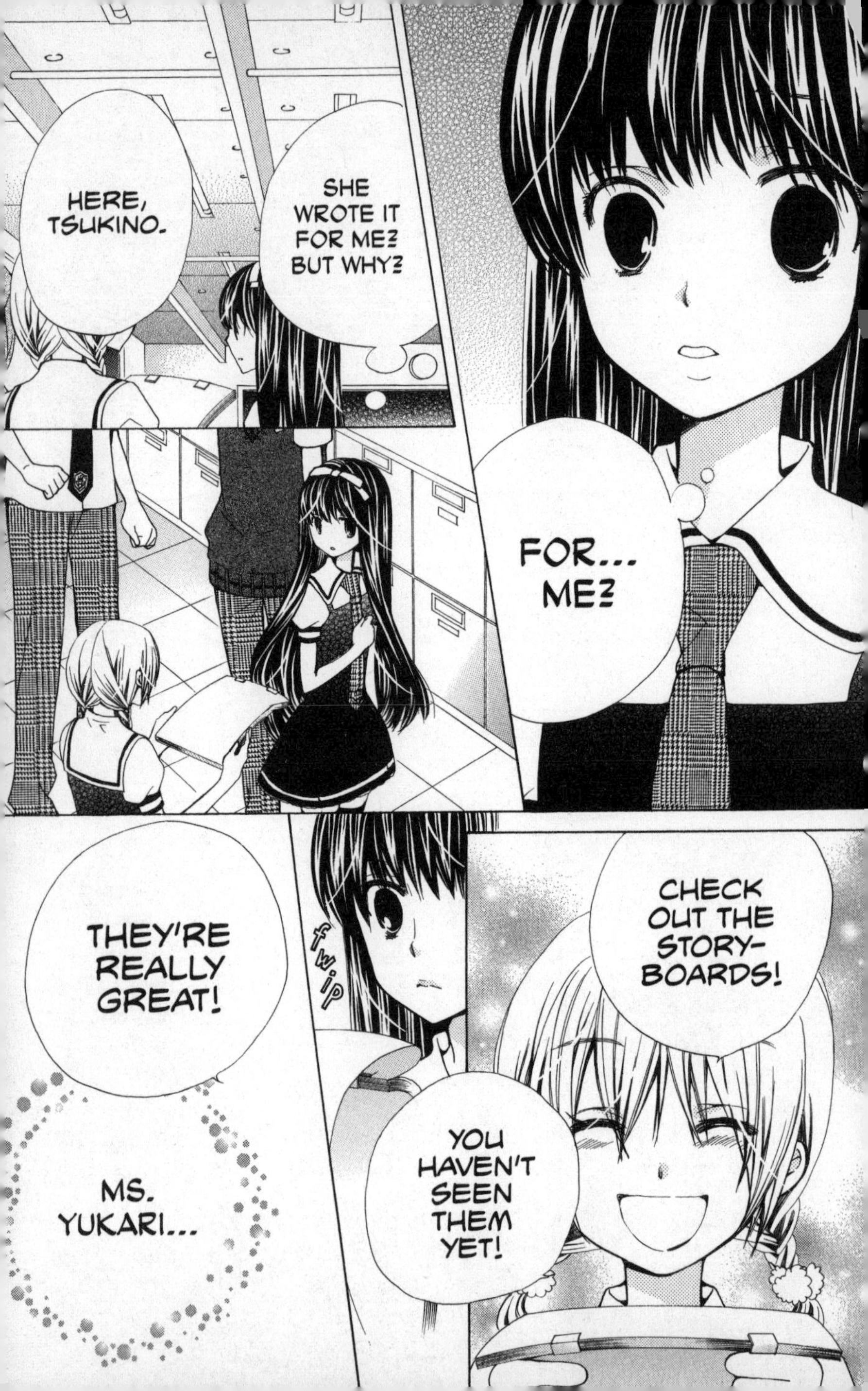
FOR... ME?
SHE WROTE IT FOR ME? BUT WHY?
HERE, TSUKINO.
CHECK OUT THE STORY-BOARDS!
YOU HAVEN'T SEEN THEM YET!
fwip
THEY'RE REALLY GREAT!
MS. YUKARI...

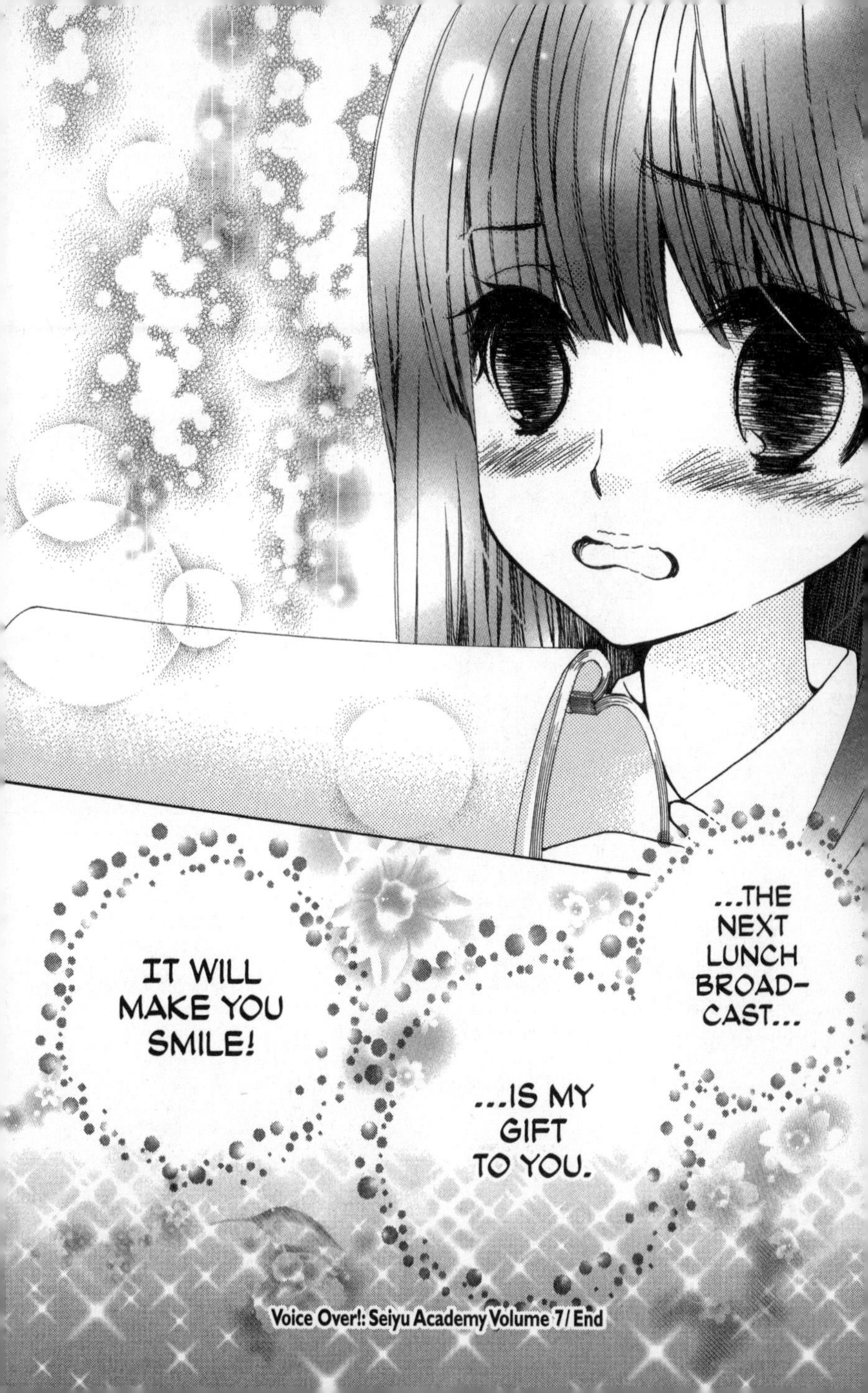
...THE NEXT LUNCH BROAD-CAST...
...IS MY GIFT TO YOU.
IT WILL MAKE YOU SMILE!
Voice Over!: Seiyu Academy Volume 7/ End

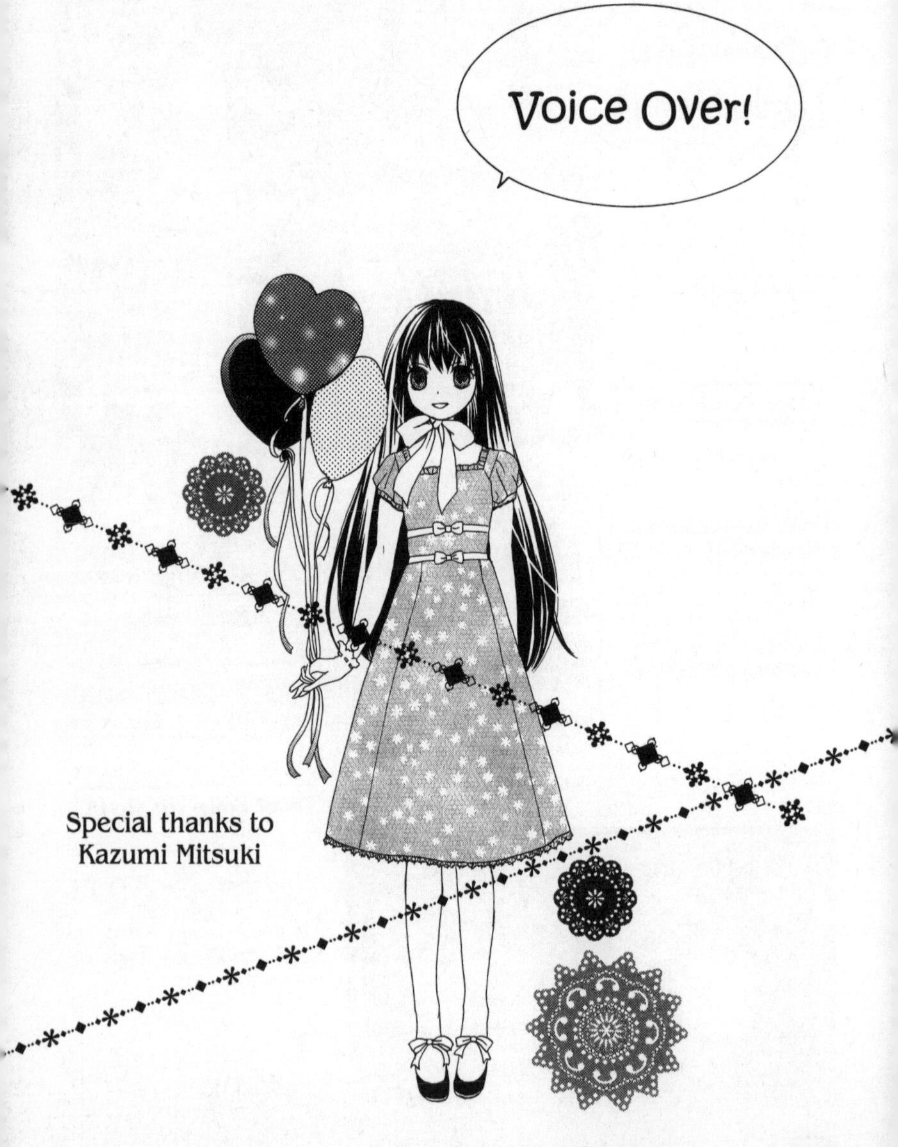
Voice Over!

Special thanks to
Kazumi Mitsuki

Sudden Bonus Content Corner!!

This time, I'm showing the poster for the hero show and the end screen for **Beast Renjai**!!

Hero show poster

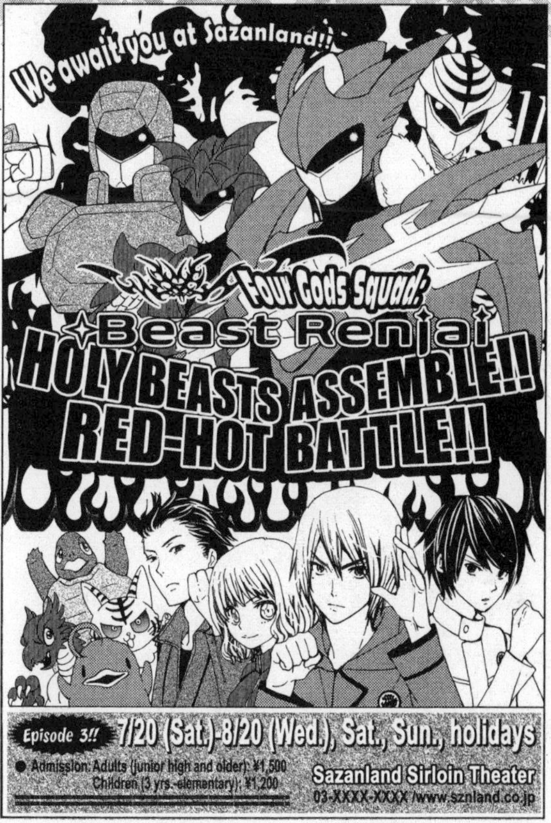

We await you at Sazanland!!
Four Gods Squad:
Beast Renjai
HOLY BEASTS ASSEMBLE!!
RED-HOT BATTLE!!
Episode 3!!
7/20 (Sat.)-8/20 (Wed.), Sat., Sun., holidays
Admission: Adults (junior high and older): ¥1,500
Children (3 yrs.-elementary): ¥1,200
Sazanland Sirloin Theater
03-XXXX-XXXX /www.sznland.co.jp

It looks like a real design!!

I-san, who designed this, is really incredible!

The sirloin theater serves all-you-can-eat meat every day.

Beast Renjai end screen

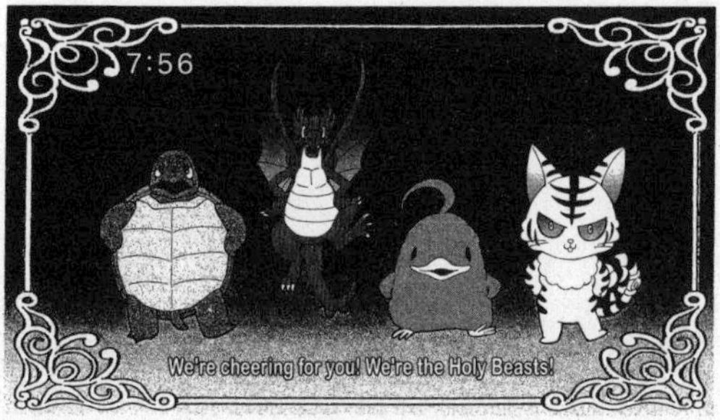

7:56
We're cheering for you! We're the Holy Beasts!

The time, 7:56, is real. M-san came up with the holy beast poses and song lyrics. They're so cute!

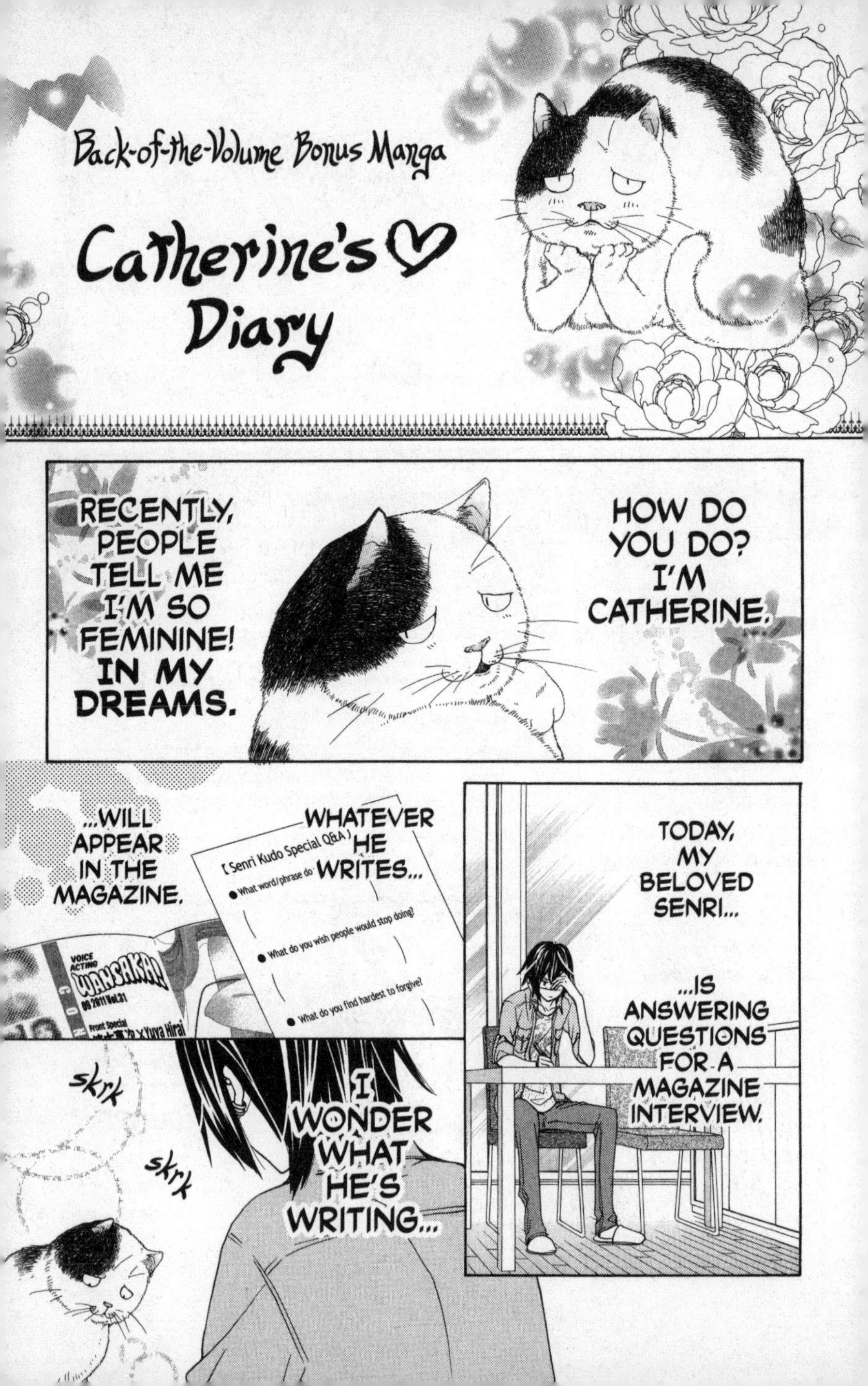
Back-of-the-Volume Bonus Manga
Catherine's ♥ Diary
HOW DO YOU DO? I'M CATHERINE.
RECENTLY, PEOPLE TELL ME I'M SO FEMININE! IN MY DREAMS.
TODAY, MY BELOVED SENRI...
...IS ANSWERING QUESTIONS FOR A MAGAZINE INTERVIEW.
WHATEVER HE WRITES...
[Senri Kudo Special Q&A]
What word/phrase do
What do you wish people would stop doing?
What do you find hardest to forgive?
VOICE ACTING
WANSAKA!!
09 2011 Vol.31
Front Special
Yuya Hirai
...WILL APPEAR IN THE MAGAZINE.
I WONDER WHAT HE'S WRITING...
skrk
skrk

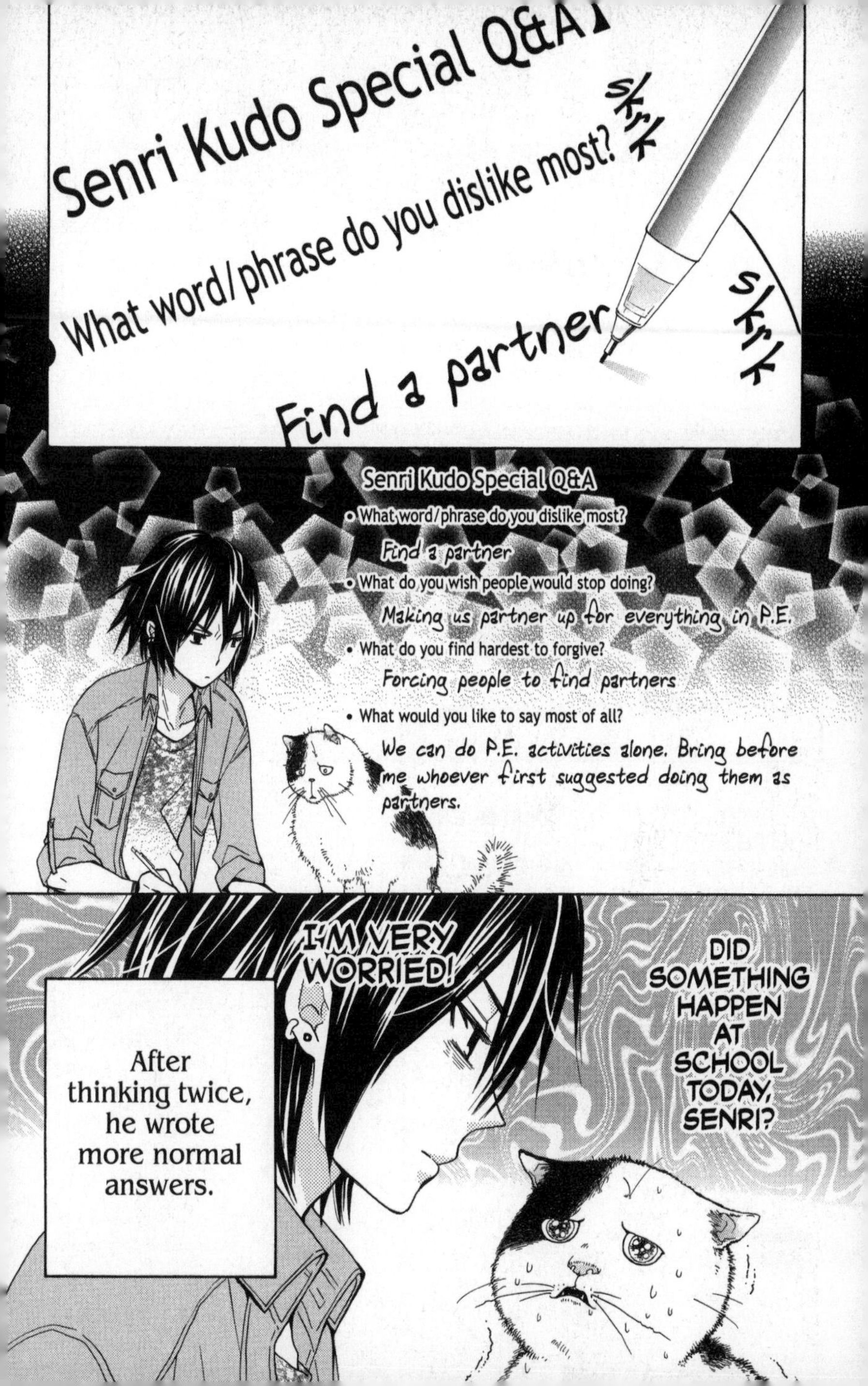
Senri Kudo Special Q&A
What word/phrase do you dislike most?
skrk
skrk
Find a partner
Senri Kudo Special Q&A
• What word/phrase do you dislike most?
Find a partner
• What do you wish people would stop doing?
Making us partner up for everything in P.E.
• What do you find hardest to forgive?
Forcing people to find partners
• What would you like to say most of all?
We can do P.E. activities alone. Bring before me whoever first suggested doing them as partners.
DID SOMETHING HAPPEN AT SCHOOL TODAY, SENRI?
I'M VERY WORRIED!
After thinking twice, he wrote more normal answers.

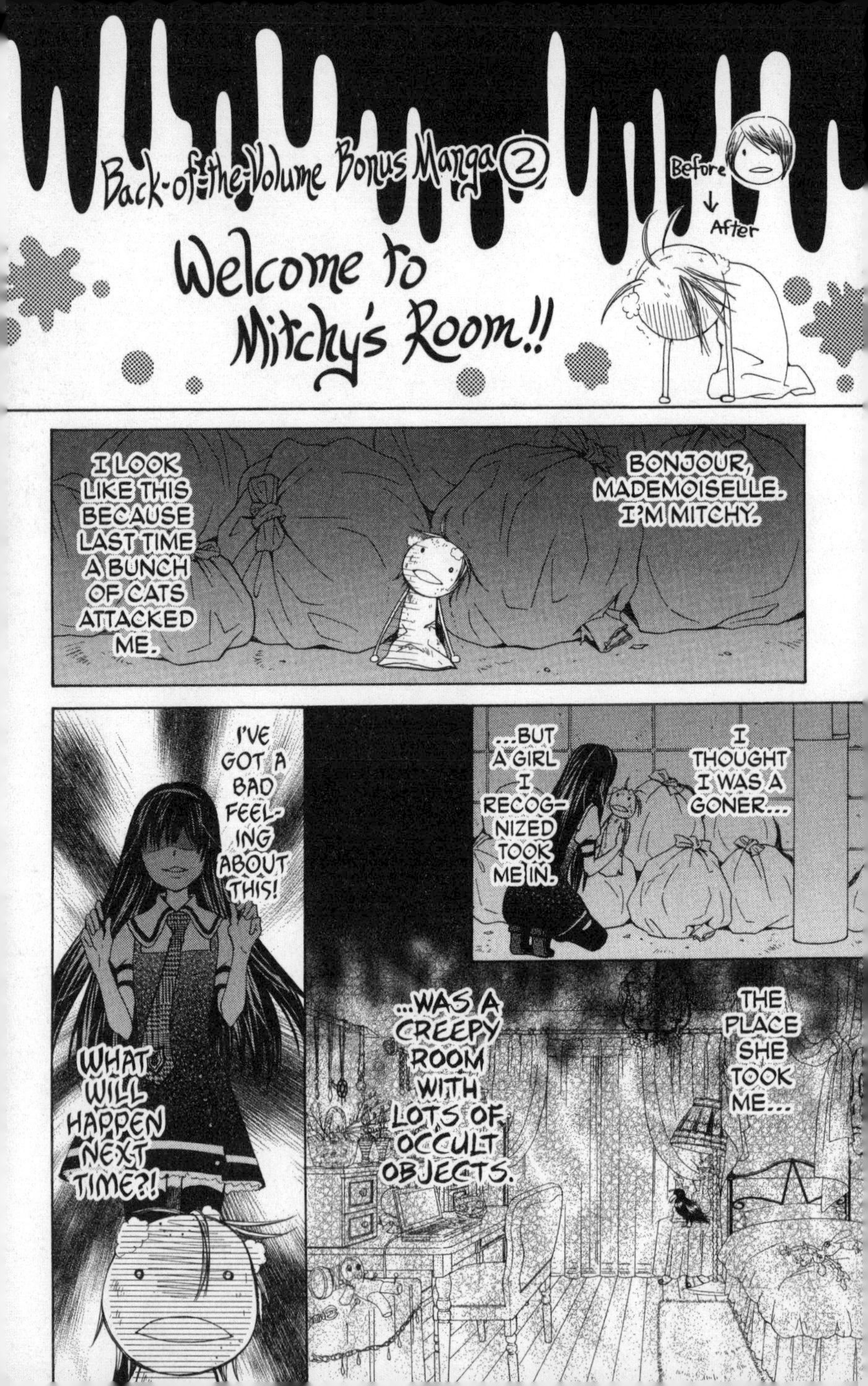
Back-of-the-Volume Bonus Manga 2
Welcome to Mitchy's Room!!
Before
After
BONJOUR, MADEMOISELLE. I'M MITCHY.
I LOOK LIKE THIS BECAUSE LAST TIME A BUNCH OF CATS ATTACKED ME.
I THOUGHT I WAS A GONER...
...BUT A GIRL I RECOGNIZED TOOK ME IN.
THE PLACE SHE TOOK ME...
...WAS A CREEPY ROOM WITH LOTS OF OCCULT OBJECTS.
I'VE GOT A BAD FEELING ABOUT THIS!
WHAT WILL HAPPEN NEXT TIME?!

*Voice Over!

★MINNAI MARU TEAM★

NOT SUITABLE FOR DO-SEE-LOW-TO

Special thanks to
Kazumi Mitsuki

WANTED

1046010

the "BLANCO"

99,999,999,

EAD or ALI

Voice Over! Seiyu Academy

End Notes

Page 104, panel 4: Takoyaki
Dough balls with pieces of octopus in them. They are made using a hot plate and are often sold at Japanese festivals. *Tako* means "octopus" in Japanese.

Page 106, panel 4: Yaki
Yaki means "fried" in Japanese, and there are many popular yaki dishes sold at festivals, such as *yakisoba* (fried soba noodles) or *yakitori* (fried chicken).

Page 129, side bar: Chankonabe
A high-protein one-pot stew commonly cooked by sumo wrestlers as part of their weight-gain regime.

Maki Minami is from Saitama Prefecture in Japan. She debuted in 2001 with *Kanata no Ao* (Faraway Blue). Her other works include *Kimi wa Girlfriend* (You're My Girlfriend), *Mainichi ga Takaramono* (Every Day Is a Treasure), *Yuki Atataka* (Warm Winter) and *S•A*, which was published in English by VIZ Media.

VOICE OVER!
SEIYU ACADEMY
VOL. 7
Shojo Beat Edition

STORY AND ART BY
MAKI MINAMI

TECHNICAL ADVISORS
Yoichi Kato, Kaori Kagami, Ayumi Hashidate,
Ayako Harino and Touko Fujitani

Special Thanks
81produce
Tokyo Animator College
Tokyo Animation College

English Translation & Adaptation/John Werry
Touch-up Art & Lettering/Sabrina Heep
Design/Yukiko Whitley
Editor/Pancha Diaz

SEIYU KA! by Maki Minami
© Maki Minami 2011
All rights reserved.
First published in Japan in 2011 by HAKUSENSHA, Inc., Tokyo.
English language translation rights arranged with
HAKUSENSHA, Inc., Tokyo.

Printed in the U.S.A.

Published by VIZ Media, LLC
P.O. Box 77010
San Francisco, CA 94107

10 9 8 7 6 5 4 3 2 1
First printing, October 2014

www.viz.com   www.shojobeat.com

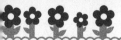 
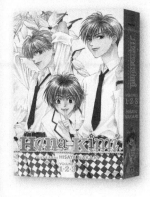 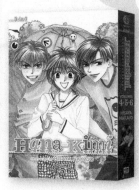 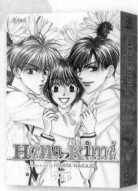

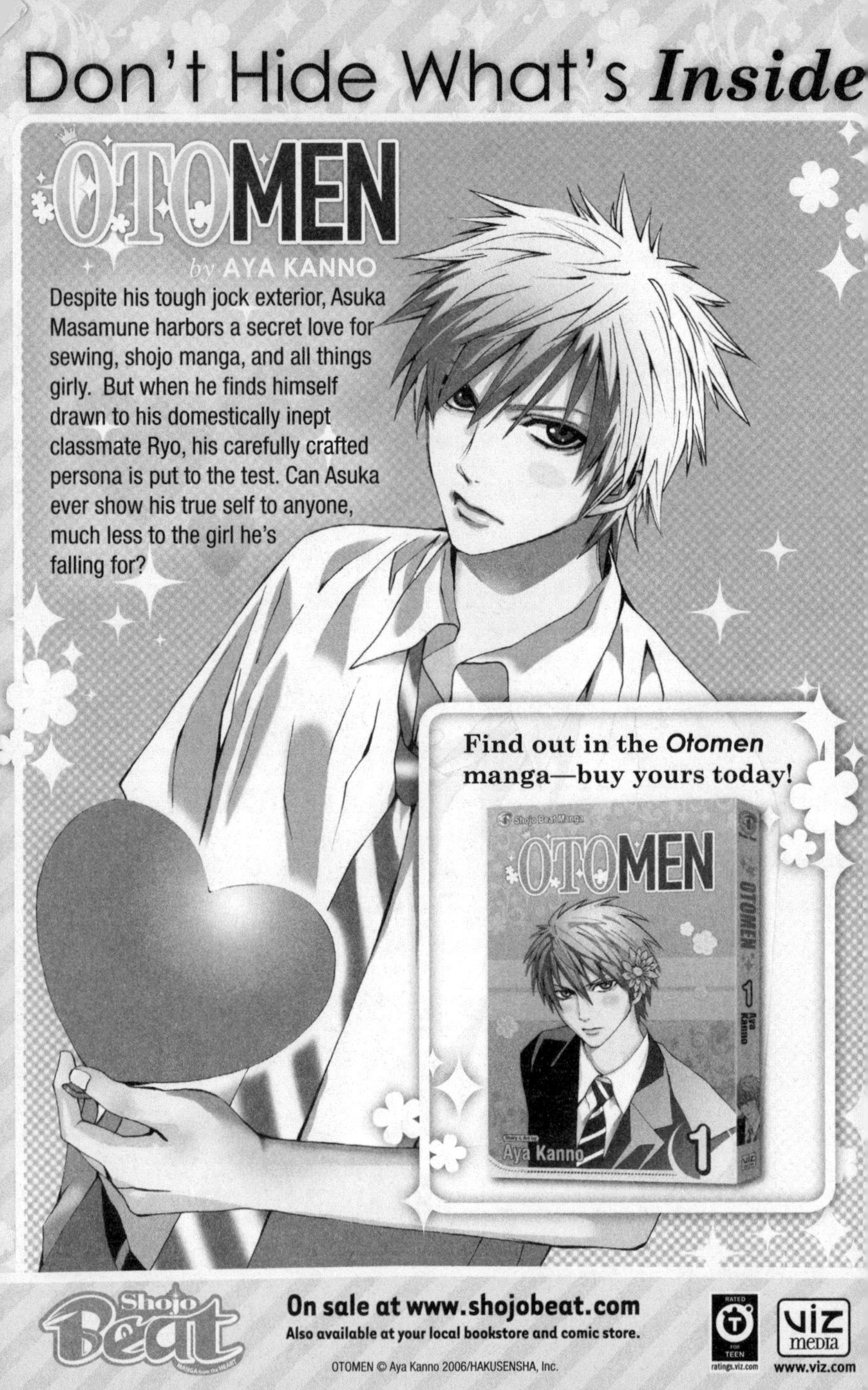
Don't Hide What's *Inside*
OTOMEN
by AYA KANNO
Despite his tough jock exterior, Asuka Masamune harbors a secret love for sewing, shojo manga, and all things girly. But when he finds himself drawn to his domestically inept classmate Ryo, his carefully crafted persona is put to the test. Can Asuka ever show his true self to anyone, much less to the girl he's falling for?
Find out in the *Otomen* manga—buy yours today!
Shojo Beat Manga
OTOMEN
1
Aya Kanno
Shojo Beat
On sale at www.shojobeat.com
Also available at your local bookstore and comic store.
OTOMEN © Aya Kanno 2006/HAKUSENSHA, Inc.
RATED T FOR TEEN
ratings.viz.com
VIZ media
www.viz.com

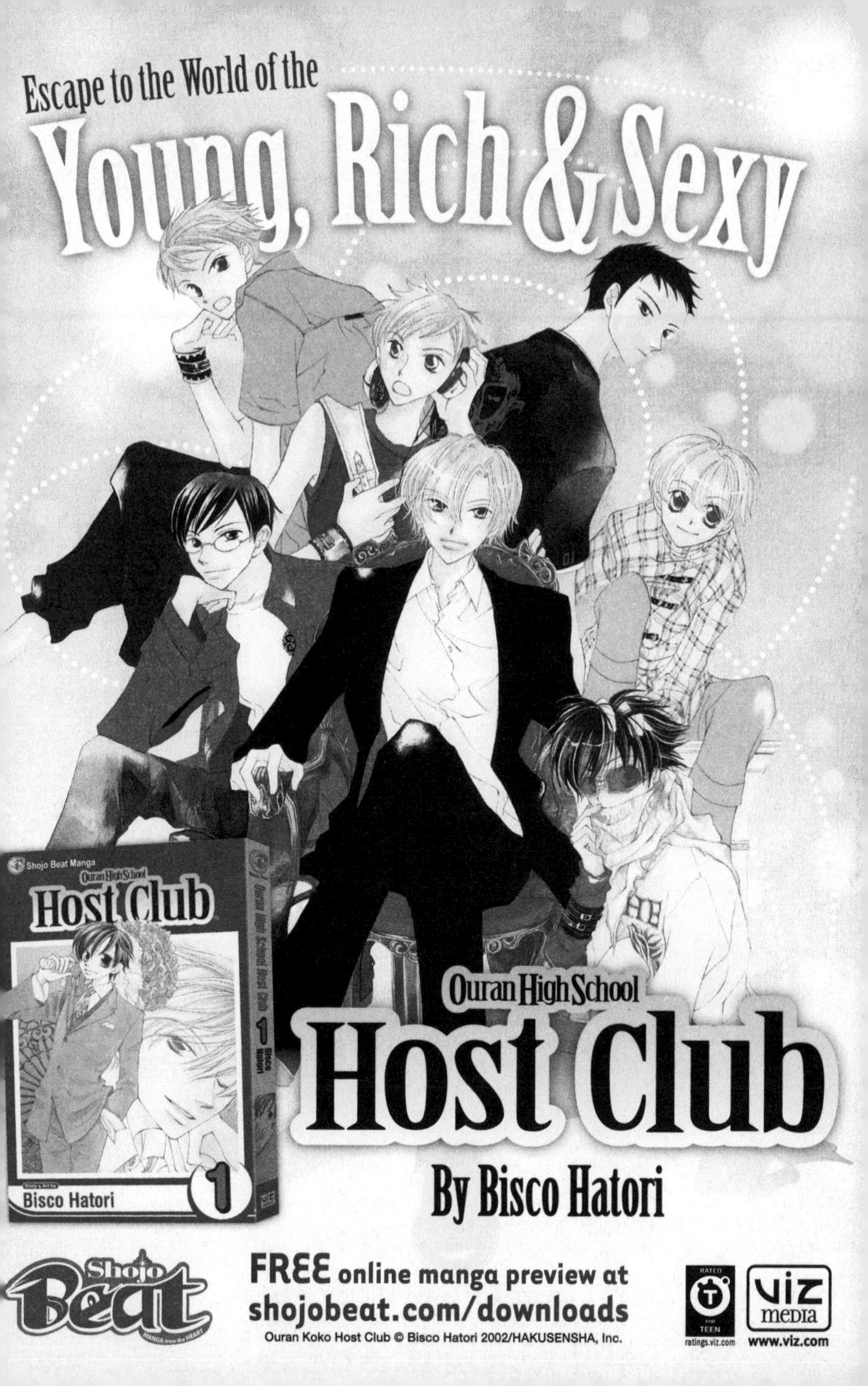
Escape to the World of the
Young, Rich & Sexy
Shojo Beat Manga
Ouran High School
Host Club
Ouran High School Host Club 1 Bisco Hatori
Story & Art by
Bisco Hatori
1
Ouran High School
Host Club
By Bisco Hatori
Shojo Beat
FREE online manga preview at
shojobeat.com/downloads
Ouran Koko Host Club © Bisco Hatori 2002/HAKUSENSHA, Inc.
RATED T FOR TEEN
ratings.viz.com
VIZ media
www.viz.com

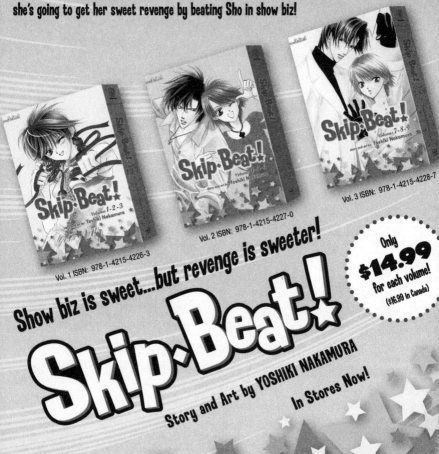

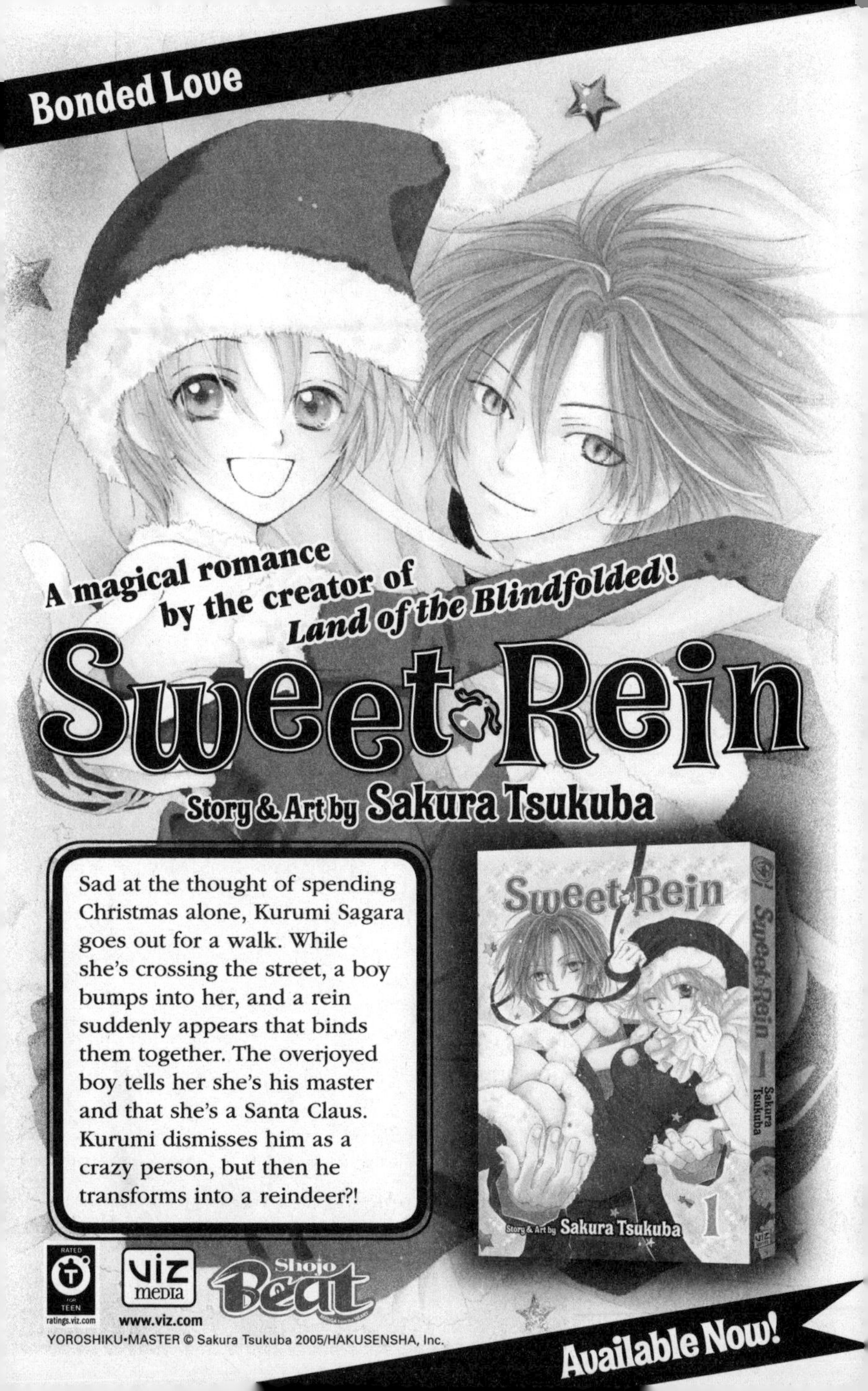
Bonded Love
A magical romance
by the creator of
Land of the Blindfolded!
Sweet Rein
Story & Art by Sakura Tsukuba
Sad at the thought of spending Christmas alone, Kurumi Sagara goes out for a walk. While she's crossing the street, a boy bumps into her, and a rein suddenly appears that binds them together. The overjoyed boy tells her she's his master and that she's a Santa Claus. Kurumi dismisses him as a crazy person, but then he transforms into a reindeer?!
Sweet Rein
Sweet Rein 1 Sakura Tsukuba
Story & Art by Sakura Tsukuba 1
RATED T FOR TEEN
ratings.viz.com
VIZ media
www.viz.com
Shojo Beat
YOROSHIKU•MASTER © Sakura Tsukuba 2005/HAKUSENSHA, Inc.
Available Now!

VIZMANGA

Read manga anytime, anywhere!

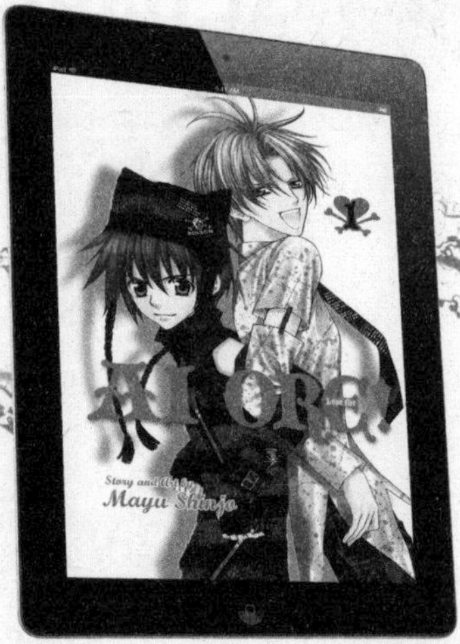

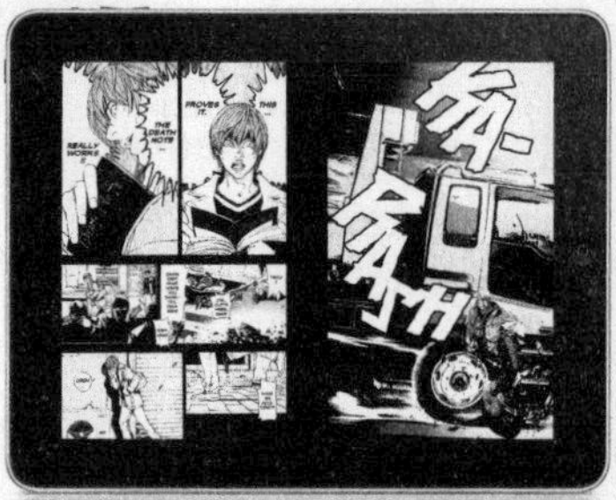

From our newest hit series to the classics you know and love, the best manga in the world is now available digitally. Buy a volume* of digital manga for your:

- iOS device (**iPad®, iPhone®, iPod® touch**) through the **VIZ Manga app**
- Android-powered device (**phone or tablet**) with a browser by visiting VIZManga.com
- **Mac or PC computer** by visiting VIZManga.com

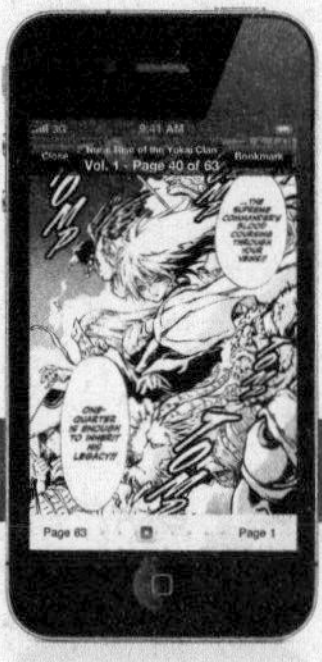

VIZ Digital has loads to offer:

- 500+ ready-to-read volumes
- New volumes each week
- FREE previews
- Access on multiple devices! Create a log-in through the app so you buy a book once, and read it on your device of choice!*

To learn more, visit www.viz.com/apps

*** Some series may not be available for multiple devices. Check the app on your device to find out what's available.**

RATED T+ FOR OLDER TEEN ratings.viz.com

viz media

viz.com/apps

This is the last page.

In keeping with the original Japanese comic format, this book reads from right to left—so action, sound effects, and word balloons are completely reversed. This preserves the orientation of the original artwork—plus, it's fun! Check out the diagram shown here to get the hang of things, and then turn to the other side of the book to get started!

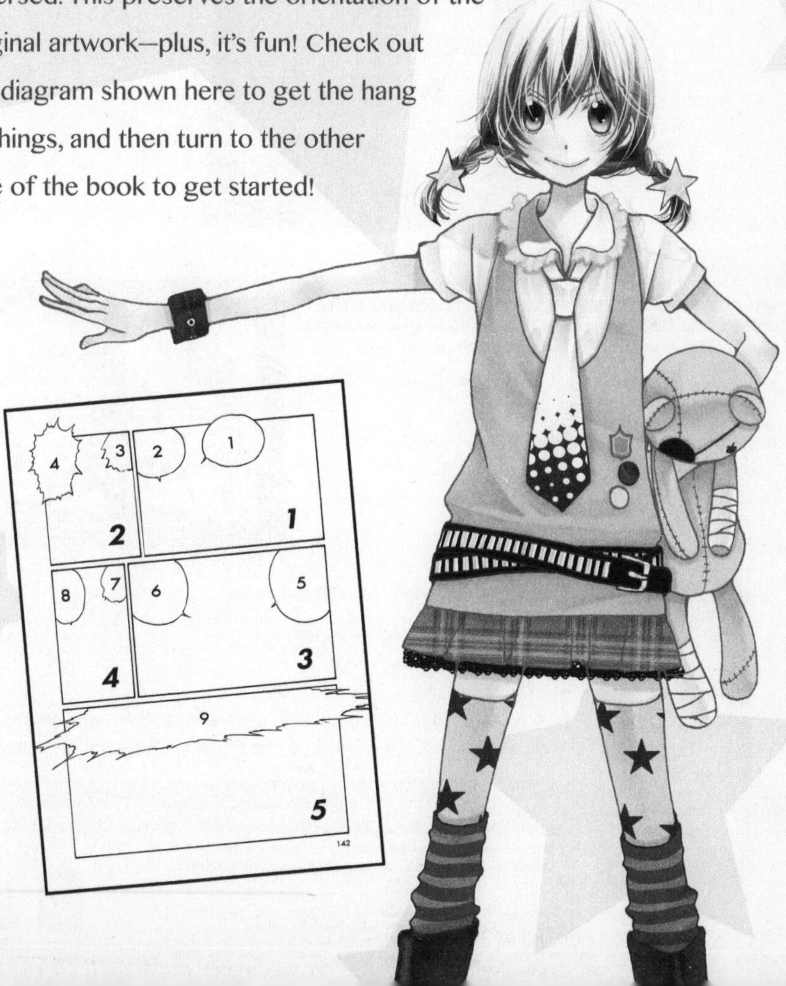
1
2
3
4
1
2
5
6
7
8
3
4
9
5
142